How Russian Came to Be the Way It Is

How Russian Came to Be the Way It Is

A Student's Guide to the History of the Russian Language

Tore Nesset

Bloomington, Indiana, 2015

© 2015 by the author. All rights reserved.

This volume was published in August 2015.

ISBN 978-0-89357-443-7

Technical Editor: Rosemarie Connolly

Library of Congress Cataloging-in-Publication Data

Nesset, Tore, author.
  How Russian came to be the way it is : a student's guide to the history of the Russian language / Tore Nesset.
      pages ; cm
  Includes bibliographical references and index.
  ISBN 978-0-89357-443-7
  1. Russian language--To 1500--History. 2. Russian language--History. 3. Proto-Slavic language--History. I. Title.
  PG2077.N47 2015
  491.709--dc23
                            2015013831

Slavica Publishers
Indiana University
1430 N. Willis Drive
Bloomington, IN 47404-2146
USA

[Tel.] 1-812-856-4186
[Toll-free] 1-877-SLAVICA
[Fax] 1-812-856-4187
[Email] slavica@indiana.edu
[www] http://www.slavica.com/

Table of Contents

Table of Contents v
Detailed Table of Contents vi
List of Tables xi
List of Figures xv
Preface xxi
Notes on Transliteration, Transcription, Orthography,
    Examples, and Abbreviations xxiii

0. Introduction: Today's Exceptions—Yesterday's Rules 1
1. The Scene: From Prehistory to Peter I "the Great" 5
2. The Texts: Writing and Literature in Kievan Rus' and Muscovy 33
3. The Toolbox: Linguistic Tools for Analyzing the History of
    Russian 61
4. Morphology: Nouns 77
5. Morphology: Pronouns 101
6. Morphology: Adjectives 113
7. Morphology: Numbers and Numerals 127
8. Morphology: Verbs 135
9. Syntax 163
10. Phonology: Pre-Slavic and Common Slavic Vowels and
    Diphthongs 195
11. Phonology: Pre-Slavic and Common Slavic Consonants 217
12. Phonology: From Old Rusian to Modern Russian 243
13. Phonology: Stress and Vowel Reduction 275
14. A Visit from Novgorod: The Language of the Birch Bark
    Letters 291
15. Epilogue: Reflections on a Triangle 303
Appendix 1: Morphological Tables 307
Appendix 2: Major Differences between Old Church
    Slavonic and Old Rusian 325
Appendix 3: Chronology of Major Sound Laws 329
Appendix 4: Example of Text Analysis 331

Bibliography 339
Indexes 349

Detailed Table of Contents

Table of Contents v
Detailed Table of Contents vi
List of Tables xi
List of Figures xv
Preface xxi
Notes on Transliteration, Transcription, Orthography,
    Examples, and Abbreviations xxiii

0. Introduction: Today's Exceptions—Yesterday's Rules 1
    0.1. Why Study the History of Russian? 1
    0.2. How to Use This Book 2

1. The Scene: From Prehistory to Peter I "the Great" 5
    1.1. Russian and Its Relatives in Present Day Europe 5
    1.2. Russian and Its Ancestors 10
    1.3. The Primordial Home of the Slavs 11
    1.4. The Slavic Migrations 13
    1.5. Rus'—The State 14
    1.6. Rus'—The People 20
    1.7. Mongols: Conflict and Collaboration 23
    1.8. The Rise of the Muscovite State 24
    1.9. Ivan IV "the Terrible": Russia in the 16th Century 26
    1.10. The "Time of Troubles" (1598–1613) 27
    1.11. Russia in the Seventeenth Century 30
    1.12. Chronology: Overview of Historical Periods and
           Events in Tabular Form 31
    1.13. Suggestions for Further Reading 32

2. The Texts: Writing and Literature in Kievan Rus' and Muscovy 33
    2.1. Overture: Cyril and Methodius, the First Slavic
         Alphabet, and Old Church Slavonic 33
    2.2. The Cyrillic Alphabet—A Practical Guide 36
    2.3. Literary Genres and Works 40
         2.3.1. Religious Literature: From Metropolitan
               Hilarion to Archpriest Avvakum 40

	2.3.2.	*The Primary Chronicle (Povest' vremennyx let)* and Other Chronicles 44
	2.3.3.	*Slovo o polku Igoreve, Zadonščina* and Military Tales 46
	2.3.4.	*Russkaja Pravda* and Other Legal Texts 48
	2.3.5.	Travel: Afanasij Nikitin's *Xoždenie za tri morja* 48
	2.3.6.	The Correspondence between Andrej Kurbskij and Ivan IV "the Terrible" 49
	2.3.7.	Birch Bark Letters 51
	2.3.8.	Summing Up: Medieval and Modern Concepts of "Literature" 51
2.4.	Standard Language: The Situation in Kievan Rus' 52
2.5.	Standard Language: Sketch of Further Development 56
2.6.	Summary: Important Concepts 58
2.7.	For Further Reading 60

3. The Toolbox: Linguistic Tools for Analyzing the History of Russian 61

- 3.1. Synchrony and Diachrony 61
- 3.2. Genetically and Typologically Related Languages 61
- 3.3. History of Standard Languages vs. Historical Dialectology 62
- 3.4. The Family Tree Model 63
- 3.5. Methodology 1: Sound Correspondences, Sound Laws, and Linguistic Reconstruction 65
- 3.6. Methodology 2: Borrowing and Analogy 67
- 3.7. Methodology 3: Grammaticalization 69
- 3.8. Methodology 4: Reanalysis 70
- 3.9. Time: Absolute and Relative Chronology 70
- 3.10. Space: The Wave Model for Innovation and Spread. Isoglosses 71
- 3.11. Summary: Historical Linguistics in a Nutshell 72
- 3.12. For Further Reading 74

4. Morphology: Nouns 77

- 4.1. Declension of Nouns in Contemporary Standard Russian 77
- 4.2. The Declension System of Common Slavic and Old Rusian 80
  - 4.2.1. The *ŏ*-Declension 81
  - 4.2.2. The *ŭ*-Declension 83
  - 4.2.3. The *ā*-Declension 84
  - 4.2.4. The *ĭ*-Declension 86
  - 4.2.5. The *ū*-Declension 87

		4.2.6.	The C-Declension 88

- 4.2.6. The C-Declension 88
- 4.2.7. Overview of Old Rusian Declensions in Tabular Form 90
- 4.3. Declension Classes: From Six to Three 90
- 4.4. Number and Case 92
- 4.5. Stems Ending in Hard and Soft Consonants 95
- 4.6. Gender 96
- 4.7. Subgender: Animacy 96
- 4.8. Summary: Overview of Changes in Tabular Form 99
- 4.9. For Further Reading 100

5. Morphology: Pronouns 101
- 5.1. Personal (1st and 2nd Persons) and Reflexive Pronouns 101
- 5.2. Personal (3rd Person) and Relative Pronouns 103
- 5.3. Demonstrative Pronouns 105
- 5.4. Possessive Pronouns 107
- 5.5. Вьсь 'all' 108
- 5.6. Interrogative Pronouns: къто and чьто 108
- 5.7. Summary 109
- 5.8. For Further Reading 111

6. Morphology: Adjectives 113
- 6.1. Short and Long Forms in Common Slavic, Old Rusian, and Contemporary Standard Russian 113
- 6.2. The Declension of Short Forms 115
- 6.3. The Declension of Long Forms 116
  - 6.3.1. Overview 116
  - 6.3.2. The Masculine Nominative and Accusative Singular: Church Slavic Influence 119
  - 6.3.3. The Feminine and Neuter Nominative and Accusative Singular: "Trivial" Forms 119
  - 6.3.4. The Masculine and Neuter Genitive, Dative, and Locative Singular: Pronominal Influence 119
  - 6.3.5. The Feminine Genitive, Dative, and Locative Singular: Pronominal Influence 120
  - 6.3.6. The Nominative, Accusative, Genitive, and Instrumental Plural: "Trivial" Forms 121
  - 6.3.7. The Instrumental Singular and the Dative and Locative Plural: Haplology and Contraction 121
  - 6.3.8. Summary: The Origin of the Long Forms in Contemporary Standard Russian 122

- 6.4. The Comparative and the Superlative 123
- 6.5. Summary 125
- 6.6. For Further Reading 126

7. **Morphology: Numbers and Numerals** 127
   - 7.1. From Nouns and Adjectives to Something in Between 127
   - 7.2. The Number 1 129
   - 7.3. The Number 2 129
   - 7.4. The Numbers 3 and 4 130
   - 7.5. The Numbers 5 to 9 131
   - 7.6. The Number 10 132
   - 7.7. The Numbers 11 to 19 132
   - 7.8. The Tens 132
   - 7.9. The Hundreds 133
   - 7.10. Thousand 133
   - 7.11. Ordinal Numbers 133
   - 7.12. Summary 134
   - 7.13. For Further Reading 134

8. **Morphology: Verbs** 135
   - 8.1. The Infinitive and the Supine 135
   - 8.2. The Present Tense 136
   - 8.3. The Four Past-Tense Forms 140
     - 8.3.1. The Aorist 140
     - 8.3.2. The Imperfect 142
     - 8.3.3. The Perfect 144
     - 8.3.4. The Pluperfect 145
     - 8.3.5. The Meaning of the Past-Tense Forms 146
     - 8.3.6. The Historical Development of the Past-Tense Forms 149
   - 8.4. The Future Tense 150
   - 8.5. Tense and Aspect 152
   - 8.6. The Imperative 154
   - 8.7. The Subjunctive 156
   - 8.8. The Participles 156
     - 8.8.1. The Structure of Participles and the Participle Suffixes 157
     - 8.8.2. The Agreement Endings 158
     - 8.8.3. The Development of Participles and Gerunds 159
   - 8.9. Summary 160
   - 8.10. For Further Reading 161

9. Syntax 163

9.1. Subject 163
9.2. Object 164
9.3. Predicative Nouns and Adjectives 166
9.4. Adverbials: Space 168
9.5. Adverbials: Time 171
9.6. Overview of Old Rusian Prepositions. Preposition
     Repetition 175
9.7. Possessive Constructions 175
9.8. Passive Constructions 179
9.9. The Dative Absolute and Other Adverbial
     Constructions with Participles 180
9.10. Agreement 181
9.11. Clitics 183
9.12. Some Notes on Complex Sentences 187
     9.12.1. Relative Clauses 188
     9.12.2. Object Clauses 188
     9.12.3. Adverbial Clauses: Time 189
     9.12.4. Adverbial Clauses: Cause 189
     9.12.5. Adverbial Clauses: Condition 190
     9.12.6. Summary: Some Important Conjunctions
             Used in Complex Sentences 191
9.13. Summary 192
9.14. For Further Reading 192

10. Phonology: Pre-Slavic and Common Slavic Vowels and Diphthongs 195

10.1. Basic Concepts: Phoneme, Allophone, Minimal Pair,
      Complementary Distribution 195
10.2. Overview: Vowel Systems for Late Proto-Indo-European,
      Proto-Slavic, Old Rusian, and Contemporary
      Standard Russian 196
10.3. The *o/a* Merger and the Loss of Vowel Quantity 198
10.4. Syllable Structure in Common Slavic: "The Law of
      Open Syllables" 200
10.5. Loss of Final Consonants 202
10.6. Oral Diphthongs: Monophthongization 203
10.7. Nasal Diphthongs: The Rise and Fall of Nasal Vowels ... 205
10.8. Liquid Diphthongs: Pleophony and Metathesis 207
     10.8.1. CORC: Word-Internal Liquid Diphthongs 207
     10.8.2. ORC: Word-Internal Liquid Diphthongs 210

  10.8.3. CЪRC: Liquids Preceded by Jers 211
  10.8.4. Summary of Liquid Diphthongs 211
 10.9. Prothetic Consonants 211
 10.10. Summary: Table of Correspondences 215
 10.11. For Further Reading 215

11. Phonology: Pre-Slavic and Common Slavic Consonants 217

 11.1. Overview: Consonant Systems for Late Proto-Indo-European, Proto-Slavic, Old Rusian, and Contemporary Standard Russian 217
 11.2. Loss of Dorsal Plosives: Centum and Satem Languages 220
 11.3. The "*Ruki* Rule" and the Emergence of /x/ 223
 11.4. More on Common Slavic Syllables: Synharmony 226
 11.5. First Palatalization of Velars 228
 11.6. *J*-Palatalization 231
 11.7. Second Palatalization of Velars 234
 11.8. Third Palatalization of Velars 236
 11.9. Fronting of Vowels after Soft Consonants 238
 11.10. Summary of Consonant Changes 240
 11.11. For Further Reading 242

12. Phonology: From Old Rusian to Modern Russian 243

 12.1. Overview: Phoneme Systems of Old Rusian and CSR 243
 12.2. The Fall and Vocalization of the Jers 246
  12.2.1. Havlik's Law 246
  12.2.2. An Approach in Terms of Feet 248
  12.2.3. Further Complications: Stress, Analogy, Tense Jers, and CЪRC Groups 250
 12.3. Some Consequences of the Fall of the Jers 251
  12.3.1. Mobile Vowels 251
  12.3.2. Emergence of Closed Syllables 252
  12.3.3. Consonant Clusters: Assimilation and Dissimilation 252
  12.3.4. Final Devoicing 254
  12.3.5. Hard and Soft Consonants Word Finally 256
  12.3.6. The Realization of /v, v'/ and the Emergence of /f, f'/ 257
  12.3.7. The Merger of /y/ and /i/ 258
 12.4. Dorsal Obstruents before /i/: [ky, gy, xy] → [k'i, g'i, x'i] 260
 12.5. Depalatalization of /š'/, /ž'/, and /c'/ 262
 12.6. Development of New Soft Post-Alveolar Fricatives 263
 12.7. Transition from /e/ to /o/: Relative Chronology 264

12.8.	The Fate of /ě/ (jat)	270
12.9.	Summary	271
12.10.	For Further Reading	273

13. Phonology: Stress and Vowel Reduction 275

13.1.	Stress Patterns	275
	13.1.1. Stress and Tone	275
	13.1.2. Contemporary Standard Russian Stress	276
	13.1.3. Common Slavic: Tone	280
	13.1.4. Old Rusian: From Tone to Stress	281
	13.1.5. The Emergence of Modern Russian Stress Patterns: Analogy	284
13.2.	Vowel Reduction: The Emergence of Akan'e	285
13.3.	Summary	289
13.4.	For Further Reading	290

14. A Visit to Novgorod: The Language of the Birch Bark Letters 291

14.1.	Orthography: бытовая система письма	291
14.2.	Phonology: The Question of the Second and Third Palatalizations	293
14.3.	Phonology: Cokan'e	295
14.4.	Phonology: Secondary Pleophony in CЪRC Groups	295
14.5.	Morphology: The Enigmatic *e*	296
14.6.	Morphology: The Ubiquitous *ě*	298
14.7.	Syntax: Clitics	299
14.8.	The Role of the Old Novgorod Dialect in the History of the Russian Language	300
14.9.	Summary: The Language of the Birch Bark Letters	301
14.10.	For Further Reading	301

15 Epilogue: Reflections on a Triangle 303

Appendix 1: Morphological Tables 307

A1.1.	Nouns	307
	A1.1.1. The ŏ-Declension	307
	A1.1.2. The ŭ-Declension	308
	A1.1.3. The ā-Declension	309
	A1.1.4. The ĭ-Declension	309
	A1.1.5. The ū-Declension	310
	A1.1.6. The C-Declension	311

A1.1.7. Overview of Old Rusian Declensions in
Tabular Form 312
A1.2. Pronouns 313
A1.2.1. Personal (1st and 2nd Persons) and Reflexive
Pronouns 313
A1.2.2. Personal (3rd Person) and Relative Pronouns 314
A1.2.3. Demonstrative Pronouns 315
A1.2.4. Possessive Pronouns 316
A1.2.5. Вьсь 'all' 316
A1.2.6. Interrogative Pronouns: къто and чьто 317
A1.3. Adjectives 317
A1.3.1. Short Forms of Adjectives 317
A1.3.2. Long Forms of Adjectives 318
A1.4. Numbers and Numerals 319
A1.4.1. The Number 1 319
A1.4.2. The Number 2 319
A1.4.3. The Numbers 3 and 4 319
A1.4.4. The Numbers 5 to 9 319
A1.4.5. The Number 10 320
A1.5. Verbs 320
A1.5.1. The Present Tense: Thematic Verbs (classes I–IV) 320
A1.5.2. The Present Tense: Athematic Verbs (class V) 321
A1.5.3. The Aorist 321
A1.5.4. The Imperfect 322
A1.5.5. The Imperative 322
A1.5.6. Participles: Suffixes 322
A1.5.7. Participles: Agreement Endings (short
forms in the nominative) 323

Appendix 2: Major Differences between Old Church Slavonic and Old Rusian 325

A2.1. Morphology: Nouns, Pronouns, and Adjectives 325
A2.2. Morphology: Verbs 326
A2.3. Syntax: The Dative Absolute Construction 326
A2.4. Phonology: Liquid Diphthongs 326
A2.5. Phonology: Prothetic Consonants in Word-Initial
Position 327
A2.6. Phonology: *J*-Palatalization and Consonant
Groups + Front Vowels 327

Appendix 3: Chronology of Major Sound Laws **329**
  A3.1. The Pre-Slavic Period 329
  A3.2. The Common Slavic Period 329
  A3.3. The Old Rusian Period 330

Appendix 4: Example of Text Analysis **331**
  A4.1. Text: Askold and Dir Attack Constantinople 331
  A4.2. English Translation 331
  A4.3. Historical Context 332
  A4.4. Morphology 332
  A4.5. Syntax 334
  A4.6. Phonology 335
  A4.7. Sociolinguistics 337

Bibliography **339**

Index of Names **349**

Subject Index **353**

List of Tables

Table 1.	Abbreviations of sources. Unless otherwise indicated, the examples are cited from *Biblioteka literatury drevnej Rusi*	xxv
Table 2.	East, West, and South Slavic languages	6
Table 3.	The Indo-European language family with example languages (not exhaustive)	10
Table 4.	Periodization (approximate) of the history of Russian	11
Table 5.	The Cyrillic alphabet (Font: Kliment Std)	38
Table 6.	The numerical values of letters	40
Table 7.	The inflectional paradigm of стол 'table' in Contemporary Standard Russian	78
Table 8.	The declension system of Contemporary Standard Russian	79
Table 9.	The Old Rusian ŏ-declension	81
Table 10.	Consonant alternations in Old Rusian nouns	82
Table 11.	The Old Rusian ŭ-declension	85
Table 12.	The Old Rusian ā-declension	85
Table 13.	The Old Rusian ĭ-declension	86
Table 14.	The ū-declension in Old Rusian	87
Table 15.	The C-declension in Old Rusian	89
Table 16.	Overview of declensions in Old Rusian	91
Table 17.	Examples of Old Rusian nominative dual forms that have become nominative plurals in Contemporary Standard Russian	94
Table 18.	Vowel correspondences in endings for hard and soft stems in Old Rusian	95
Table 19.	Schematic overview of changes concerning nouns in Old Rusian and Contemporary Standard Russian (CSR)	99
Table 20.	Declension of personal (1st and 2nd person) and reflexive pronouns in Old Rusian	102

Table 21.	The declension of personal pronouns (3rd person) in Old Rusian	103
Table 22.	The declension of demonstrative pronouns in Old Rusian	106
Table 23.	The declension of possessive pronouns in Old Rusian	107
Table 24.	The declension of Old Rusian вьсь 'all'	108
Table 25.	The declension of interrogative pronouns in Old Rusian	109
Table 26.	The distribution of short and long forms of adjectives in Common Slavic and Contemporary Standard Russian	114
Table 27.	The declension of short forms of adjectives in Old Rusian	115
Table 28.	The declension of long forms of adjectives in Old Rusian	117
Table 29.	The origin of the long forms in Contemporary Standard Russian	123
Table 30.	Properties characteristic of adjectives and nouns	127
Table 31.	Properties of adjectives, numerals, and nouns in Contemporary Standard Russian	128
Table 32.	Properties of numbers in Common Slavic and Old Rusian	129
Table 33.	The declension of дъва 'two' in Old Rusian	129
Table 34.	The declension of трье 'three' and четыре 'four' in Old Rusian	131
Table 35.	The declension of numbers 5–9 in Old Rusian	131
Table 36.	The declension of десять 'ten' in Old Rusian	132
Table 37.	The development of the category of numerals	134
Table 38.	The conjugation of thematic verbs (classes I–IV) in Old Rusian	138
Table 39.	The conjugation of athematic verbs (class V) in Old Rusian	139
Table 40.	The aorist endings in Old Rusian	141
Table 41.	The conjugation of the aorist in Old Rusian	141
Table 42.	Comparison of aorist and imperfect endings in Old Rusian	143
Table 43.	The conjugation of the imperfect in Old Rusian	144
Table 44.	Tense and aspect in Old Rusian	153
Table 45.	The conjugation of the imperative in Old Rusian	155

Table 46.	The participle suffixes in Old Rusian	158
Table 47.	The agreement endings of Old Rusian participle (nominative short forms)	159
Table 48.	The inventories of verb forms in Old Rusian and Contemporary Standard Russian	160
Table 49.	Prepositions for location vs. goal in Old Rusian	169
Table 50.	Major constructions for temporal adverbials in Old Rusian	174
Table 51.	Major Old Rusian prepositions	176
Table 52.	Conjugations and their meanings	191
Table 53.	Major syntactic differences between Old Rusian and Contemporary Standard Russian	192
Table 54.	Loss of vowel quantity—Late Proto-Indo-European and Old Rusian vowel correspondences	199
Table 55.	Effects of monophthongization of oral diphthongs	204
Table 56.	Metathesis and pleophony in CORC groups	208
Table 57.	Some pleophony and metathesis word pairs in Modern Russian	210
Table 58.	Metathesis of liquid diphthongs in word-initial position (ORC groups)	210
Table 59.	The development of CORC, ÓRC, ÕRC, and CЪRC groups in Russian	211
Table 60.	Development of Late Common Slavic word-initial /je/ in Russian	214
Table 61.	Late Proto-Indo-European consonant phoneme system	218
Table 62.	Proto-Slavic consonant phoneme system	219
Table 63.	Old Rusian consonant phoneme system	219
Table 64.	Contemporary Standard Russian consonant phoeneme system	219
Table 65.	The effect of the *ruki* rule in the Old Rusian aorist	225
Table 66.	The phonetic motivation of synharmony	227
Table 67.	Reflexes of Proto-Slavic /tj/ and /dj/ in Old Church Slavonic and Old Rusian	233

Table 68.	Comparison of the three palatalizations of velar consonants	238
Table 69.	Old Rusian vowel system	245
Table 70.	Contemporary Standard Russian vowel system	245
Table 71.	Old Rusian consonant phoneme system	246
Table 72.	Contemporary Standard Russian consonant phoneme system	246
Table 73.	Dorsal obstruents + [i] or [y] in Old Rusian and Contemporary Standard Russian	260
Table 74.	The interaction of stress and a following hard consonant for the transition from /e/ to /o/	265
Table 75.	Relative chronology of fall/vocalization of the jers, the transition from /e/ to /o/, and transition from /ě/ to /e/	266
Table 76.	Relative chronology of softness/hardness assimilation (hardening of /r'/ and the transition from /e/ to /o/	267
Table 77.	Relative chronology of depalatalization and the transition from /e/ to /o/	268
Table 78.	Present-tense forms of нести 'carry' in Contemporary Standard Russian	269
Table 79.	Main stress patterns in Contemporary Standard Russian	277
Table 80.	Strong vs. dissimilative akan'e	286
Table 81.	The ending -ѣ in the ā-declension—Comparison between Old Rusian and Old Novgorod dialect	298
Table 82.	Differences between Old Church Slavonic and Old Rusian nouns, pronouns, and adjectives	325
Table 83.	Differences between Old Church Slavonic and Old Rusian verbs	326
Table 84.	Liquid diphthongs in Old Church Slavonic and Old Rusian	326
Table 85.	Prothetic consonants in Old Church Slavonic and Old Rusian	327
Table 86.	J-palatalization in Old Church Slavonic and Old Rusian	327
Table 87.	Chronology of Pre-Slavic sound laws	329
Table 88.	Chronology of Common Slavic sound laws	329
Table 89.	Chronology of Old Rusian sound laws	330

List of Figures

Figure 1. Slavic languages in present-day Europe 8
Figure 2. The East Slavic Tribes 15
Figure 3. Kievan Rus': Rivers and cities 18
Figure 4. The explansion of the Muscovite state 28
Figure 5. Pages from the *Ostromir Gospel*, 11th century 41
Figure 6. Simple family tree model of the major Slavic languages 64
Figure 7. Graphical representation of the changes in the declension system 93
Figure 8. Loss of intervocalic [j], assimilation, and contraction in long forms of adjectives 118
Figure 9. The five verb classes in Old Rusian 137
Figure 10. Phonetic word, morphosyntactic word, and clitic 184
Figure 11. Vowel systems of Late Proto-Indo-European, Proto-Slavic, Old Rusian, and Contemporary Standard Russian 197
Figure 12. Changes concerning vowel height for short vowels and long vowels 200
Figure 13. Late Proto-Indo-European oral diphthongs ending in /i/ and /u/ 203
Figure 14. Vowel and diphthong correspondences 216
Figure 15. The reduction from nine to four dorsal plosives in the centum and satem languages 221
Figure 16. The results of *j*-palatalization in East Slavic 232
Figure 17. Development of different endings after soft consonants through vowel fronting 240
Figure 18. Main stress patterns in Contemporary Standard Russian 278
Figure 19. Development of **целый** 'whole' 294
Figure 20. The three components of the book 304

Preface

I started working on this book in 2012, when I was on sabbatical at the University of North Carolina, Chapel Hill. The idea was to write a short textbook based on teaching materials I had developed over the years. I thought it would be a simple and quick project, and I was—unsurprisingly, perhaps—wrong. However, a full draft was completed in the summer of 2013 and a revised version was submitted for publication in November 2014.

I would like to thank my employer, UiT The Arctic University of Norway, for granting me a sabbatical and the University of North Carolina for hosting me. Thanks to the U.S.-Norway Fulbright Foundation for giving me a grant, which made my stay in the United States possible. I would also like to express my gratitude to George Fowler, Vicki Polansky, Chris Flynn, and Rosemarie Connolly at Slavica Publishers for helping me realizing this project.

Special thanks are due to Laura A. Janda, Hanne M. Eckhoff, Anna Endresen, and an anonymous referee for detailed, critical comments on earlier versions of the entire book. Their input led to a number of important improvements. Thanks also to my colleagues Ingunn Lunde and Margje Post at the University of Bergen for testing out my book in class and for providing valuable comments on parts of the manuscript. I would like to thank all members of the CLEAR research group in Tromsø for continuous support and and many interesting discussions. Last but not least, I would like to thank students from courses I have taught in Oslo, Bergen, and Tromsø. Without you this book would not have appeared.

Notes on Transliteration, Transcription, Orthography, Examples, and Abbreviations

Throughout the book, Russian person names and titles of literary works are transliterated, i.e., given in Latin letters. I use the scientific transliteration system where Russian ч = č, ш = š, ж = ž, щ = šč, and х = x.[1] However, for well-known names that have conventional spellings in English I use these spellings instead of transliteration. Therefore Достоевский, Толстой, and Пушкин are rendered as Dostoevsky, Tolstoy, and Pushkin, rather than Dostoevskij, Tolstoj, and Puškin.

While transliteration involves transferring words from one alphabet to another, transcription is the representation of speech sounds by means of graphic symbols. In this book, I use the International Phonetic Alphabet (IPA), but according to standard practice in Slavic linguistics I use the symbols [č', š, ž] for the first sound in the words чистый 'clean', широкий 'wide', and жестокий 'cruel'. I mark softness (palatalization) by means of an apostrophe after the relevant consonant—hence the apostrophe in [č'], which is soft (palatalized) in Contemporary Standard Russian. Square brackets [ ] are used for phonetic transcription, while phonemic transcription is given between slashes / /. For explanation of these and other fundamental phonological notions, see section 10.1.

Unlike names and titles of literary works, example words and sentences are given in Cyrillic. Examples are cited in modernized orthography; the only letter you are not familiar with from Contemporary Standard Russian is ѣ ("jat", Russian: ять), which represented an e-like sound. More information about the Cyrillic alphabet is given in section 2.2.

Throughout the book, example sentences are given in the following format:

(1) a. **Семъ же лѣтѣ** и вятичи побѣди. (PVL 981 AD; 81,29)
    b. **В том же году** он победил и вятичей.
    c. **In the same year**, he conquered the Vjatiči too.

---

[1] For an overview of the scientific transliteration system, see http://en.wikipedia.org/wiki/Scientific_transliteration_of_Cyrillic.

In (a) you find the example itself, while (b) and (c) provide Modern Russian and English translations. For your convenience, the word or construction under scrutiny is boldfaced. The source is given in parentheses in (a); in the example above, PVL stands for *Povest' vremennyx let* (the so-called *Primary Chronicle*), while the number after PVL indicates which year AD the relevant event took place according to the chronicle. The number after the semicolon refers to the column (before the comma) and line (after the comma) of the relevant passage in the *Polnoe sobranie russkix letopisej* (1997, vol. 1). In other words, the example in (1) corresponds to column 81, line 29 in this edition. This numbering is adopted in Müller's (1977) handbook and Ostrowski's (2003) edition, and is useful if you want to compare the example in different variants of the *Primary Chronicle*. The easiest way to do this is to use the electronic version of Ostrowski's edition.[2]

The examples from the *Primary Chronicle* and most other sources are cited from *Biblioteka literatury drevnej Rusi*.[3] The Modern Russian translations are from the same source. English translations are based on Cross and Sherbowitz-Wetzor 1953 (for the *Primary Chronicle*) and Zenkovsky 1974 (for other works). However, these translations are quite free and sometimes based on other versions of the texts than those cited in the present book. Therefore, I have frequently adapted the English phrasing so as to more clearly bring out the linguistic points under scrutiny. The abbreviations in Table 1 are used to identify the sources of examples. Unless indicated otherwise, the texts are cited according to *Biblioteka literatury drevnej Rusi*.

---

[2] Ostrowski's (2003) edition is available http://pvl.obdurodon.org/pvl.html and http://hudce7.harvard.edu/~ostrowski/pvl/.

[3] *Biblioteka literatury drevnej Rusi* is published by Institut russkoj literatury Rossijskoj Akademii Nauk at http://lib.pushkinskijdom.ru/Default.aspx?tabid=2070.

Table 1. Abbreviations of sources. Unless otherwise indicated, the examples are cited from *Biblioteka literatury drevnej Rusi*

Abbreviation:	Source:
Avvakum	*Žitie protopopa Avvakuma im samim napisannoe i drugie ego sočinenija*, cited after Avvakum Petrovič 1997
BBL	Birch Bark Letter, cited after Zaliznjak 2004; number is the number used by Zaliznjak
Dom	*Domostroj*
Filofej	*Poslanija starca Filofeja*
Hilarion	*Slovo o zakone i blagodati mitropolita Ilariona*
Groznyj	*Pervoe poslanie Ivana Groznogo Kurbskomu*
GVL	*Galicko-Volynskaja letopis'*
KL	*Kievskaja letopis'*, cited after electronic version published by Institut russkogo jazyka RAN[4]
Kurbskij	*Pervoe poslanie Kurbskogo Ivanu Groznomu*
Monomax	*Poučenie Vladimira Monomaxa* (including *Monomax's letter to Oleg, son of Svjatoslav*)
PVL	*Povest' vremennyx let, Ipat'evskij spisok* (*Primary Chronicle, Hypatian Redaction*); numbers indicate year, column, and line
RPK	*Russkaja Pravda (kratkaja redakcija)*
RPP	*Russkaja Pravda (prostrannaja redakcija)*
Sergij	*Žitie Sergija Radonežskogo*
Slovo	*Slovo o polku Igoreve* (*Lay of Igor's Campaign* or *Igor Tale*)
Xoždenie	*Xoždenie za tri morja Afanasija Nikitina*

---

[4] The electronic version of the *Kiev Chronicle* is available at http://www.lrc-lib.ru/rus_letopisi/Kiev/index.php.

Introduction   Today's Exceptions—Yesterday's Rules

0.1. Why Study the History of Russian?

Time machines do not exist, but books are good substitutes. This book takes you two thousand years back in time and explains how the Russian language came to be the way it is by reviewing all major changes in the grammar and sound system. I cannot know why you are holding this book in your hands, but a reasonable guess is that you are a graduate student of Russian or Slavic linguistics. Or maybe you are still an undergraduate? Or maybe your main interest lies in Russian literature or history? Or maybe you are a linguist who wants to learn about the history of the Russian language? I have written this book with all types of readers in mind. Beyond curiosity, the only thing you need in order to read this book is some competence in the Modern Russian language. Struggling your way through Russian grammar, you may have asked yourself why there are so many exceptions to the grammatical rules. Take a simple word like **писа́ть** 'write'. Why isn't it inflected the same way as **чита́ть** 'read'? Why do some forms of **писа́ть** such as **пишу́** 'I write' have **ш** instead of **с** in the stem? And why does the stress move to the stem in some of the inflected forms, such as **пи́шешь** 'you write'? Turning from verbs to nouns, you may wonder why nouns occur in the genitive after numerals (e.g., **пять столо́в** 'five tables'). And why do some masculine nouns have the ending **-а** in the nominative plural (e.g., **рога́** from **рог** 'antler'), while most masculines have **-ы** (e.g., **столы́**)? Conversely, why do some neuter nouns such as **плечо́** 'shoulder' take **-и** in the plural (**пле́чи**), when the general rule for neuter nouns is **-а** (e.g., **места́** from **ме́сто** 'place')?

This book provides you with answers to these and many other questions. The slogan in the title of this chapter summarizes the basic pedagogical idea: today's exceptions are yesterday's rules. In other words, the exceptions in Modern Russian are the result of historical processes that are regular and can be analyzed and understood. Learning about the processes that shaped Russian will deepen and enrich your understanding of the modern language. When you have read this book, the seemingly idiosyncratic properties of **писа́ть** and other words will no longer be random facts you just have to memorize, but rather the outcome of regular and well-understood historical processes. In order to maximize the usefulness of the book, each chapter starts with a presentation of some seemingly idiosyncratic properties of Modern Russian, and then goes on to explain how they developed historically.

At this point I hope to have convinced you that the history of Russian is not an arcane or esoteric topic, but instead it provides you with useful language skills and practical facts you can use. However, after reading this book I hope you will agree that there is more to it than that. One of the most fascinating aspects of language is the fact that it always changes. Historical linguistics is the academic discipline that analyzes language change. Chapter 3 offers a brief introduction to historical linguistics, and the entire book illustrates how these principles apply to the history of Russian. When you have read this book, you will have a good idea about language change and historical linguistics in general.

Yet another reason to study the history of Russian relates to literature and history. A large body of texts has come down to us from medieval Russia, representing a wide variety of genres. These texts provide a unique window into the culture and history of Russia. Admittedly it is possible to read some medieval texts in translation, but no translation does full justice to a text, and not all texts are available in translation. This book provides you with the linguistic tools you need in order to read medieval texts in the original, and thus facilitates a deeper understanding of Russian culture and history. At the same time, knowledge of literature and history enhances your understanding of language. Learning about the intricacies of language change becomes more concrete and meaningful if you are able to situate those intricacies in their cultural and historical context. Therefore, chapter 1 of this book outlines the historical development from the Migration Period to the late 1600s when Peter I "the Great" came to power. Furthermore, chapter 2 engages the relationship between language and literature, discussing major literary works and genres, as well as the development of literacy and writing.

0.2. How to Use This Book

Since this book is designed for readers with different interests and academic backgrounds, there are many ways of using it. First and foremost, you may read it. My goal has been to create a narrative that is simple and has a logical structure, so that the book can be read from beginning to end. If you do not have a background in linguistics, do not despair. I limit the use of linguistic terminology to a minimum, and the terms I use are explained at their first occurrence. At this point a warning is in order. Since this book aims at making very complicated things accessible, I have had to simplify things. This book does not aim at providing the whole picture. However, if you want to learn more I offer some suggestions for further reading at the end of each chapter.

With regard to the structure of the book, I start with three introductory chapters that provide necessary background information on history, literature, and linguistics. If you are well versed in one or all of these fields, you may want to go straight to chapters 4–9, which discuss changes in grammar, and then proceed to changes in the sound system in chapters 10–13. The decision to discuss grammar before sounds is untraditional, but is based on my experience from the classroom. Working with historical linguistics is more efficient (and more fun) if you can read texts and work with the grammar in parallel. The chapters on grammar offer the necessary linguistic tools to get started reading texts, and I have therefore placed them before the chapters on the sound system, which is less directly relevant for your work with texts. However, if you are a die-hard phonologist, it is possible to read chapters 10–13 before 4–9. The chapters on grammar and sound changes are followed by one chapter about the Old Novgorod dialect, which is important for the birch bark letters—a fascinating body of texts from medieval Novgorod. In an epilogue in chapter 15 I reflect on the relationship between the three components of the book: the facts about the history of Russian, the tools from linguistic theory, and the background information about literature and history.

While I hope you will find it worthwhile to read the whole book, I would like to point out that individual chapters and even sections of chapters may be read in isolation. For instance, if you need to brush up your knowledge about the development of the stress patterns in Russian, you may read section 13.1 without looking at any other parts of the book. You may even benefit from the book without actually reading it, since it is designed to be useful as a reference work. It is tabular in form, and using the detailed table of contents and index, you should be able to find the information you are looking for without having to wade through long stretches of prose. Moreover, at the end of the book, there are appendices containing grammatical tables, a list of differences between Old Church Slavonic and East Slavic, as well as a chronological overview of sound changes. There is also an appendix with a short text and grammatical commentary, which helps you get started with the study of medieval texts.

In addition to the book you are holding in your hands, I have a webpage with supplementary information. Check it out at http://dx.doi.org/10.7557/se.2015.1!

Even if time machines do not exist, it is my hope that this book offers a good substitute. However you decide to make use of this book, I hope you will enjoy traveling in time with me. Have a pleasant trip!

Chapter 1

The Scene: From Prehistory to Peter I "the Great"

Language change does not happen in a vacuum. In order to understand how Russian came to be the way it is you need some background knowledge about the prehistory and history of the Russians and their Slavic relatives. In this chapter, you will learn about the Slavic and Indo-European languages in Europe (section 1.1) and the ancestor languages that Russian has developed from (section 1.2). In sections 1.3–1.4, we explore the prehistory of the Slavs, before we turn to a brief overview of Russian history before Peter I "the Great" in sections 1.5–1.11. While reading the chapter, make use of the chronological overview of important historical events and periods in section 1.12.

1.1. Russian and Its Relatives in Present Day Europe

Russian belongs to the eastern subgroup of the Slavic languages, a group of languages spoken in Eastern Europe that have developed from a reconstructed language referred to as "Proto-Slavic." It is customary to divide the Slavic languages into three groups—East, West, and South Slavic.

As shown in Table 2, the East Slavic languages include Belarusian, Russian and Ukrainian, and it has also become customary to recognize Rusyn as a separate East Slavic language. Rusyn is a minority language spoken in western Ukraine, as well as in parts of Poland, Slovakia, Hungary, Romania, and Serbia.

The western group comprises Czech, Slovak, and Polish, as well as Kashubian and Upper and Lower Sorbian. Kashubian is a minority language in Poland that is closely related to Polish. Upper and Lower Sorbian are two closely related minority languages spoken in eastern Germany. Polabian, which died out in the 18th century, was spoken around the Elbe River in Germany. Slovincian, extinct since the early 20th century, was spoken in Pomerania in what is now western Poland.

The South Slavic languages include Slovene (Slovenian), Bosnian, Croatian, and Serbian, as well as the closely related Macedonian and Bulgarian.

Table 2. East, West, and South Slavic languages

East Slavic languages:	
	Belarusian
	Russian
	Ukrainian
	Rusyn
West Slavic languages:	
	Czech
	Slovak
	Polish
	Kashubian
	Upper and Lower Sorbian
	Polabian
	Slovincian
South Slavic languages:	
	Slovene (Slovenian)
	Bosnian, Croatian, and Serbian
	Macedonian
	Bulgarian

The map in Figure 1 (see pp. 8–9) indicates the approximate geographical distribution of the Slavic languages. Notice that the South Slavic languages are separated from their eastern and western relatives by German in Austria, Hungarian in Hungary, and Romanian in Romania. The geographical distribution is the result of prehistoric migrations and later developments in European history, to which we return in section 1.3. While maps like the one in Figure 1 provide a good overview, it is important to remember that they are simplistic insofar as they suggest a one-to-one relation between state and language. However, we have already seen that Rusyn, Kashubian, and Upper and Lower Sorbian are minority languages not associated with a state. The relationship between state and language is particularly complex in the former Yugoslavia. Russian is the main language of the Russian Federation, but is also spoken by large minorities in the former Soviet republics and in diaspora populations around the world. At the same time, Russian is far from the only language spoken in Russia. The encyclopedia *Jazyki Rossijskoj Federacii i sosednix gosudarstv* (Jarceva 1997–2005) discusses 177 languages and groups of languages spoken on the territory of the former Soviet Union. According to the census of 2010, more than 150 languages are spoken in the Russian Federation, about two thirds of which are indigenous to Russia.[1] Clearly, Russia is a multilingual state.

The Slavic languages belong to the Indo-European language family, which comprises eleven branches of languages that descend from the reconstructed Proto-Indo-European language. Table 3 provides an overview. The closest relatives of the Slavic languages are the two Baltic languages, Latvian and Lithuanian, which are spoken in Latvia and Lithuania. Many researchers analyze the Slavic and Baltic languages as one "Balto-Slavic" branch of the Indo-European language family. While Slavic dominates Eastern Europe, Western Europe is dominated by the Germanic languages (in the northwest) and the Romance languages (mostly in the southwest). In the first millennium BC, Celtic languages were spoken over large areas of Europe, but are now minority languages largely confined to the British Isles and Brittany in France. In the Balkans in southeastern Europe, we find the Albanian and Hellenic (Greek) languages, while the Armenian language is spoken in the Caucasus between the Black Sea and the Caspian Sea. The large Indo-Iranian branch dominates the Indian subcontinent, and Indo-Iranian languages are furthermore spoken inter alia in Iran, Afghanistan, and Tajikistan. The Anatolian languages, of which Hittite is most well known, were spoken in what is now Turkey, but all are extinct. Hittite is attested on clay tablets dating from the eighteenth century BC—the oldest preserved written records of any Indo-European language. Tocharian, another extinct branch of Indo-European, is the easternmost Indo-European language, attested in manuscripts from the 3rd to 9th centuries AD that were excavated in the early twentieth century in what is now the Xinjiang Uyghur Autonomous Region of China.

Although the Indo-European languages are prevalent in Europe, far from all languages in Europe belong to the Indo-European family. Examples of non-Indo-European languages in Europe include Basque (spoken in Spain and France), as well as a number of languages belonging to the Finno-Ugric family, e.g., Sámi (spoken in northern Fenno-Scandinavia and on the Kola peninsula in Russia), Finnish (spoken in Finland), Estonian (spoken in Estonia), and Hungarian (spoken in Hungary). There are also a number of Finno-Ugric minority languages in Russia, e.g., Karelian and Vepsian (spoken in the western part of Russia), Mordvin and Mari (spoken along the river Volga), Komi and Udmurt (spoken in the eastern parts of European Russia), and Khanty and Mansi (spoken in Western Siberia).

---

[1] For lists of languages from the census, see http://www.gks.ru/free_doc/new_site/perepis2010/croc/perepis_itogi1612.htm.

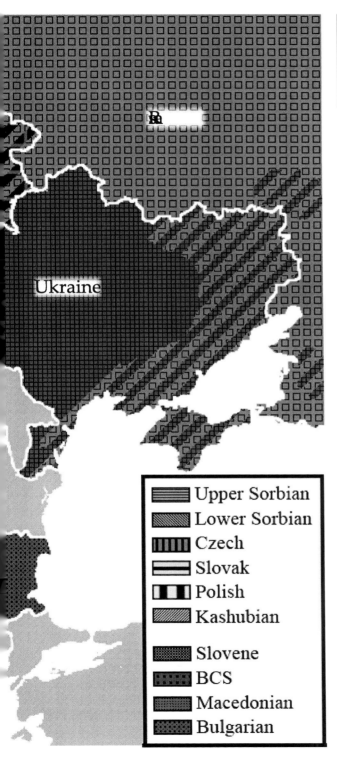

Figure 1. Slavic languages in present-day Europe

Table 3. The Indo-European language family with example languages (not exhaustive)

Branch:	Example languages:
1. Slavic	Russian, Czech, and Bulgarian
2. Baltic	Latvian and Lithuanian
3. Germanic	English, German, Dutch, and Norwegian
4. Romance	Latin, Italian, Spanish, French, and Romanian
5. Celtic	Irish, Welsh, and Breton
6. Hellenic	Greek
7. Albanian	Albanian
8. Armenian	Armenian
9. Indo-Iranian	Persian (Farsi), Hindi, and Urdu
10. Anatolian	Hittite
11. Tocharian	Tocharian

1.2. Russian and Its Ancestors

In the previous section you learned that the Slavic languages are defined as those languages that have developed from the reconstructed ancestor language Proto-Slavic. At this point it is natural to ask when this development started and which periods it can be divided into. Table 4 provides a schematic overview. "Pre-Slavic" refers to the period before the Slavic languages became different from the other Indo-European languages. "Common Slavic" is the period that covers changes that are shared by all the Slavic languages, but not by other Indo-European languages. Some scholars use the terms "Common Slavic" and "Proto-Slavic" interchangeably. However, in this book I follow Andersen (1985, 1998) and use Proto-Slavic for the reconstructed ancestor language that represents the initial state of Common Slavic. I will use the term "Late Common Slavic" about the transitional period when Slavic linguistic unity was beginning to break up. For the period after the East Slavic languages separated from their western and southern relatives I use the term "Old Rusian" (with one s), which alludes to Rus', the state that united a number of East Slavic tribes and reached its peak of power and prestige in the 11th century. Alternative terms are "(Old) East Slavic" and the traditional "Old Russian" (with double s). However, the latter term is misleading since the language in question is the ancestor of not only Russian, but also Belarusian and Ukrainian. For the period following the separation of Russian from Belarusian and Ukrainian I use the term "Middle Russian," which in turn is followed by the period of "Modern

Russian." When referring to the land and people, I avoid using "Russian" before the Muscovite period, i.e., the period when Moscow replaced Kiev as the dominant city.

Locating the periods in time would be easy if (a) languages changed abruptly after long periods of stability, and (b) these changes were detectable in written sources. However, a more realistic model assumes continuous and gradual language change. Furthermore, we have no written sources before Late Common Slavic, and even for the periods where we have written sources, these sources do not reflect language change in a way that facilitates a straightforward and simple dating of the periods in question. For these reasons, the dates given in Table 4 should be taken with more than one grain of salt. The suggested dates nevertheless give some indication of the time frame covered in this book.

Table 4. Periodization (approximate) of the history of Russian

Period:	Time span:
Pre-Slavic	Before 300 AD
Common Slavic	300–1000 AD
Old Rusian	1000–1400 AD
Middle Russian	1400–1700 AD
Modern Russian	1700–present

1.3. The Primordial Home of the Slavs

The dates suggested in Table 4 indicate that Common Slavic overlapped with the transitional period between Late Antiquity and the Early Middle Ages that historians refer to as the "Migration Period" (400–800 AD). What was the primordial home of the Slavs, and how were they affected by the extensive migrations in Europe during this period? As for the primordial home, it makes sense to distinguish between three hypotheses (cf. Schenker 1995: 1–8):

Three hypotheses about the primordial home of the Slavs:

(1) a. *The autochthonous hypothesis:*

　　　The area between the Oder and Wistula rivers in what is now Poland

　　b. *The Danubian hypothesis:*

　　　The area along the river Danube in the former Yugoslavia, Slovakia, and Hungary

(1) c. *The mid-Dnieper hypothesis*
   The area along the river Dnieper in present-day Ukraine and Belarus

The autochthonous hypothesis has mainly been defended by Polish scholars—hence its name (autochthonous means "native, indigenous"). Today, most researchers favor the mid-Dnieper hypothesis. Three sets of data are relevant:

(2) a. The shared, inherited vocabulary of the modern Slavic languages
   b. Early loanwords in Slavic
   c. Roman written sources

Andersen (1998: 415) points out that the vocabulary shared by all the modern Slavic languages "includes no detailed terminology for physical surface features characteristic of the mountains or the steppe, nor any relating to the sea, to coastal features, littoral flora or fauna, or salt water fishes." Instead, we find words relating to inland landscapes (lakes, rivers, and swamps), as well as trees, plants, and animals of the temperate forest zone (Andersen 1998: 416). On the assumption that this shared vocabulary reflects the topography, flora, and fauna of the original homeland of the Slavs, the vocabulary evidence suggests that the primordial home of the Slavs was somewhere in the temperate forest zone that stretches across Central and Eastern Europe. However, these data do not enable us to distinguish conclusively between the hypotheses in (1), since they all locate the primordial home in the vicinity of the European forest zone.

Evidence from early loanwords has more specific implications (cf. Schenker 1995: 7 and 159f.). Slavic has a number of early loanwords from Indo-Iranian languages, many of which are religious terms. Examples (cited in Modern Russian) include бог 'god', рай 'paradise', and святой 'holy'. From Germanic, there are borrowings such as купить 'buy', хлеб 'bread', and other household terms. If we assume that linguistic borrowing is the result of language contact between neighboring peoples, the primordial home of the Slavs must have been adjacent to areas occupied by speakers of Indo-Iranian and Germanic languages. The contact between Slavic and Baltic must also have been extensive in the Common Slavic period; as mentioned in section 1.1, many researchers even assume a common Balto-Slavic branch of the Indo-European language family. Accordingly, the primordial home of the Slavs must have been close to that of the Balts. As pointed out by Schenker (1995: 7), there is evidence that Baltic peoples dwelled between the Baltic Sea and the upper Dnieper. The Scythians and Sarmatians, who spoke Indo-Iranian languages, lived on the steppe north of the Black Sea, and this area was later occupied by the Germanic Ostrogoths. If we place the primordial home of the Slavs between the areas occupied by Balts, Scythians, Sarmatians, and Ostrogoths, we end up in the Dnieper area.

Written Roman sources from the first centuries AD that describe the lands of central or southeastern Europe mention Celtic and Germanic tribes, but not the Slavs. As pointed out by Schenker (1995: 6), this is hardly accidental, but "can be explained simply by the fact that the Slavs, unlike the Celts and the Germans, had not arrived on the frontiers of the classical world until after the Great Migrations." This reinforces the evidence from loanwords and favors the Mid-Dnieper hypothesis that locates the primordial home of the Slavs far away from the Roman Empire.

1.4. The Slavic Migrations

The Migration Period led to dramatic changes in Europe. Germanic tribes, originating in southern Scandinavia, among them Goths, pushed southwards through Europe and sacked Rome in 410 AD. Other Gothic tribes known as Ostrogoths migrated through present-day Poland and Ukraine until they reached the coast of the Black Sea around 200 AD. In addition to the southward Germanic migrations, there were waves of westward migrations of nomadic peoples from Asia, such as the Huns and the Avars. The Huns overran the Ostrogoths and pushed through the steppe north of the Black Sea and into Europe, where they established a short-lived empire, which dissolved after the death of Attila the Hun in 453. The Avars, a Turkic people from central Asia, founded an empire that covered large areas of Central and Eastern Europe from the late 6th to the early 9th century.

The migration waves from the north and the east affected the Slavs. If we accept the Mid-Dnieper hypothesis, the Migration Period found the Slavs in their primordial homeland in present-day Ukraine and Belarus. As a result of waves of Slavic migrations into Central Europe and the Balkans, Slavic-speaking tribes came to inhabit most of Central and Eastern Europe. As the Slavs spread over larger areas, linguistic diversity increased, and Common Slavic gradually disintegrated into West, South, and East Slavic languages. After 700 AD the areas occupied by the Slavs in Central and Eastern Europe became smaller. Gradually, Slavs became absorbed in local populations in Greece, Albania, and Romania, while Germans displaced the Slavs in Bavaria and Austria and Magyars displaced the Slavs in Hungary.

The East Slavs started an expansion to the north, where they encountered tribes speaking Baltic and Finno-Ugric languages. This expansion probably took place between 500 and 800 AD. Before the establishment of the state called "Kievan Rus'," we find a number of East Slavic tribes living in independence in the area between the Baltic and the Black Seas. These tribes include the *Poljane*, *Drevljane* (also called *Derevljane*), *Radimiči*, *Dregoviči*, *Severjane*, *Kriviči*, *Vjatiči*, and *Slovene*.[2] Their approximate geographical distribution is indicated on the map in Figure 2, opposite.

1.5. Rus'—The State

The 800–900s AD saw the first formation of a state among the East Slavs—Kievan Rus'. In order to understand this political development, we must first consider the impact of geography and the interplay between trade, farming, hunting, and gathering.

Three keywords summarize the role of geography: steppe, forest, and rivers. The landscape between the Baltic and Black Seas that was inhabited by the East Slavic tribes is part of the East European Plain that stretches from present-day Poland in the west to the Ural Mountains in the east. The steppe, which comprises the southern part of present-day Ukraine has fertile soil, but provides no protection against neighboring nomadic peoples. The soil in the forests further to the north is poorer, but better protects its inhabitants against intruders. While the large, impenetrable forests separate peoples, the role of rivers in Russian history has been to promote contact between the inhabitants of different regions. The area that became Kievan Rus' is dominated by a number of river systems, all of which originate in the Valdai Hills between present-day Moscow and St. Petersburg. The largest rivers are the Volga, which flows to the southeast into the Caspian Sea, and Dnieper, which flows southwards and ends up in the Black Sea. However, the Valdai Hills are also connected to the Baltic Sea through the Western Dvina, which enters the Baltic Sea in present-day Latvia, and the chain of rivers formed by the Lovat, Volkhov, and Neva, which runs from the Valdai Hills through Lake Ilmen and Lake Ladoga and finally enter the Baltic Sea where St. Petersburg is today. Importantly, these four river systems were connected by portages, i.e., places where it was possible to transport boats and cargo over land from one river to another.

The East Slavic tribes were farmers, but especially in the north where the soil is poorer, they were also engaged in hunting and gathering. Furs from wild animals and wax and honey from bees were valuable goods that provided the foundation for trade along the rivers. To some extent this trade was local or regional exchange of timber, fur, and wax from the north with grain and cattle from the south. However, at the same time the East Slavs found themselves lo-

---

[2] Notice that *Slovene* is used in two different senses in this book. Don't confuse the East Slavic tribe Slovene that used to live around Novgorod in the 8th–9th centuries with the speakers of the South Slavic language Slovene (Slovenian) in present-day Slovenia.

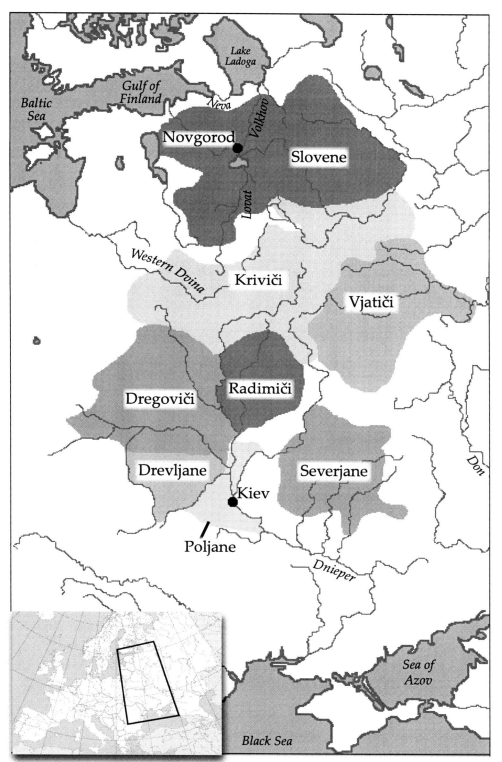

Figure 2. The East Slavic Tribes

cated along an international trade route that connected Northern Europe with the Byzantine Empire. Scandinavian Vikings known as Varangians (Russian: варяги) came up the rivers from the Baltic Sea and conducted raids on the Baltic, Finno-Ugric, and Slavic tribes in the area. They took slaves and stole valuable goods such as wax, fur, and swords, which they sold in the market centers on the Volga and the Black Sea. In return they received silver coins, as well as finished goods such as weapons and luxuries such as jewelry and spices.

While the details are not known, it seems that the relations between the raiders and their victims became regularized. The raiders became rulers or princes and started to collect regular amounts of tribute on an annual basis instead of conducting irregular plundering raids. This arrangement may have been mutually beneficial; in exchange for the tribute the tribes avoided destructive raids and received some protection against other raiders (Martin 2002: 2). It is this mutually beneficial state of affairs, which Xlevov (1997: 80) refers to as a "viable symbiosis" (Russian: жизнеспособный симбиоз), that formed the basis of the state known as Kievan Rus'. Although the majority of its inhabitants were primarily engaged in agriculture, Kievan Rus' as a state was based on trade, and in this sense it was a commercial state, rather than an agrarian state.

According to the *Primary Chronicle* (*Povest' vremennyx let*), the major written source that was compiled in the 11th or 12th century (see section 2.3.2), the first prince was Rjurik, who gave his name to the dynasty that ruled until Tsar Ivan IV "the Terrible's" son Fedor died in 1598 [3] In 862, Rjurik allegedly settled in Novgorod in the northwestern corner of Rus', but his followers established themselves further south in Kiev on the Dnieper, from which they effectively controlled the trade between Scandinavia and the Byzantine Empire. Kiev is considered the capital of Rus' from 882. The Kievan rulers conducted military campaigns against Constantinople, which resulted in treaties that made it possible for merchants from Kievan Rus' to trade not only at the Byzantine outpost Kherson on the Crimea, but also at the richer markets in Constantinople, today's Istanbul in Turkey, which was then the capital of the Byzantine Empire and the center of the Greek-Orthodox church.

The relations with the Byzantine Empire strengthened in 988, when Kievan Rus' adopted Christianity under Grand Prince Vladimir, who later became known as "the Holy." The Patriarch of Constantinople appointed a Metropol-

---

[3] In order to make it easier for you to keep the numerous Russian monarchs apart I provide their name, number, and conventional nickname, e.g., Ivan IV "the Terrible." Nicknames are given in quotes in order to emphasize that they are not necessarily accurate or objective characterizations of the monarchs' personalities. In the case of Ivan IV "the Terrible," the English nickname is not an accurate translation of грозный 'menacing, formidable', which is his traditional Russian nickname.

itan as the head of the church of Rus', and Byzantine clergymen baptized the population of Kiev in the Dnieper. From now on, Kievan Rus' was united not only through the power of the princes and their dynasty, but also through the Orthodox Church, which in the words of Martin (2007: 9) "gave shape and definition to the emerging state." The relationship between church and state is a consistent theme throughout Russian history, and is as relevant in the 21st century as it was in the 10th.

The conversion to Christianity sparked a period of cultural flourishing; the art of writing was introduced, Byzantine artists and artisans came to Kievan Rus', and churches were built in Kiev, Novgorod, and other cities. Kievan Rus' reached its peak in power and prestige under Vladimir's son, Jaroslav, who is known as "the Wise" and ruled in Kiev from 1019 to 1054. During Jaroslav's reign Kievan Rus' developed strong relations with foreign countries and their dynasties. It is symptomatic for the period that Jaroslav's sister was married to the Polish king, while his daughters married the monarchs of France, Hungary, and Norway. The marriage between Jaroslav's daughter Elizaveta and Harald "Hardrada" (Old Norse: Harðráði 'hard ruler') illustrates the crucial position of Kievan Rus' between the Byzantine Empire and Scandinavia. Before Harald became the king of Norway, he had served as a mercenary and military commander in the armies of Jaroslav and the Byzantine emperor.

The Scandinavian Vikings referred to Kievan Rus' as "Garðaríki," "the kingdom of cities," and as shown on the map in Figure 3 a number of cities emerged as trade developed. In addition to Kiev in the south, we have seen that Novgorod played an important role in the northwest. In the following centuries, Novgorod became the center of a large empire in northern Russia. In the northeastern part of Rus', Jaroslavl', Rostov, Suzdal', and Vladimir became important cities. However, as we will see in the following sections, gradually the small provincial city of Moscow became the center of gravity in the region and later the capital of the Russian empire. In a schematic, yet meaningful overview, we may consider medieval Russia a triangle defined by Novgorod, Kiev, and Moscow where the corners represent the relationship between Russia and the surrounding world. Novgorod represents the commercial relations with Scandinavia and later the Hanseatic League. Kiev represents the relationship to the Byzantine Empire and Orthodox Christianity. It became the task of Moscow to take up the challenge from Russia's most formidable antagonist in the east—the Mongols. In sections 1.7 and 1.8 you will learn more about the Mongols and the rise of Moscow, but first we must make a detour and discuss a key term in Russian history, namely Rus', which gave the state its name.

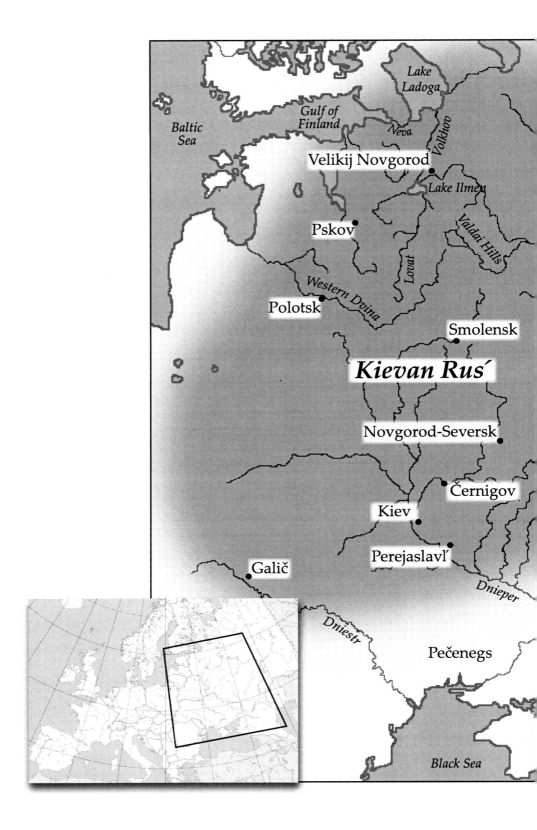

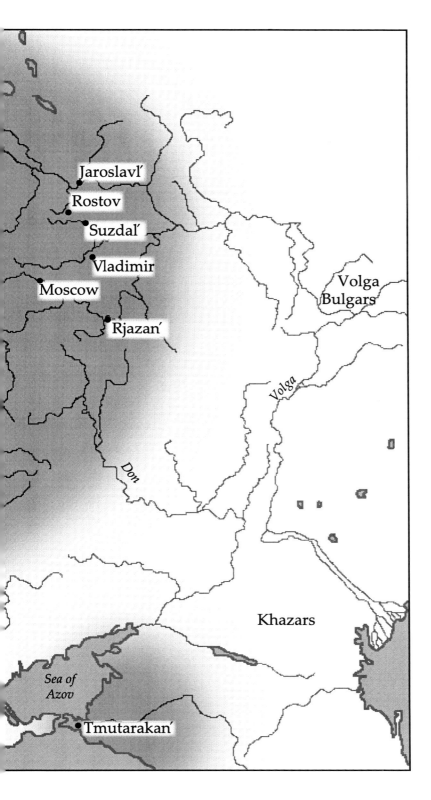

Figure 3. Kievan Rus': Rivers and cities

1.6. Rus'—The People

In Slavic linguistics, few questions of etymology have received more attention than the origin of the term *Rus'*. Who were these people? There are two positions:

(3) a. *The Normanist view:*
   The Rus' were Scandinavian Vikings.
   b. *The Anti-Normanist view:*
   The Rus' were a Slavic tribe.

It is not hard to see why this question has sparked intense debates. In the cold-war era in the second half of the twentieth century, western researchers were inclined to emphasize the importance of western influence in Russian history, whereas Soviet scholars were equally eager to deny any foreign impulses, especially from the west. Adherents of the Normanist view relate the term to the Old-Norse words *roþsmenn*, *roþskarlar* 'oarsmen, seamen' and the Swedish name of the coastal area north of Stockholm, Roslagen. Normanists also point to the Finnish words *Ruotsi* 'Sweden' and *Ruotsalainen* 'Swede'. Possibly, *Rus'* reflects the name of a group of Scandinavian Vikings used by Finno-Ugric tribes in northern Russia and adopted by their Slavic neighbors. Anti-Normanists, on the contrary, avoid relating *Rus'* to Scandinavia, for instance suggesting that *Rus'* may have originated from the name of the river *Ros'* in present-day Ukraine (cf., e.g., Grekov 1949: 443, Šaskol'skij 1965: 53–54, Šaskol'skij 1967, and Tixomirov 1979: 44–45).

Let us see what the *Primary Chronicle* says about Rus'. I give the quotes in Old Rusian and provide Modern Russian and English translations, a practice I will follow throughout the book. When you have learned more about Old Rusian grammar, you may return to this page and enjoy reading the examples in the original. The *Primary Chronicle* describes a period of conflict among the Slavic and Finno-Ugric tribes in the area. In order to solve the conflict, a group of Varangians from "overseas" is invited to serve as mediators:

(4) a. Идоша за море к варягом, к руси. Сице бо взвахуть ты варягы русь, яко се друзии зовутся свее, друзии же урмани, аньгляне, инѣи и готе, тако и си. Ркоша руси чюдь, словенѣ, кривичи и вся: «Земля наша велика и обилна, а наряда въ ней нѣтъ. Да поидете княжить и володѣть нами.» И изъбрашася трие брата с роды своими, и пояша по собѣ всю русь, и придоша къ словѣномъ пѣрвѣе. (PVL 862 AD; 19,20)

1.6. Rus'—The People

(4) b. Пошли за море к варягам, к руси. Те варяги назывались русью, как другие называются шведы, а иные — норманны и англы, а еще иные готы — вот так и эти. Сказали руси чудь, словене, кривичи и весь: «Земля наша велика и обильна, а порядка в ней нет. Приходите княжить и владеть нами.» И избрались трое братьев со своими родами, и взяли с собой всю русь, и пришли прежде всего к словенам.

c. They went overseas to the Varangians, to the **Rus'**; these particular Varangians were known as **Rus'**, just as some are called Swedes, and others Normans, English, and Gotlanders, for they were thus named. The Čud', the Slovene, the Kriviči, and the Ves' then said to the **Rus'**, "Our land is great and rich, but there is no order in it. Come and rule and reign over us." They selected three brothers, with their kinsfolk, who took with them all the **Rus'** and first came to the Slovene.[4]

In accordance with the Normanist view, this passage describes the Rus' as a subgroup of the Varangians, who were Scandinavians. There is a little snag, though. Although the *Primary Chronicle* was compiled in the 11th or 12th century, the only versions that have come down to us are from later centuries. The oldest is the so-called *Laurentian Redaction* from 1377, where the third sentence of the passage goes like this:[5]

(5) a. Рѣша русь, чюдь, словѣни, и кривичи: «Вся земля наша велика и обилна, а наряда въ неи нѣтъ. Да поидѣте княжитъ и володѣти нами.» (PVL 862 AD; 19,24)

b. Сказали русь, чудь, словене, и кривичи: «Вся земля наша велика и обильна, а порядка в ней нет. Приходите княжить и владеть нами.»

---

[4] It is not quite clear whether Old Rusian **словенѣ** in this passage should be translated as 'Slavs' (i.e., Slavic people in general) or as 'Slovene' (the East Slavic tribe around Novgorod, see map in Figure 2 on p. 15). However, the latter option seems more likely due to the fact that **словенѣ** is mentioned next to **кривичи**, another East Slavic tribe; it makes good sense that the passage is about the two northernmost East Slavic tribes, the Slovene and the Kriviči, and their non-Slavic neighbors, the Čud and the Ves' (Vepsians).

[5] The quote from the *Laurentian Redaction* is from *Polnoe sobranie russkix letopisej*, vol. 1 (1997: 19); see also Ostrowski 2003: 104.

(5) c. The **Rus'**, Čud', Slovene, and Kriviči then said, "All our land is great and rich, but there is no order in it. So come and rule and reign over us."

While in (4a) *Rus'* occurs in the dative singular, suggesting that Rus' was the addressee, in (5) *Rus'* is in the nominative singular, i.e., serves as the subject of the sentence together with the Slavic and Finno-Ugric tribes. However, in the rest of the passage, Rus' is described as Scandinavians, in the same way is in (4a). The *Laurentian Redaction* thus leaves behind a confusing impression, whereby it is unclear whether the Rus' were Scandinavians or a Slavic tribe.

The term *Rus'* is also mentioned in other sources, which offer evidence in favor of the Normanist view. Here are three of them (for more detailed discussion, see Schenker 1995: 57–60):

(6) a. Annals of St. Bertin (830–82)

b. The Rus'—Byzantine treaty of 912

c. Constantine Porphyrogenitus' (905–59) description of the Dnieper cataracts

The *Annals of St. Bertin* describe the arrival of a Byzantine diplomatic delegation to the court of emperor Louis the Pious (778–840) at Ingelheim on the Rhine. Among the men in the Byzantine delegation were men belonging to a group called "Rhos," who turned out to be Scandinavian. The treaty between Kievan Rus' and the Byzantine Empire of 912, which is included in the *Primary Chronicle*, mentions the names of the Rus' emissaries, all of whom have Scandinavian names such as Karl, Ingjald, and Gunnar. In his description of the route from Scandinavia to the Byzantine Empire, Emperor Constantine Porphyrogenitus (905–59) mentions the Dnieper cataracts, which were important, because ships would have to be carried over land, which made merchants vulnerable to attacks. The cataracts have both Rus' and Slavic names, and the Rus' names are arguably Scandinavian. These and similar sources favor the Normanist view, suggesting that the founders of the Kievan state, Rus', were Scandinavian Vikings. However, these sources do *not* suggest that the Scandinavian Vikings had a massive cultural impact on the history of Rus'. As pointed out by Christensen and Rasmussen (1986: 32), the cultural influence went in the opposite direction; the Scandinavians received cultural impulses from the Slavs, who in turn were subject to massive cultural influence from the Byzantine Empire. Within a few generations the Scandinavian princes were assimilated to the local Slavic population, and Rus' became the name of the state of the eastern Slavs.

1.7. Mongols: Conflict and Collaboration

So far we have focused on Kievan Rus' and its neighbors in the north—the Scandinavians—and in the south—the Byzantine Empire. However, neighboring states in the east were also important. Between the seventh and thirteenth centuries there was an Islamic state of Bulgars on the upper Volga, while the Khazars, a Turkic people whose ruling elite had adopted Judaism, controlled an empire stretching from the mid-Volga to the North Caucasus.[6] Both the Bulgars and the Khazars, who spoke Turkic languages, were important trade partners for Kievan Rus'. However, in 965 Prince Svjatoslav conducted an attack on the Khazars, after which the Khazarian Empire collapsed. Svjatoslav may have been pleased with his achievement, but the disintegration of the Khazarian Empire had the unfortunate consequence of destabilizing the steppe region south of Rus'—with shattering long-term consequences for Rus'.

In section 1.4, you learned about the Huns and the Avars, whose invasions from the east had a tremendous impact not only on the Slavs, but on European history in general. After the Khazarian collapse, the steppe was dominated by pagan nomads known as Pechenegs, who in the 11th century were ousted by another pagan nomadic people, the Polovtsians (Cumans). However, it was only in the 13th century that the challenge from the steppe became impossible to handle for Kievan Rus'. Since its peak under Jaroslav "the Wise" in the 11th century, Kievan Rus' had become increasingly fragmented and was not able to stop the formidable forces of the Mongols, who attacked Rus' with a large army under the command of Batu. Batu was the grandson of Chingiz Khan, who in 1206 had managed to unite the Mongol tribes and create a strong Mongol state. In December 1237, the Mongols captured their first Rus' city, Rjazan', and then moved northeast and subjugated the fortified outpost of Moscow, as well as the more important cities in the area such as Suzdal', Vladimir, and Tver'. In 1239, the Mongols attacked Perejaslavl' and Černigov in southwestern Rus', and in 1240 Kiev surrendered.

Batu's headquarters were in Sarai, and this city on the Volga became the capital of the Mongol state known as the Golden Horde. As pointed out by Martin (2007: 156), the main focus of the Golden Horde was to control the steppe, and Rus' was only interesting as a means to achieve this goal. After the Mongol invasion, the princes of Rus' remained in charge as long as they acknowledged the Mongol Khan's suzerainty and paid tribute to him. Mongol

---

[6] Do not confuse the Volga Bulgars with the South Slavic Bulgarians in Bulgaria. The first state in what is now Bulgaria was founded by Volga Bulgars, who had migrated from the Volga region in the 7th century. The immigrants became assimilated to the Slavic population and adopted their language, and the Slavs in the area became known as Bulgarians.

suzerainty lasted for more than 200 years. The battle at Kulikovo Pole in 1380 was the first victory over the Mongols, but Moscow did not stop paying tribute until 1452, and it ended all formal loyalty to the Khan in 1480—240 years after the collapse of Kiev.

The history of Rus' and the Mongols is a history of military conflict. The Khan would send punitive expeditions that would raid cities and force unwilling princes to pay tribute. The Mongols on the Volga were finally defeated in the 1550s under Ivan IV "the Terrible," but Mongol raids in southern Russia were a constant problem in the 16th and 17th centuries, and the Khanate on the Crimean peninsula was not subdued until 1783.

However, the history of Rus' and the Mongols is also a history of collaboration. The fact that the princes of Rus' kept their thrones made it possible for the Khan to play the princes against each other. This gave ambitious princes an opportunity to collaborate with the Khan in order to eliminate rivaling princes and extend their own power. In this intricate power play, the princes of Moscow turned out to be true virtuosos, and this contributed to the rise of Moscow, to which we turn in the following section.

1.8. The Rise of the Muscovite State

Two keywords summarize the history of Muscovy, the state that gradually emerges around Moscow: outward expansion and consolidation of central power. Moscow started out as a small provincial town that was first mentioned in the chronicles in 1147, i.e., about a century after Kievan Rus' was at its peak under Jaroslav "the Wise." After the Mongol conquest the center of gravity moved to the northeastern part of Kievan Rus', and in the beginning the most important city was Vladimir, which became the seat of the Grand Prince and the Metropolitan. However, in 1328 the Mongols gave Ivan I "Moneybag" (Russian: **Калита**) of Moscow the title of Grand Prince, and the same year the Metropolitan made Moscow his residence.[7] Cultivating good relations with the Mongols appears to have been Ivan's highest priority; he traveled to Sarai nine times during his lifetime, and helped the Mongols in a punitive expedition against Tver' in 1327.

During the 14th and 15th centuries Muscovy grew steadily. Some regions (e.g., Jaroslavl') were purchased, others were conquered (e.g., Perm' and Vjatka), while still others (e.g., Rjazan') were inherited. In 1456, even Novgorod, the prosperous city in the northwest that controlled a large empire in northern

---

[7] Some historians consider it more likely that in the beginning Ivan I "Moneybag" shared power with prince Aleksandr of Suzdal', and that Ivan was given the official title of grand prince only after Aleksandr's death in 1331 (see Martin 2007: 196 for discussion).

Russia, became a dependency of Moscow. After revolts in 1471 and 1478, Moscow conquered Novgorod, exiling and executing opponents to Moscow suzerainty. As a consequence of this, Novgorod became part of Muscovy for good.

As mentioned in the previous section, in 1480 the Moscow Grand Prince Ivan III "the Great" ended all formal loyalty to the Mongols. In 1493 he took the title of "Sovereign of all Russia," called himself "autocrat" (Russian: **самодержец**) and "tsar" — until then it was the Mongol Khan who was referred to as "tsar." Ivan III "the Great" was married to a Byzantine princess, and adopted Byzantine symbols such as the double-headed eagle. His reign represents the end of what historians call the "appanage era," the period after the fragmentation of Kievan Rus' until the Moscow grand princes had completed the "gathering of the Russian lands."

The Russian church became increasingly rich and powerful in the 15th century. In Western Europe, this century is characterized by religious conflict culminating with the Reformation. However, no reformation ever took place in Russia. While in Russia the main schism in the church did not occur until the second half of the 17th century, there were also conflicts around the church at the end of the 15th century, the most important being the so-called "possessor/non-possessor controversy." The non-possessors led by Nil Sorskij (1433–1508) were critical of monastic wealth, whereas the church's official position was that monastic wealth was a means to fulfill its crucial function in society. A church council held in 1503 deemed the church's official position correct.

Another important issue concerning the church and its relation to the state is the theory of Moscow as the Third Rome, which was first articulated in letters from the monk Filofej (ca. 1465–1542), who was the abbot in a monastery in Pskov. Here is the famous line (with Modern Russian and English translations):

(7) a. Два убо Рима падоша, а третий стоит, а четвертому не быти.
(Filofej)

b. Ибо два Рима пали, а третий стоит, а четвертому не бывать.

c. For two Romes have fallen, and the third stands, and there will not be a fourth.

The fall of the first Rome refers to the fact that Rome adopted catholicism, which from the perspective of the Orthodox Church amounted to heresy. The "second Rome" was Constantinople, the capital of the Byzantine Empire and the center of the Orthodox Church. However, the Byzantine Empire had gradually lost its power, and in 1453 Constantinople was taken over by the Muslim Ottoman Empire. At this point, the Russian Church was the leading branch of the Orthodox Church, so Moscow could be considered the "Third Rome." Filofej's writings could be interpreted as a warning against misconduct on the part of the princes, since the fall of the first and the second Rome was the result of God's punishment. However, the Moscow rulers instead embraced the idea of Moscow as the Third Rome, interpreting Moscow as the center of the Christian world and Muscovy as the direct continuation of the Roman and Byzantine empires.

As can be seen from the map in Figure 4 on pp. 28–29, Muscovy in the beginning of the 16th century under Ivan III's son Vasilij III comprised most of the territory that was earlier controlled by Kiev. However, Kiev itself was not under Muscovy's control, but rather part of the neighboring Grand Duchy of Lithuania, which became Russia's main rival in the following centuries. In the northwest, Sweden controlled Finland. In the east and south, Muscovy's neighbors were the Mongol Khanates of Kazan', Astraxan', and the Crimea. In other words, although Muscovy had grown large, it did not have access to the Baltic and Black Seas. The struggle to get access to the sea became a major issue for the Russian rulers in the following two centuries, to which we turn in the following section.

1.9. Ivan IV "the Terrible": Russia in the 16th Century

In 1533 began the reign of one of the most enigmatic rulers of Russia. He was three years old, his name was Ivan IV, and history knows him as "the Terrible." It makes sense to divide Ivan's reign into two phases. During the first phase, the young tsar mostly left the conduct of government to advisors, whereas in the second phase after 1560 he assumed absolute power. However, both phases are characterized by familiar Muscovy politics involving consolidation of central power and outward expansion.

The power of the central government increased. This development was in the interest of the lesser nobility, while the Boyars, the most highly ranked noblemen, were interested in preserving their independence. A new law codex (*sudebnik*) was issued in 1550, and the following year a Church council issued the *Stoglav* (Hundred chapters), a text reforming the organization of the Church and regulating its relation to the state. The army was also reorganized, and regular infantry units of loyal musketeers were established.

The reformed army became instrumental in Moscow's expansionist foreign policy. In 1552, Ivan IV's army defeated the Khanate in Kazan', thus paving the way for Russian expansion in Siberia. Siberia was important for the fur trade, and Russia's eastward expansion was to continue until the Russians reached the Pacific Ocean in 1639. At the same time Ivan IV's army was engaged in military conflicts in the Baltic area known as Livonia, pursuing its long time goal of gaining access to the Baltic Sea. The Livonian war would drag on for a quarter of a century—without ever giving the desired outcome from the Russian perspective.

Characteristic of the second phase of Ivan's reign is Russia's first (but not last) large-scale experiment with terror. In order to assume absolute power, in 1564 Ivan left Moscow and threatened to abdicate. Finally, he agreed to come back, but only on the condition that he would be granted the right to punish any opponent or enemy of the state. A second condition was even more radical. Ivan insisted that Muscovy be divided into two parts: the *Zemščina*, which kept normal institutions, and the *Opričnina* ("the exceptional area"), which would be ruled by a new administration responsible to the tsar and no one else. Ivan established a corps of personal bodyguards, *opričniki*, who numbered 6000 men dressed in black uniforms with brooms indicating their intention to sweep Russia free of traitors. With this tremendously powerful tool in his hands, Ivan took radical measures against real and imagined enemies. For instance, in 1569–70 the *opričniki* slaughtered tens of thousands inhabitants of Novgorod. The *Opričnina* experiment was a major failure and was abolished in 1572, when Ivan slaughtered the leaders of the *opričniki*.

As you may have guessed at this point, Ivan IV was a violent and brutal person. In 1581, he struck and killed his eldest son, the seventeen-year-old heir to the throne, in a rage. When Ivan died in 1584, another son, Fedor, became tsar and ruled until he died in 1598, leaving no heir to the throne. Russia was now in a threefold crisis. The *Opričnina* experiment had created a social crisis, and the lack of heirs to the throne resulted in a dynastic crisis. On top of this, Russia was in an economic crisis. During Ivan's reign the taxes that the peasants had to pay had risen by 300–400%. At the same time, Russia's expansion to the east gave peasants an opportunity to migrate to the outskirts of the empire, including the fertile areas in the south that had previously been controlled by the Mongols. Combined with crop failures and plague, these developments left Russia in a deep economic crisis at the end of the 16th century.

1.10. The "Time of Troubles" (1598–1613)

A turbulent period which is traditionally known as the "Time of Troubles" (Russian: смутное время) started in 1598, when the boyar Boris Godunov was elected tsar by a *zemskij sobor*, an assembly dominated by representatives of the Church, boyars, and gentry. Boris Godunov did not manage to stabilize the situation, and his authority was undercut by rumors that one of Ivan IV "the Terrible's" sons, Dmitrij, was still alive. In reality, Dmitrij had died at the age of nine in 1591 under unclear circumstances. However, a pretender who claimed to be Dmitrij and had miraculously escaped death in 1591, surfaced in Poland, raised an army and invaded Russia. This "False Dmitrij" (Russian:

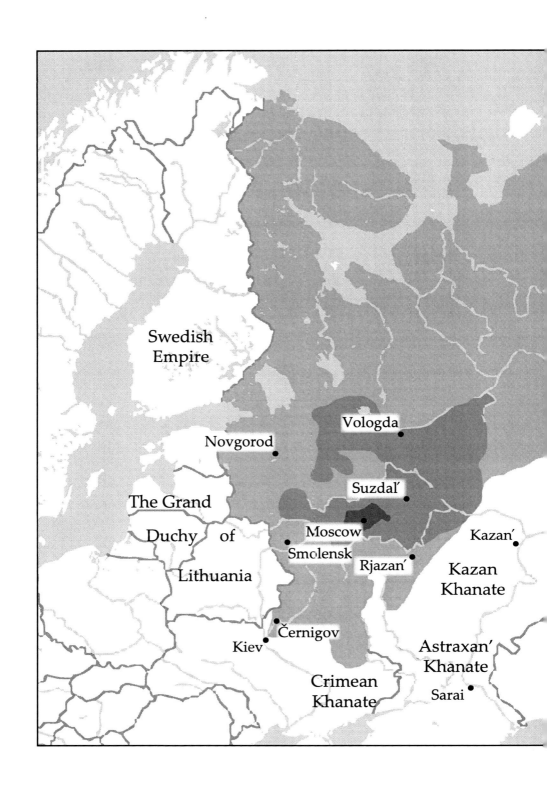

Figure 4. The explansion of the Muscovite state

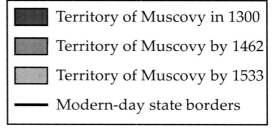

Лжедмитрий), as he is known in Russian history, ruled in Moscow from 1605 to 1606, and was then overthrown and murdered by the boyars. A second False Dmitrij, supported by Poland, attacked Russia in 1607, but was finally killed in 1610. Russia was now in a state of civil war, and Swedish and Polish intervention complicated the situation. For a while Poland controlled Moscow, but Moscow was eventually liberated by a national army in 1612. A new tsar was elected in 1613. His name was Mixail Romanov, and the Romanov dynasty would stay in power until the Russian Revolution in 1917.

1.11. Russia in the Seventeenth Century

The dynastic crisis was now solved, but the financial and social crises were not. While the military conflicts with Sweden and Poland were settled, the state was close to bankrupt, a problem it tried to solve by raising taxes. Another unpopular measure was the establishment of serfdom for the peasants. Traditionally, the peasants had been granted the right to leave their landowners in November of each year. However, as mentioned in section 1.9, peasants fleeing to the outskirts of the empire were a growing problem for the landowners, and the response to this problem was to impose tighter restrictions on the peasants. Among these restrictions were so-called "forbidden years," when the peasants were not allowed to leave their landowners at all. In the *Sobornoe uloženie* (Law Codex) of 1649, the right to leave the landowners was formally eliminated, and as a consequence of this the peasants were effectively bound to the land and to the service of the landowners. Serfdom was now in place for a long time, and was only abolished in 1861.

All these unpopular measures led to a number of uprisings, e.g., the so-called tax rebellion in Moscow in 1648 that soon spread to other cities. The most prominent uprising was led by Stepan (Stenka) Razin, a Cossack from the Don area, who advanced up the Volga, attracting on the way thousands of Cossacks, runaway peasants, and other dissenters. However, Razin was betrayed, handed over to tsarist authorities, and executed in Moscow in 1671.

Despite social unrest and the critical financial situation, Russia's territorial expansion continued in the 17th century. The Ukrainian Cossacks rebelled against the Polish-Lithuanian authorities, and their leader, hetman Bohdan Xmel'nic'kyj, appealed to Russia for help and in 1654 acknowledged the Russian tsar as his superior.

Closer contact with Kiev brought new cultural impulses to Moscow, but also the practical problem of re-establishing ritual unity with the Kiev metropolitanate. In 1653, Patriarch Nikon launched a fundamental reform of church ritual with the goal of reversing the independent development of the Russian church that had accelerated ever since the fall of Constantinople in 1453. This reform met with strong opposition, and the result was a schism within the Russian Church. As pointed out by Torke (2002: 76), the Old Believers movement and its leaders, such as Archpriest Avvakum Petrovič, represented a broad social movement, which included "a protest against enserfment, the centralizing activities of the government, and the intrusion of Western innovations." Ironically, while Nikon's reforms were approved and implemented, Nikon himself was deprived of all his sacerdotal functions because he had insisted that the patriarch be the tsar's superordinate.

The first Romanov on the throne, Mixail, ruled from 1613–45, and was then succeeded by his son, Aleksej Mixajlovič, who ruled until 1676. Under Aleksej's son Peter I, known as "the Great," Russia finally built a port on the Baltic Sea, St. Petersburg, which became the capital of the modernized and westernized Russia of the 18th century. However, as Russia's center of gravity moves from Moscow to Petersburg and the Middle Ages come to an end, we leave the history of Russia and shift our focus to an event with profound ramifications—the emergence of writing in Rus'. This is the topic of the next chapter.

1.12. Chronology: Overview of Historical Periods and Events in Tabular Form

ca. 200	Goths reach the Black Sea.
370	Huns invade Europe.
ca. 500–800	East Slavic expansion to the north.
ca. 560	Avars invade Europe.
ca. 700	Slavic westward migration reaches the Elbe.
862	Rjurik becomes the ruler of Novgorod according to the *Primary Chronicle*.
882	Kiev becomes the capital of Rus'.
965	Prince Svjatoslav defeats the Khazars.
988	Kievan Rus' accepts Christianity under Vladimir "the Holy."
1019–54	Kievan Rus' flourishes during the reign of Jaroslav "the Wise."
1147	Moscow is mentioned in the chronicles for the first time.
1237	The Mongols under Khan Batu take Rjazan'.
1240	Kiev surrenders to the Mongols.
1328	The Prince of Moscow is awarded the title of Grand Prince, and the Metropolitan makes Moscow his residence.
1380	First victory over the Mongols at Kulikovo Pole.
1452	Ivan III "the Great" stops paying tribute to the Mongols.

1453	Fall of Constantinople and Byzantine Empire; paves the way for the ideology of Moscow as the Third Rome.
1456	Novgorod becomes a dependency of Moscow.
1480	Subjugation to the Mongols ends.
1552–56	Ivan IV "the Terrible" defeats the Mongol khanates in Kazan' and Astraxan'.
1564–72	Ivan IV "the Terrible's" Opričnina in operation.
1598–1613	"Time of Troubles."
1605–06	False Dmitrij rules in Moscow.
1607	Second false Dmitrij attacks Russia.
1610	Second false Dmitrij is murdered.
1612	Moscow liberated by national army.
1613	The first Romanov, Mixail, becomes tsar.
1648	Tax rebellion in Moscow.
1654	Ukrainian hetman Bohdan Xmel'nic'kyj acknowledges the Russian tsar as his superior.
1671	Stenka Razin executed.
1653	Patriarch Nikon launches his church reform which results in the schism of the Russian Church.
1682	Archpriest Avvakum Petrovič dies, Peter I "the Great" becomes tsar.

1.13. Suggestions for Further Reading

An authoritative and very readable history of medieval Russia in English is Martin 2007; a shorter narrative by the same author is Martin 2002. A very brief overview is given in Heyman 1993. For those who read Scandinavian languages, Christensen and Rasmussen (1986) provide a good overview, and Opeide (2009) offers interesting perspectives of Russian history. For information about the primordial home of the Slavs and their early migrations, the interested reader is referred to Schenker 1995 and the short, but very informative overview in Andersen 1998. A whole monograph devoted to the topic is Gołąb 1992. Schenker (1995) offers a good overview of the etymology of *Rus'* and the Normanist/anti-Normanist debate. A balanced analysis of this debate in Russian historiography is Xlevov 1997.

Chapter 2   **The Texts: Writing and Literature in Kievan Rus' and Muscovy**

In the previous chapter, we explored the history of medieval Russia. We now turn to an important characteristic of this society—the emergence of writing and literature. Needless to say, medieval texts are interesting in and of themselves, but the texts are of particular interest to us as historical linguists, since they represent a major source of data. This chapter provides you with important background knowledge about writing, alphabets, texts, and literature. Questions we will consider include: How did writing come to Kievan Rus'? Which alphabets were used? In what language were the texts written? What was the standard language in Kievan Rus'? What kinds of texts have come down to us? Although this chapter is by no means a detailed history of medieval literature, you will learn about some important literary genres and key texts. Finally, this chapter gives you an opportunity to reflect on the differences between the medieval and modern concepts of literature.

2.1. Overture: Cyril and Methodius, the First Slavic Alphabet, and Old Church Slavonic

The history of writing in Rus' starts not in Rus', but in the Byzantine Empire. In the fall of 863 two brothers, Constantine (who later took the name Cyril when he became a monk) and Methodius, arrived in Moravia in what is now the Czech Republic. After the collapse of the Avar state in the 9th century (see section 1.4), a Slavic state had emerged in Moravia. In order to counterbalance the massive cultural influence from the Frankish empire in the west, the Moravian Duke Rostislav asked the Byzantine emperor to send missionaries who could teach the Gospel in Slavic rather than Latin. Constantine and Methodius's Moravian mission was unsuccessful, and they had to leave after forty months. Nevertheless, as pointed out by Schenker (1995: 26), "Rostislav's initiative brought about what has turned out to be the most momentous event in the cultural history of the Slavs," because Constantine and Methodius brought to Moravia key texts from the New Testament that they had translated into Slavic, using a new alphabet that had been devised for the purpose. This was the beginning of writing and literature in the Slavic world—a tradition that is still alive today, more than 1100 years later.[1]

Constantine and Methodius grew up in Thessalonica in what is now the northern part of Greece. It is believed that the two brothers were bilingual, since the countryside around Thessalonica was largely Slavic (recall from section 1.4 that Slavic tribes settled in the Balkans during the Migration Period). Constantine had made a career as a scholar in the Byzantine capital, Constantinople, while Methodius had been in civil service before he became a monk. Together the two brothers had carried out a mission to Khazaria on behalf of the Byzantine emperor. Given their experience from Khazaria, Constantine's scholarly merits and the fact that the two brothers were bilingual, they must have been an obvious choice for the Byzantine emperor when he decided to send missionaries to Moravia upon Duke Rostislav's request. In the 800s, the differences among the Slavic dialects were still small, so it seems safe to assume that the dialect spoken by Constantine and Methodius was intelligible in Moravia and elsewhere in the Slavic world.

Which alphabet did Constantine "devise"? In present-day Europe, two alphabets are used for the Slavic languages. The West Slavic languages, as well as Slovene, Croatian, and Bosnian use the Latin alphabet, while the East Slavic languages, Bulgarian, Macedonian, and Serbian are written in Cyrillic. There is a close correlation between alphabet and religion; Catholic areas use the Latin alphabet, while Cyrillic is used in areas dominated by the Orthodox Church. Since the Cyrillic alphabet has its name after Constantine's adopted monastic name, it may appear obvious that this was the alphabet that was devised for the purposes of the Moravian mission. However, in reality things are less straightforward. In addition to Cyrillic, another alphabet was used in early Slavic writing. Although this alphabet, known as Glagolitic, is not in use anymore, it was still used in religious texts in certain parts of Croatia up to the beginning of the twentieth century.

The Cyrillic alphabet is clearly an adaptation of the capital letters of the Greek alphabet with the addition of some letters for non-Greek sounds. As for the provenience of the Glagolitic alphabet, at least three hypotheses deserve mention:

---

[1] The question of whether Slavic writing existed before the Moravian mission has been the subject of lively debate, but remains unanswered. As Cubberley (1993: 21) aptly notes, "the fact is that there are few facts." Since the Slavs were surrounded by and interacted with peoples who had adopted writing, it is not unlikely that they had experimented with writing before the time of Constantine and Methodius. However, no hard evidence has been presented, so the question remains open. In any case, it is clear that the Slavic literary tradition starts with the Moravian mission.

(1) a. Glagolitic was a totally individual creation "from scratch."
   b. Glagolitic was based on Greek cursive script (the handwriting used in writing on papyrus).
   c. Glagolitic was based on Cyrillic.

Speaking in favor of the "genuine creation" hypothesis in (1a) is the fact that the written sources that describe the Moravian mission insist that Constantine *created* the alphabet. Furthermore, there may have been some political advantages to creating a new alphabet rather than adapting an existing system. The idea behind Rostislav's initiative was to support Slavic independence, and having a distinct Slavic alphabet may have been considered advantageous. As Schenker (1995: 178) points out, "in the eyes of Constantine and his contemporaries, the possession of a distinct alphabet bestowed upon Slavic the dignity requisite for undertaking the sacred task of Bible translation and secured for it a place of equality among the major languages of medieval Christendom." Finally, it should be pointed out that some other languages had independent alphabets. A case in point is Armenian, which Constantine most likely had some knowledge of.

At the same time, one cannot but wonder why Constantine, an accomplished linguist who knew several languages, would go to the trouble of creating an entirely new alphabet "from scratch." This line of reasoning suggests that Constantine would use some model as a starting point for his work. The most likely source is Greek cursive script, i.e., the hypothesis in (1b), which was first proposed by the British paleographer Isaac Taylor in 1880 and has been accepted by a number of leading scholars in the field. It should be pointed out that the difference between the hypotheses in (1a) and (1b) is a matter of degree; even if Constantine used cursive Greek as his starting point, the resulting alphabet may still have been different enough to justify talking about the creation of a new alphabet.

Although hypothesis (1c) represents an interesting idea, it is most likely incorrect, for the simple reason that the Glagolitic alphabet is older than the Cyrillic. For instance, there are palimpsests (reused manuscripts) that superimpose Cyrillic on Glagolitic, but no examples of Glagolitic on top of Cyrillic. The rejection of hypothesis (1c) has the corollary that the alphabet Constantine created or adapted was Glagolitic, not Cyrillic. Exactly how the Cyrillic alphabet became associated with Constantine (Cyril) remains unclear. However, the names of the alphabets are much later formations; according to Cubberley (1993: 29) the name *glagolica* probably developed in the Croatian area in the fourteenth century, while in Russia *glagolica* and *kirillica* are attested only in the nineteenth century.

The text canon that emerged from the work of Constantine and Methodius and their followers is referred to as "Old Church Slavonic" (often abbreviated as OCS) in English and **старославянский язык** in Russian. The oldest manuscripts that have come down to us are from the tenth century. The term Church Slavic (without "old") and its Russian equivalent **церковнославянский язык** are used about texts that belong to the Cyrillo-Methodian tradition, but are either dated after 1100 or contain numerous dialectal features. Thus, the two oldest texts preserved from the East Slavic area, the so-called *Novgorod Codex* (**Новгородский кодекс**) from between 1000 and 1025 and the *Ostromir Gospel* (**Остромирово евангелие**) from 1056–57, are usually not included in the Old Church Slavonic canon, since they include a number of East Slavic features.

Although the Moravian mission itself failed, Old Church Slavonic writing flourished in the tenth century, especially in Ohrid in Macedonia and Preslav in Bulgaria. While the more conservative Ohrid school appears to have favored the Glagolitic alphabet, Methodius's immediate disciples who settled in Preslav may have devised the Cyrillic alphabet. In view of Bulgaria's proximity to Kievan Rus', it is not surprising that the Preslav school had the strongest impact on Kievan Rus' and that it was the Cyrillic alphabet that was introduced there when Vladimir "the Holy" adopted Christianity in 988.

2.2. The Cyrillic Alphabet—A Practical Guide

Since this is a book about linguistics and not about paleography (the study of ancient writing), examples are cited in modernized orthography. In other words, I keep the use of unfamiliar letters to a minimum, since this makes it possible to describe the relevant linguistic phenomena in a simple and straightforward manner. However, when you work with medieval texts, you will frequently encounter letters you do not recognize from Modern Russian.

Table 5, on p. 38, provides an overview of the Cyrillic alphabet in the font Kliment Std, which approximates the shape of the letters in medieval manuscripts, and contains a number of letters that are not used in Contemporary Standard Russian.[2] Although the shape of the letters is somewhat different, you recognize most of them from Modern Russian. In the following we concentrate on the letters that are different.

For consonants, the letters in Table 5 provide few challenges. Notice, however, that the letter ч, which corresponds to modern ч, has an unfamiliar shape. While the letter ш is essentially the same as its modern counterpart ш, the letter щ has a different shape from the modern щ. In Old Church Slavonic, щ repre-

---

[2] The Kliment Std font is developed by the German Slavist Sebastian Kempgen, and is freely available at http://kodeks.uni-bamberg.de/aksl/Schrift/KlimentStd.htm.

sented the sequence /š't'/. In Russian, the pronunciation [šč'] was widespread and was still normative ("**литературное**") in the 19th century. However, in Contemporary Standard Russian the pronunciation as a long soft fricative [š':] is the norm. The two letters з (known as "**земля**") and ѕ (known as "**зело**," also represented as **s**) are very similar. The former is the predecessor of the letter з in modern Russian, while the latter, which originally represented the sound sequence [dz], was excluded from the Cyrillic alphabet in Russia in 1738 (Istrin 1988: 66).

With regard to vowels, there are more differences. First, you need to learn the letter ѣ ("jat," Russian: **ять**). This letter represented a narrow e-like sound, which it is customary to transcribe as [ě]. Although the phonemes /ě/ and /e/ merged in Old Rusian times, the letter ѣ was used in Russian orthography until the spelling reform in 1917–18. You will encounter ѣ frequently in the examples in this book. The merger of /ě/ and /e/ is discussed in section 12.8.

For the phoneme /i/, three letters occur in medieval Cyrillic manuscripts: **i**, **ï**, and **и**. In Kliment Std, the last has the shape н, which approximates the shape of the letter in medieval manuscripts. In this book, however, only **и** is used.

In addition to the letter **o**, which you recognize from Modern Russian, Greek omega (ѡ) was used to represent the same sound. While the most widely used letter was **o**, ѡ frequently occured in the preposition and prefix **от(ъ)**, where **т** was placed on top of the vowel: ѿ. In this book, we will only use **o**.

In medieval texts you normally find the digraph **оу** where Modern Russian has **у**. Sometimes, the two letters that constitute the digraph are placed on top of each other: ꙋ. In this book, however, we will only use modern **у**.

From Contemporary Standard Russian you are familiar with the hard sign **ъ** and the soft sign **ь**, which are part of the orthographic system without representing independent sounds. It is important to notice that these letters, which we call "jers," represented vowels in Old Church Slavonic and early Old Rusian. The hard sign (Russian: **ер**) was a short *u*-sound, which it is customary to transcribe as /ŭ/, while the soft sign (Russian: **ерь**) represented a short *i*-sound that can be transcribed as /ĭ/. The development of the jers is described in detail in section 12.2.[3]

In Modern Russian, the letter **ы** is a combination of the soft sign **ь** and the letter **i**. In medieval texts, it was more common to represent the relevant sound as **ъı**, which is a combination of the hard sign plus the letter **i**. In the present book, you will only encounter the modern variant **ы**.

The letters ѫ (Russian: **юс большой**) and ѧ (Russian: **юс малый**) represented nasal vowels in Common Slavic akin to the vowels in the French words **bon vin** 'good wine'. In transcription, we use /ǫ/ for ѫ and /ę/ for ѧ. Although

---

[3] In scholarly literature on Slavic languages in English you may come across both spellings "yer" and "jer." The latter spelling is used throughout this book.

the nasal vowels had lost their nasal quality by the Old Rusian period, especially ѫ was widely used in Old Rusian manuscripts. However, in the present book I will use **y** instead of ѫ and **я** instead of ѧ. You will learn more about nasal vowels in section 10.7.

From Table 5, you see that there was no specific letter for /j/. However, the letters ю, ꙗ, ѥ, ѭ, and ѩ represented a sequence of /j/ plus a vowel (and later also indicated that a preceding consonant was soft). Only ю has survived in Contemporary Standard Russian. The letter ꙗ has been replaced by **я**, while the sequence /je/ is represented as **e** in Modern Russian. In this book, only the modern letters **ю, я**, and **e** are used. The sequences /ji/ and /jь/ were both designated as **и**. Lunt (2001: 25) aptly characterizes the lack of a device to differentiate these two sound sequences as the "most serious defect in the writing system."

Table 5. The Cyrillic alphabet (Font: Kliment Std)

Letter	Transcription	Letter	Transcription
а	a	оу, 8	u
б	b	ф	f
в	v	ѳ	th
г	g	х	x
д	d	щ	šč, š':
є	e	ц	c
ж	ž	ч	č
ѕ (s)	dz	ш	š
з	z	ъ	ъ (ŭ)
і, ї, н	i	ы	y
к	k	ь	ь (ĭ)
л	l	ѣ	ě
м	m	ю	ju
н	n	ꙗ	ja
о, ѡ	o	ѥ	je
п	p	ѧ	ę
р	r	ѫ	ǫ
с	s	ѩ	ję
т	t	ѭ	jǫ

Words in medieval texts are often abbreviated. The first and the last letter of the stem and the entire grammatical ending can be written out and the rest omitted. For instance, **апостолъ** 'apostle' can be written as follows: **ап͠лъ**. Notice that the so-called titlo (the symbol ˜) above the stem indicates that the word is abbreviated. As pointed out by Lunt (2001: 28), according to the Greek tradition, such abbreviations were originally a way of emphasising the *nomina sacra* ("sacred names"), i.e., the names for God, Jesus, Heaven, etc., but in Slavic the practice was extended to other frequently occurring words, and thus became a space-saving device rather than a means of emphasis. Another way of saving space was to write certain letters above the others. For instance, the aorist form **бысть** of **быти** 'be' may be written as follows: **вы̊**. Notice that often only some of the omitted letters are placed on top of the word. Often an arc is placed above the small letters.

In addition to representing sounds, in medieval texts letters could also designate numbers. Each letter had a numerical value, as shown in Table 6 on p. 40. The Cyrillic number designations were taken over from Greek, and thus Cyrillic letters that lacked a Greek counterpart had no numerical value, while some Greek letters were used to represent numbers even though they were otherwise not used in the Cyrillic alphabet. Notice that Greek **s** ("stigma") represents 6 and that ϴ ("theta") equals 9, while 60 is represented as Greek ξ ("ksi") and 700 as Greek ψ ("psi").

The highest number in the table is 900. In order to represent 1000, the symbol ҂ was placed before a letter for the numbers from 1 to 9. For instance, ҂г̄ = 3000. The number ҂ѕ х̄ к̄z can be deciphered as follows: ҂ѕ (6,000) + х̄ (600) + к̄ (20) + z (7) = 6627. Notice the titlo above the letters, which shows that the letters represent numbers rather than sounds. Thus, the titlo has two functions in Cyrillic manuscripts; it indicates that we are dealing with numbers or abbreviated words.

Before we leave the Cyrillic alphabet, it should be pointed out that the shape of the letters changed considerably over time. It is customary to distinguish between three styles: uncial (Russian: **устав**), semi-uncial (Russian: **полуустав**), and cursive (Russian: **скоропись**). Uncial letters, which have a square shape, were gradually replaced by the less square semi-uncial beginning in the fourteenth century. In the Russian area, the cursive style, the forerunner of today's handwriting, developed in writing for administrative purposes from the fifteenth century. You can find good examples of the various styles in Cubberley 1993: 34–35 and Čekunova 2010.

Table 6. The numerical values of letters

Letter	Numerical value	Letter	Numerical value
а	1	ѯ	60
в	2	о	70
г	3	п	80
д	4	ҁ	90
є	5	р	100
ѕ	6	с	200
з	7	т	300
н (и)	8	оу, ѵ	400
ѳ	9	ф	500
і, ï	10	х	600
к	20	ѱ	700
л	30	ѡ	800
м	40	ц, ѧ	900
н	50		

An important reform is the introduction of the "civil script" (Russian: **гражданский шрифт**) for the printing of non-religious books under Peter I "the Great" in 1708–10. This reform eliminated some redundant letters such as ѫ and ѧ, and introduced э. Arabic numbers replaced letters for the representation of numbers. The Modern Russian orthography is due to the reforms in 1917–18, when the letters ѣ and i were finally removed.

2.3. Literary Genres and Works

In the following, we will review important literary genres and consider examples from key texts. Although such a brief overview cannot aim at representativity, it gives a flavor of the richness and variety found in the literature of Rus'.

2.3.1. Religious Literature: From Metropolitan Hilarion to Archpriest Avvakum

The existence of the *Novgorod Codex* and the *Ostromir Gospel* mentioned in section 2.1 show that copying of liturgical books started shortly after Vladimir "the Holy" adopted Christianity in 988. The oldest example of an original text written in Kievan Rus' is Metropolitan Hilarion's sermon *Slovo o zakone i blagodati*, which was written a few years before Hilarion became the first Slav to be Metropolitan in Kiev in 1051. Using Byzantine rhetorical schemes, Hilarion reflects on the victory of the grace of Christ over the Law of Moses. The sermon ends with a eulogy to Prince Vladimir "the Holy," where Hilarion compares Vladimir to Constantine "the Great," the first Roman emperor to convert to Christianity. The following quote where Hilarion addresses Vladimir is illustrative. For convenience, the quote is given in (a) Church Slavic, (b) Modern Russian, and (c) English:

(2) a. Онъ [Коньстантинъ] въ елинѣхъ и римлянѣх царьство Богу покори, ты же — в Руси: уже бо и въ онѣхъ и въ насъ Христос царемь зовется. Онъ съ материю своею Еленою крестъ от Иерусалима принесъша и по всему миру своему раславъша, вѣру утвердиста, ты же съ бабою твоею Ольгою принесъша крестъ от новааго Иерусалима, Константина града, и сего по всеи земли своеи поставивша, утвердиста вѣру. Егоже убо подобникъ сыи, съ тѣмь же единоя славы и чести обещьника сътворилъ тя Господь на небесѣхъ благовѣриа твоего ради, еже имѣ въ животѣ своемь. (Hilarion)

b. Тот [Константин] покорил Богу царство в еллинской и римской стране, ты же — на Руси: ибо Христос уже как и у них, так и у нас зовется царем. Тот с матерью своею Еленой веру утвердил, крест принеся из Иерусалима и по всему

Figure 5. Pages from the *Ostromir Gospel*, 11th century

> миру своему распространив <его>, — ты же с бабкою твоею Ольгой веру утвердил, крест принеся из нового Иерусалима, града Константинова, и водрузив <его> по всей земле твоей. И, как подобного ему, соделал тебя Господь на небесах сопричастником одной с ним славы и чести <в награду> за благочестие твое, которое стяжал ты в жизни своей.

(2) c. He [Constantine] conquered for God the empire in the Greek and Roman land, like you did in Rus': therefore Christ is called "tsar" by them and by us. He and his mother Helena confirmed the faith, bringing the cross from Jerusalem and extending it all around the world. You and your grandmother Olga confirmed the faith, bringing the cross from the New Jerusalem, Constantine's city, and erecting it all over your land. And the Lord in Heaven made you part of his same glory and honor in reward for the godliness you achieved in your life.

As shown in the quote, Hilarion treats Rus' as the continuation of Rome and Constantinople, thus suggesting a historical role for the people of Rus' and their monarch as the defenders of true Christianity. This is a theme that runs like a red thread through Russian literature from the very beginning to our times.

Hilarion's general approach to history is characteristic of the medieval conceptualization of time. In the quoted passage, Hilarion juxtaposes Rome, Constantinople, and Kiev, and throughout the sermon he builds up an elaborate set of comparisons between the Old and the New Testament. Comparisons of this sort do not uncover the causes of historical events, but instead establish a number of analogies between the present and the past, describing events in the present as repetitions of events foreshadowed in the Bible. In the words of Børtnes (1992: 7), "history understood in this way does not seek to discover the causal links between events and characters, but rather to interpret them as images of a timeless, archetypical pattern designed by God before the foundation of the world."

The same approach to history is pervasive in hagiographical texts. Hagiography can be defined as the writing and critical study of saints (apostles, martyrs, or "confessors," i.e., persons who spent their lives seeking individual perfection). The most important hagiographical genre is the vita (English: *life*, Russian: житие)—"biographies" of saints. An early Kievan example of hagiographical writing is the monk Nestor's *Reading on the Life and Slaying of the Blessed Martyrs Boris and Gleb* (**Чтение о житии и о погублении блаженную страстотерпцю Бориса и Глѣба**), where the author describes the death of Boris and Gleb, Vladimir "the Holy's" two youngest sons, who were killed by their older brother Svjatopolk in the power struggle after Vladimir's death in 1015. In the same way as Hilarion compares Vladimir "the Holy" to Constantine "the Great," Nestor compares Boris and Gleb to Joseph and Benjamin of the Old Testament, while Svjatopolk is compared to Cain. Boris and Gleb's acceptance of a violent death without resistance is furthermore described as an imitation of Christ's death on the cross—the so-called *imitatio Christi* motif. In this way, historical events in the recent history of Rus' were interpreted as repetitions of archetypical events from the Bible.

An example of a *žitie* 'saint's life' from the Muscovite period is *Žitie Sergija Radonežskogo*, which describes the life of the founder of the large Holy Trinity Monastery near Moscow. This *žitie*, which was written by the monk Epiphanius "the Wise" in 1417–18, is an example of *pletenie sloves* (word-weaving, weaving of words), the ornamental style that was fashionable in Muscovy in the fourteenth and fifteenth centuries:

(3)   a.   Благодарим Бога за премногу его благость, бывшую на нас, якоже рече апостолъ: «Благодать Богу о неизреченнѣм его дарѣ!» Паче же нынѣ длъжны есмы благодарити Бога о всем, еже дарова намъ такова старца свята, глаголю же господина преподобнаго Сергиа, в земли нашей Русстѣй, и въ странѣ нашей полунощнѣй, въ дни наша, въ послѣдняя времена и лѣта.
(Sergij)

       b.   Благодарим Бога за великую его благость, сошедшую на нас, как сказал апостол: «Благодарность Богу за неизреченный его дар!» Ныне же мы должны особенно благодарить Бога за то, что даровал он нам такого старца святого, — говорю о господине преподобном Сергии, — в земле нашей Русской, в стране нашей полунощной, в дни наши, в последние времена и годы.

       c.   We thank God for the great kindness that he has shown us as the apostle said: "gratitude to God for his ineffable gift!" Now we must thank God especially for giving us such a holy monk—I am talking about the Lord's venerable Sergij—in our Russian land, in our midnight-dark land, in our days, in the last times and years.

The leader of the Old Believers movement in the late seventeenth century (cf. section 1.11), Avvakum Petrovič, transforms the genre of saint's life. His *žitie*, which was written by himself when he was a prisoner in Pustozersk on the White Sea, is a blend of a traditional saint's life and a modern autobiography, where the author combines Church Slavic linguistic features with elements from the spoken language. Avvakum describes his sufferings, which he can only make sense of as an example of *imitatio Christi*:

(4) a. Таже ин начальник, во ино время, на мя рассвирепел, — прибежал ко мне в дом, бив меня, и у руки отгрыз персты, яко пес, зубами. И егда наполнилась гортань ево крови, тогда руку мою испустил из зубов своих и, покиня меня, пошел в дом свой. Аз же, поблагодаря бога, завертев руку платом, пошел к вечерне. (Avvakum)

b. Потом начальник в другой раз на меня рассвирепел, прибежал ко мне в дом, бил меня и у руки отгрыз пальцы, как пес, зубами. И когда глотка его наполнилась кровью, руку мою отпустил из зубов и, покинув меня, пошел в дом свой. Я ж, поблагодарив Бога, завертел руку платком и пошел к вечерне. (Mjakotin 2002: 13)

(4) c. And likewise another headman at another time became as a wild beast against me. Breaking into my house, he beat me and gnawed the fingers of my hand, like a dog, with his teeth; and when his throat was full of blood, then he loosened his teeth from my hand and, throwing me aside, went to his house. But I, blessing God, wrapped up my hand in a cloth and went to vespers.

2.3.2. *The Primary Chronicle* (*Povest' vremennyx let*) and Other Chronicles

A chronicle (Russian: **летопись**) is a recording of historical events with an entry for each year. Each entry starts with the phrase **Въ лѣто**... 'in the year...' and then follows a description of what happened that year. The chronicles counted the years from God's creation of the world, which they considered took place 5508 years before the birth of Christ. Here is the entry for the year 6392 (i.e., 884 AD) from the so-called *Primary Chronicle* (Russian: *Povest' vremennyx let*):

(5) a. В лѣто 6392. Иде Олегъ на сѣверы, и побѣди сѣверы, и възложи на нихъ дань легъку, и не дасть имъ козаромъ дани даяти, рекъ: «Азъ имъ противенъ, а вамъ не чему." (PVL 884 AD; 24,8)

b. В год 6392 (884). Пошел Олег на северян, и победил северян, и возложил на них легкую дань, и не велел им платить дань хазарам, сказав: «Я враг их, и вам <им платить> незачем."

c. In the year 6392, Oleg attacked the Severjane, and conquered them. He imposed a light tribute upon them and ordered them not to pay tribute to the Khazars, saying, "I am their enemy, and you should not pay them."

Short entries like this with down-to-earth recollections of historical events testify to the value of the *Primary Chronicle* as a historical source, although it is sometimes difficult to distinguish between what is factual and what is legendary in the chronicle. Clearly legendary are anecdotes such as Olga's revenge over the Drevljane who had murdered her husband, and the death of Oleg who was bitten by a snake that had been hiding in the skull of his favorite horse. Some of these anecdotes have correspondences in the Old Norse sagas; such similarities may reflect Byzantine influence on both Old Rusian and Old Norse literature, as suggested by the Danish scholar Adolf Stender-Petersen (1957: 100–02).

The chronicles revolve around the deeds of the princes, emphasizing the legitimacy and prestige of the ruling dynasty. At the same time, the *Primary Chronicle* illustrates the close relationship between the princes and the church. The *Primary Chronicle* starts with the story about the division of the earth among Noah's sons, thus integrating the history of Rus' into the history of the world as seen from a Christian perspective. In the same way as the sermons and saints' lives discussed in the preceding section, the *Primary Chronicle* includes the *imitatio Christi* motif, for instance, in the description of the death of Boris and Gleb. In a sense, the *Primary Chronicle* incorporates two different approaches to history: a linear and a cyclic conception of time. On the one hand, a chronicle by definition follows a chronological principle, whereby events are organized chronologically on a timeline. As pointed out by Børtnes (1992: 13), this linear conception of time is unlimited and could in principle go on forever. However, on the other hand, the Christian conception of history as cyclic repetitions of the archetypical events from the Bible also pervades the *Primary Chronicle*.

Chronicles were not restricted to Kiev; as Rus' became more and more fragmented, a number of principalities began to have their own chronicles written, often using the *Primary Chronicle* as their starting point. The *Primary Chronicle* has come down to us as the first part of a number of regional chronicles, the two oldest of which are found in the *Laurentian Codex* from 1377 and the *Hypatian Codex* from the late 1420s. The Russian philologist and linguist Aleksej Šaxmatov (1864–1920) hypothesized that the Laurentian version preserves a redaction of the *Primary Chronicle* by the monk Silvester from 1117, while the *Hypatian Codex* reflects a version prepared for Prince Mstislav Vladimirovič the following year. According to Šaxmatov's hypothesis, the redactions from 1117 and 1118 are based on the first comprehensive redaction of the *Primary Chronicle*, which may have been compiled by the monk Nestor (the author of the *Reading on the Life and Slaying of the Blessed Martyrs Boris and Gleb* discussed in the previous section) around 1113. Nestor's redaction, in turn, may have been based on earlier versions, which may go as far back as to the 1030s. With certain modifications Šaxmatov's hypothesis is still accepted by most experts today (see Ostrowski 2003: XVII–LXXIII for critical discussion).

2.3.3. *Slovo o polku Igoreve, Zadonščina,* and Military Tales

Slovo o polku Igoreve, which is often referred to as the *Lay of Igor's Campaign* or the *Igor Tale* in English, addresses a topic that is well known from religious literature and chronicles, namely Rus' as the stronghold of Christianity and the threat a fragmented Rus' faces from the non-Christian peoples of the steppe. In 1185, Prince Igor' of Novgorod-Seversk in present-day Ukraine (not to be confused with Novgorod in northwestern Russia) carried out an unsuccessful military campaign against the Polovtsians (also known as Cumans), where he was taken prisoner and manages to flee only after having spent several weeks in captivity. Historically, Igor's campaign was a minor event in the ongoing conflicts between Rus' and the peoples of the steppe. However, although the anonymous author of the *Igor Tale* treats an unoriginal topic based on an insignificant historical event, the author's literary treatment of his topic makes the *Igor Tale* a unique masterpiece of Old Rusian literature. While the description of the campaign itself is highly condensed, the narrative is interrupted by lyrical digressions that juxtapose the author's troubled present with a "golden age" represented by the legendary bard Bojan when Rus' stood united against its enemies in the steppe. The complex relationships between the temporal planes combined with rich poetic imagery in the words of Børtnes (1992: 18) enables the author to translate "his troubled premonitions of the ruin of Rus' into a poetic vision of tragic portent."

The following quote from one of the lyrical digressions illustrates the use of poetic imagery. Igor's wife, likened to a seagull, laments the loss of her husband. Although Old Rusian literature has a number of female heroes, this may be one of the earliest examples where a woman speaks to us in the first person:

(6) a. На Дунаи Ярославнынъ гласъ слышитъ, зегзицею незнаема рано кычеть. "Полечю, — рече, — зегзицею по Дунаеви, омочю бебрянъ рукавъ въ Каялѣ рѣцѣ, утру князю кровавыя его раны на жестоцѣмъ его тѣлѣ." (Slovo)

b. На Дунае Ярославнин голос слышится, одна-одинешенька спозаранку как чайка кличет. "Полечу, — говорит, — чайкою

2.3.3. *Slovo o polku Igoreve*, *Zadonščina*, and Military Tales

по Дунаю, омочу шелковый рукав в Каяле-реке, оботру князю кровавые его раны на горячем его теле.»

(6) c. At the river Danube the voice of Jaroslavna is heard. Since morning, she sings like an unknown seagull. "Like a seagull I will fly along the river Danube. I will dip my beaver-trimmed sleeve into the river Kajala. I will cleanse the bloody wounds of my prince, on his mighty body."

The reason why Igor's tale is one of the most debated works of Old Rusian literature is not only its *literary* qualities, but also the fact that its authenticity has been disputed. The *Igor Tale* is known from one manuscript that was acquired by Prince A. I. Musin-Puškin, who published it in 1800, but never really explained how he acquired it. After the manuscript perished in a fire in 1812 when Napoleon marched on Moscow, its authenticity was questioned. However, the arguments presented by the Russian linguist Andrej Zaliznjak (born 1935) have finally laid these doubts to rest. Zaliznjak argues that only a linguistic genius would have been able to forge the *Igor Tale*. In order to do so, an anonymous forger would have to (a) have known more than all linguists of the past two centuries combined, (b) have been able to acquire a foreign language (i.e., the language of Kievan Rus', which is very different from the Modern Russian language of around 1800) without access to definitive grammars or dictionaries, (c) have been able to write a literary masterpiece in this language, and (d) have been able to keep his tremendous knowledge secret to his contemporaries, since no such person is known from the relevant time period. Assessing the formidable task an anonymous forger would face, Zaliznjak concludes:

(7) Попасть из пистолета через плечо в червонного туза вслепую — сущий пустяк по сравнению с такой задачей. (Zaliznjak 2008a: 141)

'Hitting an ace of diamonds blindfolded using a pistol slung facing backwards over your shoulder is a mere trifle compared to such a task.'

Although Igor's tale is a unique specimen in Old Russian literature, there are several military tales devoted to the continuous conflicts with the peoples of the steppe. For instance, *Povest' o razorenii Rjazani Batyem* (The Tale of Batu's Sacking of Rjazan') describes the Mongols' conquest of Rjazan' in 1237, while *Zadonščina* is devoted to the victory over the Mongols at Kulikovo Pole in 1380. *Povest' o prixoždenii Stefana Batorija na grad Pskov* describes the Polish-Lituanian attack on Pskov in 1581 during Ivan IV "the Terrible's" reign.

2.3.4. *Russkaja Pravda* and Other Legal Texts

With the growth of Kievan Rus' arose a need for a legal system. The oldest law codex is known as *Russkaja Pravda*. It has been preserved in two versions, the older *Kratkaja redakcija*, which dates back to the reign of Jaroslav "the Wise," and the more recent *Prostrannaja redakcija* from the twelfth or thirteenth century. However, the written versions are based on an oral tradition, presumably of pre-Christian origin. Here is a short quote illustrating the efforts to regulate conflicts in a multi-ethnic society:

(8) a. Аще ли ринеть мужь мужа любо от себе любо к собѣ, 3 гривнѣ, а видока два выведеть; или будеть варягъ или колбягъ, то на роту. (RPK)

b. Если человек толкнет человека от себя или к себе, то 3 гривны, и пусть пострадавший приведет на суд двух свидетелей; если пострадавший варяг или колбяг, то пусть сам клянется.

c. If a man pushes another man either away from or towards himself, then he has to pay 3 grivnas if two witnesses are presented; if the aggrieved party is a varjag [Varangian, a Scandinavian warrior] or a kolbjag [a Finnic merchant], then his oath is sufficient.

Russkaja Pravda remained the core of the legal system for a long time; only in 1497 under Ivan III "the Great" was a new law codex (*sudebnik*) issued for the rapidly growing Muscovite state. Another *sudebnik* was issued under Ivan IV "the Terrible" in 1550. In 1649 a new law codex, known as *Sobornoe uloženie* was issued.

2.3.5. Travel: Afanasij Nikitin's *Xoždenie za tri morja*

Travel memoirs represent a genre of some importance in Old Rusian literature. While most of them describe pilgrimages to the Holy Land, Afanasij Nikitin's *Xoždenie za tri morja* reports on a business trip to India that Afanasij Nikitin, a merchant from the city of Tver', undertook around 1470. As a businessman Nikitin was highly unsuccessful—he was robbed by the Mongols near Astraxan', and all he managed to sell in India was his horse. However, his travel memoirs offer vivid descriptions of India twenty-five years before Portuguese explorer Vasco da Gama found a maritime route to India:

(9) a. Город же Бедерь стерегут в нощи тысяща человѣкъ кутоваловых, а ѣздят на конех в доспѣсех, да у всѣх по свѣтычю. А яз жеребца своего продал в Бедери. Да наложил есми у него шестьдесят да осмь футунов, а кормил есми его год. В Бедери же змеи ходят по улицам, а длина еѣ двѣ сажени. (Xoždenie)

b. По ночам город Бидар охраняет тысяча стражей под начальством куттавала, на конях и в доспехах, да в руках у каждого по факелу. Продал я своего жеребца в Бидаре. Издержал на него шестьдесят восемь футунов, кормил его год. В Бидаре по улицам змеи ползают, длиной по две сажени.

c. A thousand men posted by the governor guard the city of Bidar by night; they are mounted, wear armor, and carry torches. I sold my stallion at Bidar; I had been keeping him for a year, and had spent sixty-eight fanams on him. Snakes fourteen feet long crawl along the streets of Bidar.

Afanasij Nikitin died in Smolensk on his way back to Tver' after having crossed three seas—the Caspian Sea, the Indian Ocean, and the Black Sea.

2.3.6. The Correspondence between Andrej Kurbskij and Ivan IV "the Terrible"

Prince Andrej Kurbskij had been one of Tsar Ivan IV "the Terrible's" closest allies, and Kurbskij played an important role in the wars against the Mongols and Poland-Lithuania. However, in 1563 Kurbskij fled to Poland-Lithuania in order to avoid Ivan's purges against the nobility. This sparked a highly polemical correspondence between the two former allies, starting with a long letter from Kurbskij where he accuses the tsar of destroying "the strong in Israel," i.e., the nobility:

(10) a. Про что, царю, силных во Израили побил еси, и воевод, от Бога данных ти на враги твоя, различными смертми разторгнул еси, и побѣдоносную святую кровь их въ церквах Божиях пролиал еси, и мученическими кровми праги церковныя обагрил еси, и на доброхотных твоих, душа своя за тя полагающих, неслыхованные от вѣка муки, и смерти, и гонениа умыслил еси, измѣнами, и чародѣйствы, и иными неподобными облыгаа православных и тщася со усердиемъ свѣт во тму преложити, и тму в свѣт, и сладкое горко прозвати, и горкое сладко? (Kurbskij)

(10) b. Зачем, царь, сильных во Израиле истребил, и воевод, дарованных тебе Богом для борьбы с врагами, различным казням предал, и святую кровь их победоносную в церквах Божьих пролил, и кровью мученическою обагрил церковные пороги, и на доброхотов твоих, душу свою за тебя положивших, неслыханные от начала мира муки, и смерти, и притеснения измыслил, оболгав православных в изменах и чародействе и в ином непотребстве и с усердием тщась свет во тьму обратить и сладкое назвать горьким, а горькое сладким?

c. Wherefore, O tsar, have you destroyed the strong in Israel and subjected to various forms of death the *voevodas* given to you by God? And wherefore have you spilled their victorious holy blood in the churches of God, and stained the thresholds of the churches with their blood of martyrs? And why have you conceived against your well-wishers and against those who lay down their lives for you unheard-of torments and persecutions and death, falsely accusing the Orthodox of treachery and magic and other abuses, and endeavoring with zeal to turn light into darkness and to call sweet bitter?

In an eloquent defense of autocracy, where Ivan responds that his power comes from God, and that he is responsible to God only, he does not fail to convey his contempt for Kurbskij:

(11) a. И ты то все забылъ еси, собацкимъ измѣннымъ обычаемъ преступивъ крестное целование, ко врагомъ християнскимъ соединился еси; и к тому, своея злобы не разсмотря, сицевыми скудумными глаголы, яко на небо камениемъ меща, нелѣпая глаголеши.　　　　　　　　　　　　　　　　(Groznyj)

b. А ты все это забыл, собачьей изменой нарушив крестное целование, присоединился к врагам христианства; и к тому же еще, не подумав о собственном злодействе, нелепости говоришь этими неумными словами, будто в небо швыряя камни.

c. But you have forgotten everything and traitorously, like a dog, you have transgressed the oath and have gone over to the enemies of Christianity, and, not considering your wrath, you utter stupid words, hurling, as it were, stones at the sky.

Altogether, five letters have been preserved, three from Kurbskij and two from the tsar.

2.3.7. Birch Bark Letters

While Andrej Kurbskij's and Ivan IV "the Terrible's" polemic letters presumably were intended to be read by the public, we now turn to letters that are just that—letters. In 1951 a young woman who was helping out in the archeological excavations of old Novgorod found a piece of birch bark into which Cyrillic letters were carved with a stylus (a needle-like implement) of metal or bone. This was the first birch bark letter. In the more than fifty years that have elapsed since the first finding more than a thousand letters have been excavated in Novgorod, and smaller numbers of letters have been found in other cities, thus testifying to the extensive propagation of writing on birch bark in medieval Russia. Most of the birch bark letters are short personal or business letters, which represent a unique source of information about the language and life of ordinary people in medieval Novgorod. In the following letter (quoted in its entirety), a father informs his son that he has bailed him out for twenty grivnas:

(12) a. От Братятѣ къ Нежилу. Поиди, сыну, домовь — свободне еси. Паки ли не идеши, а послу на тя ябьтьникъ. Я заплатиль 20 гривьнъ, а ты свободнь. (BBL 421; Zaliznjak 2004: 293)

b. От Братяты к Нежилу. Иди, сын, домой — ты свободен. Если же не пойдешь, я пошлю за тобой судебного исполнителя. Я заплатил 20 гривен, и ты свободен.

c. From Bratjata to Nežil. Go home, son, you are free. If you don't go, I will send a law-enforcement official for you. I have paid 20 grivnas, and you are free.

We will return to the language of the birch bark letters in chapter 14.

2.3.8. Summing Up: Medieval and Modern Concepts of "Literature"

Referring to all the texts explored in the preceding sections as "literature" may be a bit of a stretch. However, even if we narrow down the scope of literature by excluding legal texts and letters, we observe a number of differences between the modern and medieval concepts of "literature." If I ask you to think of a typical example of Russian literature, you would probably come up with a novel by, say, Dostoevsky or Tolstoy or, perhaps, a poem by Pushkin. Or there are numerous other options in nineteenth or twentieth century literature. However, it is not very likely that any text from medieval times would be high up on anybody's list of typical examples of Russian literature. Why? In addition to the trivial fact that medieval literature is less well known compared to writers such as Dostoevsky, Tolstoy, and Pushkin, there are a number of systematic reasons. First of all, when we think of literature today, we first and foremost think of fiction. However, the literature of medieval Rus' is factual, not fictional. Although, for instance, hagiographic works may contain elements that at least for a modern reader may appear fantastic, these elements were intended to be taken seriously as part of reality. In the words of Børtnes (1992: 1), "'literature' in Old Russia dealt primarily with the real world as medieval men saw it, and not with fictionalized accounts of it." A second characteristic that sets the literature of medieval Rus' apart from modern literature pertains to originality. From a modern perspective, originality in literature is highly desirable, but this was not the case in Rus'. In medieval times, literature dealt with the truth according to the tradition and the ideology of the state and the church, and under such circumstances original accounts were anything but desirable. Finally, modern literature is associated with professional writers. In medieval Russia, alternatively, the authors often remain anonymous, and writing was never the main occupation of the author. Very often, for instance, writers were monks who held a number of obligations in addition to writing.

Although there are substantial differences between modern and medieval concepts of "literature," this does not mean that the literature of the Middle Ages is irrelevant for post-medieval Russian literature. We have seen that from the very beginning, literature in Kievan Rus' addressed topics such as the historical role of the Russian people as the defenders of true Christianity, topics that have played a no less important role in Russian literature in later centuries. Commenting on the character of Aleša, the youngest of the Karamazov brothers, Børtnes (1988: 280) points out that "[m]any critics have interpreted Aleša on the conventions of the realistic novel, and thereby misunderstood Dostoevsky's intentions." Instead, Børtnes insists, *The Brothers Karamazov* can only be fully understood and appreciated against the background of the medieval hagiographic tradition.

2.4. Standard Language: The Situation in Kievan Rus'

The preceding sections testify to a hectic literary activity from the times of Vladimir "the Holy" and his son, Jaroslav "the Wise." In which language were these works written? What was the standard language in Kievan Rus'? These questions are not as simple as they may seem. Although the center of the church was Constantinople, the capital of the Byzantine Empire where Greek was the

2.4. Standard Language: The Situation in Kievan Rus'

dominant language, the Greek language was not used in the Kievan church. Given the existence of the flourishing Cyrillo-Methodian tradition in the South Slavic religious centers of Ohrid and Preslav, it was natural to use a Slavic language in church in Kievan Rus' too. As mentioned in section 2.1, it is customary to refer to this variant of South Slavic as "Church Slavic." In short, while the imported religious culture was Byzantine, the imported religious language was South Slavic.

In the eleventh century the differences between East, West, and South Slavic had grown so significant that it makes sense to talk about an Old Rusian language that was different from South Slavic. Or to be more precise, we must assume that the inhabitants of Kievan Rus' spoke a number of regional East Slavic (Old Rusian) dialects, and that they would encounter the South Slavic-based Church Slavic in church.

We will return to the differences between South Slavic and Old Rusian in later chapters of this book. However, in order for you to get an idea of the differences let us consider one simple example at this point. The word for 'city' was городъ in Old Rusian, while South Slavic had градъ. Likewise, Old Rusian had молодъ for 'young', whereas the corresponding word in South Slavic was младъ. In other words, the Old Rusian sound sequence /oro/ or /olo/ corresponded to /ra/ and /la/ in South Slavic. Whenever a scribe would encounter words like these, he would have to ask himself: "should I write as I speak or use the Church Slavic form?"

In view of the co-existence of Old Rusian and Church Slavic, we must ask: what was the standard language in Kievan Rus'? For our purposes it is sufficiently precise to define "standard language" as a set of rules explicitly encoded in grammars, dictionaries, and textbooks that children learn through formal instruction. To take a pedestrian example, the spelling of English is something you have to learn in school, and you sometimes need to consult dictionaries to make sure you have spelled a word correctly. Spelling is therefore part of standard language, as are the grammatical rules that define what is considered correct English. "Standard language" is a concept from modern sociolinguistics, and it is far from unproblematic to transpose it to medieval communities. However, we will use this term in this chapter.

It makes sense to distinguish between three hypotheses about standard language in Kievan Rus':

(13) a. *The Church Slavic Hypothesis*: Church Slavic was the standard language in Kievan Rus'.

b. *The Old Rusian Hypothesis*: Old Rusian was the standard language in Kievan Rus'.

(13) c. *The Diglossia Hypothesis*: The sociolinguistic situation in Kievan Rus' was an example of diglossia between Church Slavic (the "high" variety) and Old Rusian (the "low" variety).

Although the Church Slavic Hypothesis had been proposed already in the nineteenth century, it is usually associated with Aleksej Šaxmatov, one of the most influential Russian philologists in the beginning of the twentieth century, who among other things did groundbreaking work on the *Primary Chronicle*, as we saw in section 2.3.2. Šaxmatov wrote:

(14) Получивъ изъ Болгаріи христіанство, Кіевъ одновременно заимствовалъ оттуда книжный языкъ.   (Šaxmatov 1915: xxxix)

'Having received Christianity from Bulgaria, Kiev at the same time borrowed from there their bookish language.'

I have translated **книжный языкъ** as 'bookish language' in order to show that it is problematic to relate the notion of "standard language" from contemporary sociolinguistic theory to scholarly discourse almost a hundred years ago. However, from the context it is clear that Šaxmatov had in mind something close to standard language in the modern sense of the word.

The Old Rusian Hypothesis was defended by Sergej Obnorskij (1888–1962), who had been a student of Šaxmatov. In a short and polemical article first published in 1947, Obnorskij wrote:

(15) Все эти данные [...] должны служить достаточным основанием для признания ложности старого взгляда на происхождение русского литературного языка как языка в основе нерусского.
(Obnorskij 1947: 31)

'All these facts [...] should serve as a sufficient basis for acknowledging the falsehood of the old view on the origin of the Russian standard language as a language with a non-Russian basis.'

Obnorskij's views were articulated in the Stalin era, when skepticism towards foreign influence was characteristic of the general cultural climate. At the same time, Obnorskij based his conclusions on detailed studies of *Russkaja Pravda* and other texts that show limited influence from Church Slavic.

The Diglossia Hypothesis, which has been advocated by the Russian linguist Boris Uspenskij (b. 1937) in a number of works, has been the subject of much debate in recent decades (cf., e.g., Šapir 1989 and 1997, Živov 1996). The concept of "diglossia" was first introduced in an article from 1959 by the American sociolinguist Charles Ferguson (1921–98). Diglossia can be defined as a situation where two (usually closely related) languages, a "high" (prestigious) and a "low" variety, are used by a single language community in such a way that they are in complementary distribution. One of Ferguson's examples is the relationship between Standard German and Swiss German in Switzerland, where Standard German is used in certain situations such as literature and formal education, while Swiss German prevails in everyday conversation. "Complementary distribution" indicates a division of labor, i.e., that the two varieties are used in different situations that do not overlap. In other words, under diglossia there are no situations where both varieties can be used. This criterion distinguishes diglossia from bilingualism, i.e., a situation where two languages exist side by side and compete with each other in a single language community. A classic example of bilingualism is the relationship between English and French in Canada, where both languages are official languages and are used side by side.

Uspenskij (2002) argues that the notion of "diglossia" is applicable to the linguistic situation in Kievan Rus'. Clearly, we are dealing with two different languages, Church Slavic and Old Rusian, where the former enjoyed cultural prestige as the language of the church, whereas the Old Rusian dialects were used in everyday conversation. Uspenskij (2002: 26–28) furthermore argues that the "high" variety (Church Slavic) and the "low variety" (Old Rusian) were in complementary distribution. Importantly, according to Uspenskij, there were no translations between the two varieties, since they were used in different situations and for different purposes.

The question now arises: What exactly was the division of labor between the two languages? In which environments was Church Slavic used, and for what purposes did the inhabitants of Kievan Rus' use Old Rusian? According to Uspenskij (2002), the choice of language depended on the genre. Here is a simple overview:

(16) a. Religious texts: Church Slavic
 b. Chronicles: Church Slavic
 c. Administrative and legal texts: Old Rusian
 d. Letters and correspondence: Old Rusian

The fact that Church Slavic was used for religious texts is not surprising, and it is likewise expected that Old Rusian prevailed in personal correspondence such as the birch bark letters. As pointed out by Uspenskij (2002: 100–01) the relationship between chronicles and Church Slavic has to do with the close connection between religion and history in medieval times; since history was thought to evolve according to God's perfect plan, it was natural to use the language of the church in historical annals. The legal texts such as *Russkaja Pravda*, which Obnorskij based his ideas on, were derived from an oral, pre-Christian tradition, and it was therefore natural that Old Rusian was used.

In its strongest version, the Diglossia Hypothesis presents the choice between Church Slavic and Old Rusian as an all or nothing affair, i.e., that some genres involved only Church Slavic, while others were purely Old Rusian. According to a weaker (and more realistic) version, the list of genres in (16) represents a continuum with the highest density of Church Slavic elements at the top and the weakest Church Slavic influence on the genres at the bottom. Indeed, Uspenskij (2002: 92–100) himself goes to great pains to point out that choice of language is not completely determined by the genre (i.e., the content), but also by the author's *attitude* to the content. Hence, we often see considerable variation between Church Slavic and Old Rusian elements in the same text.

The Diglossia Hypothesis incorporates insights both from the Church Slavic Hypothesis and the Old Rusian Hypothesis. Considering Church Slavic the "high" variety in the diglossia implies that Church Slavic was the standard language in Kievan Rus'. At the same time, Uspenskij's model captures Obnorskij's insight that Old Rusian prevailed in legal and administrative texts.

The merits of the Diglossia Hypothesis notwithstanding, it is not difficult to spot its weaknesses. As mentioned above, using genre as the criterion for the choice between the "high" and "low" varieties is problematic, since Church Slavic and Old Rusian elements live side by side in chronicles and other texts. Uspenskij's recourse to the author's attitude is also problematic, since it makes the Diglossia Hypothesis difficult to test empirically (Šapir 1990: 283) — after all, we cannot look into the heads of the medieval scribes and observe their attitudes. While the Diglossia Hypothesis has clearly brought new insights to the study of the sociolinguistic situation in Kievan Rus', it seems that Uspenskij's conception is too narrow and rigid to do justice to the richness of variation that can be observed in medieval texts. Instead of trying to force the facts into a rigid model, it may be more fruitful, as Živov (1996: 31–41) suggests, to analyze the "hybrid register" as a linguistic system in its own right and investigate the functions of Church Slavic and Old Rusian elements in such texts.

2.5. Standard Language: Sketch of Further Development

Already Ferguson (1959: 332) pointed out that diglossia tends to be stable over time. Uspenskij (2002: 32) argues that the diglossia lasted from around 1000 AD until ca. 1650. After a transitional period of bilingualism the Modern Russian standard language emerged in the early 1800s:

(17) a. Diglossia: 1000–1650
b. Bilingualism: 1650–1800
c. Standard language based on prestigious dialect: 1800–present

Although a schematic overview like this does not do justice to all the facts, it shows that the history of the Russian standard language has gone through three very different periods. After the long and relatively stable period of diglossia, according to Uspenskij (1994 and 2002) the complementary distribution between Church Slavic and Russian was broken in the seventeenth and eighteenth centuries when Russia was increasingly exposed to western culture. The transitional period in (17b) is referred to as "bilingualism" since, as mentioned in the previous section, this term indicates the presence of competing languages that are not in complementary distribution. The new standard language that emerges around 1800 is no longer defined in terms of its relationship to Church Slavic. What develops is rather a standard language based on the prestigious dialects of St. Petersburg and Moscow, i.e., a standard language of the same type as we find in European countries such as France, where the standard language is based on the way the cultural elite in Paris speak.

The history of the standard language is often described in terms of three "South Slavic influences" (Uspenskij 2002: 32):

(18) a. *First South Slavic influence*:

   Adoption of Christianity and the formation of the Rusian version of Church Slavic after 988.

b. *Second South Slavic influence*:

   Orthographical and grammatical changes in Church Slavic that resulted in the formation of two versions of Church Slavic (the Great Russian and the southwestern Russian) from mid 1300s.

c. *Third South Slavic influence*:

   Changes in Church Slavic as part of the religious reforms under Patriarch Nikon and Tsar Aleksej Mixajlovič; represented the end of diglossia in Russia from ca. 1650.

We have already considered the first South Slavic influence in section 2.1. The second South Slavic influence (which is sometimes called "Re-Bulgarization," Issatschenko 1980: 124–25) concerns a series of orthographical and grammatical changes in Church Slavic, which aimed at bringing the Russian version of Church Slavic closer to the Bulgarian version, perceived as purer and more archaic. Traditionally, the second South Slavic influence has been considered the result of mass immigration from the Balkans due to the Turkish occupation of the Balkan Peninsula (see, e.g., Borkovskij and Kuznecov 1963: 37). However, as demonstrated by Talev (1973), no such mass immigration ever took place. Rather, it seems that the second South Slavic influence was related to the two Bulgarian clergymen Kiprian and Grigorij Camblak, who were metropolitans in Rus' around 1400.

The second South Slavic influence increased the distance between Church Slavic and the spoken language and thus jeopardized the diglossia that normally holds between closely related languages. In the southwestern parts of Rus' (today's Ukraine, Belarus, as well as the southwestern parts of Russia), which became part of the Grand Duchy of Lithuania, the so-called *prosta mova* ("simple language") was used to some extent as a standard language in addition to Church Slavic. The result was bilingualism instead of diglossia.

In Muscovy, on the other hand, the second South Slavic influence became short-lived, and Uspenskij (2002) argues that diglossia remained in force. This has to do with the ideology of Moscow as the Third Rome. Recall from section 1.8 that after the fall of Constantinople in 1453, the Moscow rulers began to consider Moscow the center of the Christian world and Muscovy as the direct continuation of the Roman and Byzantine empires. From this perspective, it made no sense to try to adapt the Russian version of Church Slavic to the norms in Bulgaria. Rather, as a result of Muscovy's increased prestige, it was decided to cultivate the *Russian* version of Church Slavic.

The third South Slavic influence is part of the religious reforms under Patriarch Nikon and Tsar Aleksej Mixajlovič in the second half of the seventeenth century. As mentioned in section 1.11, Ukraine became more closely connected to Russia after Ukrainian hetman Bohdan Xmel'nic'kyj acknowledged the Russian tsar as his superior in 1654. Nikon and Aleksej wanted to create a unified Church Slavic norm for the whole empire, and they ended up importing the Church Slavic version from southwestern Rus' to Moscow. Since the second South Slavic influence had had a much stronger impact in southwestern Rus', the third South Slavic influence essentially amounted to recreating the second South Slavic influence in Moscow (Uspenskij 2002: 414). In other words, the third South Slavic influence is "South Slavic" only in an indirect sense; it incorporates features from southwestern Rus', which in turn were imported from Bulgaria. While the followers of Aleksej and Nikon adopted the southwestern version of Church Slavic, the Old Believers have kept the Muscovite version alive to this day.

2.6. Summary: Important Concepts

This chapter has introduced a number of concepts that are important for the history of the Russian language:

(19) Old Church Slavonic (OCS; Russian: **старославянский язык**, section 2.1): the language extrapolated from the oldest Slavic texts. The OCS text canon comprises texts from before 1100 of Bulgarian or Macedonian provenance.

(20) Church Slavic (Russian: **церковнославянский язык**, 2.1): the language in other texts that belong to the Cyrillo-Methodian tradition, but are either dated after 1100 or contain numerous dialectal features.

(21) Glagolitic (2.1): The oldest Slavic alphabet, presumably created from scratch or adapted from Greek cursive by Constantine (Cyril) for the purpose of the Moravian mission.

(22) Cyrillic (2.1): The Slavic alphabet used in present-day Russian, Belarusian, Ukrainian, Bulgarian, and Macedonian, i.e., in areas dominated by the Orthodox Church.

(23) Hagiography (2.3.1): the writing and critical study of the lives of the saints (apostles, martyrs, or "confessors," i.e., persons who spent their life seeking individual perfection).

(24) Vita (English: *life*, Russian: **житие**, 2.3.1): a "biography" of a saint.

(25) Chronicle (Russian: **летопись**, 2.3.2): a chronological recording of historical events with an entry for each year.

(26) Birch bark letter (Russian: **берестяная грамота**, 2.3.7): letter carved into birch bark by means of a stylus (a needle-like implement of metal or bone).

(27) Standard language (2.4): a set of explicit rules encoded in grammars and textbooks that children learn through formal instruction.

(28) Diglossia (2.4): a situation where two languages, a "high" (prestigious) and a "low" variety, are used by a single language community in such a way that the two varieties are in complementary distribution.

(29) Bilingualism (2.4): a situation where two languages exist side by side and compete with each other in one single language community.

(30) First South Slavic influence (2.5): adoption of Christianity and the formation of the Rusian version of Church Slavic after 988.

(31) Second South Slavic influence ("Re-Bulgarization," 2.5): orthographical and grammatical changes in Church Slavic from the mid 1300s, which aimed at bringing the Russian version of Church Slavic closer to the Bulgarian version; resulted in the formation of two versions of Church Slavic (the Great Russian and the southwestern Russian varieties).

(32) Third South Slavic influence (2.5): changes in Church Slavic as part of the religious reforms under Patriarch Nikon and Tsar Aleksej Mixajlovič in the second half of the seventeenth century; according to Uspenskij (2002), represented the end of diglossia in Russia.

2.7. For Further Reading

If you want to learn more about the Moravian mission and the relationship between the Glagolitic and Cyrillic alphabets, Cubberley 1993 and Schenker 1995 are good sources of information. Čekunova 2010 describes the development of the Cyrillic alphabet and offers numerous examples of various writing styles (uncial, semi-uncial, and cursive). Franklin 2002 contains interesting perspectives on the history of writing in Rus'. An insightful overview of the history of the literature from 988 to 1730 is Børtnes 1992, and for Scandinavian readers Svane 1989 is a rich source of information. For the texts themselves, the electronic version of *Biblioteka Drevnej Rusi* (http://lib.pushkinskijdom.ru/Default.aspx?tabid=2070) of the Institut russkoj literatury RAN is a very useful resource with good introductions and parallel Old Rusian and Modern Russian texts. Other electronic resources include the historical part of the Russian National Corpus (www.ruscorpora.ru) and TOROT—Tromsø Old Russian and OCS Treebank (http://nestor.uit.no/). Press 2007 offers excerpts of an impressive number of texts. English translations of excerpts from many important texts are found in Zenkovsky 1974. A somewhat dated English translation of the *Primary Chronicle* is Cross and Sherbowitz-Wetzor 1953. Scandinavian readers may enjoy Svane's (1983) translation of the *Primary Chronicle* and Egeberg's (2012) translation of Avvakum's *Life*. For more information on the history of the standard language, see Uspenskij 1994 and 2002 and Nuorluoto 2012. A short overview in English is provided in Issatschenko 1980.

Chapter 3   **The Toolbox: Linguistic Tools for Analyzing the History of Russian**

In chapter 1 you learned that Russian belongs to the Slavic language family, which evolved from a reconstructed ancestor language called "Proto-Slavic." You may ask how we reconstruct ancestor languages and describe language change. This chapter addresses these questions and provides you with some linguistic tools you need in order to analyze the history of Russian.

3.1. Synchrony and Diachrony

In simple terms, linguistics is the study of human language. We study linguistic phenomena from two very different perspectives. It is customary to distinguish between synchrony (synchronic linguistics) and diachrony (diachronic linguistics). On the one hand, synchronic linguistics is the study of a language system as it is at a certain point in time. In diachronic linguistics, on the other hand, we study language as a historical process, i.e., as a system that develops over time. The distinction between synchrony and diachrony goes back to the Swiss linguist Ferdinand de Saussure (1857–1913) and his seminal book *Cours de linguistique générale*, published posthumously in 1916.

A grammar of Russian in the early twenty-first century would be a good example of a synchronic linguistic description, but equally good examples are grammars of Old Rusian of the mid 1200s or Late Common Slavic of the 900s. A diachronic study of the same languages will follow the development over time from Proto-Slavic to Modern Russian, i.e., describe the historical changes that have created the Russian language that is spoken today. Notice that diachrony is not the same as the study of languages in earlier times. As shown by the examples we just considered, we work with synchronic linguistics as long as we describe a language at one point in time—regardless of whether this point is in the past or present.

3.2. Genetically and Typologically Related Languages

Linguists often say that two languages are related. It is important to note that this can mean two different things. Two languages are "genetically related" if they have developed from the same ancestor language. Russian and Bulgarian are genetically related insofar as both languages have developed from Proto-Slavic. More distant relatives of Russian are Spanish, French, English, and Norwegian, since like Russian the Romance and Germanic languages have developed from Proto-Indo-European.

If we say that two languages are "typologically related," this means that their grammars have similar structures. For instance, two languages may display the same basic word order or resemble each other insofar as the words have many or few inflected forms. Notice that even languages that are closely related genetically may be typologically different. A case in point is Russian and Bulgarian. Although these languages are closely related genetically, Russian has a complex case system for nouns, but a small system of grammatical tenses for the verb, whereas Bulgarian has lost its case system, but preserved and further developed a complex verb system.

3.3. History of Standard Languages vs. Historical Dialectology

We have now seen that in diachronic linguistics we study the development of language over time. But what does "language" mean? On one interpretation, a language is a set of explicit rules of the kind you learn in school. For instance, you have to learn how to spell *beautiful* in English (and not everybody succeeds). Language in this sense is what we call a "standard language." For Russian, we use the term Contemporary Standard Russian (often abbreviated as CSR), which corresponds to the Russian term **современный русский литературный язык**. The history of this standard language starts with the creation of the first Slavic alphabet in the 860s and takes us all the way to CSR via the introduction of writing to Kievan Rus' together with Christianity in 988. As mentioned in section 2.4, for our purposes it is sufficiently precise to define "standard language" as a set of rules explicitly encoded in grammars, dictionaries, and textbooks that children learn through formal instruction.

A different sense of language is the linguistic system that children acquire from their parents without formal instruction. For instance, children who grow up in English-speaking language communities do not need formal instruction in order to figure out how to pronounce and use the word *beautiful* in their speech. Let us, for convenience, refer to the linguistic system that children acquire naturally, without formal instruction as "non-standard language." The diachronic study of non-standard language is sometimes called "historical dialectology." The diachronic study of Russian from the perspective of historical dialectology does not have a datable starting point, since children have acquired their mother tongue as long as there have been languages. For this reason, we could say that the history of Russian (in the relevant sense) starts with Proto-Indo-European. However, in the present book we will explore some changes in the Pre-Slavic period, but mainly focus on the linguistic development from Proto-Slavic onwards.

We have briefly discussed the history of the standard language in sections 2.4 and 2.5. However, the main focus of this book is on historical dialectology, and the tools you will learn about in the remainder of this chapter are the main principles of historical dialectology.

3.4. The Family Tree Model

It is customary to describe genetic relatedness in terms of a metaphor, namely the family tree. In historical linguistics, this model, which goes back to the German linguist August Schleicher (1821–68), is sometimes referred to by its German name, the "Stammbaum model." In Figure 6 (on p. 64), you find a simple family tree for the major Slavic languages. Proto-Slavic, the reconstructed ancestor language, is the root of the tree, which branches out until we reach the Slavic languages spoken in Europe today.

It is possible to draw more detailed family trees for the Slavic languages. For instance, we could have included the minority languages Kashubian, Sorbian, and Rusyn, and the extinct Polabian and Slovincian languages. In addition, we could have undertaken a more fine-grained classification of the West and South Slavic languages. For South Slavic, it is customary to distinguish between an Eastern (Macedonian and Bulgarian) and a western subgroup (Slovene and Bosnian, Croatian, and Serbian), while West Slavic is often divided into three subgroups: (a) Upper and Lower Sorbian, (b) Czech and Slovak, and (c) Lechitic (Polish, Kashubian, Slovincian, and Polabian). However, the simple tree diagram in Figure 6 is sufficient to illustrate the strengths and weaknesses of the family tree model.

The model's main advantage is the fact that it represents the genetic relationships between languages in an intuitive way. From Figure 6, it is easy to see that Russian and Belarusian are genetically closely related since they belong to the same branch, while Czech is more distantly related to Russian since it belongs to the West Slavic branch. At the same time it is important to remember that the family tree model is exactly that—a model. The purpose of models is to simplify so as to bring out certain properties more clearly—in our case the genetic relationships between languages. However, simplification inevitably entails that other properties are left out.

It is worth noting two weaknesses of the family tree model. First, the tree diagram suggests that language development starts out from a completely homogeneous stage and then develops through increasing diversification. In other words, it looks like there was no language variation in the early stages of

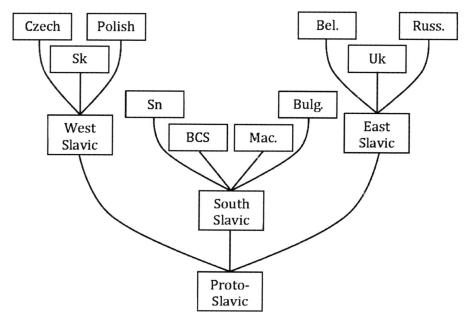

Figure 6. Simple family tree model of the major Slavic languages (Sk = Slovak, Sn = Slovene, BCS = Bosnian, Croatian and Serbian, Mac. = Macedonian, Bulg. = Bulgarian, Bel. = Belarusian, Uk. = Ukrainian, Russ. = Russian)

language development. This is not accurate; there is no evidence that language variation is a recent phenomenon. In fact, language change is hardly conceivable without language variation, since languages tend to go through a stage of variation where forms compete before they change. In English, over time many verbs have adopted the regular past-tense ending *-ed*. For instance, *help*, which today has the regular past-tense form *helped*, earlier had *holp* in the past tense. The change from irregular to regular past tense tends to proceed through a stage of variation where the irregular and regular forms compete. In some varieties of present-day English we witness such competition for verbs such as *dream*, which has two past-tense forms. Whether the regular *dreamed* will oust the irregular *dreamt* we cannot know; the point here is that variation and change probably went hand-in-hand from the very beginning of linguistic history, although the family tree model does not capture this aspect of language change.

A second weakness of the family tree model concerns language contact. As shown in Figure 6, the model has branches that become more and more distant from each other, so the model suggests that language change makes languages more and more different from each other. However, languages that are in close contact may converge over time, a fact that cannot be captured in the family tree model. A possible illustration of this point may be the relationship between the Slavic and Baltic languages. Although it is well known that Baltic is the closest relative of Slavic, scholars have debated whether there was a single Balto-Slavic branch in the Indo-European language family or not. To some extent, this debate may have resulted from taking the family tree model too literally. Rather than assuming either a stage of complete Balto-Slavic unity or no such stage, it may be more realistic to assume a prehistoric Balto-Slavic dialect continuum, which as pointed out by Andersen (1998: 420) may have been "formed in periods of gradual differentiation and [...] intermittent periods of convergence." However, the family tree model does not allow us to diagram such a dialect continuum.

3.5. Methodology 1: Sound Correspondences, Sound Laws, and Linguistic Reconstruction

How can we demonstrate that two languages are genetically related? Already in the eighteenth century many scholars were convinced that languages such as Greek, Latin, and Sanskrit must have developed from the same ancestor language. However, it was not until the 1870s that a group of German linguists known as the "Neogrammarians" devised a rigorous methodology that makes it possible to establish this with certainty. Key concepts of the Neogrammarian methodology are "systematic sound correspondences" and "sound laws." Consider the following word pairs from Latin and English, where the Latin and English words on each line have identical meanings:

(1) Latin: English:

   pater   *father*

   piscis   *fish*

   pēs, pedis *foot*

Comparing the Latin and English words you may have noticed that the Latin words begin with the sound [p], while the English words have [f] in initial position. Obviously, there exists a possibility that these correspondences are due to chance. After all, we are dealing with only three word pairs. However, the list in (1) can be extended. With a long list of correspondences the likelihood that they are due to chance is negligible, so we can safely assume that Latin and English are genetically related languages. If you want an additional argument for the systematicity of the correspondences, you may look up the relevant words in other Germanic languages, such as German, Dutch, or Norwegian. You will find out that word-initial [f] is attested across Germanic, so this is not an idiosyncratic fact about English.

There is a way of demonstrating that two languages are genetically related. We make a list of word pairs with the same (or, at least, closely related) meanings, where one language has a certain sound in a certain position, while the other language displays another sound in the relevant position. This is what we shall refer to as "systematic sound correspondences." If we can establish systematic sound correspondences between two languages, we conclude that they are genetically related. Words in lists like (1) are called "cognates." In other words, *pater* and *father* are cognates, as are *piscis* and *fish*, and *pēs/pedis* and *foot*. Cognates have developed from the same word in the ancestor language.

How did the correspondences in (1) develop historically? Was [p] the original sound that turned into [f] in the Germanic languages, or was it the other way around? Or did both [p] and [f] develop from a third sound? The dataset in (1) does not enable us to solve this question, but linguists have established that [p] represents an older stage of development, and that [f] is an innovation in Germanic. We can write this as follows:

(2) Proto-Indo-European [p] → Proto-Germanic [f]

This formula simply means that Proto-Indo-European [p] turned into Proto-Germanic [f]. This is what we call a "sound law," i.e., a rule stating that a sound at one stage turns into another sound at a later stage. In general, we can write sound laws as follows:

(3) Stage 1 X → Stage 2 Y/ Z

The arrow can be read as "turned into," while the slash stands for "in the environment of," i.e., "the sound X at stage 1 turned into Y at stage 2 in the environment Z." "Environment" refers to positions in the word, such as "the beginning of a word," "the position following a certain sound," etc. Sound laws that are restricted to a certain environment are called "conditioned." The statement in (2) does not specify any environment, because it holds across the board. Such sound laws are referred to as "unconditioned." "Stages" are, e.g., Proto-Slavic, Old Rusian, and Modern Russian or phases within a historical period such as Early Common Slavic and Late Common Slavic. It is not always necessary to include the names of the stages in the sound laws.

The sound law in (2) is part of what is called "Grimm's law," and is credited to Jacob Grimm (1785–1863), the elder of the Brothers Grimm, who evidently did more than collect fairytales. However, many of the relevant facts were known before Grimm from the Danish scholar Rasmus Rask (1787–1832). The work of Rask, Grimm, and others yielded important milestones in the development towards the Neogrammarian methodology, where "sound law" is one of the cornerstones. The Neogrammarians used the word "law" because they wished to emphasize the scientific rigor of their method. However, the implied association with scientific laws of nature, such as gravitation, is somewhat misleading. Whereas gravitation holds at any time and place, sound laws such as Grimm's law are descriptions of historical events that took place at a particular point in time at a particular geographic location. For this reason, many linguists prefer to use the term "sound change" instead of "sound law."

Before we leave sound laws, a remark is in order. Very often sound laws juxtapose stages that may be centuries apart. It is likely that the development from sound X at stage 1 to sound Y at stage 2 went through a number of intermediate steps. Since no intermediate steps are included in statements such as (2) and (3), sound laws may not provide a realistic and accurate account of the actual historical processes that take us from X to Y. However, as a way to explicate the relationships between two stages in the development of a language, sound laws are extremely useful, as will become evident in chapters 10–13, where we discuss the phonological history of Russian.

With systematic sound correspondences and sound laws in our toolbox we can start reconstructing proto-languages. On the basis of an exhaustive set of sound laws we are able to establish the sound system of the relevant proto-language. The reconstruction of the sound system then forms the basis for the reconstruction of the vocabulary and grammar of the proto-language. It is important to notice that reconstructed proto-languages such as Proto-Slavic are linguistic hypotheses. They are attempts at representing the available data as simply and elegantly as possible, but since data are never exhaustive and the available facts can be interpreted in more than one way, there is often disagreement among scholars. While sound laws are instrumental in linguistic reconstruction, the concepts of "borrowing" and "analogy" are also important. We turn to these notions in the following section.

3.6. Methodology 2: Borrowing and Analogy

Apparent counterexamples to sound laws are traditionally explained in two ways, namely as borrowings or analogy. Although English has [f] in words such as *father*, English also has the word *paternal* with [p] at the beginning. Does this force us to give up Grimm's law discussed in the previous section, which predicts [p] → [f] in English? The answer is clearly negative. Sound laws describe historical events, and historical events have limited duration. Long after Grimm's law had stopped working, English borrowed *paternal* and numerous other words of Romance origin—what is often referred to as the "Latinate vocabulary" of English. It is important to notice that you cannot simply explain away any counterexample to a sound law as borrowing. In order to make a case for borrowing, you have to show that speakers of the relevant languages were in geographical proximity and interacted with each other in the historical period in question. In the case of the Latinate vocabulary of English, the historical explanation has to do with the Norman conquest of England in 1066 and the new aristocracy William the Conqueror brought to Britain from Normandy. In section 1.3, we saw that borrowings (loanwords) from Indo-Iranian, Germanic, and Baltic play an important role in the debate about the primordial home of the Slavs.

Methodologically more important than borrowing is analogy. Let us look at a Slavic example. Originally, the noun that has become **река** 'river' in present-day Russian displayed [k] in stem-final position in all inflected forms. However, in Common Slavic [k] turned into [c'], approximately the sound denoted by the letter ц, before an e-like sound that is transcribed as [ě]. This is due to a sound law known as the second palatalization, which we will return to in section 11.7. For now it is sufficiently precise to state the sound law as follows:

(4) [k] → [c'] / __ [ě]

Since the dative and locative cases had the ending [ě] in the singular, these forms got [c'] instead of [k] at the end of the stem, while the other singular forms retained [k]:

(5) Nom: *rěk-a*, Acc: *rěk-u*, Gen: *rěk-y*, Dat: *rěc'-ě*, Inst: *rěk-oju*, Loc: *rěc'-ě*

As we can see, the sound law occasioned an alternation between [k] and [c'] in stem-final position. Since the sound law introduced an alternation, it had the effect of increasing the complexity of the inflection of the word. However, the inflection has subsequently been simplified again, since [c'] has disappeared from **река** in Modern Russian. We say that the dative and locative forms have changed by means of analogy to the other inflected forms of the word. We can define analogy as follows:

(6) Analogy:
     A morphological change, whereby one form becomes more similar (analogous) to another form.

Notice that while sound laws such as the second palatalization in (4) describe phonological changes where a sound is affected by surrounding sounds, analogies are morphological changes. Analogies do not refer to a phonological environment (surrounding sounds), but rather involve concepts such as "stem," "ending," "case," etc., which belong to the field of morphology (inflection and word-formation). Accordingly, the removal of [c'] by analogy only took place at the end of the stem of certain classes of words. In other positions, [c'] was not affected by analogy, as can be seen from words such as цена 'price' and церковь 'church'.

The example with река shows that analogy creates counterexamples to sound laws. When we come across dative and locative forms like [rěkě] instead of the expected [rěc'ě], it is tempting to give up the sound law in (4), since the sound law predicts that [k] is impossible before [ě]. However, counterexamples like these can be given an independent explanation whereby analogy has eliminated the effect of the sound law after the sound law stopped working.

3.7. Methodology 3: Grammaticalization

According to Hopper (1991: 17), the term "grammaticalization" was first used by the French Slavist and general linguist Antoine Meillet (1866–1936), although the phenomenon was known before Meillet's time. The study of grammaticalization experienced a revival in the 1970s and 1980s and has been an important topic in historical linguistics ever since. Here is a simple definition:

(7) Grammaticalization is language change whereby words develop into grammatical morphemes, such as prefixes and suffixes.

It is important to note that grammaticalization is not an abrupt change from word to grammatical morpheme, but rather proceeds along a continuum from more lexical (i.e., word-like) properties to more grammatical properties. It is customary to refer to all changes along this continuum as "grammaticalization" even if they do not start out as full-blown words or end up as full-fledged grammatical morphemes.

Let us consider a simple example from English. The expression *going to* can be used to indicate movement in space, as in *I'm going to Norway*, but has also developed into a grammatical marker of future tense. A sentence like *I'm going to buy a new car* does not necessarily involve any movement in space at all, but only indicates that the purchase will take place in the future. Although the *going to* example does not take us all the way from a word to a grammatical morpheme, as pointed out by Bybee, Perkins, and Pagliuca (1994: 6) the example exhibits two crucial properties of grammaticalization, namely semantic generalization and phonological reduction. Semantic generalization involves the development of less specific meanings of the type that is characteristic of grammatical morphemes. In the *going to* construction we observe a change from a concrete spatial meaning to the more general, grammatical meaning "future tense." Phonological reduction includes such properties as loss of stress and reduced length. This has happened in the *going to* construction; *going to* is often reduced to *gonna* when it marks the future tense.

Grammaticalization is relevant for the history of Russian as well. In section 8.4, you will see that the evolution of the future with **буду, будешь**, etc. followed by an imperfective infinitive is an example of grammaticalization that resembles the *going to* construction in English. Another example involves Old Rusian **ся** which has undergone grammaticalization towards suffix status. In Contemporary Standard Russian, -**ся** is attached to a verb, and is arguably a suffix (cf. Nesset 1998a–b for detailed discussion). In Old Rusian, in contrast, **ся** had a freer distribution and was not restricted to the position immediately after a verb, as we will see in section 9.11.

3.8. Methodology 4: Reanalysis

Sometimes language change is invisible: language users adopt a new analysis of a pattern without changing the pattern itself. This is called "reanalysis" or "reinterpretation." By way of example, consider the English word *alcoholic*, which was derived from the noun *alcohol* by the addition of the suffix -*ic*. However, instead of analyzing *alcohol* as *alcohol+ic*, many speakers have adopted an alternative analysis, *alco+holic*, whereby the element -*holic* indicates addiction to a substance or an activity. This reanalysis leaves the form of the word unaltered. However, we can tell that the reanalysis has taken place from words such as *shopaholic* and *workaholic*, which contain -*holic* and involve addiction. The formation of words like *shopaholic* and *workaholic* are examples of "actualization," the process whereby reanalysis shows on the surface. In section 8.3.6 you will see that reanalysis is relevant for Russian past-tense forms in -*l* (*delal* 'did', *pisal* 'wrote', etc.), which have developed from participles in Common Slavic and Old Rusian.

3.9. Time: Absolute and Relative Chronology

We have seen that sound laws can be understood as descriptions of historical events. The same point can be made about analogy and grammaticalization; in both cases we are dealing with historical events that took place in a certain geographical location at a certain point in time. Like any other historian, the historical linguist is interested in dating the historical events under scrutiny. Language change can be dated in two different ways. It is customary to distinguish between absolute and relative chronology.

3.9. Time: Absolute and Relative Chronology

Absolute chronology involves relating language change to datable historical events. Imagine, for example, that we encounter evidence of a certain sound law in a document. We can draw the conclusion that the relevant sound law must have been operative in the time before the document was written. If we are so lucky as to know when the document was written, we are able to provide an absolute chronology for the language change we are interested in. As mentioned in section 2.3.7, in Novgorod and some other Russian cities archeologists have excavated a large number of letters written on birch bark. The birch bark letters are found in various archeological layers, which can be dated. Analysis of birch bark letters therefore facilitates absolute chronology of certain language changes in the Old Novgorod dialect, to which we turn in chapter 14.

However, in historical linguistics absolute chronology is the exception rather than the rule. Dating of historical documents is less than straightforward, and for older periods we do not have any written sources at all. A more realistic option is relative chronology where we determine the order in which certain historical processes took place. In section 3.6, we saw that the sound law that transformed [k] to [c'] before [ě] took place before analogy changed the dative and locative forms of the word for 'river' from [rěc'ě] back to [rěkě]. This is an (admittedly somewhat trivial) example of relative chronology since we are able to say that the sound law came before the analogy. We will consider more complicated examples of relative chronology in section 12.7.

3.10. Space: The Wave Model for Innovation and Spread. Isoglosses

Language change takes place in time and space. As historical linguists we are interested not only in the temporal aspect (absolute and relative chronology), but also in the spatial implications of language change. We want to know how language change spreads through geographical space. For this purpose, linguists have devised the so-called wave model of language change. This model is based on a metaphor whereby language change is compared to the waves that occur in a pond when you throw a stone into it. Language change is said to spread through geographical space from a central area in the same way as waves emanate from the point where the stone hits the water. We can draw lines on the maps indicating how far an innovation has spread at a point in time. Such lines are called "isoglosses." Isoglosses mark the area where a particular linguistic feature is used.

What happens in the central area is an innovation, i.e., the emergence of a new linguistic feature. Innovations may be due to sound law, analogy, or borrowing and may or may not be examples of grammaticalization. What is important is that there is social prestige attached to the innovation, because otherwise it is not likely to be adopted by other speakers and spread from one place to another. Social prestige is not straightforward to define, and a detailed discussion is not required here. Suffice it to say that a similar kind of prestige that is responsible for the spread of linguistic innovations is at work in the world of fashion. People are likely to mimic the clothing, behavior, and linguistic habits of celebrities and other people they admire. In historical linguistics, it is often observed that language change has spread from cultural centers such as capital cities to remote areas that enjoy less prestige.

The wave model is attributed to the German linguist Hugo Schuchardt (1842–1927), a contemporary of the Neogrammarians who was critical of their ideas. The wave model is sometimes considered an alternative to the family tree model, which was embraced by the Neogrammarians. However, it is more meaningful to consider the two models to be complementary. The family tree and wave models are based on different metaphors (the family tree vs. waves in a pond), and they capture different aspects of language change that are equally valid. As pointed out in section 3.4 above, the family tree model provides a good overview of the relationships between genetically related languages, but does not capture the fact that related languages may influence each other due to subsequent contact after the break-up of their common ancestor language. This is exactly the aspect of language change that the wave model enables us to capture. In section 3.4 we saw that the family tree model is arguably ill-suited for representing the relationship between the Slavic and Baltic languages in prehistoric times. The wave model, alternatively, is perfectly capable of representing a dialect continuum with a complicated pattern of isoglosses dividing up the area inhabited by Baltic and Slavic tribes.

3.11. Summary: Historical Linguistics in a Nutshell

The aim of this chapter has been to fill up your toolbox, i.e., give you the linguistic tools you need in order to analyze the history of Russian. When you have mastered the concepts listed below, you are well equipped to make use of the rest of this book:

(8) Synchrony (synchronic linguistics, section 3.1):

The study of language as a system at a certain point in time.

(9) Diachrony (diachronic linguistics, 3.1):

The study of language as a historical process, i.e., as a system that develops over time.

3.11. Summary: Historical Linguistics in a Nutshell

(10) Genetically related languages (3.2):
Languages that have developed from the same ancestor language.

(11) Typologically related languages (3.2):
Languages whose grammars display similar structures.

(12) History of standard languages (3.3):
The diachronic study of standard languages, i.e., sets of explicit rules, which are encoded in grammars and textbooks, and which children learn through formal instruction.

(13) Historical dialectology (3.3):
The diachronic study of the language children in a speech community acquire without formal instruction.

(14) The family tree model (3.4):
A tree diagram representing the genetic relations among languages that have developed from the same ancestor language.

(15) Systematic sound correspondence (3.5):
A situation where for given words with (approximately) the same meanings, one language has a certain sound in a certain position, whereas another language consistently displays another sound in the relevant position.

(16) Cognate (3.5):
A word that has developed from the same historical source as another word. Latin *pater* and English *father* are cognates since they have developed from the same word in Proto-Indo-European.

(17) Sound law (3.5):
A rule stating that sound X at stage 1 turned into sound Y at stage 2, either across the board ("unconditioned sound law") or restricted to a certain environment defined by surrounding sounds ("conditioned sound law").

(18) Borrowing (3.6):

The importation of a word (a "loan word") from another language due to language contact.

(19) Analogy (3.6):

A morphological change whereby one form becomes more similar (analogous) to another form.

(20) Grammaticalization (3.7):

Language change whereby words develop into grammatical morphemes, such as prefixes and suffixes.

(21) Reanalysis (3.8):

The adoption of a new interpretation of a pattern without changing the pattern itself.

(22) Absolute chronology (3.9):

The dating of language change by relating it to datable historical events.

(23) Relative chronology (3.9):

The dating of language change by establishing in which order two or more changes took place.

(24) Innovation (3.10):

The emergence of a new linguistic feature in a speech community.

(25) The wave model (3.10):

Model for language change capturing how innovations emanate through geographical space as they are adopted by more and more speakers.

(26) Isogloss (3.10):

A line on a map that indicates the boundary of an area where a particular linguistic feature is used.

3.12. For Further Reading

A simple and up-to-date introduction to historical linguistics is Campbell 1999. More ambitious texts are Anttila 1989 and Hock 1991. Bybee (2007) discusses recent advances in historical linguistics with reference to the theory of cognitive linguistics. For grammaticalization, Heine, Claudi, and Hünnemeyer 1991 and Hopper and Traugott 2003 are good introductions.

Chapter 4   Morphology: Nouns

Learning Contemporary Standard Russian, you have struggled with all the exceptions from the rules. Where do the exceptional inflections of words such as **время** 'time', **телёнок** 'calf', and **дочь** 'daughter' come from? Why is **путь** the only masculine noun in declension III? Why do some masculines such as **рог** 'antler' and **глаз** 'eye' have **-а**, and not **-ы** in the nominative plural? And where do exceptional plural forms such as **небеса** and **чудеса** from **небо** 'heaven' and **чудо** 'wonder' come from? This chapter offers answers to these and many other questions. We start from what you are already familiar with, namely nouns in Contemporary Standard Russian (section 4.1), and then turn to changes concerning declension classes (4.2 and 4.3), number and case (4.4), hard and soft stems (4.5), gender (4.6), and animacy (4.7). You find a brief summary in section 4.8.

4.1. Declension of Nouns in Contemporary Standard Russian

Morphology is the study of the structure of words. In historical morphology we are interested in how the structure of words develops over time. A key concept in morphology is the inflectional paradigm, which we can define as a list of all the inflected forms of a word. It is customary to say that the paradigm of nouns in Contemporary Standard Russian consists of twelve forms, although as we will see below, this is an oversimplification. The paradigm of **стол** 'table' in Contemporary Standard Russian is given in Table 7 on p. 78.

    The part of the word that is shared by all the inflected forms is what we call the "stem," while the parts that are different among the inflected forms are what we call "inflectional endings." It is often helpful to separate the stem from the endings by means of a hyphen, as is done in Table 7. The content elements that distinguish between the inflected forms are referred to as "inflectional features." These are elements such as singular, plural, nominative, accusative, and so on. The inflectional features are organized in categories, such as number (singular and plural) and case (nominative, accusative, etc.). Number and case are the only inflectional categories of nouns not only in Modern Russian, but also in Common Slavic and Old Rusian.

Table 7. The inflectional paradigm of **стол** 'table' in Contemporary Standard Russian

	Singular	Plural
N(ominative)	стол	стол-ы
A(ccusative)	стол	стол-ы
G(enitive)	стол-а	стол-ов
D(ative)	стол-у	стол-ам
I(nstrumental)	стол-ом	стол-ами
L(ocative)	стол-е	стол-ах

Often a language has more than one ending for an inflectional feature. In Contemporary Standard Russian, for instance, the features dative and singular can be expressed in three different ways for nouns: **-у** (e.g., **столу** from **стол** 'table'), **-е** (e.g., **жене** from **жена** 'wife'), and **-и** (e.g., **тетради** from **тетрадь** 'notebook'). On this basis it is customary to divide Russian nouns into three inflection classes, i.e., classes of nouns that have the same endings. For nouns, adjectives, and pronouns the inflection classes are traditionally referred to as "declensions" or "declension classes." An overview of the declensions in Contemporary Standard Russian is given in Table 8. Notice that whereas there are three declensions in the singular, in the plural it is customary to assume only one declension class. In order to avoid complications that are not relevant here, Table 8 shows only endings for nouns with hard consonants in stem-final position in declensions I and II. Slashes separate endings of different genders. The symbol "Ø" ("zero") is used when a form lacks an ending. A dash (—) indicates that the relevant case is not attested in the plural.

You may find three surprises in Table 8, namely the rows marked G2, L2, and V. G1 is the "normal" genitive, while G2 (the "second genitive" or "partitive") represents forms such as **сахару** which are used to indicate an indefinite quantity of sugar in constructions such as **немного сахару** 'some sugar'. Is this a separate case? There are reasons to answer this question in the affirmative. In order for something to be a separate case, there must be a separate form with a separate meaning. In the genitive, we have two different endings, **-а** and **-у** in declension I, and they signal different meanings. While **-а** is compatible with all the functions of the genitive, **-у** indicates indefinite quantity. Since G1 and G2 have separate forms and separate meanings, we must consider them different cases. (The fact that the distinction between the two genitives is only attested for certain masculine nouns of declension I does not affect the argument. However, one may discuss whether the best analysis is to say that only masculines in declension I have two genitive cases or that the two genitives occur in all declensions, but that the endings are the same in the two cases except for masculines in declension I.)

Table 8. The declension system of Contemporary Standard Russian

	Singular			Plural
	Declension I	Declension II	Declension III	
N	-Ø/-o	-a	-Ø	-ы/-а
A	=N or G1	-y	=N	=N or G1
G1	-a	-ы	-и	-ов, -ей, -Ø
G2	-y/-a	-ы	-и	—
D	-y	-e	-и	-ам
I	-ом	-ой	-ью	-ами
L1	-e	-e	-и	-ах
L2	-y/-e	-e	-и	—
V	=N	-a or -Ø	=N	—

The analysis of the two genitives as different cases goes back to a seminal paper by the Russian-American linguist Roman Jakobson (1936). Jakobson also proposed that Contemporary Standard Russian has two locative cases; in addition to the "normal" locative, which is marked as L1 in Table 8, examples like **в лесу** 'in the forest' represent a second locative marked as L2 in the table. Although the second locative is normally found after the prepositions **в** 'in' and **на** 'on', while **при** 'by' and **о** 'about' take the first locative, Jakobson pointed out that both locatives contrast in examples of the following type:

(1) a. Сколько красоты в лесе! 'How much beauty there is in a forest!'
   b. Сколько красоты в лесу! 'How much beauty there is in the forest!'

The difference is subtle, but the example with **в лесе** describes a property of the forest—the forest has the property of being beautiful. The sentence with **в лесу** refers to a situation where beautiful things are located in the forest. If we accept that examples of this type not only have different endings, but also (slightly) different meanings, we must conclude that L1 and L2 represent different cases in Contemporary Standard Russian.

The V in Table 8 stands for "vocative," which is traditionally considered a case. Vocative is the address form, which names the person you are talking to:

(2) Мам, не волнуйся, я хорошие сигареты курю.

'Mom, don't worry, I smoke good cigarettes.' (Наши дети 2004)

In Modern Russian, nouns in declension II have separate forms like **мам!** with no ending that are used as address forms, so such forms seem to satisfy the criterion of having both a separate form and a separate meaning. However, not all researchers accept that the vocative is a *case* (cf., e.g., Andersen 2012). While the "normal" cases are connected to syntactic functions (nominative to subject, accusative to direct object, etc.), the vocative is not relevant for syntactic functions. However, since discussion of this point is beyond the scope of this book, I will follow traditional practice and treat the vocative together with the grammatical cases.

To summarize, we have seen that Contemporary Standard Russian has three declensions in the singular and one in the plural, and that there are two numbers (singular and plural), as well as nine cases (eight if the vocative is not considered a case). With this in mind we are ready to explore the situation in Common Slavic and Old Rusian.

4.2. The Declension System of Common Slavic and Old Rusian

Common Slavic and Old Rusian nouns can be divided into six declensions, i.e., three more than we have in Contemporary Standard Russian:

(3) a. The $\breve{o}$-declension

b. The $\breve{u}$-declension

c. The $\bar{a}$-declension

d. The $\breve{i}$-declension

e. The $\bar{u}$-declension

f. The C-declension

Although Common Slavic and Old Rusian had the same declension classes, the inflectional endings changed over time. In the following, we will focus on the Old Rusian endings, which are the ones you will encounter while reading medieval texts. However, the names of the declensions refer to a much older stage, when there was still a difference between long and short vowels; the symbols $\breve{o}$, $\breve{u}$, and $\breve{i}$ stand for short vowels, while $\bar{a}$ and $\bar{u}$ indicate long vowels. The capital C represents any consonant. Let us look at the endings of each declension (sections 4.2.1–4.2.6), and then compare with Contemporary Standard Russian in section 4.2.7.

4.2.1. The ŏ-Declension

This declension, which corresponds to declension I in Contemporary Standard Russian, comprises masculine nouns in -ъ or -ь and neuter nouns in -о or -е. Table 9 includes five example words, three masculines and two neuters. **Родъ** 'family, birth' (masculine) and **лѣто** 'year, summer' (neuter) have hard consonants in stem-final position, while **конь** 'horse' (masculine) and **море** 'sea' (neuter) have soft consonants stem-finally. **Вълкъ** 'wolf' (masculine) is included in order to illustrate the alternations in nouns with velar consonants (/k, g, x/) in stem-final position.

Table 9. The Old Rusian ŏ-declension

Sg	N	род-ъ	вълк-ъ	кон-ь	лѣт-о	мор-е
	A	род-ъ	вълк-ъ	кон-ь	лѣт-о	мор-е
	G	род-а	вълк-а	кон-я	лѣт-а	мор-я
	D	род-у	вълк-у	кон-ю	лѣт-у	мор-ю
	I	род-ъмь	вълк-ъмь	кон-ьмь	лѣт-ъмь	мор-ьмь
	L	род-ѣ	вълц-ѣ	кон-и	лѣт-ѣ	мор-и
	V	род-е	вълч-е	кон-ю	лѣт-о	мор-е
Du	NA	род-а	вълк-а	кон-я	лѣт-ѣ	мор-и
	GL	род-у	вълк-у	кон-ю	лѣт-у	мор-ю
	DI	род-ома	вълк-ома	кон-ема	лѣт-ома	мор-ема
Pl	N	род-и	вълц-и	кон-и	лѣт-а	мор-я
	A	род-ы	вълк-ы	кон-ѣ	лѣт-а	мор-я
	G	род-ъ	вълк-ъ	кон-ь	лѣт-ъ	мор-ь
	D	род-омъ	вълк-омъ	кон-емъ	лѣт-омъ	мор-емъ
	I	род-ы	вълк-ы	кон-и	лѣт-ы	мор-и
	L	род-ѣхъ	вълц-ѣхъ	кон-ихъ	лѣт-ѣхъ	мор-ихъ

Although the ŏ-declension resembles the modern declension I, there are a number of differences you need to focus on. First of all, Old Rusian had separate endings for the vocative (V) in the singular. Notice that for neuter nouns the vocative is the same as the nominative. Old Rusian furthermore has a dual (Du) number, which is used to refer to two entities. In Old Rusian, therefore, the plural is reserved for groups larger than two entities. As shown in the table, in the dual there are only three different case endings per noun. The remaining inflectional categories and features are the same as in Contemporary Standard

Russian, and the good news is that they are used essentially in the same way as in the modern language. This means that if you encounter, say, a preposition that governs the genitive in Contemporary Standard Russian, you can be relatively sure that it did so in Old Rusian too, and this way you know that the following noun is in the genitive.

When it comes to the individual inflectional endings, you may notice that ъ and ь are listed as endings. In Common Slavic and early Old Rusian these letters, which are called "jers," represented vowel sounds, although as you will see in section 12.2 they merged with /o/ and /e/ or disappeared, depending on the position in the word. In texts, you will therefore sometimes see that the jers are replaced by the letters **o** or **e**, or that the jers have been omitted.

The letter ѣ ("jat") represented an e-like sound that later merged with /e/. However, in Common Slavic and early Old Rusian there were still two distinct *e*-sounds, so the locative singular **родѣ** and the vocative **роде** were pronounced differently. Notice, that in **вълкъ** the locative and vocative forms have different consonants in stem-final position. This is due to the so-called first and second palatalizations, two sound laws that we will discuss in detail in chapter 11. The consonant alternations summarized in Table 10 are relevant for stems with к, г, and х (the velar consonants) in final position, and alternations are not restricted to the ŏ-declension, as we will see below.

Table 10. Consonant alternations in Old Rusian nouns

	к	г	х
Before **e**	ч	ж	ш
Before ѣ and (N pl) и	ц	з	с

Consonant alternations in the stem are not characteristic of nouns in Contemporary Standard Russian, where nouns like **волк** 'wolf' are written with a к in all inflected forms. This is a result of analogy, since restoring к in the forms that had a different consonant in Old Rusian has made these forms more similar to the remaining inflected forms (cf. section 3.6). A rare example of a noun with a consonant alternation in Modern Russian is **друг** 'friend' where the consonant alternation not only has been preserved in the nominative plural, but also has spread to the other plural forms (N pl. **друзья**, G pl. **друзей**, etc.). In the singular, on the other hand, the consonant alternation has been eliminated; the modern locative sg. is **друге**, while Old Rusian had **друзѣ**.

The Old Rusian plural endings display a number of differences from the modern language. First, for masculine nouns the nominative and accusative cases are different in the plural, since the nominative has -и, while the accusative has -ы (-ѣ for nouns with a soft consonant in stem-final position). In

Modern Russian, the accusative ending -ы has spread to the nominative. Second, the genitive plural has the endings -ъ/-ь. This is different from Modern Russian, where most masculine nouns in declension I have the endings -ов or -ей. Only a few exceptional masculines lack an ending in the genitive plural in Contemporary Standard Russian, such as ботинок 'boot' (без ботинок 'without boots') and чулок 'stocking' (без чулок 'without stockings'). The zero ending in Modern Russian is the reflection of the Old Rusian endings -ъ/-ь, so irregular genitive plurals such as ботинок and чулок are reminiscences of the Old Rusian ŏ-declension. Finally, in Contemporary Standard Russian, the dative, instrumental, and locative plural have the endings -ам, -ами, and -ах regardless of declension class. However, in Old Rusian different declensions had different endings in these forms. Notice in particular the instrumental plural ending -ы/-и, which is quite different from the modern ending in the instrumental plural. In Modern Russian, the letter ы does not occur after velar consonants (к, г, and х), but there is no such rule in (early) Old Rusian; the instrumental plural of волкъ is therefore волкы.

4.2.2. The ŭ-Declension

Whereas the ŏ-declension was a large and, in principle, unlimited class of nouns, the ŭ-declension comprised only a handful of nouns in Old Rusian, all of which were masculines with a hard consonant in stem-final position. Here are the most important nouns:

(4) Nouns in the ŭ-declension in Old Rusian:

волъ 'ox', вьрхъ 'top', домъ 'house', ледъ 'ice', медъ 'honey', полъ 'half', and сынъ 'son'

In Old Rusian, the ŭ-declension was losing ground and the nouns above were gradually assimilated to the ŏ-declension. This process illustrates two general principles of language change. First, both declensions contain masculine nouns with hard stem-final consonants followed by the ending ъ in the nominative singular. In other words, the two classes were closely related, and it is therefore not surprising that language users would start using the "wrong" endings for the relevant nouns. Let us call this the "closeness principle":

(5) *The closeness principle*:
Words tend to migrate between closely related classes.

Second, the ŏ-declension is much larger than the ŭ-declension, so it was natural that nouns would migrate from the small class to the large class. This is a widespread scenario in historical linguistics. If two classes are closely related, the larger class tends to grow at the sacrifice of the smaller class—a linguistic version of "the rich get richer, the poor get poorer" principle in economics.

(6) *The "rich get richer, poor get poorer" principle*:
Words tend to migrate from small to large classes.

The merger of the ŭ- and ŏ-declensions is due to analogy in the sense that the two classes become more similar by adopting the same inflectional endings.

Table 11, opposite, provides an overview of the inflectional endings of the ŭ-declension in Old Rusian. Notice in particular the ending -y in the genitive and the locative singular, and the ending -овъ in the genitive plural. Although the ŭ-declension disappeared as a declension class, these individual endings have survived. The -y endings have resurfaced in the second genitive (e.g., constructions like **много сахару** 'a lot of sugar') and the second locative (e.g., constructions like **в лесу** 'in the forest'). The -овъ ending has ousted the zero ending as the normal genitive plural ending for masculine nouns in a hard consonant (e.g., **много столов** 'many tables'). The zero ending, which goes back to the genitive plural ending -ъ of the č-declension, is now only attested in a few exceptional masculine nouns, as pointed out in the preceding section.

4.2.3. The ā-Declension

The ā-declension corresponds to declension II in Contemporary Standard Russian and contains feminine nouns with the endings -a/-я in the nominative singular, as well as a few masculine nouns, such as **юноша** 'young man'. As shown in Table 12, opposite, **сестра** 'sister' has the endings one would expect from Contemporary Standard Russian, although we find -ѣ in the dative and locative singular, and -ъ instead of no ending in the genitive plural. **Рук-а** 'hand, arm' is included in the table in order to show that nouns with к, г, or х in stem-final position display the same consonant alternations as the corresponding nouns in the ŏ-declension. **Воля** 'wish' illustrates the inflection of nouns with a soft consonant in stem-final position, while **душа** 'soul' and **дѣвица** 'girl' show that nouns in ш, ж, щ, ч, and ц inflect in the same way as **воля**; note, however, that we use the letter **a** after ш, ж, щ, ч, and ц, not я. In section 12.5, we will see that ш, ж, and ц originally represented soft consonants, which became hard later in the Old Rusian period and are hard in Contemporary Standard Russian.

4.2.3. The ā-Declension

Table 11. The Old Rusian ŭ-declension

Sg	N	дом-ъ	вьрх-ъ
	A	дом-ъ	вьрх-ъ
	G	дом-у	вьрх-у
	D	дом-ови	вьрх-ови
	I	дом-ъмь	вьрх-ъмь
	L	дом-у	вьрх-у
	V	дом-у	вьрх-у
Du	NA	дом-ы	вьрх-ы
	GL	дом-ову	вьрх-ову
	DI	дом-ъма	вьрх-ъма
Pl	N	дом-ове	вьрх-ове
	A	дом-ы	вьрх-ы
	G	дом-овъ	вьрх-овъ
	D	дом-ъмъ	вьрх-ъмъ
	I	дом-ъми	вьрх-ъми
	L	дом-ъхъ	вьрх-ъхъ

Table 12. The Old Rusian ā-declension

Sg	N	сестр-а	рук-а	вол-я	душ-а	дѣвиц-а
	A	сестр-у	рук-у	вол-ю	душ-ю	дѣвиц-ю
	G	сестр-ы	рук-ы	вол-ѣ	душ-ѣ	дѣвиц-ѣ
	D	сестр-ѣ	руц-ѣ	вол-и	душ-и	дѣвиц-и
	I	сестр-ою	рук-ою	вол-ею	душ-ею	дѣвиц-ею
	L	сестр-ѣ	руц-ѣ	вол-и	душ-и	дѣвиц-и
	V	сестр-о	рук-о	вол-е	душ-е	дѣвиц-е
Du	NA	сестр-ѣ	руц-ѣ	вол-и	душ-и	дѣвиц-и
	GL	сестр-у	рук-у	вол-ю	душ-у	дѣвиц-ю
	DI	сестр-ама	рук-ама	вол-яма	душ-ама	дѣвиц-ама
Pl	N	сестр-ы	рук-ы	вол-ѣ	душ-ѣ	дѣвиц-ѣ
	A	сестр-ы	рук-ы	вол-ѣ	душ-ѣ	дѣвиц-ѣ
	G	сестр-ъ	рук-ъ	вол-ь	душ-ь	дѣвиц-ь
	D	сестр-амъ	рук-амъ	вол-ямъ	душ-амъ	дѣвиц-амъ
	I	сестр-ами	рук-ами	вол-ями	душ-ами	дѣвиц-ами
	L	сестр-ахъ	рук-ахъ	вол-яхъ	душ-ахъ	дѣвиц-ахъ

4.2.4. The ĭ-Declension

This declension corresponds to declension III in Contemporary Standard Russian. In Common Slavic and Old Rusian the ĭ-declension contained both masculine and feminine nouns ending in -ь in the nominative singular. In Contemporary Standard Russian, there is only one masculine noun left in declension III, namely путь 'way'. Table 13 provides one masculine (огнь 'fire, flame') and one feminine example (ночь 'night'). Notice that masculine and feminine nouns have different endings in the instrumental singular and nominative plural. The endings in parentheses are variants.

Table 13. The Old Rusian ĭ-declension

Sg	N	огн-ь	ноч-ь
	A	огн-ь	ноч-ь
	G	огн-и	ноч-и
	D	огн-и	ноч-и
	I	огн-ьмь	ноч-ию (-ью)
	L	огн-и	ноч-и
	V	огн-и	ноч-и
Du	NA	огн-и	ноч-и
	GL	огн-ию (-ью)	ноч-ию (-ью)
	DI	огн-ьма	ноч-ьма
Pl	N	огн-ие (-ье)	ноч-и
	A	огн-и	ноч-и
	G	огн-ии (-ьи)	ноч-ии (-ьи)
	D	огн-ьмъ	ноч-ьмъ
	I	огн-ьми	ноч-ьми
	L	огн-ьхъ	ноч-ьхъ

In Old Rusian, masculine nouns in -ь could belong to either the ŏ- or the ĭ-declensions. However, the masculines migrated to the ŏ-declension, which contained the majority of masculine nouns. Once again, we see the "rich get richer, poor get poorer" and closeness principles at work. The ŏ-declension was the larger class for masculines, and both declensions were closely related insofar as they contained masculines with the -ь ending in the nominative singular. A small group of masculines escaped the influence of the ŏ-declension by changing their gender to feminine. Examples include the modern words печать 'press, seal' and степень 'degree'. As a result, the only masculine noun that has remained in the third declension to this day is путь.

4.2.5. The ū-Declension

The ū-declension comprises a handful of feminine nouns with the letter -ы at the end in the nominative singular:

(7) Nouns in the ū-declension in Old Rusian:

букы 'letter', **кры** 'blood', **любы** 'love', **мъркы** 'carrot', **свекры** 'mother-in-law', **тыкы** 'pumpkin', and **цьркы** 'church'

The ū-declension was in the process of disappearing in Old Rusian, and in Contemporary Standard Russian the relevant nouns belong to declension II (**буква, тыква**) or declension III (**кровь, любовь, морковь, свекровь, церковь**). The inflection is summarized in Table 14. In addition to the endings in the table you may come across endings from the ī-declension, especially in the genitive and locative singular, where, e.g., **цьркъви** is attested in addition to **цьркъве** (Ivanov 1995: 224).

Table 14. The ū-declension in Old Rusian

Sg	N	букы	свекры
	A	букъв-ь	свекръв-ь
	G	букъв-е	свекръв-е
	D	букъв-и	свекръв-и
	I	букъв-ию (-ью)	свекръв-ию (-ью)
	L	букъв-е	свекръв-е
Du	NA	букъв-и	свекръв-и
	GL	букъв-у	свекръв-у (-ию)
	DI	букъв-ама	свекръв-ама
Pl	N	букъв-и	свекръв-и
	A	букъв-и	свекръв-и
	G	букъв-ъ	свекръв-ъ
	D	букъв-амъ	свекръв-амъ
	I	букъв-ами	свекръв-ами
	L	букъв-ахъ	свекръв-ахъ

Characteristic of the *ū*-declension is the alternation in the stem between -ы in the nominative singular and -ъв in all other forms. Historically, both -ы and -ъв go back to a long *u*-sound (/ū/), which explains the name of the declension. Notice that the genitive, dative, instrumental, and locative case endings in the plural are the same as in the *ā*-declension. In the singular, the *ū*-declension resembles the C-declension, to which we turn in the next section.

4.2.6. The C-Declension

In Old Rusian, C-declension is an umbrella-term for four groups of nouns, which have different final consonants in the stem (in all forms except the nominative singular): N-stems, R-stems, S-stems, and T-stems. As shown below, the C-declension includes nouns of all three genders:

(8) Nouns in the C-declension in Old Rusian:
    a. *N-stems*:
        i. Masculines in -ы: **камы** 'stone', **ремы** 'strap, belt', **пламы** 'flame'
        ii. Neuters in -я: **семя** 'seed', **имя** 'name', **веремя** 'time'
    b. *R-stems*:
       Feminines: **дъчи** 'daughter', **мати** 'mother'
    c. *S-stems*:
       Neuters in -о: **коло** 'wheel', **слово** 'word', **небо** 'heaven', **тѣло** 'body', **чудо** 'wonder', **око** 'eye', **ухо** 'ear'
    d. *T-stems*:
       Neuters in -я denoting offspring of animals: **осьля** 'baby donkey', **теля** 'calf', **козля** 'baby goat'

Table 15 gives an overview of the inflection of the nouns in the C-declension. Notice that different handbooks provide different endings for some forms. This is partly because some forms are not well attested in the Old Rusian texts, and partly because C-declension nouns were in the process of migrating to other declensions (see section 4.3). Table 15 is based on Borkovskij and Kuznecov 1963: 190–97, Gorškova and Xaburgaev 1981: 151–57, Ivanov 1983: 259–60, and Ivanov 1995: 202–43. However, when working with Old Rusian texts, be prepared for other endings than those given in the table. In particular, endings from the *ĭ*-declension often replace the original C-declension endings. For instance, in addition to genitive/locative singular forms such as **камене**, you may also encounter **камени** with the -и ending from the *ĭ*-declension. For S-stems and T-stems, endings from the *ŏ*-declension are also attested. Instead of locative singular forms like **словесе** and **осьляте**, you may come across **словѣ** and **осьлѣ**.

Table 15. The C-declension in Old Rusian

Sg	N	камы	сѣмя	дъчи	кол-о	осьля
	A	камен-ь	сѣмя	дъчер-ь	кол-о	осьля
	G	камен-е	сѣмен-е	дъчер-е	колес-е	осьлят-е
	D	камен-и	сѣмен-и	дъчер-и	колес-и	осьлят-и
	I	камен-ьмь	сѣмен-ьмь	дъчер-ию	колес-ьмь	осьлят-ьмь
	L	камен-е	сѣмен-е	дъчер-е	колес-е	осьлят-е
Du	NA	камен-и	сѣмен-ѣ	дъчер-и	колес-ѣ	осьлят-ѣ
	GL	камен-у	сѣмен-у	дъчер-у (-ию)	колес-у	осьлят-у
	DI	камен-ьма	сѣмен-ьма	дъчер-ьма	колес-ьма	осьлят-ьма
Pl	N	камен-е	сѣмен-а	дъчер-и	колес-а	осьлят-а
	A	камен-и	сѣмен-а	дъчер-и	колес-а	осьлят-а
	G	камен-ъ	сѣмен-ъ	дъчер-ъ	колес-ъ	осьлят-ъ
	D	камен-ьмъ	сѣмен-ьмъ	дъчер-ьмъ	колес-ьмъ	осьлят-ьмъ
	I	камен-ьми	сѣмен-ы	дъчер-ьми	колес-ы	осьлят-ы
	L	камен-ьхъ	сѣмен-ьхъ	дъчер-ьхъ	колес-ьхъ	осьлят-ьхъ

Although in Old Rusian the C-declension is a small class, it contains some important words. Masculine N-stems such as **камы** have changed their nominative singular forms (cf. Modern Russian **камень** 'stone'). In other words, the nominative singular has been extended with **-ен-** by analogy to the remaining forms in the paradigm, and this change facilitated the migration of the masculine N-stems to the *ŏ*-declension. Among the neuter N-stems you recognize the small group of exceptional neuters such as **имя** 'name' and **веремя** 'time' that in Contemporary Standard Russian are in declension III. There are only two R-stems in Old Rusian: **дъчи** 'daughter' and **мати** 'mother'. These are part of declension III in Contemporary Standard Russian, and have kept **-ер-** in all forms except the nominative and accusative singular. S-stems such **чудо** and **слово** are now neuters in declension I, but the two religious words **небо** and **чудо** have preserved **-ес-** in the plural forms (**небеса**, **чудеса**). For **слово**, the normal plural form in Modern Russian is **слова**, but an archaic form **словеса** also exists, and **-ес-** has been preserved in some derived words, e.g., **словесность** 'literacy'. **Коло** has become **колесо**; here the stem has been extended with **-ес-** in all forms of the paradigm due to analogy. T-stems have preserved -ят- in the plural, but have -ёнок in the singular in Modern Russian (телёнок – телята). In Contemporary Standard Russian these words represent an irregular pattern within declension I, and once again the irregularity is due to historical "left-overs" from the C-declension.

4.2.7. Overview of Old Rusian Declensions in Tabular Form

Table 16, opposite, offers an overview of the inflectional endings of the six declensions explored in the previous sections.

4.3. Declension Classes: From Six to Three

Since Common Slavic and Old Rusian had six declension classes, while Contemporary Standard Russian has only three, we must ask how this reduction took place. This is a story about three "winners" and three "losers." The "winners" are the ŏ-, ā-, and ĭ-declensions, which form the basis for the three declensions in the modern language, while the ŭ-, ū-, and C-declensions lost in the competition and do not exist anymore. However, as we have seen in section 4.2, the "losers" have left a number of traces behind that make the modern declension system more complicated. The C-declension, for instance, has produced some irregular subpatterns in declensions I (телёнок – телята) and III (имя – имена and дочь – дочери). We have also seen that the ŭ-declension provided endings that have been integrated into declension I in Modern Russian, namely the second genitive singular ending -у (много сахару), the second locative ending -у (в лесу), and the genitive plural ending -ов.

The transition from six to three declensions can be broken down to the following processes:

(9) ŭ-declension → ŏ-declension:

All ŭ-declension nouns migrated to the ŏ-declension (e.g., домъ 'house').

(10) ū-declension → ĭ-declension:

Some ū-declension nouns migrated to the ĭ-declension (e.g., любы 'love').

(11) ū-declension → ā-declension:

Some ū-declension nouns migrated to the ā-declension (e.g., букы 'letter').

Table 16. Overview of declensions in Old Rusian (Endings of different genders are separated by a slash; ∅ ("zero") indicates that a form has no ending)

		ŏ-decl		ŭ-decl		ā-decl		ĭ-decl		ū-decl		C-decl	
		Hard	Soft	Hard	Soft	Hard	Soft	Hard	Soft	Hard	Soft	Hard	Soft
Sg	N	-ъ/-о	-ь/-е	-ъ	-ъ	-а	-я	-ь	-ь	-ы	-ы	-∅	-∅
	A	-ъ/-о	-ь/-е	-ъ	-ъ	-у	-ю	-ь	-ь	-ъ	-ъ	-ь/-ъ/-∅	-ь/-ъ/-∅
	G	-а	-я	-у	-у	-ы	-ѣ	-и	-и	-е	-е	-е	-е
	D	-у	-ю	-ови	-ьмь	-ѣ	-и	-и	-и	-и	-и	-и	-и
	I	-ьмь	-ьмь	-ъмь	-ьмь	-ою	-ею	-ьмь/-ию	-ьмь/-ию	-ию	-ию	-ьмь/-ию/-ьмь	-ьмь/-ию/-ьмь
	L	-ѣ	-и	-у	-у	-ѣ	-и	-и	-и	-е	-е	-е	-е
	V	-е/-о	-ю/-е	-у	-у	-о	-е	-и	-и	-и	-и	-и	-и
Du	NA	-а/-ѣ	-я/-и	-ы	-ы	-ѣ	-и	-и	-и	-и	-и	-и/-и/-ѣ	-и/-и/-ѣ
	GL	-у	-ю	-ову	-ову	-у	-ю	-ию	-ию	-у	-у	-у	-у
	DI	-ома	-ема	-ьма	-ьма	-ама	-яма	-ьма	-ьма	-ама	-ама	-ьма	-ьма
Pl	N	-и/-а	-и/-я	-ове	-ове	-ы	-ѣ	-ие/-и	-ие/-и	-и	-и	-е/-и/-а	-е/-и/-а
	A	-ы/-а	-ѣ/-я	-ы	-ы	-ы	-ѣ	-и	-и	-и	-и	-и/-и/-а	-и/-и/-а
	G	-ъ	-ь	-овъ	-овъ	-ъ	-ь	-ии	-ии	-ъ	-ъ	-ъ	-ъ
	D	-омъ	-емъ	-ъмъ	-ьмъ	-амъ	-ямъ	-ьмъ	-ьмъ	-амъ	-амъ	-ьмъ	-ьмъ
	I	-ы	-и	-ьми	-ьми	-ами	-ями	-ьми	-ьми	-ами	-ами	-ьми/-ьми/-ы	-ьми/-ьми/-ы
	L	-ѣхъ	-ихъ	-ъхъ	-ьхъ	-ахъ	-яхъ	-ьхъ	-ьхъ	-ахъ	-ахъ	-ьхъ	-ьхъ

(12) C-declension → ŏ-declension:

The S- and T-stem nouns migrated to the ŏ-declension (e.g., **коло** 'wheel' and **осьля** 'baby donkey').

(13) C-declension → ĭ-declension:

The N- and R-stem nouns migrated to the ĭ-declension (e.g., **семя** 'seed' and **мати** 'mother').

(14) ĭ-declension → ŏ-declension:

Masculine ĭ-declension nouns migrated to the ŏ-declension (e.g., **гость** 'guest'; exception: **путь** 'way').

The "rich get richer, poor get poorer" and closeness principles are at work in all these changes, insofar as nouns migrate from small to large classes that are closely related.

The disintegration of the ŭ-, ū-, and C-declensions started already in Common Slavic, and even in early Old Rusian we are only dealing with reminiscences of the original six-declension system. The migration of masculine ĭ-declension nouns to the ŏ-declension is a somewhat more recent change. The noun **дьнь** 'day' illustrates this. This noun originally belonged to the C-declension, and there are attested examples with the original genitive singular **дьне**. In later documents, however, we tend to find the ĭ-declension genitive form **дьни**, while in Modern Russian the genitive singular of **день** is **дня**, which reflects the final transition to the ŏ-declension.

Figure 7, opposite, represents the processes graphically. The solid arrows connect the "winning" declensions in Common Slavic and Old Rusian to their modern counterparts. The dashed arrows represent the processes in (9–14) above.

4.4. Number and Case

As we have seen in the previous section, Common Slavic and (early) Old Rusian had three features in the category of number: singular, dual, and plural. While singular and plural are still alive and kicking in Modern Russian, the dual has been lost. This process started in the thirteenth century, and the dual was completely lost during the fourteenth and fifteenth centuries. As a consequence, the meaning of the feature plural has changed. Originally, the plural was used to refer to three or more items, but since the disappearance of the dual, the plural has been used to indicate *two* or more items.

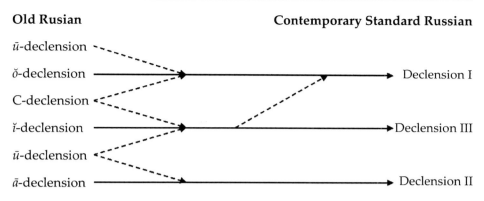

Figure 7. Graphical representation of the changes in the declension system

Although the dual was lost, there are many traces of it in Modern Russian. For most words, dual forms were replaced by plural forms, but for some nouns the dual forms ousted the plural forms. A few examples are given in Table 17 on p. 94. It is not hard to guess why the dual forms have prevailed in words like these; since these nouns denote paired items, it stands to reason that they occurred more frequently in the dual than in the plural. In other words, it is likely that the more frequent form prevailed. This is a general principle of language change:

(15) *The frequency principle*:
High-frequent forms tend to oust low-frequent forms.

For most nouns, we can assume that the plural was more frequent than the dual, but for some paired entities the dual may have been more frequent and hence ousted the plural form. Notice that although forms like **pora** have developed from Old Rusian dual forms, such forms cannot be analyzed as dual forms in Modern Russian. While in Old Rusian **pora** could be used to refer to two and only two antlers, in the modern language **pora** indicate any number of antlers larger than one.

Table 17. Examples of Old Rusian nominative dual forms that have become nominative plurals in Contemporary Standard Russian

	Old Rusian dual	Old Rusian plural	Contemporary Standard Russian plural
рог 'antler'	рога	рози	рога
глаз 'eye'	глаза	глази	глаза
берег '(river)bank'	берега	берези	берега
рукав 'sleeve'	рукава	рукави	рукава

In section 4.1 we saw that Contemporary Standard Russian has two genitive and two locative cases. In 4.2.2 you learned that the second genitive and second locative endings -y came from the ŭ-declension. Does that mean that we should say that these cases existed in Old Rusian as well? No! In Modern Russian the same nouns can have both the endings -a and -y in the genitive (сахара vs. сахару) and the endings -e and -y in the locative (в лесе vs. в лесу), and the endings signal (slightly) different meanings. In other words, there is a contrast between G1 and G2 and between L1 and L2. In Old Rusian, alternatively, there was no such semantic contrast. The endings -a and -y in the genitive had the same meaning, but were used for nouns of different declensions (although we observe some variation already in early texts). Likewise, -e and -y in the locative had the same meanings, but were used for different nouns of different declensions. Since there was no contrast in meaning in Old Rusian, we cannot analyze this as different cases.

In the previous sections, we have included the vocative among the cases in Old Rusian. As mentioned, this is controversial, but that need not concern us here. What is important is the fact that the vocative forms that Old Rusian had inherited from Common Slavic disappeared in the fourteenth and fifteenth centuries. Only a few relics of the old vocative such as **Господи** and **Боже** are left in Contemporary Standard Russian. Although the original vocative was lost, new vocatives such as **мам!** from **мама** 'mom' have developed in Modern Russian, as shown in section 4.1. As pointed out by Danièl' (2009: 243; see also Andersen 2012: 159 for discussion), these new vocatives are recorded from the mid 1800s, so we are dealing with a relatively recent innovation that has compensated for the loss of the original vocative in medieval times.

Summarizing this section, we have seen that Russian has lost one feature in the category of number, namely the dual, but developed two additional features in the category of case, namely the second genitive and the second locative. New vocative forms have replaced the Old Rusian vocative.

4.5. Stems Ending in Hard and Soft Consonants

In Contemporary Standard Russian, the endings are spelled differently depending on whether the stem ends in a hard or a soft consonant. In the genitive singular, for instance, сестра 'sister' becomes сестры, whereas воля 'will' becomes воли. However, this is merely an orthographical difference, since the endings -ы and -и represent the same phoneme /i/. In general, hard and soft stems have the same phonemes in the endings. In Old Rusian, in contrast, different phonemes occurred in the endings of hard and soft stems. In the genitive singular of the ā-declension, for instance, hard stems had -ы (сестры from сестра), whereas soft stems had -ѣ (волѣ from воля). The letters ы and ѣ represented different phonemes, as we will see in chapter 12. Since the development has been from different to same phonemes in hard and soft stems, Contemporary Standard Russian arguably has a simpler system than Old Rusian. However, the good news is that the Old Rusian system is regular; all you need to learn is the small number of correspondences given in Table 18. If you know the vowel in the endings following hard stems, you can predict the vowel in the corresponding ending for soft stems. The ending -a which corresponds to -я and the ending -у which corresponds to -ю are not included in the table since here we have the same phoneme after hard and soft stems.

Table 18. Vowel correspondences in endings for hard and soft stems in Old Rusian

Hard	Soft
-ъ	-ь
-о	-е
-ѣ	-и
-ы	-ѣ

In addition to the correspondences in Table 18, you need to memorize three exceptions concerning the ŏ-declension:

(16) a. The vocative had -e for hard stems and -ю for soft stems of masculine nouns.

b. The nominative plural had -и both for hard and soft stems of masculine nouns.

c. The instrumental plural had -ы for hard stems and -и for soft stems.

4.6. Gender

Apart from number and case, the most important category for nouns in Common Slavic, Old Rusian, and Modern Russian is grammatical gender. Genders are defined as "classes of nouns reflected in the behavior of associated words" (Hockett 1958: 231), which means that nouns of the same gender have the same agreement patterns. Let us consider the three Modern Russian nouns **корабль** 'ship', **лодка** 'boat', and **судно** 'vessel'. If you want to combine these nouns with the adjective **большой** 'big' you need to use different forms of the adjective, because the adjective must agree with the noun: **большой корабль**, **большая лодка**, and **большое судно**. Here we observe three different agreement patterns, so we can conclude that Modern Russian has three genders, which it is customary to refer to as "masculine," "feminine," and "neuter." Modern Russian has inherited this three-gender system from Old Rusian and Common Slavic, which had the same three genders.

It is important to notice that gender is *not* an inflectional category of nouns. Nouns are inflected in case and number, which means that each noun displays different endings for different cases and numbers. However, each noun has only one gender. For adjectives, on the contrary, gender is an inflectional category, since each adjective has different forms for different genders, as we saw in the example with **большой** above.

4.7. Subgender: Animacy

Another important category is animacy. From Modern Russian you know that nouns that denote living beings (animates) such as **брат** 'brother' behave differently from those denoting inanimates such as **дом** 'house':

(17) a. A=G: **Он любил своего брата.** 'He loved his brother.'

b. A=N: **Он любил свой дом.** 'He loved his house.'

The difference between animates and inanimates is only relevant in the accusative case. The pattern in (17a) is referred to as "A(ccusative)=G(enitive)," since the accusative has the same form as the genitive. "A=N" in (17b) indicates that the accusative has the same form as the nominative. The A=G pattern can be thought of as a strategy for avoiding homonymy between the nominative and the accusative, i.e., ensuring that the two cases have different endings. Arguably, this is particularly important for animates, since they typically occur as subjects (after all, only living beings can carry out actions). By using the A=G pattern for animates, the Russian language clarifies that an animate noun is not a subject in the given construction.

4.7. Subgender: Animacy

Animacy is related to grammatical gender in the sense that both categories manifest themselves through agreement; in (17), for instance, the difference between **своего** and **свой** indicates whether the noun in question is animate or inanimate. Animacy is sometimes referred to as a "subgender" (Corbett 1991: 165–68), because **брат** and **дом** represent two subgroups of the masculine gender that have different agreement patterns only in the accusative, but otherwise behave like any other masculine nouns.

As illustrated by (17), it is not only the forms of **свой** that depend on animacy; the nouns themselves also display different endings. For animate nouns like **брат**, the accusative has the same form as the genitive (A=G, i.e., **брата**), whereas for the inanimate noun **дом** the accusative has the same form as the nominative (A=N, i.e., **дом**). Simplifying somewhat, we can state the following rule for Contemporary Standard Russian:

(18) *The animacy rule of Contemporary Standard Russian*:

For masculine nouns in the singular and nouns of all genders in the plural, the accusative equals the nominative (A=N) if the noun is inanimate, but equals the genitive (A=G) if the noun is animate.

While the inherited three-gender system has remained stable since Common Slavic times, the system of subgenders has changed. Simply put, the A=G pattern has become more widespread over time. By way of illustration, consider the following example from *Povest' vremennyx let*:

(19) a. A=N: И помяну Олегъ **конь свой**.   (PVL 912 AD; 38,16)
 b. A=G: И вспомнил Олег **коня своего**.
 c. And Oleg remembered **his horse**.

Since Oleg's horse is animate, we have A=G in the Modern Russian version in (19b), but A=N is nevertheless found in (19a). However, A=G is also attested in medieval texts, as shown by the following example from *Kievskaja letopis'*:

(20) a. A=G: Онъ […] увороти **коня** направо.
 b. A=G: Он […] повернул **коня** направо.
 c. He […] turned the **horse** to the right.

The variation between the A=N and A=G patterns reflect ongoing change in Old Rusian. How did the expansion of the genitive-like accusative take place? A traditional story goes like this: The A=G pattern first indicated "a healthy, free, male person" (Lunt 2001: 56), and then spread to other humans and animals in the singular, before the pattern made its way to the plural. In the plural, humans in the masculine gender first adopted A=G, followed by humans in the feminine gender, before, finally, animals in the plural were assimilated to the A=G pattern. Schematically, this can be represented as follows:

(21) Gradual expansion of the A=G pattern (traditional account):
    a. Healthy, free, persons in the masculine singular
    b. Other persons in the masculine singular
    c. Animals in the masculine singular
    d. Humans in the masculine plural
    e. Humans in the feminine plural
    f. Animals in the plural

However, far from all researchers accept this version wholesale. According to Krys'ko (1994: 35 and 126), there is no evidence that the animacy subgender originated in a semantically restricted subset of humans. Krys'ko (1994: 47) furthermore argues that the A=G pattern was well established even for animals in early Old Rusian, but admits that A=G was less frequent for animals than for humans. This is compatible with an interpretation whereby animals adopted the A=G pattern later than humans. It is not controversial that the A=G pattern made its way to the plural after it had established itself in the singular. According to Ivanov (1983: 286) the A=G pattern spread to the plural in the 14th century, while animals in the plural adopted the A=G pattern as late as the 17th century. Krys'ko (1994: 126), contrastively, suggests that the plural was affected as early as in the 12th century.

    Another factor that is often said to be relevant for the choice between the A=G and A=N patterns is definiteness. According to this view, which goes back at least to Meillet 1897, there was a tendency to use the A=G pattern if the noun was definite, i.e., identifiable from the context. In English, we use the definite article *the* in order to signal that an entity is identifiable. In other words, if I say *I am looking for the horse* with the definite article in front of *horse*, the implication is that you should be able to identify which horse I am talking about. For instance, the horse may have been mentioned earlier. It is likely that the A=G pattern had a function in Old Rusian that resembled the function of the definite article in English, i.e., to single out identifiable entities. However, variation is extensive, so it is difficult to state simple rules.

4.8 Summary: Overview of Changes in Tabular Form

In this chapter you have learned that the changes involving nouns include both losses and additions. On the one hand, three declensions were lost, as was the dual number. The number of the cases, on the other hand, has increased. The second genitive (G2) and the second locative (L2) cases are innovations, and the loss of the old vocative has been compensated for by the emergence of new vocative forms such as мам! from мама 'mom'. The number of genders (masculine, feminine, and neuter) has remained stable, and so has the number of subgenders (inanimate and animate), although the A=G pattern that is characteristic of the animate subgender may have spread from humans to animals, and certainly spread from the singular to the plural. Table 19 summarizes these changes. The numbers in the table indicate how many declensions, numbers, cases, genders, and subgenders there were in Old Rusian and Contemporary Standard Russian (CSR).

Table 19. Schematic overview of changes concerning nouns in Old Rusian and Contemporary Standard Russian (CSR)

Category	Old Rusian	CSR	Change
Declension	6	3	Loss of $\breve{u}$-, $\bar{u}$- and C-declensions
Number	3	2	Loss of dual
Case	7	9	Addition of G2 and L2
			Loss of old V, emergence of new V
Gender	3	3	—
Subgender (animacy)	2	2	A=G pattern has expanded from humans to animals (possibly), and from the singular to the plural (certainly)

In addition to learning about concrete changes affecting nouns, you have seen three general principles of language change at work:

(22) a. *The "rich get richer, poor get poorer" principle* (section 4.2.2):
    Words tend to migrate from small to large classes.
   b. *The closeness principle* (4.2.2):
    Words tend to migrate between closely related classes.
   c. *The frequency principle* (4.4):
    High-frequent forms tend to oust low-frequent forms.

The "rich get richer, poor get poorer" principle concerns the reduction from six to three declensions; as we have seen, the three large declension classes have survived, while the three small ones have disappeared. An example illustrating the closeness principle is the migration of *ŭ*-declension nouns to the *ŏ*-declension. Both declensions contained masculine nouns with the ending -ъ in the nominative singular, so the two declensions were closely related, and it was therefore natural that the nouns from the *ŭ*-declension were absorbed into the *ŏ*-declension when the *ŭ*-declension collapsed. The relationship between the dual and the plural illustrates the frequency principle. Normally, plural forms were of higher frequency and therefore ousted the dual forms, but for paired nouns such as **рогъ** 'antler' the dual forms were presumably more frequent than the plural forms, and therefore the dual forms replaced the old plural forms.

4.9. For Further Reading

You will find overviews of the declension system of Old Rusian and the changes it underwent in all historical grammars. Gorškova and Xaburgaev (1981) and Ivanov (1983)[1] offer reader-friendly presentations in Russian; a good supplement is Galinskaja 1997 (see also Galinskaja 2014: 159–252). For an overview in English, see Townsend and Janda 1996, which compares Russian to other Slavic languages. For works on specific topics, Janda (1996) provides detailed accounts of the *ŭ*-declension and the dual in Slavic, while Andersen 2012 and Danièl' 2009 are updated works on the rise and fall of the vocative. Krys'ko 1994 is a thorough critique of the traditional treatment of animacy in the history of Russian.

---

[1] For a thorough discussion of Ivanov 1983, see Darden 1991/forthcoming.

Chapter 5   Morphology: Pronouns

Have you ever wondered whether the so-called reflexive postfix **-ся** is related to the reflexive pronoun **себя**? Do you know the etymology of **сейчас** and **сегодня**? And do you know where the **н-** in the pronoun comes from in prepositional phrases like **к нему** 'to him'? Answers to these and many other questions are offered in this chapter, which explores the declension of personal pronouns (sections 5.1 and 5.2), demonstrative pronouns (section 5.3), possessive pronouns (section 5.4), **вьсь** 'all' (section 5.5), and interrogative pronouns (section 5.6).

5.1. Personal (1st and 2nd Persons) and Reflexive Pronouns

Table 20 on p. 102 shows the declension of the Old Rusian personal pronouns corresponding to **я** 'I' and **ты** 'you' in Modern Russian. Notice that (early) Old Rusian had dual forms meaning 'we two' and 'you two'. In the same way as for nouns, the dual was lost for all pronouns. The reflexive pronoun is included in the table, since its declension parallels that of **ты** in the oblique cases singular. As in Modern Russian, the reflexive pronoun does not have a nominative form, and there are no dual or plural forms of the reflexive pronoun.

    Although the declension of the personal and reflexive pronouns resembles the declension of the corresponding words in Contemporary Standard Russian, some comments are in order. First of all, Table 20 contains two nominative singular forms meaning 'I': **я** and **язъ**, but in fact the picture is even more complicated, since these two forms compete with the Church Slavic form **азъ**. While **азъ** is clearly of South Slavic origin and **я** is East Slavic (i.e., Old Rusian), the origin of **язъ** is less clear. Some researchers argue that this is the original Old Rusian form that subsequently was shortened to **я** (cf. Ivanov 1983: 295), but others analyze **язъ** as a hybrid between **азъ** and **я** that emerged in the Russian version of Church Slavic (cf. Gorškova and Xaburgaev 1981: 247, but see Ivanov 1985: 328–32 for critical discussion). In any case, all three forms are attested in medieval texts from the Old Rusian period.

Table 20. Declension of personal (1st and 2nd person) and reflexive pronouns in Old Rusian

		1st person	2nd person	Reflexive
Sg	N	язъ, я	ты	—
	A	мене, мя	тебе, тя	себе, ся
	G	мене	тебе	себе
	D	мънѣ, ми	тобѣ, ти	собѣ, си
	I	мъною	тобою	собою
	L	мънѣ	тобѣ	собѣ
Du	N	вѣ	ва	—
	A	на	ва	—
	GL	наю	ваю	—
	DI	нама	вама	—
Pl	N	мы	вы	—
	A	насъ, ны	васъ, вы	—
	G	насъ	васъ	—
	D	намъ, ны	вамъ, вы	—
	I	нами	вами	—
	L	насъ	васъ	—

In the accusative and dative singular and plural, you find short forms like **ми** and **ти** in addition to the longer forms that resemble the relevant pronouns in Modern Russian. These short forms are what linguists call "clitics," i.e., unstressed linguistic elements that occupy an intermediate position between full-fledged words and affixes (prefixes and suffixes). We will return to clitics in section 9.11. For now it is sufficient to notice that the clitic forms of the personal pronouns have not survived in Contemporary Standard Russian, while the reflexive clitic has undergone grammaticalization and become an affix (often referred to as a "postfix" in the Russian grammatical tradition), which is found in so-called reflexive verbs in Modern Russian (e.g., **мыться** 'wash (oneself)').

It is worth noticing that the Old Rusian accusative forms **мене**, **тебе**, and **себе** have developed into **меня**, **тебя**, and **себя** in Contemporary Standard Russian. Possibly, the **-я** at the end is due to influence from the clitic forms which ended in **-я**, as shown in Table 20. Notice also the first vowel in the dative and locative forms **тобѣ** and **собѣ**. The corresponding modern forms **тебе** and **себе** which are spelled with "e" instead of "o" may be due to the influence from the Old Rusian accusative and genitive forms, or from Church Slavic. Old Church Slavonic had dative and locative forms with "e."

5.2. Personal (3rd Person) and Relative Pronouns

The personal pronoun in the third person was originally a demonstrative pronoun that already in Common Slavic started to be used in the meanings 'he', 'she', 'it', and 'they'. In addition to singular and plural forms, these pronouns also had dual forms, which, however, were lost early. In Table 21, you recognize the oblique cases, while the nominative forms are different. What happened was that another demonstrative pronoun, онъ (она, оно, они), replaced the old nominative forms. This created a so-called suppletive paradigm. Suppletion occurs when a paradigm consists of completely unrelated forms such as онъ and его. If you go back to the previous section, you will see that the personal pronouns involve suppletion in the first and second persons too (e.g., я and мене). The plural form они came to be used for all genders, and ихъ also became generalized to all genders. In other words, the gender distinctions in the plural were lost. This happened to all pronouns discussed in this chapter.

Table 21. The declension of personal pronouns (3rd person) in Old Rusian

		Masculine	Feminine	Neuter
Sg	N	и	я	е
	A	и	ю	е
	G	его	еѣ	его
	D	ему	еи	ему
	I	имь	ею	имь
	L	емь	еи	емь
Du	NA	я	и	и
	GL	ѣю	ѣю	ѣю
	DI	има	има	има
Pl	N	и	ѣ	я
	A	ѣ	ѣ	я
	G	ихъ	ихъ	ихъ
	D	имъ	имъ	имъ
	I	ими	ими	ими
	L	ихъ	ихъ	ихъ

Although as a personal pronoun и disappeared very early in the nominative case, this pronoun played an important role in the formation of long forms of adjectives, a topic you will learn more about in the following chapter. In combination with the particle же, и also served as a relative pronoun in Old Rusian:

(1) a. И бяше варягъ одинъ, бѣ дворъ его, идеже бѣ церкви святыя Богородица, **юже** създа Володимиръ.   (PVL 983 AD; 82,11)

  b. Был тогда варяг один, и был двор его, где сейчас церковь святой Богородицы, **которую** построил Владимир.

  c. Now there was a certain Varangian whose house was situated by the spot where now stands the Church of the Holy Virgin **which** Vladimir built.

In the same way as in Modern Russian, the relative pronoun adopts the gender and number of its antecedent (церковь 'church'), and occurs in the accusative since it is the direct object of the verb in the relative clause (създа in Old Rusian, построил in Modern Russian). The modern relative pronoun который goes back to an interrogative or indefinite pronoun that has ousted иже as a relative pronoun. Although relative sentences with который are attested in the 13th century, this construction was not widespread before the 16th century (Borkovskij and Kuznecov 1963: 475). You will learn more about relative clauses in section 9.12.1.

As shown in Table 21, the accusative forms equal the nominative in the masculine and neuter singular and in the feminine and neuter plural. In other words, for these forms we are dealing with the A=N pattern discussed in section 4.7. This has changed; Contemporary Standard Russian displays the A=G pattern, since the accusative forms are его and их. The emergence of the A=G pattern started early, so you may encounter его and их as accusative forms in Old Rusian texts.

Contemporary Standard Russian has a peculiar rule, whereby н is attached to a personal pronoun after prepositions. For instance, the dative form ему becomes нему after the preposition к: к нему 'to him'. The historical explanation is that the prepositions corresponding to к, в, and с in Modern Russian originally ended in н: кън, вън, and сън. Prepositional phrases such as кън ему 'to him' consisted of three syllables: къ–не–му. Since н belongs to the same syllable as the first vowel of the pronoun, н was reanalyzed as part of the pronoun instead of the preposition. This pattern has since been generalized to other prepositions.

Before we leave the personal pronouns it is worth mentioning that Old Rusian had a number of forms ending in a jer (ь or ъ). In Contemporary Standard Russian all these forms have a hard consonant at the end, so you may find it difficult to memorize which forms ended in -ъ and which ended in -ь in Old Rusian. Here is a simple mnemonic: singular forms had -ъ (cf. instrumental singular -имь and locative singular -емь), whereas plural forms displayed -ѣ (cf. genitive and locative plural -ихъ and dative plural -имъ).

5.3. Demonstrative Pronouns

Contemporary Standard Russian has a two-way distinction between proximal and distal demonstrative pronouns. The proximal этот 'this' refers to something close to the speaker (e.g., этот стол 'this table'), while the distal тот 'that' is used for reference to something further away (e.g., тот стол 'that table'). Old Rusian had a three-way distinction, where сь 'this' fulfilled the proximal function, and онъ was the distal pronoun. Some researchers describe the third pronoun, тъ, as "neutral" (Russian: безотносительное, Ivanov 1983: 301) or "distal, but visible" (Ivanov 1995: 364), while others assume that it originally indicated proximity to the addressee rather than the speaker (cf. Borkovskij and Kuznecov 1963: 221). If the latter analysis is correct, Old Rusian had a system resembling the distinction between first, second, and third persons, where сь meant 'close to me' (i.e., first person), тъ meant 'close to you' (i.e., second person), and онъ meant 'close to neither you nor me' (i.e., third person).

The transition from a three-way to a two-way system happened as follows. Сь and онъ disappeared as demonstrative pronouns, and the new proximal pronoun этот was created by attaching a particle to тот. Notice that the modern distal pronoun тот has developed through a doubling of the original form: тъ + тъ became тот. The genitive singular form того was originally pronounced with [g]. It is assumed that [g] developed into the fricative [γ] and later disappeared. Finally, [v] was inserted in order to avoid two consecutive vowels (cf. Ivanov 1983: 302 for discussion).

The masculine plural form in Table 22 (on p. 106) is ти which parallels the masculine plural of nouns in the ŏ-declension, which had the ending -и. As we saw in section 4.2.1, for nouns the masculine plural ending has been replaced by the ending -ы from the accusative. The development of the demonstrative pronoun has followed a different path, as the modern plural form is те. This form has presumably emerged as a result of the analogy to the oblique cases in the plural. As shown in the table, the oblique cases in the plural contained the vowel /ě/ spelled as -ѣ, which became /e/ through regular sound change. When тѣ became the nominative plural, /ě/ occurred in all the plural forms, and could therefore be analyzed as a plural marker. At the same time /ě/ set the pronouns apart from nouns which have generalized the vowel /a/ in the plural (cf. the Modern Russian endings -ам, -ами, and -ах) and from adjectives which have generalized /i/ (cf. the Modern Russian endings -ым, -ыми, and -ых). Admittedly, the opposition between pronouns and adjectives is neutralized after soft consonants, insofar as both pronouns such as они and adjectives such

Table 22. The declension of demonstrative pronouns in Old Rusian

		Proximal			"Neutral" (?)			Distal		
		Masc	Fem	Neut	Masc	Fem	Neut	Masc	Fem	Neut
Sg	N	сь	си	се	тъ	та	то	онъ	она	оно
	A	сь	сю	се	тъ	ту	то	онъ	ону	оно
	G	сего	сеѣ	сего	того	тоѣ	того	оного	оноѣ	оного
	D	сему	сеи	сему	тому	тои	тому	оному	онои	оному
	I	симь	сею	симь	тѣмь	тою	тѣмь	онѣмь	оною	онѣмь
	L	семь	сеи	семь	томь	тои	томь	ономь	онои	ономь
Du	NA	сия	сии	сии	та	тѣ	тѣ	она	онѣ	онѣ
	GL	сею	сею	сею	тою	тою	тою	оною	оною	оною
	DI	сима	сима	сима	тѣма	тѣма	тѣма	онѣма	онѣма	онѣма
Pl	N	си	си	си	ти	ты	та	они	оны	она
	A	сиѣ	сиѣ	си	ты	ты	та	оны	оны	она
	G	сихъ	сихъ	сихъ	тѣхъ	тѣхъ	тѣхъ	онѣхъ	онѣхъ	онѣхъ
	D	симъ	симъ	симъ	тѣмъ	тѣмъ	тѣмъ	онѣмъ	онѣмъ	онѣмъ
	I	сими	сими	сими	тѣми	тѣми	тѣми	онѣми	онѣми	онѣми
	L	сихъ	сихъ	сихъ	тѣхъ	тѣхъ	тѣхъ	онѣхъ	онѣхъ	онѣхъ

as **синий** 'dark blue' have /i/ in Modern Russian (cf. **им, ими, их** vs. **синим, синими, синих**).

The original proximal demonstrative pronoun **сь** had the alternative singular forms **сей** (masculine), **сия** (feminine), and **сие** (neuter). The masculine form has survived in expressions such as **по сей день** 'to this day', and in the adverbs **сейчас** 'now' (literally 'this hour') and **сегодня** 'today' (literally 'this day' in the genitive).

5.4. Possessive Pronouns

The declension of the possessive pronouns **мои** 'my' and **нашь** 'our' is given in Table 23. **Твои** and **свои** follow the pattern of **мои**, while **вашь** is declined in the same way as **нашь**. For possessors in the third person, Contemporary Standard Russian uses the indeclinable **его** 'his, its', **ее** 'her, its', and **их** 'their', which correspond to the genitive forms of the personal pronoun. We find the same use of genitive forms of the personal pronoun in Old Rusian as well. By way of example, consider **дворъ его** 'his house' in (1) above (p. 104).

Table 23. The declension of possessive pronouns in Old Rusian

		Masc.	Fem.	Neuter	Masc.	Fem.	Neuter
Sg	N	мои	моя	мое	нашь	наша	наше
	A	мои	мою	мое	нашь	нашу	наше
	G	моего	моеѣ	моего	нашего	нашеѣ	нашего
	D	моему	моеи	моему	нашему	нашеи	нашему
	I	моимь	моею	моимь	нашимь	нашею	нашимь
	L	моемь	моеи	моемь	нашемь	нашеи	нашемь
Du	NA	моя	мои	мои	наша	наши	наши
	GL	моею	моею	моею	нашею	нашею	нашею
	DI	моима	моима	моима	нашима	нашима	нашима
Pl	N	мои	моѣ	моя	наши	нашѣ	наша
	A	моѣ	моѣ	моя	нашѣ	нашѣ	наша
	G	моихъ	моихъ	моихъ	нашихъ	нашихъ	нашихъ
	D	моимъ	моимъ	моимъ	нашимъ	нашимъ	нашимъ
	I	моими	моими	моими	нашими	нашими	нашими
	L	моихъ	моихъ	моихъ	нашихъ	нашихъ	нашихъ

5.5. Вьсь 'all'

The declension of весь is given in Table 24. Notice that in the same way as for тъ, the nominative plural вьси was replaced by вьсѣ, which has become все in Contemporary Standard Russian.

Table 24. The declension of Old Rusian вьсь 'all'

		Masculine	Feminine	Neuter
Sg	N	вьсь	вься	вьсе
	A	вьсь	вьсю	вьсе
	G	вьсего	вьсеѣ	вьсего
	D	вьсему	вьсеи	вьсему
	I	вьсѣмь	вьсею	вьсѣмь
	L	вьсемь	вьсеи	вьсемь
Pl	N	вьси	вьсѣ	вься
	A	вьсѣ	вьсѣ	вься
	G	вьсѣхъ	вьсѣхъ	вьсѣхъ
	D	вьсѣмъ	вьсѣмъ	вьсѣмъ
	I	вьсѣми	вьсѣми	вьсѣми
	L	вьсѣхъ	вьсѣхъ	вьсѣхъ

5.6. Interrogative Pronouns: къто and чьто

The two interrogative pronouns къто 'who' and чьто 'what' were declined as shown in Table 25. Къто has the same endings as тъ, while чьто follows the same pattern as сь. Notice that къто has a genitive-like accusative, whereas for чьто the accusative equals the nominative. In the instrumental, къто has the form цѣмь with the same consonant alternation we find in nouns with the ending -ѣ (see Table 10 in section 4.2.1). This is the result of the sound law called "second palatalization" which you will learn more about in section 11.7. Under the influence of the remaining forms in the paradigm the instrumental form developed the same initial consonant as the rest of the paradigm. This is an example of analogy, since the instrumental became more similar to the other forms of къто.

Historically, both къто and чьто developed from the same root that was followed by the particle то. The root originally started with [k] in both pronouns, but since in the word meaning 'what' the root contained a front vowel, the [k] in this pronoun underwent the so-called first palatalization, a sound law we will discuss in section 11.5.

Table 25. The declension of interrogative pronouns in Old Rusian

		'who'	'what'
Sg	N	къто	чьто
	A	кого	чьто
	G	кого	чего
	D	кому	чему
	I	цѣмь	чимь
	L	комь	чемь

5.7. Summary

Although the pronouns explored in this chapter display a number of idiosyncratic properties, we can draw some general conclusions.

(2) Loss of dual number and gender in the plural:

Like nouns, by the end of the Old Rusian period the pronouns had lost

a. the dual number (section 5.1)

b. gender distinctions in the plural (5.2)

(3) Third person (5.2):

The third person was less prominent than the first and second persons in the Common Slavic and Old Rusian pronominal system.

a. Originally, there were no personal pronouns in the third person, but this hole was filled by demonstrative pronouns:

i. **И** came to be used as a personal pronoun in Common Slavic.

ii. The nominative forms of **и** were then replaced by **онъ, она, оно, они**.

b. There were no possessive pronouns in the third person; instead genitive forms of **и** were used, a system that has survived in Contemporary Standard Russian.

(4) Suppletion in personal pronouns (5.2):
   a. The introduction of **онъ, она, оно, они** in the nominative of personal pronouns created suppletive paradigms where the nominative and oblique cases are completely unrelated (e.g., **онъ** and **его**).
   b. Suppletion is also characteristic of personal pronouns in the 1st and 2nd person (e.g., **я** and **мене**).

(5) Demonstrative pronouns (5.3):
   a. Common Slavic and early Old Rusian had a three-way system:
      i. **сь**: proximal (close to speaker)
      ii. **тъ**: neutral or proximal (close to addressee)
      iii. **онъ**: distal (neither close to speaker nor addressee)
   b. The three-way system became reduced to a two-way system:
      i. **сь** and **онъ** were lost as demonstrative pronouns.
      ii. **тъ** became the distal pronoun.
      iii. **этот** emerged as a new proximal pronoun.

(6) Plural endings (5.3):
   a. Pronouns (except personal pronouns in the 1st and 2nd person) develop -ѣ (/ě/) as a plural marker, since all plural forms have this vowel.
   b. The plural marker /ě/ sets pronouns apart from
      i. nouns that generalized /a/ in the plural (cf. Modern Russian **-ам, -ами, -ах**)
      ii. adjectives that generalized /i/ in the plural (cf. Modern Russian **-ым, -ыми, -ых**)
   c. The opposition between pronominal and adjectival plural declension is neutralized after soft consonants where both pronouns and adjectives have generalized /i/ (cf. Modern Russian **-им, -ими, -их** in both soft adjectives such as **синий** 'dark blue' and possessive pronouns such as **мой** 'my').

(7) General historical processes:
   a. Grammaticalization: clitic reflexive pronoun developed into "postfix" **-ся** (5.1).

(7) b. Analogy: many examples of analogy inside paradigms, e.g., the replacement of nominative plural **ти** by **тѣ** under the influence of the remaining plural forms (5.3).

5.8. For Further Reading

Thorough overviews of the declension and history of pronouns can be found in most historical grammars, e.g., Gorškova and Xaburgaev 1981 and Ivanov 1983. Kiparsky (1967) offers detailed discussions of individual forms.

Chapter 6   Morphology: Adjectives

You may have asked yourself why Russian makes a distinction between short and long forms of adjectives. Why are the short forms only used in a limited number of constructions? Why do they only have nominative forms? Read this chapter and you will find answers to these and other questions regarding the history of adjectives. Section 6.1 explores the relationship between short and long forms, while sections 6.2 and 6.3 outline their declension. In section 6.4 you will find a discussion of the comparative and superlative degrees of adjectives. Section 6.5 sums up the main points.

6.1. Short and Long Forms in Common Slavic, Old Rusian, and Contemporary Standard Russian

One of the challenges you have faced while learning Russian is that there are two sets of adjective forms. In addition to "normal" long forms such as **новый** 'new', there are also so-called short forms like **нов** 'new'. The use of the short forms is restricted in two ways:

(1) Restrictions on the use of short forms of adjectives in Contemporary Standard Russian
   a. Syntax: Short forms are restricted to predicative function.
   b. Morphology: Short forms are restricted to the nominative case.

In order to understand the syntactic restriction, it is sufficient to distinguish between two syntactic functions of the adjective. In **новый дом** 'new house' the adjective is used attributively, while in **Дом был новый/нов** 'The house is new' the adjective occurs in the predicative function. In Contemporary Standard Russian, the short form is excluded in the attributive function, but competes with the long form in the predicative function.

The morphological restriction is easier to understand. In Contemporary Standard Russian, short forms are only attested in the nominative. The masculine nominative singular **нов** corresponds to **нова** in the feminine nominative singular, to **ново** in the neuter nominative singular, and to **новы** in nominative plural, but there are no short forms in the so-called oblique cases, i.e., the cases that are different from the nominative. (Admittedly, there are a few exceptions such as **на босу ногу** 'barefoot' with a short form in the accusative, but such exceptions are restricted to fixed expressions.)

Common Slavic and Old Rusian also had both long and short forms of adjectives, but their distribution was quite different. While in Modern Russian it is the long form that is the "normal" form with the widest distribution, i.e., what linguists call the "default," in Common Slavic it was the short form that prevailed. In other words, the history of the adjectives is the history of the expansion of the long form from a humble start in Common Slavic to its dominating position in Modern Russian. During this time, the long form has completely ousted its short competitor from the attributive function and the oblique cases, and in our times it is even dominant in the predicative nominative. Table 26 summarizes the differences between Common Slavic and Contemporary Standard Russian; texts from the Old Rusian period reflect intermediate stages in the development.

Table 26. The distribution of short and long forms of adjectives in Common Slavic and Contemporary Standard Russian

Function	Case	Common Slavic	Contemporary Standard Russian
Attributive	Nominative	SHORT/LONG	LONG
	Oblique cases	SHORT/LONG	LONG
Predicative	Nominative	SHORT	SHORT/LONG
	Oblique cases	SHORT	LONG

Since the short form has been under constant pressure from the long form, we must ask how it survived in the predicative function and in the nominative case. The long forms arose through the addition of the pronoun **и** 'this' to the adjective (see section 5.2). The feminine form of **и** was **я**, so one could form phrases like **добра я сестра** with the meaning 'this kind sister'. Notice that the meaning of the demonstrative pronoun includes the feature "definite"; it is clear that we are dealing with a particular sister, not just any sister. When the pronoun became part of the adjective, it became a marker of definiteness. In other words, **добрая сестра** (with the long form of the adjective) came to mean 'the kind sister', as opposed to **добра сестра** (with the short form of the adjective), which did not imply definiteness.

The fact that long forms started their career as definiteness markers provides the key to understanding their expansion and the decline in use of the short forms. In sentences with a subject and a predicative adjective, the adjective's only function is to describe a property (e.g., "nice" in *The man is nice*). The predicative does not serve to pick out a particular individual, and definiteness is therefore irrelevant. In the attributive function, however, both definite and indefinite meanings are possible, so here the marking of definiteness is crucial. In view of this, it was natural for the long forms to thrive in the attributive function where definiteness marking was important, but not in the predicative function where it was irrelevant. This made it possible for the short form to survive in the predicative function.

How could the short forms survive in the nominative, but not in the oblique cases? In Contemporary Standard Russian, the nominative competes with the instrumental case in the predicative function; you can say both **Успех был большой** and **Успех был большим** in order to convey the meaning 'The success was great'. However, the instrumental in this function is a relatively recent innovation; in Common Slavic and (early) Old Rusian the nominative was prevalent in the predicative function (see section 9.3). Since the short form only survived in the predicative function where the oblique cases were marginal, it is natural that the short form has been lost in the oblique cases.

6.2. The Declension of Short Forms

If you know how to decline nouns in Old Rusian, short forms of adjectives do not offer much of a challenge. As shown in Table 27, the adjectives have the same endings as nouns. In the masculine and neuter genders, the adjectives follow the ŏ-declension, while the ā-declension is used for feminine adjectives. **Добръ** 'kind' represents adjectives with a hard consonant in stem-final position, while **синь** 'dark blue' exemplifies the declension of adjectives with a soft consonant stem-finally.

Table 27. The declension of short forms of adjectives in Old Rusian

		Hard C in stem-final position			Soft C in stem-final position		
		Masculine	Feminine	Neuter	Masculine	Feminine	Neuter
Sg	N	добр-ъ	добр-а	добр-о	син-ь	син-я	син-е
	A	добр-ъ	добр-у	добр-о	син-ь	син-ю	син-е
	G	добр-а	добр-ы	добр-а	син-я	син-ѣ	син-я
	D	добр-у	добр-ѣ	добр-у	син-ю	син-и	син-ю
	I	добр-ъмь	добр-ою	добр-ъмь	син-ьмь	син-ею	син-ьмь
	L	добр-ѣ	добр-ѣ	добр-ѣ	син-и	син-и	син-и
Du	NA	добр-а	добр-ѣ	добр-ѣ	син-я	син-и	син-и
	GL	добр-у	добр-у	добр-у	син-ю	син-ю	син-ю
	DI	добр-ома	добр-ама	добр-ома	син-ема	син-яма	син-ема

Pl	N	добр-и	добр-ы	добр-а	син-и	син-ѣ	син-я
	A	добр-ы	добр-ы	добр-а	син-ѣ	син-ѣ	син-я
	G	добр-ъ	добр-ъ	добр-ъ	син-ь	син-ь	син-ь
	D	добр-омъ	добр-амъ	добр-омъ	син-емъ	син-ямъ	син-емъ
	I	добр-ы	добр-ами	добр-ы	син-и	син-ями	син-и
	L	добр-ѣхъ	добр-ахъ	добр-ѣхъ	син-ихъ	син-яхъ	син-ихъ

There is not much to add about the historical development of the short forms. The dual and all the oblique cases have been lost. Since Modern Russian does not distinguish between genders in the plural, there is only one short plural form left for each adjective. The modern plural ending -ы for hard stems corresponds to the Old Rusian masculine accusative plural and the feminine nominative and accusative plural. In sum, the Old Rusian paradigms which comprised 45 short forms have been reduced to only four short forms in Contemporary Standard Russian.

6.3. The Declension of Long Forms

The declension of the long forms is a much more complicated story. An overview is provided in section 6.3.1, and then we go through the individual forms in sections 6.3.2 through 6.3.7, before the origin of the long forms in Modern Russian is summarized in 6.3.8.

6.3.1. Overview

Table 28, opposite, offers an overview of the declension of long forms of adjectives in Old Rusian. **Добрыи** 'kind' represents adjectives with hard consonants in stem-final position, whereas **синии** 'dark blue' displays the inflection of adjectives with soft consonants stem-finally.

Before considering the complex developments of individual forms, it is useful to clarify the general processes at work. As mentioned in section 6.1, the long forms were originally created by the addition of the demonstrative pronoun и to the short form of the adjective. The problem is that a number of processes took place as the adjective and the pronoun became one word:

(2) a. Phonological processes:

Loss of intervocalic [j], vowel assimilation, vowel contraction, and haplology.

Table 28. The declension of long forms of adjectives in Old Rusian

		Hard C in stem-final position			Soft C in stem-final position		
		Masculine	Feminine	Neuter	Masculine	Feminine	Neuter
Sg	N	добр-ыи	добр-ая	добр-ое	син-ии	син-яя	син-ее
	A	добр-ыи	добр-ую	добр-ое	син-ии	син-юю	син-ее
	G	добр-ого	добр-ыѣ (-оѣ)	добр-ого	син-его	син-ѣѣ (-еѣ)	син-его
	D	добр-ому	добр-ои	добр-ому	син-ему	син-еи	син-ему
	I	добр-ымь	добр-ою	добр-ымь	син-имь	син-ею	син-имь
	L	добр-омь	добр-ои	добр-омь	син-емь	син-еи	син-емь
Du	NA	добр-ая	добр-ѣи	добр-ѣи	син-яя	син-ии	син-ии
	GL	добр-ую (-ою)	добр-ую (-ою)	добр-ую (-ою)	син-юю	син-юю	син-юю
	DI	добр-ыима	добр-ыима	добр-ыима	син-иима	син-иима	син-иима
Pl	N	добр-ии	добр-ыѣ	добр-ая	син-ии	син-ѣѣ	син-яя
	A	добр-ыѣ	добр-ыѣ	добр-ая	син-ѣѣ	син-ѣѣ	син-яя
	G	добр-ыихъ	добр-ыихъ	добр-ыихъ	син-иихъ	син-иихъ	син-иихъ
	D	добр-ыимъ	добр-ыимъ	добр-ыимъ	син-иимъ	син-иимъ	син-иимъ
	I	добр-ыими	добр-ыими	добр-ыими	син-иими	син-иими	син-иими
	L	добр-ыихъ	добр-ыихъ	добр-ыихъ	син-иихъ	син-иихъ	син-иихъ

(2) b. Morphological process:

Analogy across paradigms, whereby pronominal endings replace adjectival endings and analogy within paradigms, whereby some inflected forms become more similar to other forms of the same word.

c. Sociolinguistic process:

Church Slavic forms replace East Slavic forms.

The interaction of these processes creates a complicated situation with extensive variation, so you should not be surprised if you encounter other forms than those mentioned in Table 28 when you read medieval texts. We will return to the effect of the morphological and sociolinguistic processes in the following sections; for now it is sufficient to consider the phonological processes, which took place in Common Slavic. Let us take the masculine genitive singular as an example. If one takes the form добра and adds the masculine genitive singular form его of и, the outcome is [dobrajego], since the pronoun was pronounced with the sound [j] in the beginning. The intervocalic [j] was then lost, before [ae] became [aa]. The process whereby [ae] becomes [aa] is an example of assimilation, i.e., the phonological process where one sound becomes more similar to another sound. After the loss of intervocalic [j] and vowel assimilation had taken place, the form was shortened to [dobrago]. This process can be referred to as "contraction." The effect of these three processes is summarized in Figure 8.

The fourth phonological process, haplology, is the omission of one of two similar sound sequences. The dative plural illustrates this. If we take the short form добр-омъ and add the dative plural form имъ of и, we get [dobromъimъ]. However, as pointed out by Kiparsky (1967: 169) there are no traces of such forms in the written sources, neither in Old Church Slavonic nor in Old Rusian. Instead we find forms like добрыимъ, where one of the two sequences of the type "vowel + m + jer" has been omitted through haplology.

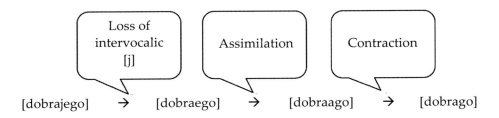

Figure 8. Loss of intervocalic [j], assimilation, and contraction in long forms of adjectives

Now that we have seen the effect of the phonological processes affecting long forms of adjectives, we will consider the individual singular and plural forms in some detail. Since the dual disappeared early, it is not necessary to discuss these forms.

6.3.2. The Masculine Nominative and Accusative Singular: Church Slavic Influence

The pronoun which is written и in Old Rusian goes back to a reconstructed jь. If we add this to the masculine nominative singular form добръ, the result is добръjь. This form undergoes the normal sound laws for jers, which we will consider in detail in section 12.2. For now, it is sufficient to note that regular sound laws produce forms like доброи, where the letter и represents the sound [j]. Such forms are indeed attested in texts from the Old Rusian period, and in adjectives with stressed endings such as молодóй 'young' the ending is spelled -ой in Contemporary Standard Russian. The ending -ыи (which corresponds to Modern Russian -ый) is the result of influence from Church Slavic. In South Slavic the jers followed a different phonetic development before [j], and this development produced forms such as добрыи given in Table 28. Although the Church Slavic ending -ый has become part of Russian orthography, many speakers of the older generation pronounce [əj] in Modern Russian with the unstressed variant of /oj/, and not /ij/ (Avanesov 1984: 194). In other words, for such speakers Church Slavic has affected Russian orthography, but not pronunciation.

6.3.3. The Feminine and Neuter Nominative and Accusative Singular: "Trivial" Forms

The forms listed in Table 28 are the result of the addition of the relevant inflected forms of и 'this' to the short forms. No additional phonological, morphological, or sociolinguistic processes take place, so in a sense we can refer to these forms as "trivial."

6.3.4. The Masculine and Neuter Genitive, Dative, and Locative Singular: Pronominal Influence

On the basis of the phonological processes outlined in section 6.3.1 we would expect the following developments:

(3) a. Genitive: [dobra-jego] → [dobrago]
    b. Dative: [dobru-jemu] → [dobrumu]
    c. Locative: [dobrě-jěmь] → [dobrěmь]

Notice that [ě] is the *e*-sound corresponding to the letter ѣ, a fact we will return to in the chapters on phonology.

While forms like the ones in (3) are attested in Old Church Slavonic, the picture is more complicated in Old Rusian, where the long forms of the adjectives came under the influence of the demonstrative pronoun тъ 'that', which corresponds to тот in Modern Russian. This pronoun had the endings -ого, -ому, and -омь in the genitive, dative, and locative cases, and these endings replaced the original adjectival endings of the long forms. This is an example of analogy in the sense that adjectival declension becomes more similar to the declension of pronouns.

Notice that the genitive ending was originally pronounced with a [g], and that this sound is preserved in some Modern Russian dialects. However, as is well known, in Contemporary Standard Russian [v] is pronounced instead of [g]. This development followed the same path as for the genitive form того of the demonstrative pronoun. As mentioned in section 5.3, it is hypothesized that [g] developed into the fricative [γ] and then disappeared. The [v] sound finally emerged in order to break up the vowel cluster [oo] to [ovo] (cf. Ivanov 1983: 302 for discussion). Before we leave the genitive singular it should be noted that the ending -аго was preserved in Russian orthography until 1918, although this spelling, of course, did not reflect the pronunciation in the beginning of the twentieth century. However, in some family names based on genitive forms [ago] is still pronounced. An example is the name of the hero in Boris Pasternak's Nobel Prize-winning novel *Doktor Živago*.

6.3.5. The Feminine Genitive, Dative, and Locative Singular: Pronominal Influence

Let us start with the dative and locative forms, which are identical. Haplology produced forms like добрѣи, and such forms are attested in texts from the Old Rusian period. However, already in the eleventh century the pronominal ending -ои from тъ 'that' is attested in long forms of adjectives.

Through haplology we get genitive forms like добрыѣ, which compete in texts with the Church Slavic forms with the ending -ыя. The alternative ending -оѣ listed in Table 28 is a pronominal ending from тъ 'that', which emerged later, but eventually was replaced by the dative and locative ending -ои.

Notice that the feminine genitive, dative, and locative singular forms display two types of analogical change. The influence from the declension of the pronoun тъ is an example of analogy across paradigms, since a pronoun exerts influence on adjectives. The adoption of -ои in the genitive is an example of analogy within a paradigm, insofar as one morphological form becomes more similar to another form of the same word. We can conclude that analogy works both across and within paradigms.

6.3.6. The Nominative, Accusative, Genitive, and Instrumental Plural: "Trivial" Forms

The long forms reported in Table 28 can be derived by the addition of the relevant inflected forms of и 'this' to the short forms of the adjective. No additional phonological, morphological, or sociolinguistic processes need to be assumed, so these forms are "trivial" in the same sense as the feminine and neuter nominative and accusative forms in the singular. The modern nominative plural ending -ые can be regarded as the continuation of the Old Rusian feminine nominal plural ending, but it may also have emerged due to the influence of the masculine accusative plural ending. Recall from section 4.2.1 that the accusative plural ending in the ŏ-declension replaced the nominative. This is an example of analogical change within the inflectional paradigm.

6.3.7. The Instrumental Singular and the Dative and Locative Plural: Haplology and Contraction

Short forms with endings consisting of more than one syllable underwent haplology:

(4) a. Masculine/neuter instrumental singular: [dobrъmь-jimь] → [dobrymь]
 b. Dative plural: [dobromъ-jimъ] → [dobryimъ]
 c. Locative plural: [dobrěxъ-jixъ] → [dobryixъ]
 d. Feminine instrumental singular: [dobroju-jeju] → [dobroju]

The instrumental form in (4a) displays contraction; we may assume an intermediate stage [dobryimь], which then lost [i]. Table 28 and (4b–c) give forms with [yi], but you will also encounter contracted forms with [i] while working with medieval texts.

Notice that the haplological forms in (4a–c) end up with the vowel [y] (spelled as ы) in the ending. The emergence of [y] may be due to the influence of the plural forms that had [y] in the endings, i.e., the forms discussed in the previous section (Kiparsky 1967: 169 and Schenker 1993: 91). The appearance of [y] unified the plural forms, giving all of them [y] in the ending. This is an example of analogy, whereby some morphological forms become more similar to other forms of the same word. In other words, we are dealing with analogy taking place within one paradigm. As a result of this analogy, [y] became present throughout the plural and could be analyzed as a plural marker. At the same time, [y] set the plural forms apart from those of nouns, which generalized [a] in the plural (cf. -ам, -ами, -ах in Modern Russian), and from pronouns such as тот and весь, which in Contemporary Standard Russian have [e] throughout the plural.

It is less obvious why the masculine and neuter instrumental singular ended up with [y], since the other oblique cases in the singular do not have [y]. However, it is possible that the similarity to the dative plural, which also includes [m], may have played a role, and the nominative and accusative singular ending -ый may also have had an impact on the instrumental singular. In any case it is clear that the emergence of [y] in the haplological forms contributed to unification of the adjectival declension. At the same time, the endings with [y] set adjectives apart from nouns, which have other vowels in the endings.

For the feminine instrumental singular in (4d), haplology yields the ending [oju], which is still attested in Modern Russian, although the shorter form [oj] is more widely used today. An alternative explanation of the feminine instrumental singular is influence from тъ 'that', which had the ending [oju] in the feminine instrumental singular.

6.3.8. Summary: The Origin of the Long Forms in Contemporary Standard Russian

The endings of the long forms in Contemporary Standard Russian have followed four different paths of development, as shown in Table 29. First of all, there are a number of "trivial" forms where the addition of -и involved no additional complications. These forms, which are given on white background in the table, include the nominative and accusative cases in singular and plural, as well as the genitive and instrumental plural. Second, there is the masculine nominative singular ending -ый, which at least on the orthographical level reflects Church Slavic influence. This ending is framed in the table. Third, there are endings that have developed through haplology and contraction. We find such forms in the instrumental singular and the dative and locative plural. In the table, these endings are given on a light gray background. Finally, the endings in the genitive, dative, and locative singular are due to influence from the pronoun тъ. These endings are given on a dark gray background in the table.

Table 29. The origin of the long forms in Contemporary Standard Russian (white = "trivial" forms; frame = Church Slavic (orthographic) influence; light gray shading = haplology and contraction; dark gray shading = pronominal endings due to influence from тъ 'that')

	Masculine sg	Feminine sg	Neuter sg	Plural
N	-ый -ой	-ая	-ое	-ые
A	=N or G	-ую	-ое	=N or G
G	-ого	-ой	-ого	-ых
D	-ому	-ой	-ому	-ым
I	-ым	-ой (-ою)	-ым	-ыми
L	-ом	-ой	-ом	-ых

6.4. The Comparative and the Superlative

In Contemporary Standard Russian comparative forms have the suffix **-ee** (e.g., добрее 'kinder' from добрый 'kind') or **-e** (e.g., хуже 'worse' that is historically related to худой, which now means 'lean'). Such comparatives are short forms that are not inflected and occur in the predicative function only. Most adjectives combine with **-ee**, while **-e** is limited to a small class of words.

In Proto-Slavic, comparatives generally consisted of four elements: (a) the stem of the adjective, (b) the comparative suffix -ējĭs-, (c) [j] following the comparative suffix, and (d) an inflectional ending:

(5)   The structure of the Proto-Slavic comparative:

   Adjective stem - ējĭs - j - inflectional ending

The inflectional endings are the "normal" short or long endings discussed in the previous sections of this chapter. Since the endings were preceded by [j], comparatives combined with the soft variety of the endings. This means that comparatives were inflected like синь 'dark blue'. Here is an example illustrating how this works:

(6)   The masculine genitive singular short form comparative:

   Proto-Slavic: **dăbr-ējĭs-j-āt** → Old Rusian: добрѣиша

The Old Rusian form follows from regular sound laws, whereby long [ē] goes to [ě] (written as ѣ), and the cluster [sj] becomes [š'] (written as ш). We will return to these sound laws in chapters 10 and 11.

Interestingly, there are some deviations from the pattern in (5). First of all, the nominative singular short forms had irregular inflectional endings; in the feminine the ending was -и in Old Rusian, thus producing forms like **добрѣиши** 'kinder', while the masculine and neuter forms lacked an ending altogether.[1] When there was no ending, there was no [j] following the comparative suffix:

(7) The masculine nominative singular short form comparative:

Proto-Slavic: **dăbr-ējĭs** → Old Rusian: добрѣи

Again, these forms follow from regular sound laws; when [s] occurs at the end of the word, it disappears.

A second deviation from the pattern in (5) concerns neuter forms, which had a slightly different comparative suffix:

(8) The neuter nominative singular short form comparative:

Proto-Slavic: **dăbr-ējĕs** → Old Rusian: добрѣе

This neuter form is important because it is the ancestor of the modern comparatives in -**ее**, such as добрее.

A third deviation from (5) involves a class of adjectives that lacked the long [ē] in the comparative suffix:

(9) The neuter nominative singular short form comparative (no [ē] in the comparative suffix):

Proto-Slavic: **xaud-jĕs** → Old Rusian: хуже

By regular sound laws, [dj] becomes [ž'] (written as **ж**). As you may have guessed, examples like (9) are the ancestors of the Modern Russian comparatives in -**е**.

Finally, we must discuss adjectives with the velar consonants [k, g, x] in stem-final position. By way of example, consider the masculine genitive singular short form of the adjective corresponding to **крепкий** 'strong' in Modern Russian:

(10) The masculine genitive singular short form comparative:

Proto-Slavic: **krēpŭk-ējĭs-j-āt** → Old Rusian: крепчаиша

---

[1] As you will see in section 8.8.1, the nominative feminine ending -**и** is also attested in active participles.

Notice that by general sound laws [ē] causes a consonant alternation in the stem-final consonant, while [ē] itself becomes [a]. You will learn more about this in section 11.5.

The history of the comparative from Old Rusian to Contemporary Standard Russian involves the complete loss of the declension. As we have seen, only the neuter nominative singular short forms have survived as comparative forms such as Modern Russian **добрее** and **хуже**. Admittedly, Modern Russian also has forms such as **добрейший** 'most kind' and **крепчайший** 'most strong', which go back to the Old Rusian comparative forms that contained **ш**. However, in Contemporary Standard Russian forms like **добрейший** and **крепчайший** may be classified as superlative, rather than comparative forms.

Old Rusian did not have a superlative suffix. Superlative meanings seem to have been expressed by combining intensifiers such as **самый**, **вельми**, or **очень**. The pattern with **самый** has survived to this day and represents the simplest way of forming superlatives in Contemporary Standard Russian (e.g., **самый добрый** 'the kindest'). Modern Russian and Old Rusian also have superlative forms with the prefix **наи-** (e.g., Modern Russian **наилучший** 'the best'), which are due to Church Slavic and/or Polish influence. The prefix **пре-** as in Modern Russian **предобрый** 'most kind' is also a Church Slavic borrowing.

6.5. Summary

Here is what you need to know about the history of adjectives in a nutshell:

(11)   Distribution of short and long forms (section 6.1):
   a.   Short forms started out as the default, but are now restricted to the predicative function in the nominative case.
   b.   Long forms started out as definiteness markers, but are now the default.

(12)   Declension of short forms (6.2):
   a.   Short forms have the same endings as nouns.
   b.   Masculine and neuter short forms follow the $\breve{o}$-declension.
   c.   Feminine short forms follow the $\bar{a}$-declension.

(13)   Declension of long forms (6.3):
   a.   Long form = short form + relevant inflected form of **и** 'this'.

(13) b. The declension of long forms are complicated by the following processes:

  i. Phonology: loss of intervocalic [j], vowel assimilation, vowel contraction, and haplology.

  ii. Morphology: analogy within and across paradigms.

  iii. Sociolinguistics: borrowing of Church Slavic forms.

 c. The long forms in Contemporary Standard Russian reflect four paths of development:

  i. "Trivial forms": the addition of **и** did not involve additional complications (e.g., feminine nominative singular **добрая**).

  ii. Haplological forms: the long form developed through haplology and contraction (e.g., dative plural **добрым**).

  iii. Pronominal forms: the long forms took their endings from the pronoun **тъ** 'that' (e.g., masculine/neuter genitive singular **доброго**).

  iv. Church Slavic form: the long form ending is due to Church Slavic influence (masculine nominative singular **добрый**).

(14) Comparative degree in Old Rusian (6.4):

 a. Masculine nominative singular forms normally had -ѣи, e.g., **добрѣи**.

 b. Neuter nominative singular forms normally had -ѣе, e.g., **добрѣе**.

 c. Other comparatives normally had -**еиш**- followed by endings of short or long forms (soft variety), e.g., **добреиша** (masculine/neuter genitive singular short form).

 d. Modern Russian comparatives in -**ее** go back to Old Rusian neuter forms in -ѣе.

6.6. For Further Reading

The development of the adjectival declension is well described in most historical grammars. Gorškova and Xaburgaev (1981) and Ivanov (1983) provide good overviews. For a detailed discussion of individual endings of long forms, Kiparsky (1967) is a good source of information. Larsen (2005) offers a thorough analysis of the changes in the distribution of short and long forms of adjectives.

Chapter 7 Morphology: Numbers and Numerals

As pointed out in section 2.2, numbers are very often rendered as letters in medieval texts. Only occasionally do you encounter numbers written out, so that we can see how they were pronounced and inflected. It is nevertheless worthwhile to explore the Common Slavic and Old Rusian number systems, because they provide historical explanations of many idiosyncracies and exceptions you have struggled with in Modern Russian. Have you ever wondered why **два**, **три**, and **четыре** combine with nouns in the genitive singular? And did you know where the numeral **сорок** 'forty' comes from? After you have read this chapter you will know the answers!

7.1. From Nouns and Adjectives to Something in Between

In Contemporary Standard Russian, numerals combine properties of adjectives and nouns. Characteristic of adjectives is the fact that they are inflected for gender; each adjective has different forms for the three genders (masculine **большой**, feminine **большая**, neuter **большое** for 'big'). A noun, alternatively, has one and only one gender. In other words, for adjectives gender is an inflectional category, while for nouns it is not (see also section 4.6). Syntactically, adjectives agree with the head noun, i.e., the noun they modify. If you want to translate *on the big ship*, you have to use the masculine locative singular form **большом** since the head noun **корабль** 'ship' belongs to the masculine gender and occurs in the locative singular in the relevant construction: **на большом корабле**. Nouns can also modify nouns, but they do not agree with the noun they modify. Instead, we have constructions such as **дым сигарет** 'cigarette smoke', where the modifying noun **сигарета** 'cigarette' occurs in the genitive. The differences between nouns and adjectives are summarized in Table 30.

Table 30. Properties characteristic of adjectives and nouns

	Adjectives	Nouns
Gender is inflectional category?	YES	NO
Agreement with head noun?	YES	NO

If we apply the criteria in Table 30 to Modern Russian numbers, it becomes clear that **один** behaves like an adjective. Not only is it inflected for gender (masculine **один**, feminine **одна**, and neuter **одно**), but it also shows agreement in the same way as **большой** (cf. **на одном большом корабле** 'on one big ship'). At the opposite end of the scale we have words such as **тысяча** 'thousand' and **миллион** 'million', which behave like nouns. **Тысяча** and **миллион** are not inflected for gender, and if they are used as modifiers they occur in the genitive, as in **дым тысячи сигарет** 'smoke from a thousand cigarettes', where **тысяча сигарет** modifies **дым**.

Numerals between 1 and 1000 display a mixture of the properties of nouns and adjectives in Modern Russian. Such numerals resemble adjectives in that they are not inflected for gender. (Admittedly, **два** 'two' is an exception since it has the feminine form **две**, but there is no separate form for the neuter gender.) With regard to agreement, things are a little more complicated. If the noun in question is in an oblique case (a case that is different from the nominative), numerals between 1 and 1000 behave like adjectives. In **на трёх больших кораблях** 'on three big ships', the numeral is in the locative in the same way as the adjective because they both modify **кораблях** in the locative. If we translate *three big ships* into a Russian nominative construction, however, we get **три больших корабля**. If **три** had behaved like an adjective, we would have expected the noun to be in the nominative, and **три** to agree with the noun. Instead, the number is in the nominative, while **корабль** occurs in the genitive. Exactly how we should analyze **три больших корабля** is not so important for our purposes. However, the example demonstrates that numbers between 1 and 1000 do not agree with nouns in the nominative, and therefore do not behave like adjectives.

Table 31 summarizes the properties of the numbers in Modern Russian. While we may analyze **один** as an adjective and **тысяча** and **миллион** as nouns, the remaining numbers can be assigned to an intermediate category, for which it is customary to use the term "numeral."

Table 31. Properties of adjectives, numerals, and nouns in Contemporary Standard Russian

	X=1	1<X<1000	X≥1000
Gender is inflectional category?	YES	NO	NO
Agreement with head noun in nominative?	YES	NO	NO
Agreement with head noun in oblique case?	YES	YES	NO
Syntactic category	Adjective	Numeral	Noun

Did Common Slavic and Old Rusian have numerals, i.e., words with the mixed properties summarized in Table 31? No! As you will see in this chapter, the Common Slavic and Old Rusian numbers either behaved like adjectives in the same way as Modern Russian **один**, or they behaved like nouns in the same way as **тысяча** and **миллион** in Modern Russian. As shown in Table 32, numbers smaller than 5 were adjectives, while the remaining numbers were nouns. How did the simple system in Common Slavic and Old Rusian develop into the more complicated system we find in Contemporary Standard Russian? This question will occupy us in the following sections, where you will learn more about the declension of numbers in Old Rusian.

Table 32. The properties of numbers in Common Slavic and Old Rusian

	X<5	X≥5
Gender is inflectional category?	YES	NO
Agreement with head noun?	YES	NO
Syntactic category	Adjective	Noun

7.2. The Number 1

Одинъ was originally inflected in the same way as the demonstrative pronoun **тъ** explored in section 5.3. However, while **тъ** generalized /ě/ (spelled as ѣ) throughout the plural forms, **одинъ** came under the influence of the soft variety of the pronominal declension and developed plural forms with /i/, cf. the modern forms **одни, одних, одним, одними,** and **одних**.

7.3. The Number 2

The Old Rusian declension of **дъва** 'two' is outlined in Table 33. Notice that feminine and neuter genders had the form **дъвѣ**, and that gender distinctions are only attested in the nominative and accusative cases. Given its meaning, it is not surprising that **дъва/дъвѣ** belonged to the dual number.

Table 33. The declension of **дъва** 'two' in Old Rusian

		Masculine	Feminine	Neuter
Du	NA	дъва	дъвѣ	дъвѣ
	GL	дъвою	дъвою	дъвою
	DI	дъвѣма	дъвѣма	дъвѣма

The oblique case forms in Table 33 are very different from the oblique cases in Modern Russian, so a number of changes have taken place. Quite early the genitive and locative form дъвою received competition from дъву, which may have adopted the dual genitive/locative ending -y of nouns in the ŏ- and ā-declensions. The form дъву was then extended to дъвухъ under the influence of genitive plural forms of adjectives and pronouns. The forms дъву and дъвухъ must then have formed the basis for the development of the modern dative and instrumental forms двум and двумя.

In Contemporary Standard Russian, the nominative forms of два combine with nouns in the genitive singular—a rule that is quite counterintuitive. Why would the numeral 2, which denotes more than one entity, combine with a noun in the singular? The historical explanation is simple. Phrases like дъва рога 'two antlers' originally contained a number in the dual followed by a noun in the dual. However, when the dual was lost as a grammatical category, рога was reanalyzed as a genitive singular form, since the genitive singular also had the ending -a. The rule that the number 2 combines with nouns in the genitive singular was then generalized to all nouns and furthermore spread to the numbers 3 and 4.[1]

7.4. The Numbers 3 and 4

The declension of трье 'three' and четыре 'four' given in Table 34 show that these forms had endings characteristic of the plural, which, however, have undergone a number of changes. The gender distinction was only attested in the nominative, and was later lost here too. Very early the genitive forms трии and четыръ were replaced by the locative forms трьхъ and четырьхъ, possibly under the influence of дъва or pronouns and long forms of adjectives, which had the same endings in the locative and genitive plural. The modern instrumental forms тремя and четырьмя may have developed under the influence of двумя.

---

[1] Notice that the noun governed by два (and три and четыре) does not always occur in a form that is identical to the genitive singular in modern Russian. While in the constructions два ряда́ 'two rows', два следа́ 'two traces', два часа́ 'two hours', два шага́ 'two steps', and два шара́ 'two globes' the nouns receive stress on the ending, the normal genitive singular forms of these nouns have stress on the stem: ря́да, сле́да, ча́са, ша́га, and ша́ра. In Russian, the term "счётная форма" is sometimes used to refer to the nouns governed by два, три, and четыре (cf. Zaliznjak 1967: 46). A possible English term is "paucal" (cf., e.g., Franks 1995).

Table 34. The declension of **трьє** 'three' and **четыре** 'four' in Old Rusian

		Masc.	Fem.	Neuter	Masc.	Fem.	Neuter
Pl	N	трьє	три	три	четыре	четыри	четыри
	A	три	три	три	четыри	четыри	четыри
	G	трии	трии	трии	четыръ	четыръ	четыръ
	D	трьмъ	трьмъ	трьмъ	четырьмъ	четырьмъ	четырьмъ
	I	трьми	трьми	трьми	четырьми	четырьми	четырьми
	L	трьхъ	трьхъ	трьхъ	четырьхъ	четырьхъ	четырьхъ

7.5. The Numbers 5 to 9

The numbers 5 to 9 were inflected like singular forms of feminine nouns of the *ī*-declension, as shown in Table 35, and their inflection in present-day Russian is a direct continuation of this pattern. Notice that in Old Rusian 'eight' was **осмь**; modern **восемь** is based on dialectal/colloquial form with [v] in the beginning. The following example from the *Novgorod Chronicle* (cited after Kiparsky 1967: 177) shows that words like **пять** were perceived as feminine nouns in the singular, since the demonstrative pronoun **та** is in the feminine singular, and the verb also is a singular form (which you will learn more about in the following chapter):

(1) a. **Изоиде та пять** лѣтъ.

   b. **Прошли те пять** лет.

   c. **Those five** years **passed**.

Notice that the numbers 5–9 combine with nouns in the genitive, as shown in the example where **лѣтъ** is in the genitive plural.

Table 35. The declension of numbers 5–9 in Old Rusian

Pl	N	пять	шесть	семь	осмь	девять
	A	пять	шесть	семь	осмь	девять
	G	пяти	шести	семи	осми	девяти
	D	пяти	шести	семи	осми	девяти
	I	пятию (-ью)	шестию (-ью)	семию (-ью)	осмию (-ью)	девятию (-ью)
	L	пяти	шести	семи	осми	девяти

7.6. The Number 10

Десять 'ten' was originally declined like nouns in the C-declension discussed in section 4.2.6. Десять has lost its distinction between singular, dual, and plural, and has adopted the same declension as the numbers 5–9 in Contemporary Standard Russian. Syntactically десять behaved like nouns in the same way as the numbers 5–9 explored in the previous section.

Table 36. The declension of десять 'ten' in Old Rusian

	Singular	Dual	Plural
N	десять	десяти	десяте (-и)
A	десять	десяти	десяти
G	десяте (-и)	десяту	десятъ
D	десяти	десятьма	десятьмъ
I	десятью	десятьма	десятьми
L	десяте	десяту	десятьхъ

7.7. The Numbers 11 to 19

In Old Rusian these numbers were expressed by numbers 1–9 + the prepositional phrase **на десяте** (the locative singular of **десять** 'ten'). The logic behind this system is not hard to grasp: 'eleven', 'twelve', 'thirteen', etc. was conceptualized as 'one', 'two', 'three', etc. "on ten," i.e., in addition to 'ten'. The Modern Russian forms are the result of the contraction of these expressions into single words such as **одиннадцать** 'eleven', **двенадцать** 'twelve', and **тринадцать** 'thirteen'.

7.8. The Tens

The numbers 20, 30, 40, 50, etc. consisted of the numbers 1–9 followed by an inflected form of **десять** 'ten'. For 'twenty', this was the nominative dual **десяти**, while for 'thirty' the nominative plural form **десяте** was used. In the case of 'fifty' and up, **десять** occurred in the genitive plural. These constructions developed into the numerals we know from Modern Russian, such as **двадцать**, **тридцать**, and **пятьдесят**.

Сорок 'forty' is the odd man out in the modern numeral system. What is the story behind this word? The expected form **четыре десяте** (with the nominative plural of **десять**) occur in medieval texts, but receive competition from **сорокъ**, which is attested from the 1200s. The etymology of **сорок** has been debated; the most widely accepted hypothesis appears to be that **сорокъ** originally meant 'bundle of forty sable skins', and then developed the more abstract meaning 'forty' (Vasmer 1964–73).

In Modern Russian, 'ninety' is **девяносто**. This numeral also has a disputed etymology. One hypothesis is that **девяносто** derives from **девять до ста** or, perhaps, **девять на сто**, while other researchers have suggested that **девяносто** goes back to the reconstructed Proto-Indo-European word *newenədk'mtə* 'ninth ten' (cf. Vasmer 1964–73).

Both **сорокъ** and **девяносто** were inflected like nouns of the ŏ-declension, but have lost all oblique forms but the genitive singular. The genitive form has been generalized to all the oblique cases, and in Modern Russian **сорока** and **девяноста** are used for all cases except for the nominative and accusative.

7.9. The Hundreds

Old Rusian **съто** 'hundred' was inflected as a neuter noun in the ŏ-declension, and originally had both singular, dual, and numeral forms in the same way as, e.g., **лѣто** 'year, summer' discussed in section 4.2.1. For 'two hundred' **дъвѣ** was followed by the nominative dual form **сътѣ** from **съто**. 'Three hundred' and 'four hundred' were formed in the same way, except that here we have the nominative plural form **съта** instead of the dual form **сътѣ**. Numbers from five and up combined with the genitive plural form **сътъ**.

7.10. Thousand

The word **тысяча** 'thousand' is attested in texts from the Old Rusian period. It was inflected like nouns of the ā-declension with a soft consonant in stem-final position and behaved syntactically like a noun.

7.11. Ordinal Numbers

So far we have focused on cardinal numerals. In Contemporary Standard Russian, ordinal numerals such as **первый** 'first', **второй** 'second', **третий** 'third' are adjectives, and the same is true for Old Rusian. Notice, however, that Old Rusian ordinal numbers (like other adjectives) had both short and long forms. In other words, you may encounter both **пьрвъ** and **пьрвыи** for 'first'.

7.12. Summary

In this chapter you have learned that Common Slavic and Old Rusian did not have a category of numerals, in the sense that numbers were either adjectives or nouns. However, over the centuries a class of numerals has developed; today's numerals are neither adjectives, nor nouns, but rather something in between, since they display a mixture of the properties of adjectives and nouns. Modern Russian **один** is still an adjective, while **тысяча** is a noun. The development is presented schematically in Table 37.

Table 37. The development of the category of numerals

	Common Slavic/Old Rusian	Contemporary Standard Russian
1	Adjective	Adjective
2–4	Adjective	Numeral
5–999	Noun	Numeral
1000	Noun	Noun

We have seen that a crucial difference between adjectives and nouns is that adjectives agree with the noun they modify, whereas nouns do not. Thus, in Common Slavic and Old Rusian the numbers 2–4 agreed with a head noun, whereas the numbers 5–999 behaved like nouns. In Contemporary Russian, on the other hand, both groups of numbers show agreement in the oblique cases, but not in the nominative.

In Contemporary Standard Russian, the numbers 2–4 combine with nouns in the genitive singular. This is due to the fall of the dual, after which dual forms like **рога** in **дъва рога** 'two antlers' were reanalyzed as genitive singular forms, which also had the ending -a. The rule was then extended to all nouns, and also spread to 'three' and 'four', which originally combined with nouns in the plural.

7.13. For Further Reading

The chapters about numerals in historical grammars such as Gorškova and Xaburgaev 1981 and Ivanov 1983 offer good overviews of the development of numerals from Old Rusian to present-day Russian. Kiparsky (1967) provides elaborate discussions of individual forms.

Chapter 8   Morphology: Verbs

Numerous exceptions and idiosyncrasies make the verb a major challenge in Modern Russian. Why are present-tense forms inflected for first, second, and third person, while past-tense forms are inflected for masculine, feminine, and neuter gender? Where do all the consonant alternations in verbs come from? Why is the particle бы used to form subjunctive constructions? You will find answers to these and many other questions in this chapter, which explores all the verb forms in Old Rusian, and explains how the modern verb system has developed.

8.1. The Infinitive and the Supine

We start with the infinitive, the verb form listed in dictionaries. The infinitive goes back to the dative singular of a deverbal noun, which was reinterpreted as a verb form. In Contemporary Standard Russian, the infinitive normally ends in -ть (стать 'become', знать 'know', хвалить 'praise', etc.), but a small group of verbs has -ти́ with stress on the infinitive suffix (e.g., нести́ 'carry'). In Common Slavic and Old Rusian, both types of verbs had -ти in the infinitive regardless of stress: ста́ти 'become', зна́ти 'know', хвали́ти 'praise', and нести́ 'carry'. The unstressed ending lost the final vowel, and only a soft /t'/ spelled as -ть remained in Contemporary Standard Russian.

A small class of verbs in Contemporary Standard Russian has infinitives like печь 'bake' and мочь 'be able'. These are difficult to segment into stem and suffix—is [č'] (spelled as ч) part of the stem or the suffix? In Old Rusian the corresponding infinitives were печи and мочи, which go back to Proto-Slavic [pěktei] and [măgtei]. The reconstructed Proto-Slavic forms are easily segmentable insofar as they have stems in [k] and [g] followed by the regular infinitive suffix /tei/. When the consonant clusters [kt] and [gt] merged to [č'] in the infinitives, the boundary between the stem and the suffix became obscured.

In addition to the infinitive, Common Slavic and (early) Old Rusian had a form called "supine," which had the suffix -тъ (notice the back jer ъ, not the front jer ь we find in Modern Russian infinitives). The supine is attested in combination with motion verbs, where Modern Russian uses the infinitive:

(1) a. А Ростиславича Мстислава вьведоша Смоленьску **кнѧжитъ**.
(KL 1175 AD)

b. А Мстислава Ростиславича ввели в Смоленск **княжить**.

c. But Mstislav Rostislavič was sent to Smolensk **to rule** there.

The supine started disappearing as early as the 11th century, and was gradually replaced by the infinitive.

8.2. The Present Tense

Common Slavic and Old Rusian present-tense forms had the following structure, where parentheses indicate elements that were not found in all verb classes:

(2) Stem + (consonant) + (theme vowel) + ending

In addition to the stem, all verbs had an ending, which expressed the inflectional categories of number (singular, dual, and plural) and person (first, second, and third). In the vast majority of the verbs, the ending was preceded by a so-called theme vowel. Such verbs are referred to as "thematic," whereas verbs without a theme vowel are called "athematic." There were only five athematic verbs: **быти** 'be', **дати** 'give', **ѣсти** 'eat', **вѣдѣти** 'know', and **имѣти** 'have'. The thematic verbs are divided into four classes according to the consonant and the theme vowel. Classes I–III have the thematic vowel /e/ (/o/), while for class IV the thematic vowel was /i/. Class IV, which contained Old Rusian verbs like **хвалити** 'praise', forms the basis for the second conjugation ("the i-conjugation") in Contemporary Standard Russian (cf. modern present-tense forms such as **хвалю, хвалишь,** and **хвалят**). Classes I–III contained all the verbs that belong to the first conjugation ("the e-conjugation") in Contemporary Standard Russian. These three classes had the theme vowel /e/ (/o/), but differed with regard to the consonant intervening between the stem and the theme vowel. In class I, which contained Old Rusian verbs like **нести** 'carry' and **мочи** 'be able', there was no intervening consonant. Class II contained Old Rusian verbs such as **стати** 'become', **съхнути** 'dry', and **двинути** 'move', which all displayed the consonant /n/ before the theme vowel. Finally, class III included verbs such as **знати** 'know', **дѣлати** 'do', and **мазати** 'smear', all of which had /j/ before the theme vowel. The classification into five classes is summarized in Figure 9, and the conjugation of one verb in each thematic class is given in Table 38 on p. 138. Table 39 on p. 139 shows the conjugation of all five athematic verbs.

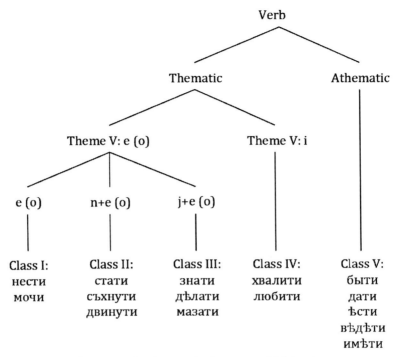

Figure 9. The five verb classes in Old Rusian

The thematic vowel in classes I–III was /e/ in the majority of the present-tense forms. However, there was no thematic vowel in the first person singular, while the third person plural had /o/ in Proto-Slavic. However, this /o/ merged with the original ending /ntĭ/, and the result was Old Rusian third person plural forms in /ut'/, such as **несуть**. The third person plural forms in -**ять** (class IV) are due to the merger of /i/ with /ntĭ/. The sound law behind these developments is referred to as "monophthongization of nasal diphthongs" (see section 10.7).

The inflectional endings of the thematic verbs have not changed much since Old Rusian times. However, three comments are in order. First, the dual has disappeared in verbs, as it disappeared in other parts of speech. Second, the second person singular ending -**ши** has lost the final vowel. In Contemporary Standard Russian, the ending is spelled with a soft sign at the end, which, however, does not affect the pronunciation of the preceding /š/. Third, Old Rusian had a soft /t'/ in the third person singular and plural endings, while Contemporary Standard Russian has a hard /t/. Old Church Slavonic and Common Slavic had hard /t/. In Modern Russian dialects, hard /t/ occurs in northern dialects, while southern dialects display soft /t'/. In order to explain these facts, we are forced to assume a softening of the endings from Common Slavic to Old Rusian, and then a subsequent hardening of the same endings in the northern dialects and the standard language. The historical processes behind these changes are not well understood. Concerning the change from Old Rusian to Modern Russian, two approaches have been proposed in the literature. Some researchers, notably Aleksej Šaxmatov (1915: 320–21), have tried to explain the hardening in terms of a sound law. However, this approach runs into problems, because Modern Russian has preserved word-final soft /t'/ in words such as **опять** 'again' and **чуть** 'scarely'. In order to make the sound law work, one would have to come up with a phonetic environment that *included* third person forms of verbs, but *excluded* words such as **опять** and **чуть**. No one has been able to solve this problem in a fully satisfactory way.

An alternative approach tries to explain the hardening of the soft /t'/ in the third person in terms of analogy. The question is: analogy to what? The most widespread answer, mentioned already by Šaxmatov (1915: 320–21), is the demonstrative pronoun **тъ**, but it is not quite clear why a verb ending would come under the influence of a demonstrative pronoun, although both the ending and the pronoun are used to refer to entities in the third person and quite often co-occur in the same sentence.

Table 38. The conjugation of thematic verbs (classes I–IV) in Old Rusian

		I: нести	II: стати	III: знати	IV: хвалити
Sg	1	несу	стану	знаю	хвалю
	2	несеши	станеши	знаеши	хвалиши
	3	несеть	станеть	знаеть	хвалить
Du	1	несевѣ	станевѣ	знаевѣ	хваливѣ
	2	несета	станета	знаета	хвалита
	3	несета	станета	знаета	хвалита
Pl	1	несемъ	станемъ	знаемъ	хвалимъ
	2	несете	станете	знаете	хвалите
	3	несуть	стануть	знають	хвалять

A major obstacle to learning Modern Russian is the consonant alternations we find in verbs deriving from the Common Slavic and Old Rusian classes I, III, and IV. Class I included a number of verbs with the velar consonants /k, g/ in stem-final position such as **печи** 'bake' and **беречи** 'guard'. These verbs displayed alternations before the theme vowel /e/ (cf. **печеши** and **бережеши**), but kept /k, g/ in the first singular and the third plural where the stem was followed by /u/ (cf. пеку, пекуть and берегу, берегуть). This alternation is due to the so-called first palatalization, a sound law you will learn more about in section 11.5. While the alternation has been preserved in Contemporary Standard Russian (cf. печёшь, бережёшь), forms like пекёшь and берегёшь exist in non-standard and dialectal speech.

Although most verbs in class III had a vowel in stem-final position, one subclass had a consonant, which in Proto-Slavic was followed by /j/ in all present-tense forms. In Common Slavic, the combination consonant + [j] underwent a sound law called "j-palatalization," which we will return to in section 11.6. This sound law created a number of consonant alternations, which we still find in verbs like мазать 'smear' and писать 'write' in Modern Russian (cf. modern present-tense forms such as мажу, мажешь, мажут and пишу, пишешь, пишут).

Verbs of the second conjugation in Modern Russian also show the results of j-palatalization, but the only present-tense form with a consonant alternation is the first singular (cf. люблю from любить in Modern Russian). In Common Slavic the thematic vowel in class IV became /j/ before the vowel of the first person singular ending, and the result was a consonant + /j/ cluster, which underwent j-palatalization and produced the consonant alternations we still find in Modern Russian.

Table 39. The conjugation of athematic verbs (class V) in Old Rusian

		быти	дати	ѣсти	вѣдѣти	имѣти
Sg	1	есмь	дамь	ѣмь	вѣмь	имамь
	2	еси	даси	ѣси	вѣси	имаши
	3	есть	дасть	ѣсть	вѣсть	имать
Du	1	есвѣ	давѣ	ѣвѣ	вѣвѣ	имавѣ
	2	еста	даста	ѣста	вѣста	имата
	3	еста	даста	ѣста	вѣста	имата
Pl	1	есмъ	дамъ	ѣмъ	вѣмъ	имамъ
	2	есте	дасте	ѣсте	вѣсте	имате
	3	суть	дадять	ѣдять	вѣдять	имуть

Turning to the athematic verbs shown in Table 39, we notice that имѣти has migrated to class III (иметь, имею, имеешь, etc. in Modern Russian), while вѣдѣти is no longer used. Быти has lost all its present-tense forms except the third person singular есть and, to some extent, the third person plural суть, which is only used in very bookish style today. Notice that быти, as opposed to all other verbs, has preserved the soft /t'/ in the third person. Дати and ѣсти have survived, but all forms have undergone changes. In the first person singular, the soft /m'/ has become hard (cf. дам and ем in Modern Russian). In the second person singular, the verbs have adopted the same ending as the thematic verbs, as shown in the modern forms дашь and ешь. The third person has replaced the soft /t'/ with hard /t/, in the same way as the thematic verbs (cf. the modern forms даст and ест). In the plural, both verbs have extended the stem in the first and second person. Compare the old forms дамъ, дасте, ѣмъ, and ѣсте with the corresponding forms дадим, дадите, едим, едите in Modern Russian. The extension of the stem is presumably due to analogy to the third person plural. The third person plural of дати has changed from Old Rusian дадять to Contemporary Standard Russian дадут, while ѣсти has only replaced the soft /t'/ with the hard /t/: едять became едят. In summary, the five athematic verbs have yielded three highly irregular verbs in Modern Russian.

8.3. The Four Past-Tense Forms

This section presents forms first (8.3.1–8.3.4), meanings later (section 8.3.5), before we finally turn to the historical development (section 8.3.6). While contemporary Standard Russian has only one past-tense form, Old Rusian inherited from Common Slavic four different past-tense forms:

(3) a. Aorist
    b. Imperfect
    c. Perfect
    d. Pluperfect

Make sure you don't confuse the Common Slavic and Old Rusian past-tense forms "imperfect" and "perfect" with the "imperfective" and "perfective" aspects.

8.3.1. The Aorist

In Old Rusian, the aorist was the most widely used past-tense form. It was formed by the addition of the endings in Table 40 to the infinitive stem. Simply put, the infinitive stem is what remains of a verb when you remove -ти, e.g., **нес** of **нести** 'carry', **ста** of **стати** 'become', **зна** of **знати** 'know', **хвали** of хвалити 'carry', and бы of быти. The aorists of these verbs are shown in Table 41.¹

Table 40. The aorist endings in Old Rusian. The symbol "∅" ("zero") is used when a form lacks an ending.

		Aorist endings
Sg	1	-хъ
	2	-∅
	3	-∅
Du	1	-ховѣ
	2	-ста
	3	-ста
Pl	1	-хомъ
	2	-сте
	3	-ша

Table 41. The conjugation of the aorist in Old Rusian

		I: нести	II: стати	III: знати	IV: хвалити	V: быти (Athematic)
Sg	1	несохъ	стахъ	знахъ	хвалихъ	быхъ
	2	несе	ста	зна	хвали	бы(сть)
	3	несе	ста	зна	хвали	бы(сть)
Du	1	несоховѣ	стаховѣ	знаховѣ	хваликовѣ	быховѣ
	2	несоста	стаста	знаста	хвалиста	быста
	3	несоста	стаста	знаста	хвалиста	быста
Pl	1	несохомъ	стахомъ	знахомъ	хвалихомъ	быхомъ
	2	несосте	стасте	знасте	хвалисте	бысте
	3	несоша	сташа	знаша	хвалиша	быша

If the infinitive stem ended in a vowel, the aorist endings were attached directly to the stem. This is the case in classes II–V, as shown in Table 41. In

---

¹ It is worth pointing out that Common Slavic had a richer aorist system, which to some extent was preserved in Old Church Slavonic. Although some archaic forms are attested in the oldest texts from Rus', such forms are not included in Table 41. If you want to learn more about the archaic aorists, you may consult a grammar of Old Church Slavonic (e.g., Lunt 2001: 102–08).

class I, however, the infinitive stem ended in a consonant, and the vowel **о** was inserted between stem and ending, as shown by forms such as **несохъ** in Table 41. In the second and third person singular, there was no ending, and the vowel **-е** was added instead of **-о** (cf. **несе**).

For verbs such as **печи** 'bake' and **беречи** 'guard' we may reconstruct the velar consonants /k, g/ at the end of the infinitive stem. As mentioned in section 8.1, in Proto-Slavic these verbs had /ktei/ and /gtei/ which became **-чи** in Old Rusian and **-чь** in Contemporary Standard Russian. The Old Rusian aorists of such verbs are **пекохъ** and **берегохъ** (first person singular) and **пече** and **береже** (second and third persons singular). Notice the consonant alternations in the second and third person singular. These alternations are due to the so-called first palatalization, which we will discuss in detail in section 11.5.

In Table 40 you can see that the first consonant in the aorist endings is either **с**, **х**, or **ш**. These consonants all go back to /s/, as you will see in section 11.3, where you will learn more about the so-called *ruki* rule.

Before we leave the aorist, a note on **быти** is in order. In addition to the forms shown in Table 41, you may also encounter aorists with the stem **бѣ**. These aorists were used in the same way as the imperfect. In the second and third person singular, **быти** and other athematic verbs also have alternative aorist forms in **-сть**, such as **бысть** and **дасть**.

The formation of the aorist can be summarized as follows:

(4) a. Infinitive stem + aorist ending = aorist
 b. If the infinitive stem ends in a consonant, the following special rules apply:
  i. **-о** is inserted between stem and ending (cf. **несохъ** from **нести** 'carry').
  ii. In the second and third person singular, there is no ending; **-е** is added to the stem instead of **-о** (cf. **несе** from **нести** 'carry').
  iii. Verbs with a velar consonant in stem-final position display consonant alternations **к~ч** and **г~ж** before **-е** in the second and third person singular (cf. **пече** from **печи** 'bake').

8.3.2. The Imperfect

The imperfect resembles the aorist, since both forms are created by adding endings to the infinitive stem, and the endings of the imperfect and the aorist are very similar. As shown by the shaded cells in Table 42, there are different endings in the second and third person singular and the third person plural,

8.3.2. The Imperfect

but elsewhere the endings are the same. In the third person singular and plural, the endings that Old Rusian inherited from Common Slavic are -ше and -ху, but these endings are sometimes extended to -шеть and -хуть, presumably by analogy to the third person ending -ть in the present tense.

Table 42. Comparison of aorist and imperfect endings in Old Rusian

		Aorist endings	Imperfect endings
Sg	1	-хъ	-хъ
	2	-∅	-ше
	3	-∅	-ше(ть)
Du	1	-ховѣ	-ховѣ
	2	-ста	-ста
	3	-ста	-ста
Pl	1	-хомъ	-хомъ
	2	-сте	-сте
	3	-ша	-ху(ть)

The formation of the imperfect is complicated by the fact that the imperfect suffix -я is inserted between the stem and the ending. The inserted element goes back to /ěa/ or /aa/ in Common Slavic. The Old Rusian insertion rule can be stated as follows:

(5) a. Insert я between stem and ending, unless the stem ends in a.
 b. Delete any vowel preceding the inserted я.

The following examples illustrate vowel insertion:

(6) a. Infinitive stem in a (no imperfect suffix inserted):

Infinitive: зна-ти 'know' – imperfect: зна-хъ (1st person singular)

 b. Infinitive stem in consonant (я inserted):

Infinitive: нес-ти 'carry' – imperfect: нес-я-хъ (1st person singular)

 c. Infinitive stem in vowel other than a (я inserted, preceding vowel deleted):

Infinitive: хвали-ти 'praise' – imperfect: хвали-я-хъ → хвал-я-хъ (1st person singular)

In (6a) the stem ends in **a**, and the ending is therefore attached directly to the stem. Since verbs of this type do not have vowel insertion in the aorist or imperfect, these forms are identical. For instance, знахъ can be interpreted both as an aorist or an imperfect. However, in the second and third person singular and the third person plural the imperfect and aorist have different endings, so here it is easy to tell the forms apart. All the imperfects of the verbs in (6) are given in Table 43, which in addition shows the imperfect forms of **быти** 'be'.

Table 43. The conjugation of the imperfect in Old Rusian

		знати	нести	хвалити	быти
Sg	1	знахъ	несяхъ	хваляхъ	бяхъ
	2	знаше	несяше	хваляше	бяше
	3	знаше(ть)	несяше(ть)	хваляше(ть)	бяше(ть)
Du	1	знаховѣ	несяховѣ	хваляховѣ	бяховѣ
	2	знаста	несяста	хваляста	бяста
	3	знаста	несяста	хваляста	бяста
Pl	1	знахомъ	несяхомъ	хваляхомъ	бяхомъ
	2	знасте	несясте	хвалясте	бясте
	3	знаху(ть)	несяху(ть)	хваляху(ть)	бяху(ть)

Verbs in class IV display consonant alternations in all imperfect forms. For instance, ходити 'walk' has the first person singular imperfect хожахъ. The consonant alternation is due to *j*-palatalization, which we return to in section 11.6.

8.3.3. The Perfect

As opposed to the aorist and imperfect, the perfect and pluperfect are periphrastic forms, i.e., forms that consist of an auxiliary verb in addition to the main verb. While the English perfect (e.g., *have done*) and pluperfect (e.g., *had done*) are periphrastic forms using the verb *to have* as the auxiliary, the auxiliary verb in the corresponding forms in Old Rusian, however, was **быти** 'be'. The following template shows how the perfect was formed in Old Rusian:

(7) The Old Rusian perfect:

Present tense of **быти** + *l*-participle (short form, nominative)

The auxiliary verb has the inflectional categories person and number, as shown in Table 39 in section 8.2 above. You will learn more about the *l*-participle in section 8.8. For now it is sufficient to note that although this form is the ancestor of the modern past-tense forms (e.g., **знал**, **знала**, **знало**, and **знали** of **знать** 'know'), it was a participle in Common Slavic and Old Rusian. Like all other participles it was inflected in the same way as adjectives, and therefore had the category *gender* instead of person. The following examples show that the auxiliary verb was inflected for person, while the *l*-participle was inflected for gender:

(8) a. На Давыда **пришелъ есмь**, а с вама хощю имѣти миръ и любовь. (PVL 1097 AD; 270,3)

  b. На Давыда **пришел** я, а с вами хочу иметь мир и любовь.

  c. I **have come** only to attack David, but am desirous to maintain peaceful and friendly relations with you.

(9) a. Азъ уже **мьстила есмь** мужа своего. (PVL 946 AD; 58,24)

  b. Я уже **мстила** за обиду своего мужа.

  c. I **have** already **avenged** the misfortune of my husband.

In both (8) and (9) the auxiliary **есмь** is in the first person singular, since the subject in both sentences is **азъ** 'I' (although the subject is not explicitly mentioned in (8)). In (8), the *l*-participle has the masculine form **пришелъ** that indicates that the subject is a man. In (9), on the other hand, we find the feminine form **мьстила** of the *l*-participle, since the subject is a woman.

8.3.4. The Pluperfect

There were two ways to form the pluperfect in Old Rusian:

(10) The Old Rusian pluperfect:

  a. Imperfect of **быти** + *l*-participle in the nominative

  b. Perfect of **быти** + *l*-participle in the nominative

The following example illustrates the option with the imperfect as the auxiliary verb:

(11) a. И Стародубу идохом на Олга, зане ся **бяше приложилъ** к полоцем. (Monomax)

(11) b. И к Стародубу ходили на Олега, потому что он **сдружился** с половцами.

c. And they went against Oleg in Starodub, because he **had been on friendly terms** with the Polovtsians.

Notice that instead of the imperfect, you will sometimes encounter the aorist with the stem бѣ, which as was pointed out in section 8.3.1 was used in the same way as the imperfect.

Here is an example with the perfect instead of the imperfect as the auxiliary verb:

(12) a. Но **реклъ** ми **есь былъ** в Ляхохъ, коли есмь былѣ с Телебугою и Алгуемь. (GVL)

b. Но **сказал** ты об этом в Ляшской земле, когда мы были с Телебугой и Алгуем.

c. But you **had told** me about this in the Polish lands, when I was there with Telebuga and Alguj.

Instead of pluperfects like **реклъ есь былъ** in (12) you will frequently come across "shortened" forms of the type **реклъ былъ**. These shortened forms are particularly widespread in the third person, but in later texts they are attested in the first and second persons as well. A reminiscence of the shortened pluperfects in Modern Russian is the formula **жил-был** 'once upon a time there lived', which is used in fairytales. It is also likely that the Modern Russian construction **было сказал** 'was about to say' has developed from the pluperfect.

8.3.5. The Meaning of the Past-Tense Forms

It is customary to assume that the difference between the aorist and imperfect was an aspectual distinction that resembles the difference between perfective and imperfective past-tense forms in Contemporary Standard Russian. The aorist described bounded events, i.e., events that were completed, whereas the imperfect did not describe events as bounded. Gorškova and Xaburgaev (1981: 301) use the following passage from the *Primary Chronicle* as an illustration. For convenience, the relevant verb forms are boldfaced; aorists are shown with spaced type, while imperfects are italicized.

(13) a. В си же времена **быша** и обре, иже *воеваша* на цесаря Ираклия и мало его не **яша**. Си же обри *воеваша* на словѣны и **примучиша** дулѣбы, сущая словѣны, и насилье

8.3.5. The Meaning of the Past-Tense Forms

творяху женамъ дулѣбьскымъ: аще поѣхати *бяше* обрину, не *дадяше* въпрячи коня, ни волу, но *веляше* въпрячи 3, или 4, ли 5 женъ в телѣгу и повести обрина, и тако *мучаху* дулѣбы. **Бяху** бо обри тѣломъ велицѣ, а умомъ горди, и **потреби** я Богъ, и **помроша** вси, и не **оста** ни единъ обринъ. […] По сихъ бо **придоша** печенизѣ, и пакы **идоша** угри чернии мимо Киевъ послѣже при Ользѣ.   (PVL (no year); 11,22)

(13) b. **Были** в те времена и обры, **воевали** они с цесарем Ираклием и чуть было его не **захватили**. Эти обры **воевали** и против славян и **притесняли** дулебов — также славян, и *творили* насилие женщинам дулебским: *бывало* когда поедет обрин, то не *позволял* запрячь коня или вола, но *приказывал* впрячь в телегу трех, или четырех или пять женщин и везти обрина, и так *мучили* дулебов. **Были** же эти обры велики телом, а умом горды, и Бог **истребил** их, **вымерли** все, и не **осталось** ни одного обрина. […] После обров **пришли** печенеги, а затем **прошли** черные угры мимо Киева, но было это после, уже при Олеге.

c. The Avars, who **attacked** Heraclius the Emperor and nearly **captured** him, also **lived** at this time. They **made war** upon the Slavs and **harrassed** the Dulebians, who were themselves Slavs. They even *did* violence to the Dulebian women. When an Avar *made* a journey, he *did not let* either a horse or a steer be harnessed, but *gave command* instead that three or four or five women should be yoked to his cart and be made to draw him. Even thus they *harassed* the Dulebians. The Avars *were* large of stature and proud of spirit, and God **destroyed** them. They all **perished**, and not one Avar **remained**. […] The Pechenegs **came** after them, and the Ugrians **passed by** Kiev later during the time of Oleg.

In this passage, aorists describe bounded (completed) events. These events may be sequentially ordered as in the final part of the quote where the Avars first died out, and then were replaced by the Pechenegs, who in turn were followed by Ugrian tribes. However, the aorist is used about parallel events as well, such as the fighting with the Slavs and the oppression of the Dulebians in the second sentence of the quote, where the translator has used imperfective verbs in Modern Russian. Even the aorist **быша** in the beginning of the quote can be interpreted as a bounded event, insofar as it describes the existence of the Avars in the areas north of the Black Sea. Recall from section 1.4 that this existence had a limited duration; the Avars appeared in the steppe and then disappeared a few centuries later.

The imperfect is used in the description of *how* the Avars oppressed the Dulebians. This is background information—it provides an example that illustrates the main point of the story, namely the cruelty of the Avars. The imperfect бяху is also used in the description of the Avars as tall and proud; these are characteristics of this people that are not limited in time, i.e., unbounded.

The passage in (13) facilitates three observations. First, we have seen that the aorist presented events as bounded, while the imperfect did not have this function. Second, the aorist had a foregrounding function since it described the main events, while the imperfect served as a backgrounding device. Third, comparison of (13a) and (13b) indicates that although the Old Rusian imperfect resembles the modern imperfective and the aorist the modern perfective aspect, we are not dealing with a one-to-one relationship. For instance, the Old Rusian imperfect does not always correspond to the imperfective aspect in Modern Russian, as shown in (13a–b). This being said, there is a strong tendency for imperfects to be formed from imperfective verbs in Old Rusian. You will learn more about the status of the perfective and imperfective aspects in Old Rusian in section 8.5.

The meaning of the Old Rusian perfect is close to the meaning of the perfect in English, so it may be useful to consider English examples before we turn to Old Rusian:

(14) a. Simple past: *John lost his knife.*
b. Perfect: *John has lost his knife.*

While both sentences describe an event in the past (the loss of John's knife), the perfect *has lost* in addition implies that the knife is still lost in the present. Therefore, it seems unnatural to say *??John has lost his knife, but then found it*, whereas *John lost his knife, but then found it* sounds fine. In other words, the meaning of the perfect has two components. The perfect describes (a) an event in the past (e.g., the loss of John's knife) and (b) a state in the present that results from the event in the past (e.g., the knife still being lost). The meaning of the Old Rusian perfect also involved these two components. The perfect **пришелъ есмь** 'I have come' in (8) implies that the subject arrived in the past and is still there in the present. In (9), **мьстила есмь** 'I have avenged' indicates that revenge was carried out in the past, and that it is still in effect in the present. It is customary to treat the perfect as a past-tense form, but it also makes sense to classify the perfect as a present-tense form, since it describes both an event in the past and a resultant state in the present.

The meaning of the Old Rusian pluperfect also resembles its English counterpart. While *John has lost his knife* relates the event to the present, the corresponding sentence with the pluperfect, *John had lost his knife*, relates the event to the past. The pluperfect **бяше приложилъ** 'had been on friendly terms' in (11) indicates that Oleg's fraternization with the Polovtsians had taken place before another event in the past (the attack on Oleg), and that the content was still relevant at that time in the past. Since the pluperfect relates an event in the past to a point in the past, we may call the pluperfect a "past perfect," while the perfect may be referred to as a "present perfect," because it relates past events to the present.[2]

We have now seen that Old Rusian had four different forms that all signaled past tense. Does this mean that Old Rusian had four different past tenses? No! The difference between the aorist and imperfect is an aspectual difference, similar—but not identical—to the distinction between the perfective and imperfective aspects we are familiar with from Modern Russian. The difference between the simple and periphrastic past-tense forms involves "current relevance"—as we have seen, the perfect and pluperfect indicate that a resultant state is still relevant at a later point in time. Some researchers also argue that "current relevance" is an aspectual notion (cf. Comrie 1976: 52 for discussion). If one accepts this argument, Old Rusian had four past-tense forms that differed with regard to aspect, but not tense.

8.3.6. The Historical Development of the Past-Tense Forms

The past-tense forms of Contemporary Standard Russian are continuations of the Old Rusian perfect. As you remember, the perfect consisted of an auxiliary verb (the present tense of **быти** 'be') and an *l*-participle. Simply put, two things happened:

---

[2] As mentioned in section 8.3.4, there were two ways to form the pluperfect. Did the two types of pluperfect have the same meaning? This question has been subjected to lively debate in recent years (Petruxin and Sičinava 2006 and 2008, Sičinava 2007 and 2013, Ševeleva 2007 and 2008). While it is clear that the pluperfect formed from the imperfect served as a past perfect in the sense discussed above, according to Petruxin and Sičinava (2006: 202) the version formed from the perfect of *byti* typically had an "antiresultative meaning." For instance, forms of this type frequently described events that took place in the past, but where the result was subsequently cancelled out. An interesting example is **умерлъ былъ** 'had been dead' (Petruxin and Sičinava 2006: 203, Sičinava 2007: 114, Sičinava 2013: 197). You might think that the result of dying cannot be cancelled out afterwards, but in the only attestation of this example we are dealing with the Biblical story about Lazarus, who was brought back to life four days after his burial.

(15) The formation of the Modern Russian past tense:
   a. The auxiliary verb disappeared.
   b. The *l*-participle was reanalyzed as a finite past-tense form.

The second step is an example of what historical linguists sometimes call "reanalysis," i.e., the reinterpretation of an entity, which changes its meaning, but not its form (Harris and Campbell 1995: 61; see section 3.8). In our case, the *l*-participle changed its meaning from a participle to a normal ("finite") past-tense form. However, the *l*-participle did not change its form. Importantly, Russian past-tense forms have preserved the category of gender. As mentioned in section 8.3.3, participles inflect like adjectives, and characteristic for adjectives is the category of gender. In other words, the reanalysis of the *l*-participle explains why past-tense forms in Modern Russian have gender as an inflectional category.

The history of the remaining Old Rusian past-tense forms is a sad sequence of deaths:

(16) a. 1100s: the imperfect disappears.
   b. 1300s: the pluperfect with imperfect as auxiliary verb disappears.
   c. 1300–1400s: the aorist disappears.

The dates are meant as rough estimates; it is difficult to pinpoint the time when these forms disappeared since medieval texts often preserve forms long after they have been lost in the spoken language. However, it seems uncontroversial that the imperfect was lost first, and that the aorist survived longer than the other forms. Notice that the pluperfect consisting of the perfect and *l*-participle is not on the list of lost past-tense forms. Although this form is not attested in Contemporary Standard Russian, it has survived in some Russian dialects.

8.4. The Future Tense

In Contemporary Standard Russian, a periphrastic construction with буду (будешь, будет, etc.) and an imperfective infinitive expresses future tense. In other words, буду читать indicates that the act of reading will take place in the future. This construction is an innovation from the Middle Russian period (cf. Andersen 2006: 245ff. and 2009: 132 for discussion).

In earlier texts, a construction with a prefixed form of the verb чати 'begin' (e.g., почати and начати) and an imperfective infinitive was a widespread means of expressing future tense. Here is an example from *Russkaja Pravda*:

8.4. The Future Tense

(17) a. Которая ли вервь **начнеть платити** дикую виру, колико лѣтъ заплатить ту виру, зане же безъ головника имъ платити. (RPP)

b. Если которая-либо вервь **будет платить** дикую виру, пусть выплачивает ту виру столько времени, сколько будет платить, потому что они платят без преступника.

c. If a local commune **will pay** a death fee, then it should pay this fee as long as it takes, because they are paying in absence of a criminal.

The Modern Russian translation **будет платить** indicates that the translator has interpreted **начнеть платити** as a periphrastic future.

According to Andersen (2006), the construction in (17) is characteristic of (early) Old Rusian and is still attested in modern Ukrainian. However, in texts from the Old Rusian period you may also encounter another construction, which consists of **имѣти** 'have' and an imperfective infinitive:

(18) a. Просимъ мира в руси, яко крѣпко ся **имуть бити** с нами, мы бо много зла створихомъ Руской земли.   (PVL 1102 AD; 278,5)

b. Попросим мира у руси, так как крепко они **будут биться** с нами, ибо много зла причинили мы Русской земле.

c. We will make peace with the Russes, since they **will offer a violent combat** in view of the fact that we have done so much damage to Rus'.

Finally, the combination of **хотѣти** 'want, wish' and an imperfective infinitive may indicate future tense:

(19) a. Нарекль же есть Богъ един день, в он же **хощет судити**, пришедый, живым и мертвым.   (PVL 986 AD; 105,23)

b. Установит же Бог и день единый, в который **будет судить** живых и мертвых.

c. God has appointed a day, in which he **shall come from heaven to judge** both the living and the dead.

We see that there is considerable variation in Old Rusian texts, but that the construction with **буду** takes over in the Middle Russian period. This development is an example of grammaticalization, whereby a free combination of a finite verb and an infinitive develops into a periphrastic future tense.

In addition to the periphrastic future discussed above, you may also encounter a future perfect in texts from the Old Rusian period. The future perfect consisted of **буду** and an *l*-participle:

(20) a. Но паче убо да възметь свое, иже **будеть погубилъ**.
(PVL 912 AD; 35,5)
b. Но пусть пострадавший возьмет то свое, что **потерял**.
c. The victim of the loss shall recover the stolen property (lit. "that which he **will have lost**").

The meaning of this construction resembles the meaning of the perfect constructions discussed in section 8.3.5. Recall that the pluperfect (past perfect) relates an event in the past to a point in the past, while the (present) perfect describes events in the past that are relevant in the present. The future perfect construction describes an event which takes place before an event in the future, and which is still relevant at that point in the future. Sentence (20), which addresses legal regulations in the case of theft, describes two events in the future: the loss due to theft and the legitimate owner taking the goods back. The loss is in the future perfect, since it will have happened before the owner takes the goods back, and since the loss is still relevant at the point in time when the owner takes the stolen goods back. Notice that the *will have happened* construction conveys the future perfect meaning in English.

8.5. Tense and Aspect

The Old Rusian forms we have considered in the preceding sections can be organized as in Table 44, where the category of tense occupies the horizontal dimension and aspect the vertical dimension. In the category of tense, three features are considered: past, present, and future. For aspect, we may distinguish between actual and perfect. The actual describes events in the past, present, or future, while the perfect describes both events and states resulting from these events. If we organize the Old Rusian verb forms like this, we see that the only cell in the table that contains two forms is the actual past tense, where we have the aorist and the imperfect. Recall from section 8.3.6 that this is an aspectual difference, and that the imperfect was the first past-tense form to disappear. After the loss of the imperfect, one form remains in each cell in Table 44. Notice that the (present) perfect is classified as a present-tense form in Table 44. As mentioned in section 8.3.6, the (present) perfect has one foot in the past (since it describes events in the past) and one in the present (since it describes a resultant state in the present).

Table 44. Tense and aspect in Old Rusian

	Past tense	Present tense	Future tense
Actual:	Aorist Imperfect	Present	Future
Perfect:	Past perfect (=pluperfect)	(Present) perfect	Future perfect

When you think of aspect, you probably think about the distinction between imperfective and perfective verbs that you are familiar with from Modern Russian. How old is this distinction? Did Common Slavic and Old Rusian distinguish between imperfective and perfective verbs? Different scholars have come to different conclusions. In a seminal study, the Czech linguist Antonín Dostál (1954) concluded that there was a consistent distinction between imperfective and perfective verbs in Old Church Slavonic. This suggests that Late Common Slavic distinguished between imperfective and perfective verbs, since the Old Church Slavonic texts, to some extent at least, reflect the linguistic situation in the Late Common Slavic period. However, other scholars have emphasized the differences between the Common Slavic, Old Rusian, and Modern Russian aspectual systems, and placed the birth of the Modern Russian aspectual system much later in time (cf., e.g., Bermel 1997 and Nørgård-Sørensen 1997).

Although a detailed discussion of the history of the imperfective-perfective distinction is beyond the scope of this book, two arguments from recent years support Dostál's idea about an early birth of the imperfective-perfective distinction. The first argument comes from the periphrastic future forms. Recall from section 8.4 that there is a fair amount of variation in texts from the Old Rusian period. Andersen (2006 and 2009), who has studied the development of the periphrastic futures in detail, shows that across East Slavic the periphrastic future is only formed from imperfective verbs. This suggests that the imperfective-perfective distinction must have been part of the grammar at the time when the periphrastic futures emerged. Since different dialects of Old Rusian have different periphrastic future constructions, it stands to reason that the imperfective-perfective distinction was part of the grammar already in Common Slavic, i.e., before or during the East Slavic expansion to the north between 500 and 800 AD (Andersen 2009: 132).

The second argument in favor of an early birth of the imperfective-perfective distinction comes from a statistical study of verbs in Old Church Slavonic by Eckhoff and Janda (2014). Eckhoff and Janda observe that the distribution of forms is different for the two aspects; past tense forms dominate the perfective aspect, while present-tense forms dominate the imperfective aspect. Eckhoff and Janda's study of a large number of Old Church Slavonic verb forms demonstrated that with regard to their behavior the verbs fell into two distinct categories, which to a large extent coincide with the imperfective and perfective verbs as classified by Dostál. In other words, since imperfective and perfective verbs behave differently, this suggests that the imperfective-perfective distinction was part of the grammar in Late Common Slavic.

Although the studies by Andersen (2006 and 2009) and Eckhoff and Janda (2014) suggest an early birth of the imperfective-perfective distinction, it does not follow from these studies that the difference between imperfective and perfective verbs was exactly the same as in Modern Russian. Dickey (2000) has demonstrated that there are significant differences across the aspectual systems of the modern Slavic languages, although all languages distinguish between imperfective and perfective verbs. This suggests that the imperfective-perfective distinction must have undergone different paths of development in different Slavic languages. Characteristic of Russian are so-called atelic perfective verbs, i.e., perfective verbs that do not culminate in a change of state. A case in point is the so-called delimitative aktionsart, i.e., verbs like **почитать** 'read for a while'. **Почитать** indicates that the reading goes on for some time, but not that the reader finishes whatever s/he is reading. According to Dickey (2008), atelic perfectives are a relatively late development in Russian. If this is correct, it indicates that the imperfective-perfective distinction has expanded so as to cover more and more types of verbs over time.

Where does the imperfective-perfective distinction come from? Many aspectual prefixes are related to prepositions with spatial meanings. By way of example, consider **войти в дом** 'enter a house' where both the prefix **в(о)** and the preposition **в** indicate movement along a path into a three-dimensional space (in this case a house). It is likely that the aspectual meaning of the perfective aspect has developed from the concrete spatial meaning. When you are struggling to complete an action (e.g., the reading of a book), in a sense you are moving along an imagined path toward completion, which resembles the path into the house in **войти в дом**. Another source of perfective verbs is the so-called semelfactive aktionsart with the suffix **-ну-**, which describes perfective events occurring once (e.g., **плюнуть** 'spit once'). Nesset (2013) has shown that at least some of these verbs had semelfactive meanings already in Old Church Slavonic, and that the semelfactive aktionsart seems to have expanded to new groups of verbs over time.

8.6. The Imperative

It is customary to assume that there were five different forms of the imperative in Old Rusian, as shown in Table 45. Today, only two forms remain, namely the second person in the singular and plural. The two dual forms have been lost, and the first person plural has been replaced by a construction with the first person plural present tense, which may be followed by -те: пойдем(те) 'let us go'. The original form that was used in both second and third person singular has survived in the second person only; in the third person the construction with пусть is now used to convey the meaning 'let him/her ...': Пусть он придёт и посмотрит сам 'let him come and see for himself'.

Table 45. The conjugation of the imperative in Old Rusian

		I: нести	II: стати	III: знати	IV: хвалити	V: дати	V: ѣсти
Sg	2–3	неси	стани	знаи	хвали	дажь	ѣжь
Du	1	несѣвѣ	станѣвѣ	знаивѣ	хваливѣ	дадивѣ	ѣдивѣ
	2	несѣта	станѣта	знаита	хвалита	дадита	ѣдита
Pl	1	несѣмъ	станѣмъ	знаимъ	хвалимъ	дадимъ	ѣдимъ
	2	несѣте	станѣте	знаите	хвалите	дадите	ѣдите

The following template illustrates the structure of imperative forms:

(21)   The Old Rusian imperative:
       Stem + и/ѣ + present-tense ending

Table 45 shows that in Old Rusian the imperative had -ѣ- in the dual and plural of classes I and II, while -и- was attested elsewhere. After -и-/-ѣ- followed the endings -вѣ, -та, -мъ, and -те, which are the same endings as we have in the corresponding present-tense forms. Notice, however, that there is no ending in the second and third person singular.

Old Rusian imperatives had consonant alternations if the verb stem ended in a velar consonant; thus печи had the imperative пьци and жечи 'burn', жьзи. The alternations between к and ц and between г and з are due to the sound law called the "second palatalization," which we will return to in section 11.7. Reflexes of the second palatalization is mostly found before /ě/, but occur before /i/ in two important morphological forms, namely the masculine plural of ŏ-declension nouns (cf. section 4.2.1) and the imperative, as we have just seen. In Contemporary Standard Russian, due to analogy these consonant alternations have disappeared both in plural forms of nouns and in the imperative forms of verbs; today, the imperative of печь is пеки(те), while жечь has the imperative жги(те).

Дати 'give' and ѣсти 'eat' illustrate the imperative of athematic verbs. As can be seen from Table 45, the relevant forms have undergone a number of changes. The Old Rusian imperatives of дати in Table 45 have been replaced by дай and дайте in Modern Russian; these forms are created by analogy to verbs in class III such as знати 'know'. The modern imperatives ешь and ешьте are continuations of the corresponding Old Rusian forms ежь and ежьте. The change from ж to ш reflects a sound law called "devoicing," which took place after the jer (ь) was no longer pronounced. We will return to this sound law in section 12.3.4.

8.7. The Subjunctive

As we have seen, in Old Rusian the *l*-participle combined with the present tense of быти was used to form the perfect, while an imperfect or perfect of быти was used to form the pluperfect. The aorist also combined with the *l*-participle. This combination yielded the subjunctive:

(22) The Old Rusian subjunctive:

Aorist of быти + *l*-participle in the nominative

Here is an example from Vladimir Monomax's *Poučenie*:

(23) a. Аще **бы** тогда свою волю **створилъ**, и Муромъ **налѣзлъ**, а Ростова **бы** не **заималъ**, а **послалъ** ко мнѣ, отсюда ся **быхом уладили**. (Monomax)

b. Если **бы** тогда ты свою волю **сотворил** и Муром **добыл**, а Ростова **бы** не **занимал** и **послал бы** ко мне, то мы бы отсюда и **уладились**.

c. If in that case you **had done** as you wanted and **taken** Murom and not **occupied** Rostov and **sent** for me, then we **would have made peace** from that time on.

As shown in (23a), the subjunctive described hypothetical events. In Modern Russian the construction with the particle бы and a past-tense form of the verb is used for this purpose, as can be seen from (23b). The modern construction is a direct continuation of the Old Rusian subjunctive; the third person singular aorist бы has been reanalyzed as an uninflected particle, while the *l*-participle has been reanalyzed as a finite past-tense form.

8.8. The Participles

Participles are adjectival forms of verbs. Contemporary Standard Russian has four participles:

(24) a. Present active participle, e.g., **читающий**
b. Present passive participle, e.g., **читаемый**
c. Past active participle, e.g., **(про)читавший**
d. Past passive participle, e.g., **прочитан(ный)**

All these participles existed in Common Slavic and Old Rusian, but in addition Common Slavic and Old Rusian had a fifth participle, the *l*-participle, which was used in the pluperfect, the (present) perfect, and the future perfect, as well as the subjunctive. As we have seen, the *l*-participle has undergone reanalysis and become a finite past-tense form, so although the form itself has survived in Modern Russian, we cannot include it in the list of participles.

In the following, you will learn about the structure of the participles and the participle suffixes (section 8.8.1), the agreement endings (8.8.2), and the development of participles and gerunds (8.8.3).

8.8.1. The Structure of Participles and the Participle Suffixes

Participles had the same structure in Common Slavic and Old Rusian as they have in Modern Russian:

(25) The structure of participles:
Stem + participle suffix + adjectival agreement ending

If we take a modern example such as the past passive participle **прочитана**, this form consists of the stem **прочита** followed by the participle suffix -**н**-, which in turn is followed by the adjectival agreement ending -**а**. The participle suffix tells us that we are dealing with a past passive participle, while the agreement ending carries the features "singular," "feminine," and "nominative."

Table 46 on p. 158 displays the Old Rusian participle suffixes. Notice that like in Modern Russian there are two allomorphs (variants that occur in different environments) for the past active participle. After vowels, -**въш**- was used, while -**ъш**- occured after consonants. This resembles the situation in Contemporary Standard Russian, as shown by forms such as **прочитавший** (with vowel-final stem) and **принесший** (with a consonant in stem-final position). The past passive participle also had two allomorphs, -**н**- and -**т**-, and this situation has been preserved to this day (cf. **унесен** 'carried away' vs. **взят** 'taken'). In Contemporary Standard Russian, the -**л**- suffix is omitted in the masculine singular if the stem ends in a consonant. In other words, the past tense of **нести** is **нёс**, not "**нёсл**." In Old Rusian, on the other hand, the masculine singular form always kept the -**л**- suffix, as in **неслъ**.

Table 46. The participle suffixes in Old Rusian

	Participle suffix		Example (N sg feminine)
Present active:	-ч-		несучи, хвалячи
Past active:	-въш-	(after vowel)	знавъши
	-ъш-	(after consonant)	несъши
Present passive:	-м-		несома, хвалима
Past passive:	-т-	(after rounded V or monosyllabic stem)	взята
	-н-	(elsewhere)	несена
l-participle:	-л-		несла

8.8.2. The Agreement Endings

An adjectival agreement ending followed the participle suffix. In the same way as for adjectives, masculine and neuter forms have the endings of the ŏ-declension, while ā-declension endings were used in the feminine gender. The present and past active and passive participles were attested as both short and long forms; the long forms are created in the same way as the corresponding forms of adjectives. However, *l*-participles are only attested as short forms, and were only used in the nominative.

Table 47 provides an overview of the nominative short forms in the singular and the plural of all five participles. For the present and past active participles, the nominative singular has unexpected forms, as shown in the shaded cells in the table:

(26) a. Masculine and neuter singular of present active participle: **неса** (**нося**)

      b. Masculine and neuter singular of past active participle: **несъ**

      c. Feminine singular of present and past active participle has the ending -**и** (**несучи, несъши**)[3]

In addition to **неса** and the more recent variant **нося** you may encounter Old Church Slavonic forms in -**ы**, such as **несы**.

---

[3] As you saw in section 6.4, the feminine nominative ending -**и** is also attested in comparative forms of adjectives.

Table 47. The agreement endings of Old Rusian participle (nominative short forms)

		Masculine	Feminine	Neuter
Present active:	sg.	неса (неся)	несучи	неса (неся)
	pl.	несуче	несучѣ	несуча
Past active:	sg.	несъ	несъши	несъ
	pl.	несъше	несъшѣ	несъша
Present passive:	sg.	несомъ	несома	несомо
	pl.	несоми	несомы	несома
Past passive:	sg.	несенъ	несена	несено
	pl.	несени	несены	несена
l-participle:	sg.	неслъ	несла	несло
	pl.	несли	неслы	несла

8.8.3. The Development of Participles and Gerunds

In Contemporary Standard Russian, active participles generally do not have short forms. (Exceptions are forms such as **блестяще** 'outstanding', which are used as adverbs.) Although the short forms of the Old Rusian active participles were lost, they did not disappear without leaving traces behind. Contemporary Standard Russian has two gerunds ("adverbial participles" or "converbs") that have developed from short forms of active participles. Modern imperfective gerunds like **неся** 'carrying' go back to masculine/neuter short forms of present active participles such as Old Rusian **неся**. Modern perfective gerunds like **похвалив** 'having praised' are, historically speaking, masculine/neuter short forms of Old Rusian past active participles, such as **хваливъ**. The feminine short form of the Old Rusian present active participle has survived in the irregular gerunds **будучи** and **едучи** from **быть** 'be' and **ехать** 'drive'. Over time, these participles have lost agreement with nouns and have become gerunds.

The Old Rusian participle suffixes resemble their modern counterparts closely, as can be seen from Table 46 in section 8.8.1. However, one important difference deserves mention. The Old Rusian present active participle had the suffix -ч-, while the corresponding participles in Modern Russian have -щ- as in **несущий** 'carrying' and **хвалящий** 'praising'. The modern participles are due to Church Slavic influence. We find the expected -ч- in forms such as **летучий** 'flying', which have become adjectives. In Modern Russian, 'bat' is **летучая мышь** (literally 'flying mouse'). The contrast between participles and adjectives is clear in pairs such as **горящий** 'burning' (a participle with the

Church Slavic -щ-) and **горячий** 'hot' (an adjective which has inherited the Old Rusian -ч-).

8.9. Summary

Table 48 compares the inventories of verb forms in Old Rusian and Contemporary Standard Russian. While the differences are not large, the following observations can be made. First, Modern Russian has lost the supine. Second, the number of tense forms (past, present, and future) has decreased. Third, the number of participles has been reduced due to the reanalysis of the *l*-participle as a finite past-tense form. Fourth, the category of gerunds has emerged in Modern Russian from participles that have lost agreement.

Table 48. The inventories of verb forms in Old Rusian and Contemporary Standard Russian

	Old Rusian	Contemporary Standard Russian
Infinitive	1	1
Supine	1	0
Present tense	1	1
Past tense	4	1
Future tense	2	1
Imperative	1	1
Subjunctive	1	1
Participle	5	4
Gerund	0	2

The fate of the past-, present-, and future-tense forms are of particular interest, since they shed light on the relationship between tense and aspect. The table lists four past-tense forms (aorist, imperfect, perfect, and pluperfect), but as pointed out in sections 8.3.6 and 8.5, the perfect may also be classified as a present-tense form. In any case, the number of tense forms has decreased. Importantly, however, this does not mean that the number of tenses has decreased. Rather than tense loss we have witnessed aspect loss. The aspectual distinction between aorist and imperfect was lost early, and the distinction between actual and perfect has also been lost. The imperfective-perfective distinction, alternatively, has expanded to new classes of verbs over time.

The following templates make it easier for you to identify the verb forms:

(27) a. Infinitive (section 8.1): Stem + **ти**

b. Supine (8.1): Stem + **тъ**

c. Present tense (8.2): Stem + (consonant) + (theme vowel) + present-tense ending

d. Aorist (8.3.1): Stem + aorist ending

e. Imperfect (8.3.2): Stem + imperfect suffix **я** + imperfect ending

f. Perfect (8.3.3): Present tense of **быти** + *l*-participle

g. Pluperfect (8.3.4):

   i. Imperfect of **быти** + *l*-participle

   ii. Perfect of **быти** + *l*-participle

h. Future (8.4):

   i. **Почати/начати** + imperfective infintive (Old Rusian)

   ii. Future of **быти** + imperfective infinitive (Middle Russian)

i. Future perfect (8.4): Future of **быти** + *l*-participle

j. Imperative (8.6): Stem + **ѣ/и** + present-tense ending

k. Subjunctive (8.7): Aorist of **быти** + *l*-participle

l. Present active participle (8.8.1): Stem + **ч** + adjectival agreement ending

m. Present passive participle (8.8.1): Stem + **м** + adjectival agreement ending

n. Past active participle (8.8.1): Stem + **въш/ъш** + adjectival agreement ending

o. Past passive participle (8.8.1): Stem + **н/т** + adjectival agreement ending

q. *l*-participle (8.8.1): Stem + **л** + adjectival agreement ending

The historical development of verbs has shown a number of general principles at work. You have seen that the verbs have been affected by both sound laws and analogy. Grammaticalization is relevant for the development of the periphrastic future. Another principle is reanalysis, i.e., what happens when an entity changes its meaning, but not its form. As we have seen, the Common Slavic and Old Rusian *l*-participle has survived, but has undergone reanalysis, since it is no longer a participle in Contemporary Standard Russian.

8.10. For Further Reading

You will find thorough discussions of the verb system in Old Rusian and its historical development in all historical grammars. Good presentations in Russian are Gorškova and Xaburgaev 1981 and Ivanov 1983. Andersen (2006 and 2009) offers interesting analyses of the development of periphrastic future forms across Slavic.

Chapter 9   Syntax

In this chapter you will learn about the structure of sentences in Old Rusian. We will focus on case usage (sections 9.1–9.6), important syntactic constructions (sections 9.7–9.9), as well as agreement, clitics, and complex sentences (sections 9.10–9.12). As you read along, you will gain a better understanding of Modern Russian too. You will see that modern adverbs such as **домой** 'homewards', **сегодня** 'today', and **вчера** 'yesterday' are relics of Old Rusian syntactic constructions. Among the curious facts explained in this chapter is also why **ся** is always attached to the end of the verb in Modern Russian.

9.1. Subject

As in Contemporary Standard Russian, the subject in Old Rusian sentences is normally in the nominative case:

(1) a. И **Всеславъ** Смолнескъ ожьже.   (Monomax)
    b. И **Всеслав** Смоленск пожег.
    c. And **Vseslav** set Smolensk on fire.

A difference between Modern Russian and Old Rusian is that in Old Rusian personal pronouns are normally omitted as the subject of the sentence. As you can see from the following example, there is no pronoun in (2a) that corresponds to the subject **он** 'he' in the Modern Russian sentence (2b):

(2) a. И Стародубу идохом на Олга, зане ся бяше приложилъ к половцем.   (Monomax)
    b. И к Стародубу ходили на Олега, потому что **он** сдружился с половцами.
    c. And we went against Oleg in Starodub, because **he** had been on friendly terms with the Polovtsians.

Linguists often refer to the omission of pronouns as "pro-drop." Pro-drop is the rule not only in the third person, but also in the first and second persons:

(3) a. Послушахъ сына своего, написахъ ти грамоту: аще ю приимеши с добромь, ли с поруганьемь, свое же узрю на твоемъ писаньи.
(Monomax)

b. Послушал **я** сына своего, написал тебе грамоту: примешь **ли ты** ее по-доброму или с поруганием, то и другое увижу из твоей грамоты.

c. **I** have listened to my son and written this letter to you: Whether **you** will receive it in good faith or not, I will see from your letter.

Although it is customary to say that Old Rusian was a pro-drop language, while Contemporary Standard Russian is not, it is worth pointing out that personal pronouns are sometimes omitted in Modern Russian too. For instance, **увижу** '(I) will see' in (3b) does not have a subject. In Old Rusian, the personal pronoun was *not* omitted if there was contrast between two subjects. This is the case in the following sentence, where there is a contrast between **мы** 'we' and **ты** 'you':

(4) a. Оже ли не поидеши с нами, то **мы** собѣ будемъ, а **ты** собѣ.
(Monomax)

b. Если же не пойдёшь с нами, то **мы** — сами по себе будем, а **ты** — сам по себе.

c. If you don't join us, then **we** will be on one side and **you** on the other.

9.2. Object

As in Contemporary Standard Russian, the direct object (**Менескъ** 'Minsk') is normally in the accusative, while the indirect object (**ему** 'to him') is in the dative:

(5) a. Володимеръ […] вдасть **ему Менескъ**. (PVL: 1116 AD)

b. Владимир […] дал **ему Минск**.

c. Vladimir […] gave **him Minsk**.

When a verb is negated, its object is in the genitive. As shown in the following example, this rule is relevant for both Old Rusian and Contemporary Standard Russian, since in both (6a) and (6b) the genitive form **дани** 'tribute' is the object. However, while in Common Slavic and Old Rusian the genitive for the object of a negated verb was (almost) obligatory, the use of the accusative has become increasingly more widespread from the seventeenth century (Borkovskij 1978: 347 and Krasovitsky et al. 2011: 574).

(6) a. И изгнаша варягы за море, и не даша имъ **дани**.
    (PVL 862 AD; 19,14)
  b. И изгнали варягов за море, и не дали им **дани**.
  c. And they drove the Varangians back beyond the sea and did not give them **tribute**.

There are some differences between Old Rusian and Contemporary Standard Russian with regard to the case of the object. First of all, nouns in the *ā*-declension sometimes occur in the nominative as objects of infinitives. In the following sentence, for instance, **гривна** (a monetary unit) is in the nominative, although it is the object of the infinitive **взяти** 'take':

(7) a. Ярославъ былъ уставилъ убити и, но сынове его по отци уставиша на куны, любо бити и розвязавше, любо ли взяти **гривна** кунъ за соромъ. (RPP)
  b. Ярослав постановил его убить, но сыновья после смерти отца постановили выкуп деньгами, либо бить его, развязав, либо взять **гривну** кун за оскорбление.
  c. Jaroslav had instructed that he should be killed, but after their father's death the sons instructed that a ransom should be paid, or that he should be beaten after his release, or that a **grivna** should be taken for the insult.

The infinitive + nominative object construction has survived in northern Russian dialects to this day. Notice that the construction is not consistently attested; you will also encounter accusative forms as objects of infinitives.

A second difference between Old Rusian and Modern Russian concerns verbs of cognition, speaking, and perception. In Old Rusian, these verbs are frequently attested with a direct object in the accusative where Modern Russian would use the preposition **о** + the locative case. The following example illustrates this; here Old Rusian has **слышавъ вълъхвы** 'having heard about the sorcerers', whereas in Modern Russian one must say **услышав о волхвах**:

(8) a. Слышавъ же Ярославъ **вълъхвы** ты, и приде к Суждалю.
    (PVL 1024 AD; 147,29)
  b. Ярослав же, услышав о **волхвах**, пришел в Суздаль.

(8) c. Having heard about the **sorcerers**, Jaroslav came to Suzdal'.

A final difference between Old Rusian and Modern Russian concerns the supine. Recall from section 8.1 that this verb form only occurred as the object of a verb of motion. Although the supine was in the process of being replaced by the infinitive in Old Rusian, there are some examples showing that the supine governed the genitive case:

(9) a. Посла Олегъ мужи свои построитъ **мира**.   (PVL 912 AD; 32,24)

    b. Послал Олег мужей своих заключить **мир**.

    c. Oleg sent his men to arrange **peace**.

Notice that in this example some versions of the *Primary Chronicle* have **построити мира** with the infinitive instead of the supine (cf. Ostrowski 2003: 186). This shows that sometimes an infinitive that has replaced an older supine still takes a genitive object. In general, however, the infinitive does not require the genitive.

9.3. Predicative Nouns and Adjectives

Characteristic of Modern Russian is the competition between the nominative and instrumental for predicative nouns and adjectives. Reading Modern Russian texts you may come across examples like **он был студент** 'he was a student' with the predicative noun **студент** 'student' in the nominative, but you will also find sentences of the type **он был студентом** with the predicative noun in the instrumental. Likewise, for predicative adjectives both nominative (e.g., **звук был приятный** 'the sound was pleasant') and instrumental (e.g., **звук был приятным**) are possible.

    The competition between the nominative and the instrumental cases for predicative nouns and adjectives is the result of a long historical development whereby the instrumental case has gradually been ousting the nominative. In Old Rusian, the nominative was the rule for both predicative nouns and adjectives. In the following description of Prince Vladimir "the Holy," for instance, we first learn that he was **несытъ** 'insatiable' (an adjective in the nominative), and then that he was **женолюбець** 'womanizer' (a noun in the nominative):

(10) a. И бѣ **несытъ** блуда, и приводя к себѣ мужьскыя жены и дѣвици растляя. Бѣ бо **женолюбець**, яко и Соломонъ.

                                                                                 (PVL 980 AD; 80,9)

(10) b. И **был** он **ненасытен** в блуде, приводя к себе замужних женщин и растлевая девиц. **Был** он такой же **женолюбец**, как и Соломон.

c. He **was insatiable** in vice. He even seduced married women and violated young girls, for he **was a womanizer** like Solomon.

Old Rusian examples with predicative nouns in the instrumental are relatively few and far between, but they do exist:

(11) a. И у Ярополка жена **грѣкини** бѣ, и бяше была **черницею**.
(PVL 977 AD; 75,13)

b. У Ярополка же была жена **гречанка**, а перед тем была она **монахиней**.

c. Now Jaropolk had a **Greek** wife who had been a **nun**.

This sentence is interesting because it juxtaposes a predicative noun in the nominative (**грѣкини** 'Greek woman') to a predicative noun in the instrumental (**черницею** 'nun').[1] The nominative is used about a permanent property (the wife's nationality), while the noun in the instrumental denotes a temporary property (she was a nun only for a while). One may speculate that the spread of the instrumental started with temporary properties, since even in Modern Russian the nominative is the preferred case for nationalities and other permanent properties, as shown in the modern translation in (11b) (see Borkovskij and Kuznecov 1963: 335).

Predicative adjectives in the instrumental represent a more recent innovation. According to Borkovskij and Kuznecov (1963: 338), this construction is attested from the seventeenth century.

The predicative nouns and adjectives we have considered so far describe the subjects of the sentences, but there are also constructions where the predicative noun or adjective describes the grammatical object. In the following sentence, for instance, the predicative noun **епископъ** 'bishop' describes **Анфилохыи** (a person's name), who is the grammatical object of the sentence.

---

[1] Notice that **грѣкини** 'Greek woman' belongs to a small class of nouns in the $\bar{a}$-declension that have the ending -**и** in the nominative singular. As you saw in sections 6.4 and 8.8.2, this ending is also attested in comparative forms of adjectives and active participles.

(12) a. В се же лѣто постави митрополитъ Анфилохыя **епископа** Володимерю. (PVL 1105 AD; 280,28)

b. В том же году поставил митрополит **епископом** Амфилохия во Владимир.

c. In the same year the Metropolitan appointed Amphilochius as **Bishop** of Vladimir.

As shown by this example, in Old Rusian the predicative noun or adjective was in the accusative when they described an accusative object. In Contemporary Standard Russian, in contrast, the instrumental has taken over, as indicated in the Modern Russian translation which has the instrumental form **епископом**. The spread of the instrumental started early, so you can come across Old Rusian examples like the following with the predicative noun in the instrumental:

(13) a. Постави Ярославъ Лариона **митрополитомъ** Руси въ святѣй Софьи, собравъ епископы. (PVL 1051 AD; 155,26)

b. Поставил Ярослав Илариона русским **митрополитом** в святой Софии, собрав епископов.

c. Jaroslav, after assembling the bishops, appointed Hilarion **Metropolitan** of Rus' in St. Sophia.

When the verb is negated and the object is in the genitive, the predicative noun or adjective also occurs in the genitive. Old Rusian examples of this type are not numerous, but they do exist:

(14) a. И не заста отца **живого**. (KL 1164 AD)

b. И он не застал отца **живым**.

c. And he did not find his father **alive**.

In this sentence, we have the genitive form **живого** of the predicative adjective in Old Rusian, whereas the Modern Russian translation uses the instrumental case.

9.4. Adverbials: Space

Like Modern Russian, Old Rusian often used prepositional phrases to specify where an event took place and to express other relations between events and places. Characteristic of both Old Rusian and Contemporary Standard Russian is a set of prepositions that take locative or instrumental case to indicate the location of an event (the answer to a question with **где?** 'where?'), but combine with the accusative to express movement towards a goal (the answer to a question with **куда?** 'where to?'). The relevant Old Rusian prepositions are listed in Table 49.

Table 49. Prepositions for location vs. goal in Old Rusian

Preposition	Gloss	Location	Goal
въ	'in(to)'	Locative	Accusative
на	'on(to)'	Locative	Accusative
за	'behind'	Instrumental	Accusative
передъ/прѣдъ	'in front of'	Instrumental	Accusative (Instrumental)
подъ	'under'	Instrumental	Accusative
надъ	'over'	Instrumental	Accusative (Instrumental)

The prepositions that govern the instrumental and accusative cases are of particular interest. In Modern Russian, **за** 'behind' and **под** 'under' take the accusative or instrumental, while **перед** 'in front of' and **над** 'over' only combine with the instrumental. In Old Rusian, however, all four took both cases, as indicated in Table 49. Here is an example that illustrates the use of Old Rusian **передъ (прѣдъ/предъ)** 'in front of' with the accusative:

(15) a. И възлозъше на вариманътью, вынесоша **предъ пещеру**.
(PVL 1091 AD; 211,11)

b. И, положив его на мантию, вынесли его **перед пещерой**.

c. They laid him in a cloak and carried him out **in front of the crypt**.

A more complicated example with Old Rusian **надъ** 'over' describes a "fiery pillar" appearing in the sky:

(16) a. [Столпъ огненъ] ста на тряпезници камянѣй, яко не видити хреста бяше, и стоя мало, ступи на церковь и ста **надъ гробомъ Федосьевомъ**, и потомъ **надъ верхъ** сступи.
(PVL 1110 AD; 284,10)

b. [Столп огненный] стал над трапезной каменной, так что не видно было креста, и, постояв немного, перешел на церковь, и стал **над гробом Феодосьевым**, и потом перешел **на верх** церкви.

(16) c. [The fiery pillar] stood over the stone refectory, so that its cross could not be seen. Then it stayed for a while, moved to the church, and halted **over the tomb of Theodosius**. Then it placed itself **on top of** the church.

As you can see, **надъ** first combines with a noun phrase in the instrumental (**гробомъ Федосьевомъ** 'the tomb of Theodosius'), and then with a noun phrase in the accusative (**верхъ** 'the top (of the church)'), although in both cases we are dealing with movement into a location (goal). This illustrates that the instrumental started ousting the accusative at an early time after **передъ** (**прѣдъ/предъ**) 'in front of' and **надъ** 'over'. This is why for these prepositions "instrumental" is given in parentheses in the rightmost column of Table 49. While the process of ousting the accusative started early, examples with the accusative are attested as late as the 18th century (for examples, see Mikhaylov 2012: 215–20).

In spatial adverbials, the use of the prepositions **въ** 'in(to)' and **на** 'on(to)' closely resembles Modern Russian. However, the **въ** + locative construction competed with the bare locative, i.e., a noun phrase in the locative without a preposition:

(17) a. Володимеръ Мономахъ сѣде **Киевѣ** в недѣлю. (PVL 1113 AD)

b. Владимир Мономах сел **в Киеве** в воскресенье.

c. Vladimir Monomax took his place **in Kiev** on a Sunday.

Although according to Toporov (1961: 10; see also Pavlova 1977, 197ff.), the use of the bare locative was still a "living phenomenon" ("**живое явление**") in Old Rusian it was gradually replaced by the **въ** + locative construction. The bare locative was used longer with place names than with common nouns, and names of large and well-known towns such as Kiev were most resilient to change (Pavlova 1977: 200f.).

In combination with a verb of motion, the bare dative sometimes describes the goal of motion:

(18) a. Прочии же идоша **Цесарюграду**. (PVL 980; 79,5)

b. Остальные же отправились **в Царьград**.

c. The others departed **for Tsar'grad** (Constantinople).

This construction has been replaced by prepositional phrases in Modern Russian. However, the adverb **домой** 'homeward' goes back to Old Rusian **домови**, the dative singular of the *ŭ*-declension noun **домъ** 'house'.

A further difference in the expression of the goal of motion concerns motion verbs with the prefix до. While in Modern Russian such verbs require a prepositional phrase with до + genitive, in Old Rusian we find examples with the bare genitive:

(19) a. И дошедше Воиня, воротишася. (PVL 1110 AD; 284,4)
 b. И, дойдя до Воиня, возвратились.
 c. And after **reaching Voin'** they returned.

The bare genitive was also used to express the source of motion:

(20) a. Се азъ **отхожю свѣта** сего. (PVL 1054 AD; 161,3)
 b. Вот я **покидаю мир** этот.
 c. I am about to **quit** this **world**.

In Modern Russian, motion verbs with the prefix от combine with prepositional phrases with the preposition от 'from' (e.g., отходить от окна 'walk away from the window').

9.5. Adverbials: Time

In Contemporary Standard Russian, the preposition в 'in(to)' is used to specify when an event takes place. In response to a question with когда? 'when?', you may encounter answers such as в двадцатом веке 'in the twentieth century', в этом году 'in this year', в январе 'in January', во вторник 'on Tuesday', в тот день 'on that day', в эту минуту 'in this minute', etc. Notice that в combines with the locative for time spans longer than a week, while shorter time spans are in the accusative case. (For неделя 'week', Modern Russian uses the preposition на followed by the locative case, e.g., на прошлой неделе 'last week'.)

In Old Rusian, the въ + accusative construction was very frequent, and it was not restricted to time spans shorter than a week. In the chronicles, for instance, the description of each year begins with въ + a number in the accusative representing the year (counted from God's creation of the world; see section 2.3.2):

(21) a. **В лѣто 6415**. Иде Олегъ на Грѣкы, Игоря оставивъ Кыевѣ.
 (PVL 907 AD; 29,19)
 b. **В год 6415** (907). Пошел Олег на греков, оставив Игоря в Киеве.

(21) c. **In the year 6415** (907). Oleg attacked the Greeks, having left Igor' in Kiev.

The **въ** + accusative construction also occurs in examples of the following type where the year has been mentioned before:

(22) a. **В се же лѣто** родися Святославъ у Игоря.   (PVL 942 AD; 45,12)

b. **В том же году** родился Святослав у Игоря.

c. **In the same year** Svjatoslav was born to Igor'.

The **въ** + locative construction, which is used in Modern Russian, is only marginally attested in *Povest' vremennyx let*, but the bare locative, i.e., the locative case without a preposition, occurs frequently:

(23) a. **Семъ же лѣтѣ** и вятичи побѣди.   (PVL 981 AD; 81,29)

b. **В том же году** он победил и вятичей.

c. **In the same year**, he conquered the Vjatiči too.

Yet another competing construction is the bare genitive:

(24) a. **Того же лѣта** заложи Володимеръ Мономахъ городъ на Въстри.   (PVL 1098 AD; 273,9a)

b. **В том же году** заложил Владимир Мономах крепость на Востри.

c. **In the same year**, Vladimir Monomax founded a castle on the Vostr'.

The bare genitive construction was particularly frequent in the combination with the demonstrative pronouns **сь** and **тъ**, but in the words of Grannes (1986: 60) made a "swift decline" in the in the 18th century and is mostly used for dates in Modern Russian (e.g., **это случилось первого апреля** 'this happened on the first of April'). However, the adverbs **сегодня** 'today' (from **сего дьня** 'this day' in the genitive) and **вчера** 'yesterday' (from the genitive form of **вечеръ** 'evening') represent "fossilized" genitives, i.e., genitive phrases that have become adverbs and are no longer analyzed as genitive forms.

The preceding examples all involve **лѣто** 'year', but the constructions discussed above are not restricted to this noun. A construction we have not considered so far is the bare instrumental, which in Modern Russian is used for day parts (**утром** 'in the morning', **днем** 'during daytime', **вечером** 'in the evening', and **ночью** 'in the night') and seasons (**весной** 'in the spring', **летом** 'in the summer', **осенью** 'in the fall', and **зимой** 'in the winter'). Since day parts and seasons relate to the diurnal and annual cycles of the sun, we can refer to them as "cyclic time spans." How did cyclic time spans behave in Old Rusian? While the bare instrumental construction is attested (Schmalstieg 1995: 168), these nouns also frequently occurred in the **въ** + accusative construction, and also the bare locative. The bare locative was used as late as in the 16th century, as can be seen from the following example from *Domostroj*:

(25) a. И тѣ суды **зимѣ** в лед засекати. (Dom)

b. И все то в посуде **зимой** льдом завалить.

c. And all in this vessel should be sprinkled with ice **in the wintertime**.

The bare accusative is also sometimes used to indicate that an event took place within a cyclic time span:

(26) a. Азъ **утро** пошлю по вы. (PVL 945 AD; 56,11)

b. **Утром** я пошлю за вами.

c. I shall send for you **in the morning**.

However, a more important function of the bare accusative is to describe the duration (**как долго?** 'for how long?') and frequency of events (**как часто?** 'how often?'). These functions have been preserved in Contemporary Standard Russian, as illustrated by the following example where the bare accusative describes the duration of the event in both Old Rusian and Modern Russian:

(27) a. И ту моляше Бога беспрестани **день и нощь** со слезами.
(PVL 1074 AD; 192,8)

b. И там молил Бога со слезами непрестанно **день и ночь**.

c. And there he prayed to God with tears without stopping, **day and night**.

As in Modern Russian, **на** + accusative was used in temporal adverbials involving ordinal numbers:

(28) a. И кончана бысть **на третьее лѣто** мѣсяца июля въ 1 день.
(PVL 1075 AD; 198,19)

b. И окончена была она **на третий год**, месяца июля в 1-й день.

(28) c. And it was completed on July 1 of **the third year**.

The **на** + accusative construction was also used with church holidays, as it still is:

(29) a. Приходи Ярополкъ ко Всеволоду **на Великъ день**.
                                                            (PVL 1084 AD; 205,8)
      b. Приходил Ярополк к Всеволоду **на Пасху**.
      c. Jaropolk came to visit Vsevolod **on Easter Day**.

In Modern Russian, **на** combines with **неделя** 'week' (e.g., **на прошлой неделе** 'last week'). The original primary meaning of **неделя** was 'Sunday', i.e., the 'day for rest' (cf. **не** 'not' and **дело** 'activity'), and the meanings 'Sunday' and 'week' coexisted in Old Rusian until **воскресение/воскресенье** 'resurrection' replaced **неделя** as the word for 'Sunday' in the fifteenth century (Flier 1984: 146; see also Flier 1985). One may speculate that the reason why **неделя** in Contemporary Standard Russian combines with **на** in Modern Russian is the fact that it originally meant 'Sunday', since Sundays are related to the Church holidays that took **на** in Old Rusian.

Table 50. Major constructions for temporal adverbials in Old Rusian

Construction	Type	Comment
Въ + accusative	Point	The most frequent construction, occurring with a wide variety of time spans (also longer than a week)
Bare locative	Point	A frequent construction, also with cyclic time spans
Bare genitive	Point	A frequent construction, especially with demonstrative pronouns
Bare accusative	Point Duration Frequency	Occurs with cyclic time spans
На + accusative	Point	Occurs with ordinal numerals and Church holidays

The major constructions explored above are summarized in Table 50. In the middle column I distinguish between three types of temporal adverbials. The adverbials labeled as "point" answer questions in **когда?** 'when?', while "duration" and "frequency" refer to questions in **как долго?** 'for how long' and **как часто?** 'how often?', respectively. The rightmost column provides information about frequency and what kinds of time spans the relevant construction combines with.

9.6. Overview of Old Rusian Prepositions. Preposition Repetition

In the two previous sections you have learned about a number of constructions with prepositions. Table 51 on p. 176 provides an overview of the major prepositions in Old Rusian and the cases they govern. Examples for each preposition are given as well.

A phenomenon that sets Old Rusian apart from Modern Russian is "preposition repetition," "the multiple occurrence of prepositions in constructions that in Modern Standard Russian would normally take only one" (Klenin 1989: 185). Consider the following example where Old Rusian **на словены на дунайскые** (with two occurrences of **на**) corresponds to **на славян дунайских** (where **на** is not repeated) in the Modern Russian translation:

(30) a. Волохомъ бо нашедшим **на словены на дунайскые**, и сѣдшимъ в нихъ и насиляющимъ имъ. (PVL no date; 6,7)

b. Когда волохи напали **на славян дунайских**, то поселились среди них, и стали притеснять их.

c. When the Voloxi attacked **the Danube Slavs**, they settled among them and started oppressing them.

It is belived that preposition repetition was characteristic of the spoken language in Rus', since the phenomenon is very widespread in birch bark letters and other texts that display little influence from Church Slavic, but is rare in chronicles and especially in religious texts. Notice that preposition repetition does not indicate emphasis (Worth 1982, Zaliznjak 2004: 164); there is no particular emphasis on the adjective **дунайскые** in (30). In the example, the adjective follows after the noun it modifies, **словены**. This is no coincidence, since preposition repetition is most widely attested in phrases where a noun is followed by a modifying adjective, pronoun, or noun (Zaliznjak 2004: 164–66).

9.7. Possessive Constructions

In order to express possession in Modern Russian you may use the following constructions:

Table 51. Major Old Rusian prepositions (A = accusative, D = dative, G = genitive, I = instrumental, L = locative)

Preposition	Case	Example
Безъ	G	безъ тебе 'without you'
Близъ	G	близь тебе 'close to you'
Въ	A & L	въ Смолиньскѣ 'in Smolensk'
Възлѣ	G & A	возлѣ горы 'near the mountain'
До	G	до Рима 'to Rome'
За	A & I	за олътаремь 'behind the altar'
Изъ	G	изъ города 'from the city'
Кромѣ	G	кромѣ двою брату 'without two brothers'
Къ	D	къ Святославу 'to Svjatoslav'
Межи/межъ/между/межу	G & I	межи Асура и Вавилона 'between Assyria and Babylon'
Мимо	G & A	мимо Киевъ 'past Kiev'
На	A & L	на горѣ 'on the mountain'
Надъ	A & I	надъ городомь 'above the city'
О	A & L	о Бозѣ 'about God'
Около	G	около города 'near the city'
Опричь/опрочь	G	опричь бояръ 'except the boyars'
Отъ	G	отъ нихъ 'from them'
По	D, A & L	по празницѣ 'after the feast'
Подлѣ	G & A	подлѣ Волховъ 'close to the Volxov river'
Подъ	A & I	подъ горами 'under the mountains'
Послѣ	G	послѣ рати 'after the war'
При	L	при князѣ Мьстиславѣ 'under Prince Mstislav'
Про	A	про вѣру 'about faith'
Противу/противъ	G & D	противу Болеславу 'against Boleslav'
Прѣдъ/передъ	A & I	предъ пещерою 'in front of the cave'
Развѣ	G	развѣ Михаила 'apart from Michael'
Сквозѣ	A	сквозѣ страшно мѣсто 'through a dangerous place'
Съ	A, G & I	съ Игоремъ 'with Igor', съ креста 'from the cross'
У	G	у Смоленьска 'near Smolensk'
Черезъ	A	черезъ лѣсъ 'through the forest'

(31) Possessive constructions in Contemporary Standard Russian:
   a. Possessive genitive: комната мамы 'mom's room'
   b. Possessive adjective: мамина комната 'mom's room'

The most widespread option is the possessive genitive construction, where the possessor (the person the room belongs to, i.e., мама) is in the genitive. In the alternative construction in (31b), the possessor is a so-called possessive adjective formed by the addition of the suffix -ин- to the stem of the noun. The possessive adjective is in the same gender, number, and case as the noun it modifies, here комната 'room'. In Contemporary Standard Russian, possessive adjectives are mostly formed from second declension nouns in -а-/-я-, especially kinship terms such as мама 'mom' and person names such as Саша.

Both constructions in (31) existed in Old Rusian, but their distribution was different. While in Modern Russian the genitive construction is the most frequent way of expressing possession, in Old Rusian possessive adjectives were the most widely used option. There were three major suffixes:

(32) Possessive adjective suffixes in Old Rusian:
   a. -ин (from $\bar{a}$-declension nouns, e.g., Ольжинъ городъ 'Olga's city')
   b. -ов (from $\breve{o}$-declension nouns, e.g., солъ Игоревъ 'Igor's envoy')
   c. -j (from $\breve{o}$-declension nouns, e.g., мати Ярославля 'Jaroslav's mother')

The -j suffix in (32c) is cited in its Proto-Slavic form. Through a Common Slavic sound change called "j-palatalization," to which we return in section 11.6, the suffix merged with the stem-final consonant and produced possessive adjectives like Ярославль from the man's name Ярославъ. Notice that the name of the city Ярославль north-east of Moscow comes from the Old Rusian possessive adjective. In Old Rusian, the -ов suffix was gradually taking over for the older -j suffix as the main means of forming possessive adjectives from $\breve{o}$-declension nouns.

It is not simple to formulate rules for the choice between the possessive genitive construction and the possessive adjective construction. The following is a rule of thumb:

(33) Possessive adjective vs. possessive genitive in Old Rusian:
   a. If the possessor is one word, the possessive adjective construction is preferred.

(33) b. If the possessor consists of two or more words, the possessive genitive construction is preferred.

The following example illustrates the division of labor between the two constructions:

(34) a. От пѣрьваго лѣта **Михаила сего** до пѣрваго лѣта **Олгова рускаго князя**, лѣт 29, от пѣрваго лѣта **Олгова**, понелѣже сѣде в Киевѣ, до пѣрваго лѣта **Игорева** лѣто 31.   (PVL 852 AD; 18,11)

b. От первого года **Михайлова** до первого года княжения **Олега, русского князя**, 29 лет, от первого года княжения **Олега**, с тех пор как он сел в Киеве, до первого года **Игорева** 31 год.

c. Twenty-nine years passed between the first year **of Michael's reign** and the accession **of Oleg, Prince of Rus'**. From the accession **of Oleg,** when he took up residence in Kiev, to the first year of **Igor's reign**, thirty-one years elapsed.

In the first possessive construction, **пѣрьваго лѣта Михаила сего** '(literally) this Michael's first year', we find the genitive since the possessor consists of two words, **Михаила сего**. In the next possessive construction, **пѣрваго лѣта Олгова** we have the possessive adjective **Олгов** (**Ольговъ**), which is as expected since the possessor is a single noun (the name **Олегъ**). However, this possessor is extended with an apposition, **рускаго князя** 'Prince of Rus'', which is in the genitive, since it consists of two words. (An apposition is a noun phrase that gives an additional description of another noun phrase. In Modern Russian, the apposition is separated from the other noun phrase by means of commas, as shown in (34b)). In the two last possessive constructions in (34), we have single words as possessors, and as expected we find possessive adjectives: **Олгов** and **Игорев**. All the possessive adjectives in (34a) are in the genitive singular neuter, since they modify the genitive singular form of the neuter noun **лѣто** 'year'. While the passage in (34) illustrates the generalization in (33) neatly, it should be pointed out that (33) represents a tendency, rather than an absolute rule. In a large empirical study, Eckhoff (2011) notes that there are quite a few attestations of the possessive genitive even when the possessor is a single word.

A complicating factor is a third construction, the so-called possessive dative. In the following example, the *ŭ*-declension dative form **конєви** of **конь** 'horse' represents the possessor:

(35) a. И копье летѣвъ сквози уши **коневи** и удари в ногы **коневи**.
(PVL 946 AD; 58,5)

b. И копье пролетело между ушей **коня** и ударило **коня** по ногам.

c. But the spear barely cleared the **horse's** ears, and struck against **his** legs.

The possessive dative is used regardless of whether the possessor consists of one or several words. The construction is often considered a result of influence from South Slavic, and the possessive dative is most frequently attested in texts that show a high degree of Church Slavic influence.

Over time the possessive dative construction lost ground, and the genitive construction gradually took over for the possessive adjective construction. However, we are dealing with a slow development; Eckhoff (2011: 162ff.) shows that the possessive adjective construction is relatively frequent as late as in the seventeenth century. In Modern Russian, there is still some limited use of the possessive dative in expressions like **Платон мне друг, но истина дороже** 'Platon is my friend, but I value truth more', where the dative pronoun **мне** corresponds to the possessive *my* in English.

9.8. Passive Constructions

In the same way as in Modern Russian, Old Rusian had passive constructions with participles. Here is an example with the past passive participle **посланъ** from **послати** 'send':

(36) a. Нѣсть се Олегъ, но святый Дмитрий, **посланъ** на ны от Бога.
(PVL 907 AD; 30,19)

b. Это не Олег, но святой Дмитрий, **посланный** на нас **Богом**.

c. This is not Oleg, but St. Demetrius, **sent** upon us **by God**.

Notice that whereas the agent (the person who performs the action) is in the instrumental case without preposition in Modern Russian, the Old Rusian example has the preposition **от** (**отъ**) plus the genitive case. However, already in Old Rusian the bare instrumental was in the process of replacing **отъ** plus genitive, and there are numerous Old Rusian attestations of passive constructions with the agent in the bare instrumental case. Here is one such example:

(37) a. **Заложена** бысть церкви святаго Михаила Золотоверхая **Святополкомъ княземъ** мѣсяца июля въ 11.   (PVL 1090 AD)

b. **Заложена** была церковь святого Михаила Златоверхая **Святополком князем**, месяца июля 11-го.

c. Upon July 11, the Church of St. Michael with the golden tower was **founded by Prince Svjatopolk**.

If you want to form a passive construction with an imperfective verb in Modern Russian, you normally use -ся: Этот журнал читался всеми людьми театра 'This magazine was read by everybody in theater'. Passive constructions with ся existed in Old Rusian too, but they were not very frequent; according to Gorškova and Xaburgaev (1981: 283; see also Zarickij 1961: 107), only about 20–23% of the occurrences of ся involve passive constructions.

9.9. The Dative Absolute and Other Adverbial Constructions with Participles

A construction you will come across in texts that show some degree of Church Slavic influence is the so-called dative absolute. This construction consists of a participle in the dative case and a noun phrase in the dative, which represents the subject of the action denoted by the participle. Consider the following passage from *Povest' vremennyx let*:

(38) a. Иде Асколдъ и Диръ на Грѣкы, и приде въ 14 лѣто Михаила цесаря. **Цесарю** же **отшедъшю** на агаряны, и **дошедшю ему** Черное рѣкы, вѣсть епархъ посла ему, яко русь идеть на Цесарьград, и воротися цесарь.   (PVL 865 AD; 21,10)

b. Пошли Аскольд и Дир на греков и пришли к ним в четырнадцатый год царствования Михаила. **Цесарь** же **был** в это время в походе на агарян, **дошел** уже до Черной реки, когда епарх прислал ему весть, что Русь идет на Царьград, и возвратился цесарь.

c. Askold and Dir attacked the Greeks during the fourteenth year of the reign of the Emperor Michael. When **the emperor had set forth** against the Hagarites and **had arrived** at the Black River, the eparch sent him word that the Russes were approaching Tsar'grad (Constantinople), and the Emperor turned back.

The forms **отшедъшю** and **дошедшю** (**дошедъшю**) are past active participles in the dative singular masculine, and **Цесарю** and **ему**, also in the dative, represent the person who carried out the action, namely the Emperor. There is no corresponding construction in Modern Russian; the dative absolute can often be rendered with a **когда** 'when' clause, although the Modern Russian translation in (38b) has chosen a different solution.

The dative absolute resembles gerund constructions in Modern Russian, such as **прочитав газету, Ваня пошел на работу** 'having read the newspaper, Vanja went to work'. However, while modern gerunds have the same subject as the verb in the main clause (**Ваня**), dative absolute constructions normally do not share the subject with the main clause. Example (38a) illustrates this; the logical subject of the dative absolute construction (**цесарю/ему**) is different from that of the main clause (**епархъ**).

Other constructions with participles also resemble the use of gerunds in Modern Russian:

(39) a. И **въшедъ** на горы сиа, и благослови я, и постави крестъ.
(PVL no date; 8,10)

b. И **взойдя** на горы эти, благословил их и поставил крест.

c. **Having walked up** on these mountains, he blessed them and erected a cross.

The participial construction **въшедъ на горы сиа** 'having walked up on these mountains' is an adverbial that specifies what happened before the main events **благослови** 'blessed' and **постави** 'erected'. In adverbial constructions of this type, Modern Russian uses gerunds, as shown in (39b), where the translator has used the perfective gerund **взойдя**. Since, as you learned in section 8.8.3, Modern Russian gerunds have developed from participles, you may not be surprised to find participles in Old Rusian adverbial constructions of the type illustrated in (39a).

In (39a), the participle **въшедъ** is connected to the aorists **благослови** and **постави** with the conjunction **и** 'and'. This is a widespread pattern in Old Rusian, but impossible in Modern Russian. If you add **и** between **взойдя на горы эти** and **благословил** in (39b), the result is an ungrammatical sentence in Modern Russian.

9.10. Agreement

From Modern Russian you know that the verb in a sentence agrees with the subject of the sentence. If, for instance, the subject is the second person singular pronoun **ты** 'you', you must choose a second person singular form of the verb, e.g., **читаешь** '(you) read'. If you want to combine the adjective **новый** 'new' with **машина** 'car', you will have to use the feminine singular nominative form **новая**. This relationship between subject and verb and between noun and adjective is called "agreement." The Old Rusian agreement rules are very similar to the ones you have learned for Modern Russian, as illustrated by the following example:

(40) a. Аще **ты крестишися, вси имут** то же створити.
$\hspace{20em}$ (PVL 955 AD; 63,25)

    b. Если **ты крестишься**, то и **все сделают** то же.

    c. If **you are converted, all other subjects will do** the same.

Here we find agreement between **ты** and the second person singular verb form **крестишься** and between **вси** and the third person plural verb form **имут** (**имуть**)—exactly like in Modern Russian.

A difference between Old Rusian and Contemporary Standard Russian concerns subjects containing numerals. In Modern Russian, you can say both **пришло пять человек** and **пришли пять человек**, where the use of the singular emphasizes that the five persons constituted a homogeneous group, whereas the verb in the plural presents them as five individuals. There is no corresponding variation in Old Rusian. As you remember from chapter 7, strictly speaking Old Rusian did not have numerals as a separate part of speech, insofar as numbers from 1 to 4 were adjectives, while higher numbers were nouns. In the following example, the subject **двя варяга** 'two Varangians' is in the third person dual and so is the verb:

(41) a. **Подъяста и два варяга** мечема подъ пазусѣ.
$\hspace{20em}$ (PVL 980 AD; 78,12)

    b. **Два варяга подняли** его мечами под мышки.

    c. **Two Varangians lifted** him up with their swords under his armpits.

Since numbers from 5 and up are nouns in the singular, they agree with third person singular forms of verbs. Kiparsky (1967: 177) provides the following example from the *Novgorod Chronicle*, where the singular form **изоиде** (**изъиде**) is used:

(42) a. **Изоиде** та пять лѣтъ.

    b. **Прошли** те пять лет.

    c. **Those five** years **passed**.

While for numerals Modern Russian displays more variation than Old Rusian, the opposite is true for collective nouns, i.e., nouns in the singular such as дружина 'retinue' which denote groups of individuals. In Modern Russian, collectives combine with verbs in the singular, and you can encounter such examples in Old Rusian too. In the following sentence, дружина agrees with the third person singular aorist собрася 'gathered':

(43) a. Къ Мьстиславу **собрася дружина** въ тъ день и въ другий.
 (PVL 1096 AD; 239,8)
 b. К Мстиславу же **собралась дружина** в тот день и в другой.
 c. On that day and the next, Mstislav's **retinue rallied** about him.

However, quite often collectives take verbs in the plural like the third person plural present-tense form начнут (начнуть) 'begin' in the following example:

(44) a. А **дружина моя** сему смѣяти **начнут**. (PVL 955 AD; 63,23)
 b. А **дружина моя станет** насмехаться.
 c. My **retinue will** laugh at that.

The agreement pattern in (43) is sometimes referred to as "formal" or "syntactic" agreement, since дружина is a singular form (it has singular endings). The relationship between дружина and the plural form начнут (начнуть) in (44) is called "semantic agreement," since it is based on the meaning of дружина, which denotes several individuals (cf. Corbett 2000: 187). Example (44) is particularly interesting since it combines semantic agreement between subject and verb with formal agreement between дружина and the possessive pronoun моя 'my', which is a nominative feminine singular form. In sentences that combine formal and semantic agreement, it is always the verb that shows semantic agreement.

9.11. Clitics

In section 5.1, you learned that Old Rusian had short and unstressed forms of personal pronouns such as мя in addition to regular forms such as мене. The short and unstressed forms are clitics. In this section we will see that Old Rusian had a number of clitics. Understanding their behavior and historical development is important when you read Old Rusian texts.

Let us first get a better understanding of what a clitic is. It is helpful to consider the following two Modern Russian sentences with the clitic *ли*:

(45) a. Он спросил, готово **ли** всё. 'He asked if everything was ready.'
   b. Он спросил, всё **ли** готово. 'He asked if *everything* was ready.'

Готóво ли and **всё ли** are pronounced as one word (with one stress). In other words, **ли** is part of the first phonetic word in the subordinate clauses in (45). This makes **ли** similar to suffixes. However, it does not make sense to analyze **ли** as a suffix. Suffixes normally attach to words of a certain part of speech. For instance, nouns and verbs have very different suffixes in Russian. However, **ли** can attach to any part of speech. In (45) it is attached to an adjective and a pronoun, but it can also combine with nouns (**Иван ли готов?** 'Is Ivan ready?') and verbs (**Знает ли Иван?** 'Does Ivan know?'). Since **ли** is not a suffix, we will say that it is not part of the same morphosyntactic word as the word it is attached to. Now we can define a clitic as an element that is part of the phonetic, but not the morphosyntactic word it attaches to. In Figure 10, the outer box represents the phonetic word **готóво ли**, while the inner box stands for the morphosyntactic word **готóво**.

In addition to **ли**, the emphatic marker **же** and the subjunctive marker **бы** are good examples of clitics in Modern Russian. Clitics like these, which attach to the preceding morphosyntactic word, are called "enclitics." Clitics that attach to the following word are referred to as "proclitics." An example of a proclitic is the preposition **на** 'on(to)', which attaches to the following noun phrase (e.g., **на столе** 'on the table'). However, in the following we will focus on enclitics.

An important property of enclitics in many languages is their tendency to be part of the first phonetic word in the clause. The principle that requires enclitics to appear in this position is called "Wackernagel's Law" after the Swiss linguist Jacob Wackernagel (1853–1938). The position at the end of the first pho-

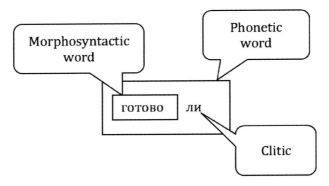

Figure 10. Phonetic word, morphosyntactic word, and clitic

netic word of a clause is often referred to as the "Wackernagel position." As you can see from (45), **ли** in Modern Russian obeys Wackernagel's law since it is found in the Wackernagel position right after **готово** (45a) and **всё** (45b).

According to Zaliznjak (2008b: 28), Old Rusian had a number of enclitics that obeyed Wackernagel's law:

(46) Old Rusian enclitics:
1. **же**
2. **ли**
3. **бо**
4. **ти**
5. **бы**
6. dative pronouns: **ми, ти, си, ны, вы, на, ва**
7. accusative pronouns: **мя, тя, ся, ны, вы, на, ва, и, ю, е**
8. auxiliary verbs: **есмь, еси, есть**, etc.

The first four enclitics on the list are particles of various types, for which it is difficult to provide precise English glosses. From Modern Russian you recognize **же** and **ли** under 1 and 2. **Бо** under 3 is related to the causal conjunction **ибо** 'for, because' in Modern Russian, while the particle **ти** under 4 does not have a corresponding word in Modern Russian. In Old Rusian, the particle **ти** (which should not be confused with the dative pronoun **ти**) was used to emphasize that something actually happened (see Zaliznjak 2008b: 32). Under number 5 you find **бы**, which is the subjunctive particle that was in the process of developing in Old Rusian from the 3rd person singular aorist of **быти** 'be'. The three last groups contain clitic pronouns and auxiliary verbs. The numbers in the list reflect their internal order when two or more clitics occur in the Wackernagel position. The higher up on the list, the further to the left the relevant clitic occurs in the sentence. Let us consider some examples:

(47) a. Крести **же ся** въ церкви святое Софьи.   (PVL 988 AD; 111,18)
    b. Крестил**ся же** он в церкви святой Софии.
    c. He was baptized in the Church of St. Sophia.

Here there are two enclitics in the Wackernagel position right after **крести** 'baptized'. Since **же** has rank 1, while **ся** is of rank 7, **же** comes before **ся**. As shown in (47b), **ся** has developed into a suffix ("postfix") in Modern Russian and therefore comes closer to the verb stem than **же**, which is still a clitic (cf. section 5.1).

The following example consists of three clauses. We are interested in the second clause, which starts with **и дай** 'and give'. In the Wackernagel position immediately after **и дай** come two enclitics, namely **же** (rank 1) and **ми** (rank 6):

(48) a. Приими молитву мою и дай **же ми** смерть таку, якоже вдалъ еси брату моему, Борису и Глѣбови. (PVL 1087 AD; 207,7)

b. Прими молитву мою и ниспошли мне смерть такую **же**, какую даровал и братьям моим Борису и Глебу.

c. Receive my prayer and grant me a death like that of my brothers Boris and Gleb.

Finally, consider a more complex example with three clitics in the Wackernagel position, viz. **же** (rank 1), followed by **ми** (rank 6), and **ся** (rank 7):

(49) a. Сему **же ми ся** дивлящю, рекоша ми: «Се не дивно.»
(PVL 1114 AD)

b. Когда я дивился этому, они сказали мне: «Это не удивительно.»

c. When I wondered about that, they said to me: "That is not surprising."

This example involves a dative absolute construction. **Дивлящю** is a participle in the dative, and the dative pronoun **ми** represents the logical subject of the participle. **Сему** is in the dative because the verb governs the dative case. The order of the clitics follows from Zaliznjak's ranking in (46).

If you are able to identify the Wackernagel position you are in principle able to predict the placement of the Old Rusian enclitics by means of the ranking in (46). However, two factors complicate the picture. First of all, Zaliznjak's analysis concerns the spoken language in Kievan Rus', and his rules work best for texts that reflect the spoken language, such as birch bark letters. The clitic systems in East Slavic and South Slavic are different, so it is not surprising that texts that show Church Slavic influence do not follow the rules completely.

A second complication has to do with what we may call "rhythmic-syntactic barriers" (Zaliznjak 2008b: 47: "**ритмико-синтаксические барьеры**"), which cannot have enclitics to their left. In the following example, one might expect clitics after the vocative **княже** 'prince!':

(50) a. Княже, ты **ся** на нас не гнѣваи. (KL 1147 AD)
  b. Князь, не гневай**ся** на нас.
  c. Prince, do not be wrathful with us.

However, Zaliznjak (2008b: 54) argues that there is a barrier after the vocative, and that the clitic **ся** therefore comes after **ты**. Zaliznjak's analysis of barriers is quite complex; for our purposes it is sufficient to notice that barriers occur between constituents in the sentence, and that they force clitics to be placed further to the right than one would expect based on Wackernagel's law alone.

If you look at the inventory of enclitics in (46), you will see that most of the clitics have disappeared. The only surviving clitics in Contemporary Standard Russian are **же, ли,** and **бы**. In addition, **ся** has survived, but, as mentioned above, it is no longer a clitic. How can this development from clitic to affix be explained? An important generalization is that in cases where Old Rusian had synonymous pairs of clitic and non-clitic forms, only the non-clitic forms survived. In other words, in pairs of clitic and non-clitic pronouns such as **мя** and **мене** only the latter has survived as the modern accusative form **меня**, since the two forms were synonyms. The pair **ся–себе** were synonyms after prepositions, so phrases like **за ся** were ousted by **за себе**, which turned into **за себя** in Contemporary Standard Russian. In combination with verbs, however, the clitic form developed meanings that were different from the non-clitic form, and therefore could not be replaced by non-clitic forms. Simplifying somewhat, these functions are reflected in the passive use of -**ся** in Modern Russian (e.g., **Этот журнал читался всеми людьми театра** 'This magazine was read by everybody in theater'), and in the so-called middle voice (e.g., verbs like **мыться** 'wash (oneself)'). As pointed out in section 3.7, what happened was that **ся** underwent grammaticalization, and became more closely connected to the verb. In Contemporary Standard Russian, -**ся** can be analyzed as a suffix (Nesset 1998a: 264ff. and 1998b). However, the fact that -**ся** is always found at the very end of the verb is a consequence of its status as a clitic in Old Rusian.

9.12. Some Notes on Complex Sentences

When reading Old Rusian texts you will frequently encounter complex sentences, i.e., sentences consisting of more than one clause. In the following we focus on some widespread patterns that differ from those you would recognize from Modern Russian.

9.12.1. Relative Clauses

From Contemporary Standard Russian you know that relative clauses are often formed with the pronoun **который**. As mentioned in section 5.2, this construction became widespread from the 16th century. In older texts you frequently encounter relative clauses with **иже**. A simple example of this construction was given in section 5.2. Here is a more complex example where a relative pronoun combines with a preposition:

(51) a. Да соиметь съ себе и ты самыя порты своя, **в нихъже** ходить.
(PVL 912 AD; 34,25)

      b. Пусть снимет с себя и те самые одежды, **в которых** ходит.

      c. He shall be deprived even of the very clothes he wears.

The plural form of **иже** is chosen because the pronoun refers back to the plural noun **порты** 'clothes'. The locative form **нихъже** is due to the preposition **в** (**въ**), which, as in Modern Russian, combines with the locative case.

9.12.2. Object Clauses

In Modern Russian, clauses with **что** 'that' frequently occur as the object of verbs of speech (e.g., **сказать** 'say'), perception (e.g., **увидеть** 'see'), or cognition (e.g., **думать** 'think'). Constructions with **чьто** existed in Old Rusian too, but the conjunction **яко** is also frequently used for 'that':

(52) a. И увидѣ Олгъ, **яко** Осколдъ и Диръ княжита.
(PVL 882 AD; 23,5)

      b. И увидел Олег, **что** княжат тут Аскольд и Дир.

      c. And Oleg saw **that** Askold and Dir reigned there.

An alternative construction in Old Rusian has **оже** instead of **яко**:

(53) a. И от тѣхъ да увѣмы и мы, **оже** с миромъ приходят.
(PVL 945 AD; 48,14)

      b. Из этих [грамот] мы узнали, **что** пришли они с мирными целями.

      c. From these [certificates] we discovered **that** they came with peaceful intent.

9.12.3. Adverbial Clauses: Time

Clauses with **когда** 'when' are frequently used in Modern Russian to locate an event in time. This construction is attested in Old Rusian too, but just as frequent in Old Rusian texts is **егда** 'when':

(54) a. **Егда** же прокопахъ, объдержашет мя ужасть.
(PVL 1091 AD; 210,14)

b. **Когда** же прокопал, охватил меня ужас.

c. **When** I had dug down to them, fear came over me.

The conjunction **донележе** is used in the meaning 'until':

(55) a. И не смѣяше Ярославъ в Кыевъ ити, **донележе** смиристася.
(PVL 1024 AD; 149,6)

b. И не решился Ярослав идти в Киев, **пока не** помирились.

c. But Jaroslav did not dare to return to Kiev **until** they were properly reconciled.

9.12.4. Adverbial Clauses: Cause

In causal constructions you frequently encounter the clitic **бо** 'because', which occurs in the Wackernagel position (see section 9.11):

(56) a. И копье [...] удари в ногы коневи, бѣ **бо** велми дѣтескъ.
(PVL 946 AD; 58,6)

b. И копье [...] ударило коня по ногам, **ибо** был Святослав еще совсем мал.

c. But the spear [...] struck against his legs, **for** the prince was but a child.

While (56a) can be analyzed as two main clauses connected by the clitic **бо**, we also find subordinate clauses with causal meanings. Above you learned that **яко** and **оже** were used in 'that'-sentences, but these conjunctions are also attested in the meaning 'because':

(57) a. О семъ бо увѣдахом, **яко** при сем цесари приходиша Русь на Цесарьград.
(PVL 852 AD; 17,28)

(57) b. Узнали мы об этом **потому, что** при этом царе приходила Русь на Царьград.

c. We have learned about this, **because** in the reign of this Emperor Russes attacked Tsar'grad (Constantinople).

(58) a. Поидѣта к Городцю, да поправимъ сего зла, еже ся сотвори у Русьской земли и в насъ, братьи, **оже** уверже в ны ножь.
(PVL 1097 AD; 262,13)

b. Приходите в Городец, да поправим зло, случившееся в Русской земле среди нас, братьев, **ибо** нож в нас ввержен.

c. Come to Gorodets, that we may avenge this crime which has occurred in the land of Rus' among us kinsmen, **because** it has cast a sword among us.

In example (58), you may also enjoy analyzing the relative clause beginning with **еже**.

Further conjunctions introducing causal clauses are **зане** and **понеже**, which can both be glossed as 'because':

(59) a. Не хощем ти вдати стола Володимерьскаго, **зане** увергъ еси ножь в ны. (PVL 1099 AD; 274,9)

b. Не хотим тебе дать стола Владимирского, **ибо** вверг ты нож в нас.

c. We do not wish to grant you the domain of Vladimir, **because** you cast a sword among us.

(60) a. Сѣди ты на столѣ своемь Кыевѣ, **понеже** ты еси старѣй братъ.
(PVL 1024 AD; 149,3)

b. Сиди ты на своем столе в Киеве, **поскольку** ты старший брат.

c. Stay you in your domain in Kiev, **because** you are the older brother.

9.12.5. Adverbial Clauses: Condition

In Modern Russian, **если** 'if' is the primary means for forming conditional clauses. **Если** is the result of the merger of the verb form **есть** and the clitic **ли** and was not widespread as a conditional conjunction before the 17th century (Borkovskij and Kuznecov 1963: 488). In earlier times you frequently encounter **аще (аче)** 'if' in conditional constructions:

(61) a. **Аще** ли руку не дадят и противятся, да убьени будуть.
(PVL 945 AD; 48,18)

b. **Если** же не дадутся нам и сопротивятся, то убьем их.

c. **If** they do not surrender, but offer resistance, they shall be killed.

Оже is also attested in the meaning 'if':

(62) a. **Оже** ми будуть берендичи, и торци и печенѣзи, и реку брату своему Володареви и Давыдови: «Дайта дружину свою моложьшюю.» (PVL 1097 AD; 266,13)

b. **Если** у меня будут берендеи, и торки, и печенеги, то скажу брату своему Володарю и Давыду: «Дайте мне дружину свою младшую.»

c. **If** the Berendiches, Torks and Pechenegs were approaching, I would say to my kinsmen Volodar' and David: "lend me your younger retainers."

9.12.6. Summary: Some Important Conjunctions Used in Complex Sentences

Although the examples given above do not provide a comprehensive account of complex sentences in Old Rusian, they illustrate two important properties of the system: polysemy and synonymy. Polysemy occurs when a word has multiple related meanings. As we have seen, **яко** and **оже** serve several functions, so they are polysemous. At the same time, Old Rusian had several conjunctions with the same meanings. For instance, **яко**, **зане**, and **понеже** are all used in the meaning 'because'. This is an example of synonymy, since different words have the same meanings. Table 52 offers an overview of the most important conjunctions and their meanings.

Table 52. Conjunctions and their meanings

Conjunction	Meanings
яко	'that', 'because'
оже	'that', 'because', 'if'
егда	'when'
донележе	'until'
зане	'because'
понеже	'because'
аще (аче)	'if'

9.13. Summary

This chapter has shown that in many ways the structure of Old Rusian sentences is similar to the syntactic structures we find in Contemporary Standard Russian. However, there are substantial differences too. The most important of them are summed up in Table 53.

Table 53. Major syntactic differences between Old Rusian and Contemporary Standard Russian

Topic	Difference
Subject (section 9.1)	Pro-drop in Old Rusian
Object (9.2)	1. Infinitive + nominative of *ā*-declension nouns 2. Verbs of cognition, speech and perception + accusative instead of **о** + locative 3. Supine + genitive
Predicative noun (9.3)	Instrumental less widely used compared to Modern Russian
Spatial adverbial (9.4)	1. **Передъ/прѣдъ** and **надъ** + accusative/instrumental 2. The bare locative used for major cities
Temporal adverbial (9.5)	1. **Въ** + accusative, bare genitive and bare locative widely used 2. **Въ** + locative marginal
Possessive construction (9.7)	Possessive adjectives more widely used than today
Passive construction (9.8)	Agent expressed as **отъ** + genitive
Dative absolute construction (9.9)	A construction with no equivalent in Modern Russian
Agreement (9.10)	Collective nouns with singular or plural agreement
Clitics (9.11)	A large number of clitics of eight different ranks in the Wackernagel position
Complex sentence (9.12)	A set of conjunctions showing extensive polysemy and synonymy

9.14. For Further Reading

Borkovskij and Kuznecov (1963) provide a comprehensive chapter on Old Rusian syntax. A shorter overview is found in Ivanov 1983. In English, Schmalstieg (1995) offers a compact description. An up-to-date analysis of possessive constructions is found in Eckhoff 2011, while the best source of information about clitics is Zaliznjak's (2008b) masterful study.

Chapter 10

Phonology: Pre-Slavic and Common Slavic Vowels and Diphthongs

Now that you have learned about morphology and syntax, you are ready for phonology—the study of sound systems. Phonology is the topic of this and the following three chapters. We start with vowels and diphthongs in the Pre-Slavic and Common Slavic periods. You will learn how the difference between short and long vowels disappeared, and how a number of sound laws created a special type of syllables called "open syllables." In addition, this chapter gives you the answer to a number of questions about Modern Russian. Why are there no words beginning with the letter ы in Contemporary Standard Russian? Why is 'city' represented as град in Leningrad and Stalingrad, but город in Novgorod? Why does the letter н show up in the inflected forms of nouns like имя and время (cf. nominative singular имя vs. genitive singular имени)?

10.1. Basic Concepts: Phoneme, Allophone, Minimal Pair, Complementary Distribution

Before we consider the historical phonology in detail, let us discuss a few terms that you will need in this and the following three chapters. If you are familiar with the concepts of "phoneme," "allophone," "minimal pair," and "complementary distribution," you may skip this section.

If we compare the pronunciation of a random word such as *cake* across speakers, we will find out that no two speakers pronounce it exactly the same. Moreover, if we analyze the pronunciation of one single speaker who is asked to repeat the same word many times, it will become clear that no two exemplars are identical. In other words, variation is ubiquitous. However, not all differences are equally important, because only some sounds distinguish between different meanings. It is customary to use the term "phoneme" for sounds that distinguish between words with different meanings. In more technical terms, we may define the phoneme as the "smallest contrastive linguistic unit that may bring about change of meaning" (Cruttenden 2008: 41).

In order to establish the phonemes in a language, we may look for so-called minimal pairs, i.e., pairs of words with different meanings that differ in only one sound. Consider the two Modern Russian words тут 'here' and тот 'that'.

Since only the vowel distinguishes between the words in this minimal pair, we are dealing with two different vowel phonemes, which we can represent as /u/ and /o/. In minimal pairs, phonemes occur in the same phonetic environments, i.e., they are flanked by the same sounds. Notice that we write phonemes between slashes.

It may be helpful to think of phonemes as families of closely related sounds. The members of one such family are said to be the allophones of the phoneme. In order to establish that two sounds are allophones of the same phoneme, we can show that they have complementary distribution. In section 2.4, you saw that complementary distribution is a key to understanding diglossia, and complementary distribution is equally important in phonology. Let us consider the vowels in the Modern Russian words мат 'checkmate' and мять 'crumple'. We may represent the vowel in мат as [a], while the vowel in мять, which has a more fronted articulation, can be written as [ä]. These two sounds occur in different environments; [a] is found between hard consonants, whereas [ä] is flanked by soft consonants. When two sounds do not occur in the same environment, they have complementary distribution. In other words, [a] and [ä] have complementary distribution. Since two sounds in complementary distribution never occur in the same environment, they cannot form minimal pairs, and hence belong to the same phoneme. Notice that we write allophones in square brackets.

10.2. Overview: Vowel Systems for Late Proto-Indo-European, Proto-Slavic, Old Rusian, and Contemporary Standard Russian

By means of the concepts introduced in the previous section you are able to detect all the phonemes of a language, e.g., the five vowel phonemes of Contemporary Standard Russian: /i, e, a, o, u/. However, just listing phonemes in a random order is not satisfactory, because phonemes constitute systems, and as linguists we are interested in capturing the systematic aspects of language. For instance, /i/ and /e/ are more closely related than /i/ and /o/, since both /i/ and /e/ are articulated in the front part of the mouth, while /o/ is articulated further back. At the same time, /o/ is articulated with rounded lips, whereas /i/ and /e/ are not. Groups of phonemes that share one or more properties of this kind ("front," "rounded," etc.), are called "natural classes." When we organize the phonemes of a language according to natural classes, we get the phoneme system of that language. Figure 11 on p. 197 juxtaposes the vowel phoneme systems (or vowel systems for short) of Late Proto-Indo-European, Proto-Slavic, Old Rusian and Contemporary Standard Russian. As you can see, the relevant sounds vary along four parameters:

10.2. Overview: Vowel Systems

Late PIE	Front		Non-front	
	Unrounded		Rounded	
High	ĭ, ī		ŭ, ū	
Mid	ĕ, ē		ŏ, ō	
Low		ă, ā		

Old Rusian	Front		Non-front	
	Unrounded		Rounded	
High	i	y		u
High-Mid	ě			
Mid	e, ь			o, ъ
Low	ä	a		

Proto-Slavic	Front		Non-front	
	Unrounded		Rounded	
High	ĭ, ī		ŭ, ū	
Non-high	ě, ē		ă, ā	

CSR	Front		Non-front
	Unrounded		Rounded
High	i		u
Mid	e		o
Low		a	

Figure 11. Vowel systems of Late Proto-Indo-European (upper left), Proto-Slavic (upper right), Old Rusian (lower left), and Contemporary Standard Russian (lower right)

(1) a. Height: high vs. high-mid vs. mid vs. low phonemes (is the vowel articulated high or low in the mouth?)

b. Frontedness: front vs. non-front phonemes (is the vowel articulated in the front or back part of the mouth?)

c. Rounding: rounded vs. unrounded phonemes (is the vowel articulated with rounded lips or not?)

d. Quantity: short vs. long phonemes (does the vowel have short or long duration?)

For our purposes, it is useful to start with the vowel system of Late Proto-Indo-European, i.e., the system that existed in the Pre-Slavic period before the Slavic languages grew distinct from the other Indo-European languages. This system comprises five short /ĭ, ĕ, ă, ŏ, ŭ/ and five long vowel phonemes /ī, ē, ā, ō, ū/. This means that the difference between a short and a long vowel was enough to distinguish between words with different meanings. The Proto-Slavic vowel system is very similar, but lacks two phonemes: /ŏ, ō/. In the Old Rusian and Modern Russian systems, the distinction between short and long vowel phonemes has been lost. In Old Rusian, the only trace of the short-long distinction is the jers /ь, ъ/, which were probably shorter than their "neighbors" /e, o/. However, the main difference between /ь, ъ/ on the one hand and /e, o/ on the other may have been qualitative rather than quantitative. We will assume that /ь, ъ/ had the property "lax" and that their shorter duration was a secondary effect of their lax pronunciation. Lax vowels are pronounced with less muscular energy than so-called tense vowels, and lax vowels therefore tend to have shorter duration (see Laver 1994: 417 for discussion). While the quantitative short-long distinction was lost, Old Rusian had developed a number of phonemes not found in Late Proto-Indo-European: /ě, y, ä/, which are associated with the letters ѣ ("jat"), ы, and я (ѧ), respectively. As shown in Figure 11, these phonemes were subsequently lost in Contemporary Standard Russian. As a result, we end up with a modern system that is exactly half the size of the Late Proto-Indo-European system, insofar as it lacks the quantitative short-long distinction, but has the same qualitative differences between /i, e, a, o, u/.

10.3. The *o/a* Merger and the Loss of Vowel Quantity

As we have just seen, the distinction between short and long vowel phonemes was lost during the Common Slavic period. This loss was the joint effect of a number of sound changes that started in the Pre-Slavic period. The first change that undermined the short-long distinction was the *o/a* merger:

10.3. The *o/a* Merger and the Loss of Vowel Quantity

(2) The *o/a* merger:
   a. Late Proto-Indo-European /ō, ā/ → Proto-Slavic /ā/
   b. Late Proto-Indo-European /ŏ, ă/ → Proto-Slavic /ă/

The result of the *o/a* merger was that the four Late Proto-Indo-European phonemes /ŏ, ō, ă, ā/ were reduced to two phonemes. The resulting vowels were probably unrounded, and are therefore represented as /ă, ā/ in Proto-Slavic, although some researchers assume weakly rounded vowels and use symbols such as /å/ (cf. Townsend and Janda 1996: 47). While in Early Common Slavic the difference between these two phonemes was quantitative (short vs. long), the short phoneme later became rounded. In Late Common Slavic, the quantitative opposition became replaced by a qualitative opposition between a rounded mid vowel (/o/) and a low unrounded vowel (/a/). Loanwords from the Late Common Slavic period illustrate this. For example, the Iranian word *tăpăra* (with short [ă]) became *toporъ* 'axe' in Old Church Slavonic (with rounded vowels). Old Church Slavonic *korablь* 'ship' and *krovatь* 'bed' are borrowed from Greek, which had long [ā] where the Slavic words have [a]. More examples are given in Townsend and Janda 1996: 47f.

For our purposes it is not necessary to consider in detail the individual changes that occasioned the loss of vowel quantity in the Common Slavic period. However, Table 54 offers an overview of the correspondences between Late Proto-Indo-European and Old Rusian vowels. These correspondences show that all the short-long oppositions where reinterpreted as qualitative differences.

Table 54. Loss of vowel quantity—Late Proto-Indo-European and Old Rusian vowel correspondences

Late Proto-Indo-European	Old Rusian
ā, ō	a
ă, ŏ	o
ē	ě
ĕ	e
ī	i
ĭ	ь
ū	y
ŭ	ъ

In addition to eliminating the short-long distinction, the correspondences in Table 54 indicate that vowels changed with regard to lip rounding and vowel height. Let us first consider rounding, which is relevant for the Late Proto-Indo-European non-front vowel phonemes /ā, ō, ū, ă, ŏ, ŭ/. As shown in the table, the three long vowels end up as unrounded vowels in Old Rusian (/a, y/), whereas the three short vowels become rounded in Old Rusian (/o, ъ/). (We assume that /ъ/ was a lax rounded vowel.) The following formulas summarize this generalization:

(3) Changes concerning rounding (non-front vowels):
   a. Late Proto-Indo-European long /ā, ō, ū/ → Old Rusian unrounded /a, y/
   b. Late Proto-Indo-European short /ă, ŏ, ŭ/ → Old Rusian rounded /o, ъ/

Figure 12 visualizes the changes regarding vowel height. The arrows show which phonemes underwent change, and in which direction they changed. As you can see, the short vowels in the left portion and the long vowels in the right portion of the figure display opposite developments. For the short vowels, the phonemes at the periphery (i.e., high or low vowels) undergo change, and they become mid vowels. For the long vowels, alternatively, it is the mid vowels that are transformed, and they move towards the periphery of the system. The long /ō/ moves down and becomes /a/, while the long /ē/ moves upwards and becomes the high-mid /ě/.

10.4. Syllable Structure in Common Slavic: "The Law of Open Syllables"

The syllable plays a key role in the sound changes we will discuss in the remainder of this chapter, so it is necessary to clarify this concept before we consider the individual sound laws. It is far from simple to give a precise definition

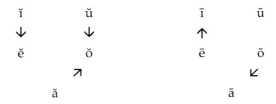

Figure 12. Changes concerning vowel height for short vowels (left) and long vowels (right)

10.4. Syllable Structure in Common Slavic: "The Law of Open Syllables"

of "syllable," but for our purposes it is sufficient to say that a syllable is a group of sounds that constitute a rhythmic unit. In Modern Russian we can generally say that a word has as many syllables as there are vowels. In other words, the Russian word **алфавит** 'alphabet' has three syllables: **ал–фа–вит**.

Notice that syllables are organized around the most sonorous sounds, which are called "syllable peaks." We can rank sounds according to their sonority, i.e., how easy it is to sing them. Low vowels are highly sonorous, while plosive consonants like [p] are very hard to sing.[1] Here is a simple sonority hierarchy, where the value 6 represents maximal sonority and 1, minimal sonority:

(4) Sonority hierarchy:
   6. Low vowels, e.g., [a]
   5. Mid vowels, e.g., [e, o]
   4. High vowels, e.g., [i, u]
   3. Sonorant consonants, e.g., [m, n, r, l]
   2. Fricative consonants, e.g., [f, s]
   1. Plosive ("stop") consonants, e.g., [p, t]

Let us assign sonority values to the sounds in **алфавит**:

(5) 63–2 6–241
   ал–фа–вит

The first syllable—**ал**—has falling sonority, since the sonority values go down from 6 to 3. The second syllable—**фа**—has rising sonority, insofar as sonority goes up from 2 to 6. The third syllable—**вит**—has first rising sonority from 2 to 4 and then falling sonority from 4 to 1.

An important constraint on syllable structure in Common Slavic can be stated as follows:

(6) The Law of Open Syllables (**закон открытого слога**):
   Common Slavic syllables had rising sonority.

It follows from this constraint that syllables such as **ал** were prohibited in Common Slavic, since they show falling sonority. Likewise, **вит** was impossi-

---

[1] Throughout the book I use the term "plosive" for sounds like [p, b, t, d, k, g], which are often referred to as "(oral) stops."

ble, since it involves falling sonority towards the end. Of the three syllables in **алфавит**, only the second syllable—фа—displays rising sonority and would be acceptable in Common Slavic. The constraint is referred to as the "Law of Open Syllables," since it only allows syllables ending in a vowel. Syllables ending in a vowel are called "open," whereas syllables ending in a consonant are "closed." A number of the sound laws we will discuss in this chapter transform closed syllables into open syllables as prescribed by the Law of Open Syllables.

10.5. Loss of Final Consonants

Proto-Slavic inherited words ending in consonants:

(7) Loss of word-final consonants:
   a. /m/: Proto-Slavic /sūnŭm/ → Old Rusian /synъ/ 'son (acc sg)'
   b. /d/: Proto-Slavic /stălād/ → Old Rusian /stola/ 'table (gen sg)'
   c. /x/: Proto-Slavic /sūnŭx/ → Old Rusian /synъ/ 'son (nom sg)'
   d. /s/: Proto-Slavic /stălăs/ → Old Rusian /stolъ/ 'table (nom sg)'

In all these examples, the final syllable consisted of consonant + vowel + consonant. If we let C stand for any consonant and V for any vowel, we see that all the final syllables had the same structure, namely CVC. Such syllables were closed and had falling sonority from the vowel to the final consonant. For instance, the final syllable /nŭm/ had the sonority values 3–4–3. Since the final syllables in (7) violated the Law of Open Syllables, they underwent change in Common Slavic, whereby the final consonants were lost. However, the loss of final consonants did not happen in one fell swoop at one point in time. Rather, Shevelov (1964: 229) distinguishes between three stages. First, final nasal consonants were lost early in the Common Slavic period, then final dental consonants such as /d/ disappeared before, finally, /s/ and /x/ were lost.

Since the final consonant was often part of an ending, the loss of final consonants had consequences for the morphological system of Common Slavic and Old Rusian. The examples in (7) illustrate two such consequences. First, both the accusative singular /sūnŭm/ and the nominative singular /sūnŭx/ became /synъ/ in Old Rusian. Due to loss of the final consonant, the difference between nominative and accusative singular disappeared in several declensions, not only in *ŭ*-declension nouns such as **сынъ** 'son'. The later development of the genitive-like accusatives for animates that you learned about in section 4.7, reintroduced a difference between the two cases. Could it be possible that the animacy subgender would never have developed in Slavic if the loss of final consonants had not wiped out the differences between the nominative and accusative singular forms in Common Slavic?

The second consequence illustrated by the examples in (7) concerns the relationship between the ŭ- and ŏ-declensions. In Proto-Slavic, the nominative singular ending in the ŭ-declension was /ŭx/ (cf. /sūnŭx/), while the ŏ-declension had /ŏs/. After the final consonants were lost, the two endings became more similar. However, based on the correspondences discussed in 10.3, we would expect the ŏ-declension ending to become /o/, not /ъ/ in Old Rusian. Exactly how the ŏ-declension came to adopt the same ending as the ŭ-declension remains one of the unsolved mysteries of Slavic linguistics. However, it is possible that grammatical gender played a role in the development, since the result was a system where all the masculine nouns in the ŭ- and ŏ-declensions adopted the ending /ъ/, whereas the neuters had the ending /o/ (e.g., лѣто 'year, summer' discussed in section 4.2.1). In other words, the difference between the masculine and neuter genders became clearer as a result of the changes.

10.6. Oral Diphthongs: Monophthongization

In addition to the ten vowel phonemes shown in Figure 11 in section 10.2, Late Proto-Indo-European had a number of diphthongs. Diphthongs are gliding transitions between two vowels in the same syllable. As you can see from Figure 13, Late Proto-Indo-European had diphthongs consisting of a mid or low vowel followed by a high vowel. We may refer to these diphthongs as "oral diphthongs" as opposed to the so-called nasal and liquid diphthongs we will explore in the following sections. As indicated in Figure 13, the oral diphthongs could be short or long. Notice that the features mentioned in the figure (mid, low, front, non-front, unrounded, and rounded) refer to the first part of the oral diphthongs.

Due to the o/a merger discussed in section 10.3, the six pairs of short and long diphthongs in Figure 13 were reduced to four pairs in Proto-Slavic: /ĕi, ēi, ăi, āi, ĕu, ēu, ău, āu/. These diphthongs were at variance with the Law of Open Syllables. By way of example, consider the first syllable /răi/ in /răikā/ 'river'.

	Front	Non-front		Front	Non-front
	Unrounded	Rounded		Unrounded	Rounded
Mid	ĕi, ēi	ŏi, ōi	Mid	ĕu, ēu	ŏu, ōu
Low		ăi, āi	Low		ău, āu

Figure 13. Late Proto-Indo-European oral diphthongs ending in /i/ (left) and /u/ (right)

If we assign sonority values to /răi/, we get 3–6–4. In other words, the syllable has falling sonority at the end. However, this problem was overcome through a sound law called "monophthongization," i.e., a process whereby a diphthong becomes a monophthong. (A monophthong is a fancy word for an "ordinary vowel," i.e., a vowel that is not a diphthong.) In the case of /răikā/, we end up with /rěka/ in Old Rusian. Now the first syllable is /rě/, which has rising sonority, since the sonority values are 3–5.

The results of monophthongization are summarized in Table 55. There are three generalizations you should notice. First, short and long diphthongs behave the same way. Second, the diphthongs ending in /i/ end up as the vowel /ě/ (jat) or /i/. Third, the diphthongs ending in /u/ become /u/, which in the case of /ĕu, ēu/ is preceded by /j/. However, /j/ later disappears due to so-called *j*-palatalization, and is therefore included in parentheses in the table. You will learn more about *j*-palatalization in section 11.6.

Table 55. Effects of monophthongization of oral diphthongs

Proto-Slavic	Late Common Slavic/ Old Rusian	Examples
ěi, ēi	i	krěiv- → krivъ 'crooked'
ăi, āi	ě (i)	snăig- → sněgъ 'snow'
ěu, ēu	(j)u	běud- → bjudu → bl'udu 'I observe'
ău, āu	u	ăux- → uxo 'ear'

At this point you may wonder what the /i/ in parentheses in Table 55 means. For /ăi, āi/, the normal outcome of monophthongization is indeed /ě/, but /i/ is attested word-finally in some grammatical forms:

(8) Monopthongization of /ăi, āi/ to /i/ instead of /ě/:

a. Nominative plural of masculine ŏ-declension nouns, e.g., Old Rusian столи 'tables'

b. 2nd/3rd person singular imperative, e.g., Old Rusian пьци 'bake!'

c. The dative singular enclitic pronouns ми, ти, and си

It is unclear whether monophthongization of /ăi, āi/ to /i/ is due to sound law or analogy. On the one hand, the fact that /i/ is restricted to certain grammatical forms suggests that we are dealing with analogy. On the other hand, all the cases listed in (8) involve a diphthong at the end of the word, and some researchers have suggested a sound law whereby /ăi, āi/ become /i/ in word-final position if the diphthong had falling intonation (see Shevelov 1964: 288 for critical discussion).

Monophthongization of oral vowels gave rise to alternations that are still important in Modern Russian grammar. By way of example, consider verbs like **ковать** 'forge', where /ova/ in the infinitive alternates with /uj/ in present-tense forms such as **кую** 'I forge'. How did this alternation emerge? Let us look at the 1st person singular present tense first. We can reconstruct the Proto-Slavic form /kauiām/, which consists of two syllables: /kau-iam/. The first syllable involves an oral diphthong, which becomes /ku/ in Old Rusian. In the latter syllable, /i/ becomes /j/, while /am/, as we will see in the next section, turns into a nasal vowel and later into /u/. The resulting Old Rusian form is /kuju/, which has been preserved in Modern Russian. For the infinitive, we can reconstruct Proto-Slavic /kauātei/. This form consists of three syllables: /ka-ua-tei/. Importantly, the sequence /au/ here is split between two different syllables, and therefore does not constitute a diphthong. In Old Rusian, /ka/ becomes /ko/, /ua/ becomes /wa/, and /tei/ turns into /ti/. This yields /kowati/, which corresponds to the modern verb **ковать**, which has /ova/. In this way, we get verbs where /ova/ alternates with /uj/. This pattern has become tremendously productive in Modern Russian, and has attracted numerous loan words, such as **абонировать** 'subscribe', **атаковать** 'attack', and **нокаутировать** 'knock out'.

10.7. Nasal Diphthongs: The Rise and Fall of Nasal Vowels

Late Proto-Indo-European and Proto-Slavic had combinations of a vowel + a nasal consonant (/m, n/), which it is customary to refer to as "nasal diphthongs," although they are not, strictly speaking, gliding transitions between two vowels. Like the oral diphthongs explored in the previous section, the nasal diphthongs violated the Law of Open Syllables. In Late Proto-Indo-European /g'ŏmbhŏs/ 'tooth', the first syllable /g'ŏm/ has the sonority values 1–5–3, so this is not a syllable with rising sonority. However, this problem was eliminated by a process of monophthongization, which turned the nasal diphthongs into nasal vowels before a syllable boundary (marked as $):

(9) Creation of nasal vowels in Common Slavic:
    a. front vowel + nasal consonant → /ę/ / __ $
    b. non-front vowel + nasal consonant → /ǫ/ / __ $

Nasal vowels are vowels that are articulated so that air escapes through the nose and the mouth at the same time. Possibly, Common Slavic /ę/ and /ǫ/

sounded approximately like the vowels in French *vin* 'wine' and *bon* 'good', respectively, although there are reasons to believe that the pronunciation of the nasal vowels displayed considerable variation across the Common Slavic dialects. In the modern Slavic languages, nasal vowels have been preserved in Polish and Kashubian.

Why did we have to specify in (9) that nasal vowels only emerged before a syllable boundary, i.e., at the end of a syllable? The answer is simple: Only nasal consonants at the end of the syllable were at variance with the Law of Open Syllables. Consider Modern Russian neuters in the third declension such as **семя** 'seed', **имя** 'name', and **время** 'time'. The Proto-Slavic nominative singular forms such as /sēmĕns/ 'seed' contained the syllable /mĕns/ with the sonority values 3–5–3–2. The first nasal consonant (/m/), which is in the beginning of the syllable, is not a problem for the Law of Open Syllables, since we have rising sonority from /m/ to /ĕ/. However, the second nasal (/n/) is at variance with the Law of Open Syllables, since sonority falls from /ĕ/ to /n/. After the final consonant was lost (as explained in section 10.5), the nasal consonant ended up at the end of the syllable and became /ę/, according to the sound law in (9a).

Although the nasal vowels eliminated violations of the Law of Open Syllables, the nasal vowels were a relatively short-lived success. At the end of the Common Slavic period, the nasal vowels turned into regular vowels:

(10) Loss of nasal vowels:
   a. Common Slavic /ę/ → Old Rusian /ä/
   b. Common Slavic /ǫ/ → Old Rusian /u/

It is interesting to note that the two nasal vowels turned into vowels that are at opposite ends of the vowel system. While the low front vowel /ä/ is in the lower left corner of the vowel space, the high non-front vowel /u/ is in the upper right corner.

Even though nasal vowels disappeared from Old Rusian phonology, they left traces in orthography, as mentioned in section 2.2. When the Old Church Slavonic texts were written down, nasal vowels were still pronounced, and both the Glagolitic and Cyrillic alphabets have letters for nasal vowels. The Cyrillic letter ѫ ("юс большой") represented /ǫ/, while ѧ ("юс малый") stood for /ę/. Due to the influence from Old Church Slavonic, especially ѧ was widely used in Old Rusian texts too, although nasal vowels were not pronounced in Old Rusian.

The sound laws in (9) and (10) have given rise to interesting alternations in Modern Russian. The **семя**, **имя**, and **время** class is a good illustration. We have just seen that in the nominative singular a nasal vowel was formed. This vowel became /ä/ in Old Rusian and /a/ (spelled as **я**) in Modern Russian. In the oblique cases, however, the *n*-sound has been preserved: **семени**. It is not hard to understand why. In **семени**, the *n*-sound was and still is in the beginning of the syllable (**се-ме-ни**). Since it therefore did not violate the Law of Open Syllables, it has remained unchanged to this day.

Another example involves verbs such at **взять** 'take'. If we reconstruct the Proto-Slavic infinitive as /vŭzĭmtěi/, we can break it up into three syllables: /vŭ-zĭm-těi/. Since the second syllable has a nasal consonant at the end, the nasal diphthong turned into the nasal vowel /ę/, which then became /a/ (spelled as **я**) in Modern Russian. However, in modern forms such as **возьму** the nasal was in the beginning of a syllable (as it still is in Modern Russian), and therefore remained unchanged.

10.8. Liquid Diphthongs: Pleophony and Metathesis

Late Proto-Indo-European and Proto-Slavic combinations of a mid or low vowel + a liquid consonant (/l, r/) are traditionally referred to as "liquid diphthongs." If we use the symbol C to represent any consonant, and let O represent any mid or low vowel and R represent any liquid consonant, we can write word-internal liquid diphthongs as CORC and word-initial liquid diphthongs as ORC. Since CORC and ORC groups display different developments, we will discuss them separately in sections 10.8.1 and 10.8.2. In section 10.8.3, we turn to liquid consonants preceded by the jers (/ъ, ь/). Such groups can be represented as CЪRC.[2]

10.8.1. CORC: Word-Internal Liquid Diphthongs

Consider the reconstructed Common Slavic form /korva/ 'cow'. The first syllable, /kor/, which involves a liquid diphthong, violates the Law of Open Syllables, since sonority falls from /o/ to /r/. Not unexpectedly, therefore, liquid diphthongs were transformed. As shown in Table 56 on p. 208, the South, West, and East Slavic languages chose different strategies to eliminate the violations of the Law of Open Syllables. In South and West Slavic, the vowel and the liquid consonant changed places, as shown in the Bosnian, Croatian, and Serbian (BCS) and Polish words for 'cow': *krava* and *krowa*. This process is referred to as "metathesis" (Russian: **метатеза**). Metathesis repairs the violation of the Law of Open Syllables, since the resulting syllables /kra/ and /kro/ involve rising sonority. In East Slavic, a different strategy was chosen. As shown

---

[2] Notice that in Slavic linguistics the liquid diphthongs are often represented as TORT, ORT and TЪRT, with a T instead of C. I prefer C, which is the most common symbol for a consonant in general linguistics.

by Russian корова 'cow', the East Slavs inserted an extra vowel after the liquid. The result was a word with three syllables (/ko-ro-va/), which all display rising sonority. This process is called "pleophony" (Russian: полногласие).

Table 56. Metathesis and pleophony in CORC groups

Common Slavic	South Slavic (BCS)	West Slavic (Polish)	East Slavic (Russian)
kor-va 'cow'	kra-va	kro-wa	ko-ro-va
gol-va 'head'	gla-va	gło-wa	go-lo-va
ber-za 'birch'	bre-za	brzo-za	be-re-za
mel-ko 'milk'	mle-ko	mle-ko	mo-lo-ko

Although both South and West Slavic have metathesis, the results are slightly different; while Bosnian, Croatian, and Serbian (BCS, South Slavic) has /a/ in the words for 'cow' and 'head', Polish (West Slavic) has /o/. The South Slavic /a/ is the result of so-called compensatory lengthening. When the liquid after the vowel disappeared, the vowel was lengthened so as to compensate for the loss of the liquid consonant. The compensatory lengthening is not visible in the BCS forms for 'birch' and 'milk' in Table 56. However, in Old Church Slavonic, the earliest attested South Slavic language, we find forms such as *mlěko* 'milk'. This form contains the vowel jat (/ě/), which as you learned in section 10.3, goes back to a long /ē/ in Proto-Slavic.

If you look at the Russian results of pleophony in Table 56, you see that the vowel that was added after the liquid consonant normally is the same as the vowel in the corresponding Common Slavic forms. In other words, /korva/ became /korova/ and /berza/ turned into /bereza/. However, in combination with /l/ Russian always has /olo/—no matter whether Common Slavic had /o/ as in /golva/ or /e/ as in /melko/. The reason for this development is that /l/ is velarized, i.e., articulated with the back of the tongue relatively far back in the mouth, and this made the flanking vowels more back too. In section 6.3 you learned about assimilation, the phonetic process where one sound becomes more similar to another sound. The backing of /e/ to /o/ in CORC groups with /l/ is an example of assimilation, since the vowel became more similar to /l/ (i.e., articulated closer to where /l/ is articulated).

One exception from the rule that Common Slavic /el/ yielded /olo/ in East Slavic occurs after /k, g, x/. As you will learn in the next chapter, such consonants underwent palatalization before /e/, and after a palatalized consonant non-front vowels like /o/ were banned in Common Slavic. The result was /elo/ as in Old Rusian желобъ (which corresponds to Modern Russian жёлоб 'rain gutter').

10.8.1. CORC: Word-Internal Liquid Diphthongs

When did the elimination of the liquid diphthongs take place? Whereas the oral and nasal diphthongs displayed identical developments across Slavic, the liquid diphthongs underwent different changes in South, West, and East Slavic. This suggests that the elimination of the liquid diphthongs occurred later than the monophthongization of oral and nasal diphthongs, when Common Slavic was in the process of splitting up into South, West, and East Slavic. Evidence from loanwords confirms this. Finnish words such as *palttina* 'linen' and *varpunen* 'sparrow', which were borrowed from Slavic, correspond to Modern Russian **полотно** 'linen' and **воробей** 'sparrow'. Since the Finnish words have vowel + liquid sequences, they must have been borrowed before pleophony took place. In other words, pleophony must have happened after the Slavs had migrated so far north as to come in contact with Finno-Ugric peoples in what is now northwestern Russia. Recall from section 1.4 that the Slavic expansion to the north took place before the ninth century.

The most famous example of a loanword involving a liquid diphthong is **король** 'king', which comes from Germanic *Karl*, the name of Charlemagne (742–814), the king of the Franks. Since this word has metathesis in South and West Slavic (cf. BCS *kralj* and Polish *król*), but pleophony in East Slavic, it must have been borrowed into Slavic before the transformation of the liquid diphthongs took place. Since the word cannot have been borrowed before Charlemagne became king, this word indicates that "metathesis and pleophony were not completed during the early ninth century" (Shevelov 1964: 416). On the basis of loanwords and other evidence, Shevelov places the elimination of liquid diphthongs in the mid-ninth century.

It is easy to find examples of pleophony forms in Modern Russian, as demonstrated in Table 57 on p. 210. However, as shown in the table Russian quite often has metathesis forms as well. Such forms are the result of Church Slavic influence in the sense that metathesis came to Russian from Church Slavic. In Old Rusian texts, you often find a mixture of pleophony and metathesis forms, and many metathesis forms have become part of the Russian language. Very often, the "slavonicisms" as the words showing Church Slavic influence are called, display a more abstract meaning than the corresponding pleophony forms. A case in point is the Church Slavic metathesis form **глава** 'chapter, head (leader)', which corresponds to the East Slavic pleophony form **голова** 'head (body part)'. Notice that even if the slavonicisms have their roots in a language that was imported to Rus' for religious purposes, the slavonicisms are not limited to religious discourse. When the Bolsheviks decided to use the slavonicism **град** instead of the pleophony form **город** in the names Leningrad and Stalingrad, this was certainly not for religious reasons.

Table 57. Some pleophony and metathesis word pairs in Modern Russian

Russian word (pleophony)	Slavonicism (metathesis)
голова 'head (body part)'	глава 'chapter, head (leader)'
сторона 'side'	страна 'country'
молоко 'milk'	Млечный путь 'Milky way'
здоровье 'health'	здравоохранение 'healthcare'
хоромы 'mansion'	храм 'temple, church'
голос 'voice'	гласность 'publicity, openness'

10.8.2. ORC: Word-Initial Liquid Diphthongs

In word-initial position, liquid diphthongs underwent metathesis in all Slavic languages. However, South Slavic on the one hand and West and East Slavic on the other display slightly different results of metathesis, depending on the tonal contour of the diphthong in Common Slavic. This is shown in Table 58. Whereas South Slavic always has /a/, West and East Slavic develop /a/ from a diphthong with so-called acute tone, but /o/ if the diphthong had a so-called circumflex contour. The acute may have been a rising tone or a rising tone followed by a falling tone (see Galinskaja 1997: 59 for discussion). It is generally agreed that the circumflex contour was a falling tone. An acute accent (´) represents the acute contour, while the circumflex accent (˜) is used to symbolize the circumflex type. The accent marks are often placed on top of the liquid consonant, but for convenience in Table 58, the preceding vowels carry the accent marks.

Table 58. Metathesis of liquid dipthongs in word-initial position (ORC groups)

	Common Slavic	South Slavic (BCS)	West Slavic (Polish)	East Slavic (Russian)
/õl/	õlkъtь 'elbow'	lakat	łokieć	lokot'
/ól/	ólnь 'doe'	[lani]	łania	lan'
/õr/	õrbota 'work'	rabota	robota	[robota]
/ór/	órdlo 'plough'	ralo	radło	ralo

Two words are placed in square brackets in Table 58. The reflex of Common Slavic /ólnь/ 'doe' is not attested in Bosnian, Croatian, and Serbian, but for completeness the OCS form *lani* is included in square brackets to show the effect of metathesis in South Slavic. For East Slavic, the form робота is given in square brackets. This is a Ukrainian form; the corresponding **работа** in Contemporary Standard Russian is the result of Church Slavic influence.

10.8.3. CъRC: Liquids Preceded by Jers

The development of CъRC groups is a complicated story in Slavic linguistics, where individual languages show different developments. Luckily, Russian and the other East Slavic languages represent the easy part of the story. In these languages, the jer and the liquid diphthong did not change places. Hence, Late Common Slavic forms such as *sъmьrtь* 'death' became **смерть** in Modern Russian, where /е/ (which developed from /ь/) is still placed in front of the liquid consonant. The only complication involves CъRC groups with the front jer /ь/ followed by /l/. Although, as you will see in section 12.1, /ь/ normally turns into /e/ in Modern Russian, in CъRC groups /ьl/ becomes /ol/ in Modern Russian. An example is **волк** 'wolf', which has developed from Common Slavic /vьlkъ/. This development is due to assimilation of the same type as in CORC groups with /el/ (e.g., **молоко** from Common Slavic /melko/, see section 10.8.1).

10.8.4. Summary of Liquid Diphthongs

Since this book is about the history of Russian, it makes sense to summarize the development of the liquid diphthongs that are relevant for the Russian language. Table 59 shows the Russian reflexes of CORC, ÓRC, ÕRC, and CъRC groups.

Table 59. The development of CORC, ÓRC, ÕRC, and CъRC groups in Russian (O = /o/ or /e/, A = /a/, R = /r/ or /l/, C = any consonant, and Ъ = /ъ/ or /ь/. Boldface identifies the relevant sounds in the examples).

Common Slavic	Modern Russian	Process	Modern Russian exx
CORC	COROC	pleophony	ко**ро**ва 'cow'
ÓRC	RAC	metathesis and lengthening	**ра**ло 'plough'
ÕRC	ROC	metathesis	**ло**коть 'elbow'
CъRC	CORC	—	см**е**рть 'death'

10.9. Prothetic Consonants

In the two preceding sections on nasal and liquid diphthongs, we have seen that syllables consisting of consonant + vowel + consonant turn into syllables containing only consonant + vowel. In other words, we can summarize the transformations of the nasal and liquid diphthongs as follows: CVC → CV. How about syllables that contained only a single vowel? Such syllables were also at variance with the Law of Open Syllables, since they did not have rising sonority. In view of this, one would expect such syllables to undergo change: V → CV. This is exactly what happens. The consonants that emerge through this process are referred to as "prothetic consonants."

There are two prothetic consonants: /j/ and /w/. The choice between them depends on the following vowel. If the vowel is unrounded, /j/ is selected. If the vowel is rounded, the prothetic consonant is /w/. This choice is well motivated. While /j/ does not involve rounded lips, /w/ is bilabial, i.e., a *v*-sound articulated with rounded lips in the same way as rounded vowels. The formation of prothetic consonants starts early in the Common Slavic period, and develops over a long time. It makes sense to distinguish between three stages.

The first stage involves high vowels:

(11) Formation of prothetic consonants (stage 1):
   a. /ī/ → /ji/: Proto-Slavic /īn-/ → Common Slavic /jin-/ 'other'
   b. /ĭ/ → /ji/: Proto-Slavic /ĭgrā/ → Common Slavic /jьgra/ 'game'
   c. /ū/ → /wu/: Proto-Slavic /ūdrā/ → Common Slavic /wydra/ 'otter'
   d. /ŭ/ → /wu/: Proto-Slavic /ŭx-/ → Common Slavic /wъx-/ 'louse'

Notice that /j/ is the consonantal "mirror image" of /i/; the two sounds are exactly the same, except that /j/ is a consonant and /i/ is a vowel. Likewise, /u/ and /w/ are identical, except that /w/ is a consonant and /u/ is a vowel. What happened in (11), therefore, is that a vowel places its consonantal mirror image in front of itself. In this way V becomes CV, but nothing else changes, since the two sounds in each new sequence are identical apart from the fact that the first member of the sequence is a consonant and the second is a vowel.

Although the changes in (11) are straightforward, there is a snag. If you compare the reflexes of w-prothesis in (11c–d) with the corresponding Modern Russian words **выдра** 'otter' and **вошь** 'louse', you see that the prothetic consonant is still in place (although it is /v/, not /w/). However, for (11a–b) the corresponding Modern Russian words, **иной** 'other' and **игра** 'game' do not show any traces of *j*-prothesis. This is the result of a later loss, which has undone the effect of *j*-prothesis before /i/ in most Slavic languages, including Russian. At this point, you may wonder why we assume *j*-prothesis at all, if it has been annulled in almost all Slavic languages. However, evidence from words like **язык** 'tongue', which has preserved the prothetic /j/ to this day, indicates that there must have been *j*-prothesis before /ī/ and /ĭ/ in Common

Slavic. In Proto-Slavic, this word started with /ĭn/. After *j*-prothesis this became /jin/, which then turned into /ję/ since the nasal diphthong was at variance with the Law of Open Syllables. Later /ję/ became /jä/ in Old Rusian and /ja/ in Modern Russian. The creation of the nasal vowel protected /j/ from disappearing, because the result of *j*-prothesis was only undone before /i/. Since the *j*-prothesis is retained in words that originally had /ī/ or /ĭ/, but where these vowels later underwent change, we must conclude that Common Slavic had *j*-prothesis before /ī/ and /ĭ/.

The relevant changes must have taken place early in the Common Slavic period. As we have just seen, they occurred before the transformation of the nasal diphthongs. They also took place before Proto-Slavic /ū/ became /y/. If the emergence of prothetic consonants had occurred after /ū/ lost its roundness and became /y/, we would have expected *j*-prothesis instead of w-prothesis in words like **выдра** 'otter'. The reason why no words in Modern Russian begin with the letter **ы** is the fact that w-prothesis occurred in Common Slavic before /ū/ turned into /y/.

Further development involves spread of *j*-prothesis to new environments. However, w-prothesis did not spread. In the second stage in the development of prothetic consonants, *j*-prothesis spread from high vowels to mid vowels:

(12) Formation of prothetic consonants (stage 2):

  a. /ē/ → /jě/: Proto-Slavic /ēdmĭ/ → Late Common Slavic /jěmь/ 'I eat'
  b. /ĕ/ → /je/: Proto-Slavic /esmĭ/ → Late Common Slavic /jesmь/ 'I am'

In the third and last stage, which took place at the very end of the Common Slavic period, *j*-prothesis spread to /a/:

(13) Formation of prothetic consonants (stage 3):

  /ā/ → /ja/: Proto-Slavic /āblŭkă-/ → Late Common Slavic /jablъko/ 'apple'

This change affects only the long /ō/ in Proto-Slavic, which turned into /a/. Recall from section 10.3 that the Proto-Slavic short /ŏ/ became /o/. No prothetic consonant emerged before /o/. Since /o/ is rounded, it was not affected by *j*-prothesis, which only took place before unrounded consonants. W-prothesis also did not affect /o/, since it never spread beyond Proto-Slavic /ū/ and /ŭ/.[3]

---

[3] Admittedly, Modern Russian has a prothetic /v/ in a few words like **вот** 'here' and **восемь** 'eight', but this is a later development in East Slavic, whereby /v/ was inserted in front of a stressed /o/ in word-initial position in some words (Kiparsky 1967: 147). In

Before we leave the prothetic consonants, it should be pointed out that prothetic /j/ was subsequently lost in some environments in Russian and the other East Slavic languages. This loss took place in the transitional period between Common Slavic and Old Rusian when the Law of Open Syllables was loosening its grip on the phonology. As shown in Table 60, a number of Late Common Slavic words in /je/ correspond to words in /o/ in Modern Russian. However, the table also shows that the change from /je/ to /o/ did not happen across the board, since there are many words that have kept /je/ in Modern Russian. Three such words are listed below the dashed line in the table. It is not easy to state a sound law so that it includes the words that change from /je/ to /o/, but not the words that do not change. However, it seems clear that two conditions had to be met in order for the change to take place. First, one of the first two syllables must carry stress. Second, there must be a front vowel in the second syllable, and this front vowel must not be /ь/. Although the Late Common Slavic words /jestь/, /jego/, and /jemu/ in the table had stress on one of the two first syllables, they did not undergo the change to /o/, because they did not have the right vowel in the second syllable.

Table 60. Development of Late Common Slavic word-initial /je/ in Russian

Late Common Slavic	Modern Russian	Gloss
/jezero/	óзеро	'lake'
/jesenь/	óсень	'autumn'
/jesetrъ/	осётр	'sturgeon'
/jelenь/	олéнь	'deer'
/jedinь/	одúн	'one'
/jestь/	есть	'is'
/jego/	егó	'him'
/jemu/	емý	'to him'

It should be pointed out that analogy and linguistic borrowing complicates the picture. While the word for 'sturgeon' had stress on the second syllable in the nominative singular, the other case forms had stress on the third syllable (cf. the Modern Russian genitive form осетрá). Here we should expect /je/ in Modern Russian, but Contemporary Standard Russian nevertheless has /o/ throughout the paradigm. This is presumably the effect of analogy from the nominative singular.

Old Church Slavonic and Old Rusian, 'eight' had the form осмь, which has been preserved in Modern Russian осьминог 'octopus' (see also section 7.5).

As for the effect of linguistic borrowing, consider Modern Russian **еди́ный** 'single, unified', which has /je/, although it contains the same root as **оди́н** and meets the criteria for the shift to /o/. The reason why we have /je/ in **еди́ный** is that it is a borrowing from Church Slavic.

10.10. Summary: Table of Correspondences

In this chapter, you have learned about a number of sound laws that are either related to the disappearance of the short-long distinction or the creation of open syllables with rising sonority. The following sound laws concern short and long vowels, insofar as quantitative distinctions are replaced by qualitative differences:

(14) Changes concerning the loss of the short-long distinction:
   a. The *o/a* merger (section 10.3)
   b. Changes affecting vowel height (10.3)
   c. Changes affecting rounding (10.3)

The following groups of sound laws create open syllables with rising sonority:

(15) Changes creating open syllables with rising sonority:
   a. Loss of final consonants (10.5)
   b. Monophthongization of oral diphthongs (10.6)
   c. Monophthongization of nasal diphthongs (10.7)
   d. Metathesis and pleophony of liquid diphthongs (10.8)
   e. Emergence of prothetic consonants (10.9)

The changes in (15) can be seen as responses to a general constraint on syllable structure in Common Slavic:

(16) The Law of Open Syllables (**закон открытого слога**, 10.4):
   Common Slavic syllables had rising sonority.

The correspondences between Late Proto-Indo-European and Old Rusian vowels and diphthongs are summarized in Figure 14 on p. 216.

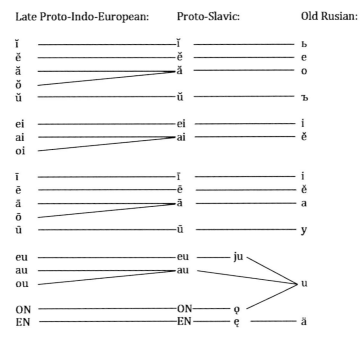

Figure 14. Vowel and diphthong correspondences (ON = nasal diphthong with non-front vowel + nasal consonant; EN = nasal diphthong with front vowel + nasal consonant)

10.11. For Further Reading

Townsend and Janda (1996) offer a pedagogical overview with comparisons across the Slavic languages. A compact survey is provided in Andersen 1998. Galinskaja 2009 and 2014: 18–24 are reader-friendly and up-to-date presentations in Russian. An unsurpassable source of information about Common Slavic phonology is Shevelov's (1964) monumental study.

Chapter 11

Phonology: Pre-Slavic and Common Slavic Consonants

While studying Modern Russian grammar, you have no doubt struggled with the consonant alternations in verbal stems. Why does the stem have different shapes in **могу** 'I can' and **можешь** 'you can'? Why are there consonant alternations in verbs like **писать** 'write' (**пишу, пишешь, пишут**) and **любить** 'love' (**люблю, любишь, любят**)? And why are alternations characteristic of verbs, but not of nouns? In order to find answers, we have to go back in time. This chapter compares the consonant system of Contemporary Standard Russian with those of Late Proto-Indo-European, Proto-Slavic, and Old Rusian (section 11.1), and then takes you through consonant changes in Pre-Slavic (sections 11.2–11.3) and Common Slavic (sections 11.4–11.9).

11.1. Overview: Consonant Systems for Late Proto-Indo-European, Proto-Slavic, Old Rusian, and Contemporary Standard Russian

Before we consider the changes affecting consonants, it is helpful to look at the consonant phoneme systems for Late Proto-Indo-European, Old Rusian, and Contemporary Standard Russian. In the same way as for vowels, we organize the consonant phonemes according to natural classes, i.e., classes of sounds that share properties such as "labial," "plosive," or "voiced." We can group the properties we need in six groups:

(1) a. Place of articulation: labial, dental, post-alveolar, palatal, and velar

b. Manner of articulation: plosive, affricate, fricative, nasal, liquid, and glide

c. Voicing: voiced and voiceless

d. Aspiration: aspirated and unaspirated

e. Palatalization: palatalized (soft) and non-palatalized (hard)

f. Labialization: labialized and non-labialized (plain)

The properties in (1a) tell us where in the mouth the relevant sounds are articulated. Consonants such as [p, b] are labial, since they are articulated with the lips, dentals such as [t, d] are articulated with the tip of the tongue behind the teeth, while post-alveolars, palatals, and velars are articulated further back. I will use the term "dorsal" as an umbrella term for palatal and velar consonants. Under the heading "manner of articulation" in (1b), we distinguish between plosives such as [t, d] and fricatives such as [s, z]. Affricates are combinations of plosives + fricatives, such as [c] (or [ts], the first sound in the Modern Russian word царь 'tsar'). An umbrella term for plosives, affricates, and fricatives is "obstruent," as opposed to nasals, liquids, and glides that are "sonorants." Recall from section 10.4 that these sounds are sonorous, in the sense that they are easier to sing than the obstruents. Voicing in (1c) has to do with the vocal chords. If the vocal chords vibrate, the relevant sound is voiced (e.g., [b, d]); if not, the sound in question is voiceless (e.g., [p, t]). In (1d) we distinguish between aspirated consonants, where a strong burst of air accompanies the sound, and unaspirated consonants, which lack such a burst of air. Palalization in (1e) is the distinction between hard and soft consonants that you are familiar with from Modern Russian. The final consonant in сталь 'steel' is palatalized (soft), while the corresponding consonant in стал 'became' is non-palatalized (hard). Labialization in (1f) refers to consonants that have lip rounding in addition to their primary place of articulation.

Let us start with the Late Proto-Indo-European consonant system in Table 61 below (similar tables summarizing later consonant phoneme systems follow on the opposite page). Characteristic of this system is the imbalance between plosives and fricatives. There are fifteen plosives, but only one fricative! Among the plosives, you notice the row of aspirated voiced consonants: /b^h, d^h, g'^h, g^h, g^{wh}/, where the superscript ^{h} represents the additional burst of air that is characteristic of aspirated consonants. Some researchers also assume a row of unvoiced aspirated plosives /p^h, t^h, k'^h, k^h, k^{wh}/, but since this is of little

Table 61. Late Proto-Indo-European consonant phoneme system

			labial	dental	palatal	velar	
						plain	labialized
plosive	voiceless	unaspirated	p	t	k'	k	k^w
plosive	voiced	unaspirated	b	d	g'	g	g^w
plosive	voiced	aspirated	b^h	d^h	g'^h	g^h	g^{wh}
fricative	voiceless			s			
nasal	voiced		m	n			
liquid	voiced			l, r			
glide	voiced		w		j		

11.1. Overview: Consonant Systems

Table 62. Proto-Slavic consonant phoneme system

		labial	dental	dorsal
plosive	voiceless	p	t	k
plosive	voiced	b	d	g
fricative	voiceless		s	x
fricative	voiced		z	
nasal	voiced	m	n	
liquid	voiced		l, r	
glide	voiced	w		j

Table 63. Old Rusian consonant phoneme system

		labial	dental		post-alveolar	dorsal
			hard	soft	soft	
plosive	voiceless	p	t			k
plosive	voiced	b	d			g
affricate	voiceless			c′	č′	
fricative	voiceless		s	s′	š′	x
fricative	voiced		z	z′	ž′	
nasal	voiced	m	n	n′		
liquid	voiced		l, r	l′, r′		
glide	voiced	w				j

Table 64. Contemporary Standard Russian consonant phoneme system

		labial		dental		post-alveolar		dorsal
		hard	soft	hard	soft	hard	soft	
plosive	voiceless	p	p′	t	t′			k
plosive	voiced	b	b′	d	d′			g
affricate	voiceless			c			č′	
fricative	voiceless	v	v′	s	s′	š	š′	x
fricative	voiced	f	f′	z	z′	ž		
nasal	voiced	m	m′	n	n′			
liquid	voiced			l, r	l′, r′			
glide	voiced							j

importance for Slavic, these consonants will not be discussed in the following (cf. Voyles and Barrack 2009: 13f.). The consonant system in Table 61 comprises nine palatal and velar plosives. The palatals were presumably close to the first sound in Modern Russian words such as кислый 'sour' and гибкий 'flexible', while the plain velars resembled the initial sounds in короткий 'short' and горький 'bitter'. The labialized velars (often referred to as "labiovelars") displayed additional lip rounding symbolized as a superscript ^{w}.

The Proto-Slavic consonant system in Table 62 is more balanced than the Late Proto-Indo-European system. The number of plosives has been reduced to nine, while the number of fricatives has increased to three. Notice in particular that the number of palatal and velar plosives has been reduced drastically; all the aspirated, palatal, and labialized phonemes have disappeared through sound changes you will learn about in section 11.2. An important new consonant phoneme is the velar fricative /x/ (the sound you find in the beginning of хороший 'good' in Modern Russian). We will discuss the emergence of /x/ in section 11.3. Notice that I use the term "dorsal" in the Proto-Slavic system to refer to the velar obstruents /k, g, x/ and the palatal glide /j/.

The Old Rusian consonant system in Table 63 is larger than the Proto-Slavic system. A number of new affricates and fricatives have emerged through a series of palatalization processes—sound laws we will explore in detail in sections 11.4–11.7. The Old Rusian consonant system also shows that the difference between hard and soft consonants had started developing in Old Rusian. This difference has been further developed in Contemporary Standard Russian, as shown in Table 64. We will return to the consonant phonemes in Contemporary Standard Russian in the next chapter, but it is useful to have the four systems from Late Proto-Indo-European to Contemporary Standard Russian next to each other. As you can see from the four tables, the development goes from the large consonant inventory of Late Proto-Indo-European via the smaller consonant systems of Proto-Slavic and Old Rusian to the sizeable system of Contemporary Standard Russian.

11.2. Loss of Dorsal Plosives: Centum and Satem Languages

Since the Late-Indo-European consonant system had so many plosives and so few fricatives, it may not come as a surprise that the first changes that took place reduced the number of plosives. As a result of these changes in the Pre-Slavic period, two groups of Indo-European languages were formed. These groups are traditionally referred to as the "satem" and "centum" languages:

11.2. Loss of Dorsal Plosives: Centum and Satem Languages

(2) a. Satem languages: Slavic, Baltic, Indo-Iranian, Armenian, and Albanian

b. Centum languages: Germanic, Celtic, Romance, Hellenic (Greek), Anatolian, and Tocharian

The terms "satem" and "centum" (pronounced "kentum") are the Avestan (an Indo-Iranian language) and Latin words for 'hundred'. As the terms suggest, the satem languages have fricatives where centum languages have plosives. The Russian word for 'hundred', сто, shows that Russian and the other Slavic languages belong to the satem group, since the word starts with the fricative /s/. (If you are wondering why English and other Germanic languages have the fricative /h/ in the word for 'hundred' although they belong to the centum group, this is due to later developments in Germanic.) Other Russian words that show that Slavic belongs to the satem languages include сердце, which corresponds to English *heart*, where /h/ has developed from /k/, and зерно, which corresponds to English *grain*. Traditionally, the division between satem and centum languages was considered an East-West split, but the discovery that Tocharian, the easternmost Indo-European language, belonged to the centum group undermined this theory.

In both the centum and satem groups the number of dorsal plosives was reduced from nine to four. However, as shown in Figure 15, the two groups did not eliminate the same phonemes. While the centum languages got rid of palatal plosives, the satem languages lost labialized plosives. Aspirated plosives disappeared in both groups.

At this point we leave the centum languages and focus on the so-called satem assibilation, a sound law that turned the palatal plosives into fricatives in the satem languages, possibly via an intermediate stage where the relevant sounds were affricates. "Sibilant" is a cover term for affricates and fricatives, and "assibilation" is a process that produces sibilants. Notice that the assibilation of palatals could only happen in the satem languages, since the centum languages had lost their palatal plosives already. We can write the sound law as follows:

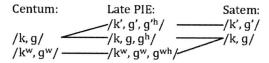

Figure 15. The reduction from nine to four dorsal plosives in the centum and satem languages

(3) The satem assibilation:
   a. Palatal voiceless plosive /k'/ → Voiceless fricative /s/
   b. Palatal voiced plosives /g', g'ʰ/ → Voiced fricative /z/

While the /s/ phoneme already existed, (3b) created a new phoneme: /z/. (As pointed out in Voyles and Barrack 2009: 37, Late Proto-Indo-European probably had a [z] allophone of the /s/ phoneme, but it was only after the satem assibilation the voiced fricative became a phoneme.)

Before we leave the reduction of the number of plosives, let us consider a couple of examples involving palatal plosives in Late Proto-Indo-European:

(4) a. Late Proto-Indo-European: /k'rdĭkŏs/ → Late Common Slavic /sьrdьce/ 'heart'
   b. Late Proto-Indo-European: /g'ŏmbʰŏs/ → Late Common Slavic /zǫbъ/ 'tooth'

In (4a), we see that /k'/ turns into /s/. The emergence of the affricate /c/ is a result of palatalization—the phenomenon we will explore in the sections 11.5–11.8. Now that you have learned that the /s/ in Russian **сердце** 'heart' has developed from /k/ in Late Proto-Indo-European, you probably recognize the same root in the English word *cordial* (of Latin origin), which still has /k/ at the beginning. However, as mentioned, **сердце** also corresponds to English *heart*.

In (4b), /g'/ turns into /z/. The nasal diphthong /ŏm/ becomes the nasal vowel /ǫ/ through monophthongization (see section 10.7), and then turns into /u/ in Modern Russian. The resulting Modern Russian word is therefore **зуб**. The corresponding English word, which has kept both the velar plosive and the nasal diphthong intact, is *comb*. On the face of it, the meaning difference between 'tooth' and 'comb' may seem considerable. However, after all, combs are implements that have teeth!

Examples such as those in (4) are numerous, so there is no doubt that Slavic belongs to the satem languages. However, there are some apparent counter-examples such as Modern Russian **корова** 'cow' and **город** 'city' that have kept a plosive even though they must have contained palatal plosives in Late Proto-Indo-European. How these and similar words have kept the plosive despite the satem assibilation rule in (3) is one of the remaining mysteries in Slavic linguistics known by its German name Gutturalwechsel (literally "velar alternation"). A possible theory is that such words represent early borrowings from centum languages (cf. Gołąb 1992: 78–90).

11.3. The "*Ruki*" Rule and the Emergence of /x/

Now that you have learned about the emergence of /z/, we will turn to another fricative that came on stage in the Pre-Slavic period, namely /x/. This sound was the result of a sound change that affected /s/ after the phonemes /r, u, k, i/:

(5) The "*ruki*" rule:

$$\text{Late PIE /s/} \rightarrow \text{Proto-Slavic /x/ / } \begin{Bmatrix} r \\ u \\ k \\ i \end{Bmatrix} \_\_ \text{ non-plosive}$$

Since this sound law involves the phonemes /r, u, k, i/, it is helpful to use the traditional mnemonic "*ruki* rule." However, the rule is also sometimes called "Pedersen's rule" after the Danish linguist Holger Pedersen (1867–1953). Notice that the *ruki* rule applies after both short /ŭ, ĭ/ and long /ū, ī/, and that it is the only sound law that produces /x/ in Slavic.

By way of example, consider the Modern Russian word **ухо** 'ear', where /x/ has developed from /s/ due to the *ruki* rule. We can reconstruct the root in Proto-Indo-European as /ous/, which became /aux/ in Proto-Slavic and /ux/ in Old Rusian and Modern Russian. The original /s/ has been preserved in some Indo-European languages, e.g., Greek where we have *aus* and Lithuanian where we have *ausis* for 'ear'. If you are guessing that English *ear* and Russian **ухо** are cognates that have developed from Proto-Indo-European /ous/, you are right; the /r/ you find in the English word for 'ear' has developed from /s/.

According to (5), the *ruki* rule applies only if /s/ is followed by a non-plosive. This is another way of saying that a plosive after /s/ blocks the application of the rule. The Russian word pair **тусклый** 'dim' and **тухнуть** 'go out (of light)' illustrates this. In **тусклый**, the following /k/ has blocked the application of the *ruki* rule and /s/ remains, while in **тухнуть** /s/ has become /x/ since there was no plosive after /s/.

Different scholars state the *ruki* rule differently, but regardless of which version one assumes, it is clear that we are dealing with a peculiar sound law. Typically, sound laws involve natural classes. In the following sections of this chapter, for instance, we will be concerned with sound laws that take place before the natural class of front vowels. However, the phonemes /r, u, k, i/, which condition the application of the *ruki* rule, do not seem to form a natural class. Why did the sound law apply after this seemingly arbitrary group of sounds? Andersen (1968) suggests an elegant solution to this problem. His proposal is that the most "marked" sounds in each subpart of the phoneme system were involved in the *ruki* rule. Simply put, "marked" here means that the sounds in question differ from what is typical in each class. Andersen argues that /i, u/ are marked vowels, and that /r/ and /k/ are marked consonants. Furthermore, /s/ was a highly marked phoneme, since it was the only fricative in Late Proto-Indo-European. What happened, according to Andersen's analysis, is that a marked phoneme (/s/) developed a marked allophone ([x]) when following marked sounds. Later the marked allophone [x] became the phoneme /x/.

In order to gain a better understanding of how the *ruki* rule works, consider the Old Rusian aorist endings discussed in section 8.3.1. Table 65, opposite, shows that the first consonant in the endings is either /s/, /x/, or /š'/ (spelled as ш). Since we know that the *ruki* rule turned /s/ into /x/, it stands to reason that all the aorist endings in the table originally contained /s/. Notice that in the endings that have preserved /s/ (2nd and 3rd person dual -ста and 2nd person plural -сте), /s/ is followed by the plosive /t/. As mentioned above, a following plosive blocked the application of the *ruki* rule, so it is not surprising that /s/ has been preserved in -ста and -сте. In the endings with /x/ (1st person singular -хъ, 1st person dual -ховѣ, and 1st person plural -хомъ), the second sound is a vowel, so here the *ruki* rule has turned /s/ into /x/.

The 3rd person plural ending with /š'/ is harder to explain, but a possible scenario is this. If we assume that in Late Proto-Indo-European the 3rd person plural form ended in /sīnt/, /s/ was followed by a vowel, and thus underwent the *ruki* rule and became /x/. The resulting /x/ then became palatalized to /š'/ due to a sound law we will discuss in the following section. In addition to this, the final consonant of the ending disappeared and the nasal diphthong became a nasal vowel, which later turned into /ä/ in Old Rusian. If you do not remember the last two changes, go back to section 10.7.

According to an alternative scenario, the *ruki* rule took place in two steps. First, /s/ turned into /š'/ unless followed by a plosive. As a result, all the endings with /x/ or /š'/ in Table 65 developed /š'/. Then, a second step turned /š'/ into /x/ if the following sound was a non-front vowel or sonorant. Since in the 3rd person plural /š'/ was followed by a front vowel, in this form /š'/ was not affected by the second step.

Table 65 contains two example verbs. The *ruki* rule clearly applies to the endings of хвалити 'praise', since here the stem ends in /i/—one of the four phonemes /r, u, k, i/ mentioned in the rule in (5). However, how could we end up with /x/ in the aorists of verbs like нести 'carry', which did not have any of the four phonemes /r, u, k, i/ in stem-final position? In section 3.6 you learned that when a historical linguist comes across something that cannot be explained by sound law, s/he first thinks about analogy. Indeed, a likely scenario is that the *ruki* rule first affected verbs where the conditions in (5) were met, and then spread to other verb classes by analogy.

11.3. The "Ruki" Rule and the Emergency of /x/

Table 65. The effect of the *ruki* rule in the Old Rusian aorist

		Aorist endings	Example: хвалити	Example: нести
Sg	1	-хъ	хвалихъ	несохъ
	2	-Ø	хвали	несе
	3	-Ø	хвали	несе
Du	1	-ховѣ	хвалиховѣ	несоховѣ
	2	-ста	хвалиста	несоста
	3	-ста	хвалиста	несоста
Pl	1	-хомъ	хвалихомъ	несохомъ
	2	-сте	хвалисте	несосте
	3	-ша	хвалиша	несоша

We face a similar problem in the endings of nouns, pronouns, and adjectives. In Contemporary Standard Russian, nouns have the ending /ax/ in the locative plural (**в комнатах** 'in the rooms', etc.). Since Late Proto-Indo-European did not have /x/, we are forced to assume that the ending originally contained /s/. The only sound law that produces /x/ is the *ruki* rule. However, how could /x/ emerge after /a/ in the modern ending /ax/? Since the *ruki* rule, as formulated in (5), did not apply after /a/, it is reasonable to assume that endings such as /ax/ are due to analogy. Recall from sections 4.2.2 and 4.2.4 that the ŏ-, ŭ-, and ĭ-declensions had the locative plural endings -ѣхъ, -ъхъ, and -ьхъ in Old Rusian. If we reconstruct these endings as /oisŭ/, /ŭsŭ/, and /ĭsŭ/, we understand how the *ruki* rule turned /s/ into /x/, since here /s/ was preceded by /oi, ŭ, ĭ/ (/ě, ъ, ь/ in Old Rusian) and followed by a non-front vowel (/ъ/ in Old Rusian from Late Proto-Indo-European /ŭ/). Possibly, /x/ spread to other declensions by analogy, and has survived in the modern ending /ax/, which goes back to the ā-declension.

Another problem is /x/ in the beginning of a word. Since the *ruki* rule applies after /r, u, k, i/, the rule cannot apply to a word-initial consonant. Yet it is not hard to find Modern Russian examples of /x/ in the beginning of the word. In addition to **хвалить** 'praise', mentioned above, examples include verbs such as **ходить** 'walk', adjectives such as **худой** 'thin' and **холостой** 'unmarried', and nouns such as **хлеб** 'bread' and **холм** 'hill'. How could /x/ develop in the beginning of such words?

For verbs, a possibility is that the *ruki* rule applied to prefixed verbs; if the prefix ended in one of the /r, u, k, i/ sounds, the rule would apply. The ancestors of the modern prefixes **у-** and **при-** are good candidates, since they ended in /u/ and /i/. In order for this analysis to work, we must assume that /x/ later appeared in unprefixed verbs due to analogy. A classic example of this development is **ходить** (Shevelov 1964: 134, Gołąb 1973: 130).

Another possible solution to the problem of initial /x/ is to assume that the relevant words started with the cluster /ks/, which became /kx/ by means of the *ruki* rule, before the initial /k/ was lost, so as to create a word with initial /x/. An example of this development is **худой** (Gołąb 1973: 129).

A number of other accounts of word-initial /x/ have been proposed. However, as pointed out by Gołąb (1973), besides the explanations involving prefixes and initial /ks/, the only certain source of Slavic words beginning in /x/ is borrowing. Some loanwords are from the Indo-Iranian languages spoken by Scythians and Sarmatians. A possible example is **холостой** (Gołąb 1973: 138). Other loanwords are of Germanic origin. A good example is **хлеб** 'bread'; as pointed out in section 1.3, this word was most likely borrowed from Gothic *hlaifs* (which corresponds to *loaf* in modern English). Another example of an early Germanic borrowing is **холм** 'hill', which is related to modern Norwegian *holme* 'small island'. If you wonder how a word meaning 'hill' can be related to a word meaning 'island', think of islands as "hills" in the sea!

11.4. More on Common Slavic Syllables: Synharmony

After the discussion of the Pre-Slavic changes that gave rise to /z/ and /x/, we are now ready to consider the changes that took place in Common Slavic. In the previous chapter, you learned about the Law of Open Syllables and saw that syllable structure played a key role in the changes concerning vowels and diphthongs in Common Slavic. In this and the following sections, you will see that syllable structure is equally important for consonants.

According to the Law of Open Syllables, the preferred type of syllable in Common Slavic was CV, i.e., a consonant followed by a vowel. However, Common Slavic did not accept all combinations of consonants and vowels. The restriction can be stated as follows:

(6) The Law of Syllabic Synharmony (**Закон слогового сингармонизма**):

In Common Slavic, a syllable could consist of:

a. Soft consonant + front vowel

b. Hard consonant + non-front vowel

In order to see how this principle works, it may be helpful to consider some examples from Modern Russian. Since Russian has soft and hard consonants and front and non-front vowels there are four possible combinations of consonants and vowels:

(7) Four types of CV syllables:
    a. Soft consonant + front vowel: те, пели
    b. Hard consonant + non-front vowel: то, помощь
    c. Soft consonant + non-front vowel: тётя, пёстрый
    d. Hard consonant + front vowel: кафе, купе

While Contemporary Standard Russian accepts all four types, only (7a–b) were well-formed in Common Slavic according to the Law of Syllabic Synharmony. I hasten to add that although (7) provides a good overview, it may exaggerate the differences between Common Slavic and Modern Russian. First, it should be pointed out that there exist counterexamples to the Law of Syllabic Synharmony in Common Slavic, such as *jutro* 'morning' with soft /j/ followed by non-front /u/. Second, the four syllable types are not equally well entrenched in Modern Russian; syllables with a hard consonant followed by front vowel are not characteristic of Contemporary Standard Russian, and it is not a coincidence that the examples in (7d) are loanwords. These caveats notwithstanding, it is clear that the Law of Syllabic Synharmony in Common Slavic describes an important tendency that is reflected in a number of sound changes.

What is the phonetic motivation for the Law of Syllabic Synharmony? Why do soft consonants combine with front vowels, and hard consonants with non-front vowels? Simply put, the Law of Syllabic Synharmony is a version of the principle that "birds of a feather flock together," since it requires consonants and vowels in a syllable to be articulated close to each other. Soft consonants are articulated with the mid body of the tongue raised towards the palate (the front part of the roof of the mouth), which is also where front vowels are articulated. Hard consonants are articulated with the body of the tongue raised towards the velum (the area behind the palate), and this is close to where non-front vowels are articulated. This is summarized in Table 66.

Table 66. The phonetic motivation of synharmony

Consonant	Vowel	Location of the body of the tongue
soft	front	palate (front part of the roof of the mouth)
hard	non-front	velum (back part of the roof of the mouth)

The term "synharmony" has to do with the Greek word for 'together' and *harmony*, which means 'agreement, concord of sounds'. When we say that something is "harmonic," we mean that its parts go together well. This is suitable for the Law of Syllabic Synharmony, which states that the consonants and vowels in a syllable are in harmony when they are articulated close to each other. In the following sections, we turn to sound changes motivated by the Law of Syllabic Synharmony.

11.5. First Palatalization of Velars

With reference to Common Slavic it is customary to distinguish between four sound changes that all affect consonants followed by front vowels or /j/. As mentioned in the previous section, front vowels and the soft consonant /j/ are articulated at the palate. Sound laws that bring consonants closer to the palate are called "palatalizations." The so-called first palatalization can be summarized as follows:

(8) The first palatalization of velar consonants in Common Slavic:
   a. /k/ → /č'/ / ___ front vowel or /j/
   b. /g/ → /ž'/ / ___ front vowel or /j/
   c. /x/ → /š'/ / ___ front vowel or /j/

The first palatalization is an example of a regressive sound change. This means that a sound affects the preceding sound. As you will see in section 11.8, Common Slavic also experienced a progressive palatalization, where a vowel affected the following consonant.

Let us consider some examples of the first palatalization:

(9) Examples of first palatalization:
   a. /k/ → /č'/: Proto-Slavic /kěsātei/ → Old Rusian /č'esati/ 'to comb'
   b. /g/ → /ž'/: Proto-Slavic /gīv-/ → Old Rusian /ž'ivъ/ 'alive'
   c. /x/ → /š'/: Proto-Slavic /graixĭn-/ → Old Rusian /grěš'ьnъ/ 'sinful'

Notice that the outcome is always a soft consonant, as indicated by the apostrophe. In Modern Russian /ž/ and /š/ have become hard consonants, and words such as жив 'alive' and шило 'awl' are pronounced as if the vowel would be spelled as ы instead of и. The hardening ("depalatalization") of /ž', š'/ to /ž, š/ took place in the Old Rusian period. You will learn more about this in section 12.5.

In the chapters on morphology, you have learned about some alternations that are due to the first palatalization. For nouns in the ŏ-declension, you have seen that the vocative had the ending -e (cf. section 4.2.1). Since the ending was a front vowel, nouns with velars in stem-final position underwent the first palatalization. An example is **Богъ** 'God', which had the vocative **Боже** (which is still used in Modern Russian). In pronouns, you see the effect of the first palatalization in **чьто** 'what'. As mentioned in section 5.6, the two pronouns **чьто** 'what' and **къто** 'who' had the same root, but with different vowels. The first palatalization applied before a front vowel, thus producing /č'/ in **чьто**, but not in **къто**. In verbs, we find traces of the first palatalization in the inflection of Modern Russian verbs such as **мочь** 'be able', **печь** 'bake', and **беречь** 'guard' (cf. section 8.2). In the present tense, these verbs have forms such as **можешь** and **может**, which show the result of the first palatalization before /ě/ in Common Slavic. In Old Rusian, such verbs also display the effect of the first palatalization in the aorist (cf. section 8.3.1). For instance, in **пече** and **береже** (second and third persons singular) we have /č'/ and /ž'/ before a front vowel, whereas /k/ and /g/ have been preserved in **пекохъ** and **берегохъ** (first person singular) where the following vowel is non-front. In section 11.3, you learned that /š'/ in the 3rd person plural aorist ending -**ша** in Old Rusian may be due to the first palatalization if we assume that this ending first had developed /x/ through the *ruki* rule.

It is likely that the changes in (8) went via an intermediate stage, whereby [k, g, x] became [k', g', x'], which later turned into [č', ž', š']. The first step is a clear example of palatalization, since [k', g', x'] are palatal consonants. The second step involves lenition, a process whereby sounds become more sonorous. Lenition means "weakening," and a widespread version of lenition turns plosives into affricates, which then become fricatives. Recall from section 10.4, that fricatives are slightly more sonorous than plosives. We can represent this as follows (see Townsend and Janda 1996: 84):

(10) First palatalization as lenition:

	Plosive	→	Affricate	→	Fricative
a.	[k]	→	[č']		
b.	[g]	→			[ž']
c.					[x] → [š']

There are two things to notice. First, [x] was already a fricative and did not undergo further lenition. Second, while both [k] and [g] underwent lenition, [k] only became an affricate ([č']), while [g] went all the way and turned into a fricative. It is possible that [g] first became an affricate and then turned into a fricative, but this is uncertain. Either way, it is clear that the first palatalization started out with two plosives and a fricative and ultimately yielded a system with one affricate and two fricatives.

An important complication concerns the first palatalization before Proto-Slavic /ē/, which turned into Late Common Slavic and Old Rusian /ě/:

(11) First palatalization before Proto-Slavic /ē/:
   a. /kē/ → /č'ě/: /krīkētei/ → /krič'ati/ 'shout'
   b. /gē/ → /ž'ě/: /lěgētei/ → /lež'ati/ 'lie'
   c. /xē/ → /š'ě/: /dūxētei/ → /dyš'ati/ 'breathe'

While these examples display the expected results of the first palatalization, the long /ē/ that triggered the palatalization turned into /a/ after a soft consonant. Since /a/ is a non-front vowel that would not have occasioned palatalization, we must assume that /ē/ → /a/ took place after the palatalization proper. According to Andersen (1969; see Townsend and Janda 1996: 78 for discussion), this change from /ē/ to /a/ may have gone through a number of intermediate steps, say:

(12) From /ē/ to /a/ via diphtongization:
   [kē] → [k'ē] → [č'ea] → [č'ᵉa] → [č'a]

Similar intermediate steps can be postulated for /g/ and /x/. Notice that we are dealing with diphthongization here, since the two intermediate steps involve gliding transitions between vowels. However, unlike the diphthongs you learned about in the previous chapter, the diphthongs in (12) have rising sonority, so they are not at variance with the Law of Open Syllables.

There are three things to notice about the change from /ē/ to /a/. First, regardless of which intermediate steps one assumes, it is clear that the ultimate result is a syllable consisting of a soft consonant followed by the non-front vowel /a/. Such a syllable violates the Law of Syllabic Synharmony. Although the Law of Syllabic Synharmony represents a strong tendency in Common Slavic, it evidently was not an obligatory requirement at the time when /ē/ became /a/.

The second reason why the change from /ē/ to /a/ is important concerns the status of soft consonants as phonemes. When the first palatalization produced [k', g', x'] and later [č', ž', š'], these soft consonants were only found before front vowels and /j/. In other words, we had a situation of complementary distribution where the soft consonants occurred before front vowels, while the hard [k, g, x] were found elsewhere. Since the relevant soft and hard consonants were in complementary distribution, the soft consonants were not independent phonemes, but rather allophones of /k, g, x/. However, when /ē/ became

/a/ after soft consonants, both soft and hard consonants were found before /a/. As a result, the soft and hard consonants were no longer in complementary distribution, and /k', g', x'/ and later /č', ž', š'/ became independent phonemes.

The third reason why the /ē/ to /a/ change is important, is that it has left interesting traces in the grammar of Modern Russian verbs and adjectives. Russian verbs with infinitives in /at'/ generally belong to the first conjugation, i.e., they take present-tense endings like **-ешь** (2 sg), **-ет** (3 sg), **-ем** (1 pl), etc. However, a number of verbs in /č', ž, š/ such as **кричать** 'shout', **лежать** 'lie', and **дышать** 'breathe' are exceptions since they belong to the second conjugation and take endings like **-ишь** (2 sg), **-ит** (3 sg), **-им** (1 pl), etc. You now understand how this exception came about. The exceptional verbs originally had /ē/ and belonged to the same class as second conjugation verbs like **смотреть** 'look' and **сидеть** 'sit'. After /ē/ turned into /a/, the relevant verbs retained their second conjugation endings in the present tense. In this way, the change from /ē/ to /a/ created an exception in the grammar of verbs in Modern Russian.

In adjectives, we see the effect of the change from /ē/ to /a/ after soft consonants in superlative forms. From the Modern Russian adjective **новый** 'new' we can form the superlative form **новейший** 'very new'. However, if the stem of the adjective ends in velar consonant such as /k/, the suffix is not **-ейший**, but **-айший** (cf. **великий** 'great'—**величайший** 'very great'). The reason behind the **-ейший**/**-айший** variation is the fact that /ē/ turned into /a/ after the soft consonant that emerged from the first palatalization in Common Slavic.

11.6. *J*-Palatalization

Under the heading "*j*-palatalization" we will consider palatalizations of consonants before /j/. The phenomenon is also known as "yodization," "jotation," and "deiotation." In the previous section, the first palatalization was stated so as to apply before front vowels or /j/. Whether one considers the mutation of /kj, gj, xj/ to /č', ž', š'/ examples of the first palatalization or the *j*-palatalization is of little consequence, since the outcome of both processes is the same. The reason why we need to consider *j*-palatalization separately is that it affects other consonants than velars. As opposed to the first palatalization, which yields the same sounds across the Slavic languages, *j*-palatalization creates different outputs in different languages. However, in the following we will focus on the results of *j*-palatalization in East Slavic. For a discussion of the other Slavic languages, you may consult Townsend and Janda 1996: 86–91. Figure 16 on p. 232 provides an overview of the changes.

As shown in Figure 16, *j*-palatalization divided the Proto-Slavic consonant phonemes into three groups. The non-labial (i.e., dental and velar) obstruents

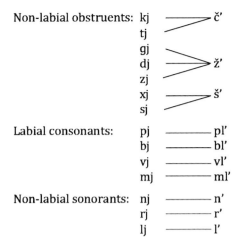

Figure 16. The results of *j*-palatalization in East Slavic

produced /č', ž', š'/, while labial + /j/ became labial + soft /l'/ and non-labial sonorants yielded soft /n', r', l'/. Here is an example for each of these groups:

(13) Examples of *j*-palatalization:
   a. Non-labial obstruent + /j/: Proto-Slavic /māzjām/ → Old Rusian /maž'u/ 'I smear'
   b. Labial + /j/: Proto-Slavic /zĕmjā/ → Old Rusian /zeml'a/
   c. Non-Labial sonorant + /j/: Proto-Slavic /mărjŏs/ → Old Rusian /mor'e/

An important property of *j*-palatalization is the fact that /j/ itself disappeared as part of the change. This sometimes gave rise to combinations of soft consonants + non-front vowels, such as in /zeml'a/ in (13b). This suggests that the Law of Syllabic Synharmony was not an absolute requirement. At the same time, *j*-palatalization paved the way for soft consonants as independent phonemes. Since they were no longer only found before front vowels, soft and hard consonants were no longer in complementary distribution, and soft consonants therefore established themselves as phonemes.

As mentioned in section 8.2, *j*-palatalization has had important consequences for Russian verbs. In Modern Russian verbs like мазать 'smear' and писать 'write', we have a consonant alternation throughout the present tense (мажу, мажешь, мажет and пишу, пишешь, пишет, etc.). This is because these verbs had /j/ after the verb root throughout the present tense in Common

Slavic. The root-final consonant merged with the following /j/, yielding the consonant alternations that learners of Russian have struggled with to this day.

Second conjugation verbs in Modern Russian display consonant alternation in the first person singular, as illustrated by verbs such as возить 'transport', носить 'carry', and любить 'love' (вожу, возишь; ношу, носишь; люблю, любишь). These verbs had /j/ in the first person singular, but not in the rest of the present-tense forms, and therefore the consonant alternation occurs only in the first person singular in Modern Russian verbs in the second conjugation.

I mentioned that *j*-palatalizations produced different sounds in different Slavic languages. While our main focus is on the East Slavic reflexes, it is also interesting to consider some of the results of *j*-palatalization in South Slavic, since they made their way into Old Rusian and Modern Russian through the influence from Old Church Slavonic. Of particular interest is the development of /dj/ and /tj/, which gave /ž'd'/ and /š't'/ in Old Church Slavonic, but /ž'/ and /č'/ in East Slavic. Table 67 summarizes the differences.

Table 67. Reflexes of Prpto-Slavic /tj/ and /dj/ in Old Church Slavonic and Old Rusian

Proto-Slavic	Old Church Slavonic	Old Rusian	Gloss
/dj/: mĕdjā	/ž'd'/: /mež'd'a/	/ž'/: /mež'a/	'boundary'
/tj/: swaitjā	/š't'/: /svĕš't'a/	/č'/: /svĕč'a/	'candle'

It is not hard to find examples with the Church Slavic reflexes of /dj/ and /tj/ in Modern Russian. A simple example is the preposition между 'between', which has /žd/ as opposed to межа 'boundary' with the same root. We also find the Church Slavic version in verbs. While судить (сужу, судишь, суженный) 'judge' has the East Slavic /ž/, the related verb обсудить (обсужу, обсудишь, обсужденный) displays the East Slavic /ž/ in the first person singular, but the Church Slavic /žd/ in the past passive participle. Since the influence from Old Church Slavonic came through a written language used in a religious context, it is not too surprising that we encounter the Church Slavic /žd/ in the participle. After all, participles are characteristic of written language.

When it comes to Proto-Slavic /tj/, we find the Old Church Slavonic influence in Modern Russian words with the letter щ, which goes back to the Old Church Slavonic /š't'/, although it is pronounced as a long soft fricative [š':] in Modern Russian. As pointed out in section 8.8.3, the suffix -щий of present active participles such as летящий 'flying' is a slavonicism as opposed to adjectives such as летучий 'flying', which has the East Slavic /č/. With regard to the root свет 'light', which, as shown in Table 67, displays the East Slavic reflex in **свеча** 'candle', it is helpful to consider the verb **просветить**. In the concrete meaning 'X-ray, screen', this verb has forms with the East Slavic reflex: **просвечу, просвеченный**. However, in the more abstract meaning 'enlighten' we find Church Slavic forms: **просвещу, просвещенный**. Again, since Old Church Slavonic was a written language used in a religious context, you are probably not surprised to learn that it is the more abstract meaning that testifies to the Church Slavic influence. This squares well with slavonicisms such as **глава** 'chapter, head (leader)', which have more abstract meanings than the corresponding East Slavic forms such as **голова** 'head (body part)', as we saw in section 10.8.1 on liquid diphthongs.

Before we leave *j*-palatalization, a few words on the development of the consonant groups /kt/ and /gt/ before /i/ are in order. Although this is not an example of *j*-palatalization, these groups underwent a similar change which yielded /č'/ and /ž'/ in Old Rusian. Important examples include the infinitives of such Old Rusian verbs as **печи** 'bake' and **мочи** 'be able', which ended in the sound sequences /kti/ and /gti/ in Common Slavic.

11.7. Second Palatalization of Velars

After the first palatalization was no longer operative, the monophthongization of /ăi, āi/ to /ě/ or /i/ took place (see section 10.6). This created combinations of hard /k, g, x/ followed by the front vowels /ě/ or /i/. Since hard consonants followed by front vowels violated the Law of Syllabic Synharmony, it is not surprising that /k, g, x/ underwent palatalization:

(14) The second palatalization of velar consonants in Common Slavic:
  a. /k/ → /c'/ / ___ front vowel
  b. /g/ → /z'/ / ___ front vowel
  c. /x/ → /s'/ / ___ front vowel

You may wonder why the environment in (14) is given as "before any front vowel," when the only relevant vowels are /ě/ and /i/. However, phonologists prefer to state sound laws as generally as possible, and the general version in (14) will work since after the first palatalization and the monophthongization of /ăi, āi/ the only front vowels that could follow /k, g, x/ were /ě/ and /i/.

In section 11.5, you learned that the first palatalization involved both palatalization proper and lenition and that the sound change probably went through intermediate stages. The same holds for the second palatalization. In particular, it is worth noting that /g/ probably first changed to the affricate /dz'/, which then became the fricative /z'/. If you find it hard to memorize which sounds were created by which palatalization, here is a simple mnemonic. The first palatalization created sounds that are transcribed with diacritics (/č′, ž′, š′/), whereas the output of the second palatalization lacks diacritics: /c′, z′, s′/.

Here are some examples:

(15) Examples of second palatalization before /ě/:
   a. /k/ → /c′/: Proto-Slavic /**kai**nā/ → Old Rusian /**c′ě**na/ 'price, value'
   b. /g/ → /z′/: Proto-Slavic /nă**gai**/ → Old Rusian /noz′**ě**/ 'foot (dative/locative sg)'
   c. /x/ → /s′/: Proto-Slavic /**xai**r-/ → Old Rusian /**s′ě**r-/ 'gray'

Although monophthongization of /ăi, āi/ normally produces /ě/, in section 10.6 you learned that we have /i/ in nominative plural of masculine ŏ-declension nouns and in the second and third person singular imperative. In these forms, palatalization took place if the stem ended in a velar consonant. Thus, the nominative plural of Old Rusian **пророкъ** 'prophet' is **пророци** with /c′/ spelled as **ц**, and the imperative of **печи** 'bake' is **пьци**.

The second palatalization had important consequences for Common Slavic and Old Rusian morphology. Before the endings /ě/ and /i/ that go back to /āi, ăi/, the second palatalization took place, whereas in other forms of the same words the original /k, g, x/ remained. The result was alternations in stem-final position. Examples include the dative and locative singular of nouns like **нога** 'foot' (Old Rusian dative and locative **нозѣ**), the nominative plural of nouns like **пророкъ** 'prophet' (Old Rusian nominative plural **пророци**), and the imperative of verbs like **печи** 'bake' (Old Rusian imperative **пьци**). Importantly, however, all these alternations have been eliminated by analogical change. Thus, in Contemporary Standard Russian we have dative and locative forms like **ноге**, plurals like **пророки**, and imperatives like **пеки**, which show no traces of the second palatalization. In fact, there are almost no alternations due to the second palatalization left in Modern Russian morphology. A rare example is the alternation between /g/ and /z′/ in Modern Russian **друг** 'friend' (nominative plural: **друзья**, cf. section 4.2.1 for discussion).

How can we know that the second palatalization took place after the first palatalization? If we look at verbs such as **кричать** 'shout', we can establish a relative chronology. Recall from section 11.5 that we can reconstruct the Proto-Slavic form /krīkētei/, with /k/ followed by /ē/, which later turned into /ě/. If the second palatalization had occurred earlier than the first palatalization, we would have had /c/ in the Modern Russian verb. However, the modern verb is not "**крицать**," but **кричать**. This we can explain only if we assume that the first palatalization happened first. The second palatalization came later when monophthongization had created new instances of velar consonants before front vowels. In other words, the relative chronology is as follows:

(16) Relative chronology of the first and second palatalizations:
   a. First palatalization of /k, g, x/ to /č', ž', š'/ before front vowels
   b. Monophthongization of /ăi, āi/ to /ě/ (/i/)
   c. Second palatalization of /k, g, x/ to /c', z', s'/ before front vowels

Another argument suggesting that the second palatalization came after the first palatalization is the fact that the second palatalization yielded different outputs in different Slavic languages, while the first palatalization produced the same sounds for all Slavic languages. Since the Slavic languages were in the process of splitting up during the Late Common Slavic period, it stands to reason that changes that covered the whole Slavic territory are older than changes that produced different results for different languages. For our purposes, it is sufficient to consider two examples where the second palatalization did not yield uniform results across Slavic. The first one is interesting because it shows that the second palatalization applied even if /w/ intervened between the velar consonant and the front vowel. Modern Russian цвет(ок) 'flower' and звезда 'star' go back to Proto-Slavic /kwait-/ and /gwaizd-/. However, palatalization through an intervening /w/ did not take place in West Slavic, as shown by the Czech words *květ* 'flower' and *hvězda* 'star'.

The second example that shows that the second palatalization did not yield the same results across Slavic concerns the Old Novgorod dialect of Old Rusian. Whereas in general Old Rusian displays the effect of the second palatalization in forms such as цѣлъ 'whole', birch bark letters from Novgorod have corresponding forms without palatalization, e.g., кѣле 'whole'. This suggests that the second palatalization never reached the northeastern corner of the Slavic area. You will learn more about this in section 14.2, where we discuss the language of the birch bark letters in more detail.

11.8. Third Palatalization of Velars

The so-called third palatalization can be stated as follows:

(17) The third palatalization of velar consonants in Common Slavic:
   a. /k/ → /c'/ / high front vowel (nasal) ____ low non-front vowel
   b. /g/ → /z'/ / high front vowel (nasal) ____ low non-front vowel
   c. /x/ → /s'/ / high front vowel (nasal) ____ low non-front vowel

As stated in (17), the third palatalization takes place between a high front vowel (i.e., Proto-Slavic /ī, ĭ/) and a low back vowel (i.e., Proto-Slavic /ā, ă/). Some scholars describe the following vowel in terms of lip rounding instead of vowel height (high vs. low), but for our purposes it is not necessary to go into this (see, however, Townsend and Janda 1996: 80–81 for discussion). The feature "nasal" is mentioned in parentheses. This means that a nasal consonant may intervene between the high front vowel and the velar that undergoes palatalization. In other words, the third palatalization took place after /ĭ, ī/ or a nasal diphthong beginning in /ĭ, ī/.

By way of illustration, consider the development of the Old Rusian words отьць 'father', кънязь 'prince', and вьсь 'all':

(18) Examples of third palatalization:
  a. /k/ → /c′/: Proto-Slavic /ătĭkăs/ → Old Rusian /otьc′ь/ 'father'
  b. /g/ → /z′/: Proto-Slavic /kŭnĭngăs/ → Old Rusian /kънäz′ь/ 'prince'
  c. /x/ → /s′/: Proto-Slavic /vĭxăs-/ → Old Rusian /vьs′ь/ 'all'

Of particular interest is /kŭnĭngăs/ 'prince' in (18b). In this Germanic loanword, /g/ is preceded by the nasal diphthong /ĭn/. This word shows that the third palatalization took place after nasal diphthongs beginning in /ĭ, ī/.

The third palatalization resembles the second palatalization insofar as both produce /c′, z′, s′/. At the same time, you should be aware of the following three differences. First, the third palatalization is progressive in the sense that the change is caused by a preceding front vowel. As we have seen, both the first and the second palatalizations are regressive since the change is caused by a following front vowel. A second difference is that the third palatalization applies across a syllable boundary, while the first and second palatalizations take place inside the syllable. In Proto-Slavic /vĭxăs-/, for instance, /ĭ/ and /x/ belong to different syllables. It is customary to say that the first and second palatalizations were intrasyllabic, while the third was intersyllabic. A third difference between the third palatalization on the one hand and the first and the second on the other is the fact that the third palatalization was triggered by a high front vowel (i.e., Proto-Slavic /ī, ĭ/), while the first and the second palatalizations were caused by any front vowel, i.e., Proto-Slavic /ī, ĭ, ē, ĕ/. The similarities and differences are summarized in Table 68 on p. 238.

Table 68. Comparison of the three palatalizations of velar consonants

	1st palatalization	2nd palatalization	3rd palatalization
Output:	/č', ž', š'/	/c', z', s'/	/c', z', s'/
Direction:	Regressive	Regressive	Progressive
Domain:	Intrasyllabic	Intrasyllabic	Intersyllabic
Triggering vowel:	Front	Front	High front

When did the third palatalization take place? In the previous section, you saw that there are solid arguments for assuming that the first palatalization occurred before the second. Both palatalizations appear before front vowels, and verbs such as **кричать** 'shout' indicate that the first palatalization took precedence. However, since the third palatalization took place in a different environment, we cannot construct simple arguments like the one with **кричать**. As a consequence, different scholars have proposed different relative chronologies (> means 'before', while a comma indicates that two processes overlapped in time):

(19) Proposed relative chronologies for the third palatalization:
- a. First > second > **third** (traditional view)
- b. First > **third** > second (Trubetzkoy 1922: 432)
- c. **Third** > first > second (Channon 1972, Lunt 1981, 1985)
- d. First > second, **third** (Vaillant 1950: 49–52, Andersen 1998: 432)

The chronology in (19a), which follows the traditional numbering, represents what has been the mainstream view since Jan Baudouin de Courtenay (1894) first described the conditions for the third palatalization, but the relative chronologies in (19b–d) have also been defended by major experts in the field. A detailed discussion of the subtle arguments that have been advanced in favor of these chronologies is beyond the scope of this book. However, the fact that the second and third palatalizations produced the same sounds suggest that they were close in time, and is compatible with (19d), according to which the second and third palatalizations overlapped in time.

11.9. Fronting of Vowels after Soft Consonants

In this section we will consider a final sound change motivated by the Law of Syllabic Synharmony:

(20) Fronting of vowels after soft consonants in Common Slavic:
Non-front vowel → front vowel / soft consonant ___

Here are two examples:

(21) Examples of vowel fronting:
 a. /ŭ/ → /ь/: Proto-Slavic /jŭgă-/ → Old Rusian /jьgo/ 'yoke'
 b. /ū/ → /i/: Proto-Slavic /sjūtei/ → Old Rusian /š'iti/ 'sew'

Vowel fronting can be triggered by any soft consonant. In the Proto-Slavic examples in (21), the triggering consonant is /j/. However, vowel fronting took place towards the end of the Common Slavic period, i.e., after *j*-palatalization had created soft consonants from combinations of consonant + /j/ (cf. section 11.6). In (21b), for instance, we can assume that /sj/ became /š'/, and that /š'/ then triggered vowel fronting. The examples in (21) involve high vowels, but as you will see below, the fronting rule affected all non-front vowels regardless of vowel height.

Since vowel fronting is triggered by a preceding sound, we are dealing with a progressive sound change. Since the preceding consonant and the vowel that undergoes fronting belong to the same syllable, the fronting rule is an example of an intrasyllabic change. Although the fronting rule is motivated by the Law of Syllabic Synharmony in the same way as the palatalizations explored in the preceding sections, there is a crucial difference. In the case of the first, second, and third palatalizations, a vowel occasioned changes in a consonant. The fronting rule represents the opposite strategy for repairing violations of the Law of Syllabic Synharmony: a consonant brings about a change in a vowel.

Vowel fronting has important morphological consequences. In section 4.2.1, you learned that the ŏ- and ā-declensions had both hard and soft variants, which had different vowel phonemes in the endings. An example is the nominative singular of neuter nouns in the ŏ-declension. In Old Rusian, words with a hard consonant in stem-final position had the ending /o/ (e.g., лѣт-о 'summer, year'), while the ending after soft consonants was /e/ (e.g., мор-е 'sea'). However, if we go back to Proto-Slavic, both words had the same ending, which we can reconstruct as /ă/. The difference between the two types of nouns is that /j/ preceded the ending in words like /mărjă/ 'sea'. Figure 17 on p. 240 illustrates the development from Proto-Slavic to Old Rusian. First, /ă/ became /o/ (section 10.3), /rj/ became /r'/ due to *j*-palatalization (section 11.6), and the final consonant was lost (section 10.5). Later, the vowel in the ending was fronted from /o/ to /e/ since it follows after the soft consonant /r'/. The result is

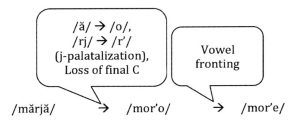

Figure 17. Development of different endings after soft consonants through vowel fronting

the Old Rusian system where nouns in the ŏ- and ā-declensions have different endings after hard and soft consonants.

11.10. Summary of Consonant Changes

In this chapter, you have learned about the development of consonants in the Pre-Slavic and Common Slavic periods, i.e., from the Late Proto-Indo-European system via Proto-Slavic to Old Rusian. The development goes from a very large consonant system in Late Proto-Indo-European to a much smaller system in Proto-Slavic. During the Common Slavic period, new consonant phonemes developed, and as you will learn in the next chapter, this growth continued from Old Rusian to Modern Russian. In short, therefore, the development was from a large consonant system via smaller systems back to a large system.

The Pre-Slavic period was characterized by loss of plosives and emergence of fricatives:

(22) Pre-Slavic consonant changes:

    a. The satem assibilation: emergence of /z/ (section 11.2)

    b. The *ruki* rule: emergence of /x/ (section 11.3)

The Common Slavic period witnessed a number of changes that were motivated by the Law of Syllabic Synharmony (**Закон слогового сингармонизма**, section 11.4):

(23) The Law of Syllabic Synharmony (**Закон слогового сингармонизма**):

    In Common Slavic, a syllable could consist of:

    a. Soft consonant + front vowel

    b. Hard consonant + non-front vowel

The relevant sound laws in Common Slavic are:

(24) Common Slavic consonant changes:
  a. The first palatalization of velars (section 11.5)
  b. The *j*-palatalization (section 11.6)
  c. The second palatalization of velars (section 11.7)
  d. The third palatalization of velars (section 11.8)
  e. Vowel fronting after soft consonants (section 11.9)

Characteristic of consonant changes in Pre-Slavic and Common Slavic is the fact that they had far-reaching consequences for the morphology:

(25) Morphological consequences of phonological changes in Pre-Slavic and Common Slavic:
  a. The *ruki* rule: alternations of /s/, /x/, and /š'/ in the aorist (section 11.3)
  b. The first palatalization of velars:
    i. Nouns: alternations in the vocative, e.g., Боже from Бог 'God' (sections 4.2.1 and 11.5)
    ii. Pronouns: the difference between чьто 'what' and къто 'who' (sections 5.6 and 11.5)
    iii. Verbs: alternations in the present tense of, e.g., мочь 'be able' (могу, можешь, могут; sections 8.2 and 11.5).
  c. The *j*-palatalization (section 11.6):
    i. First conjugation verbs: alternations in the present tense of verbs like писать 'write' (пишу, пишешь, пишут)
    ii. Second conjugation verbs: alternations in the present tense of verbs like любить 'love' (люблю, любишь, любят)
  d. The second palatalization of velars (section 11.7):
    i. Nouns: alternations before endings in /ě/ or /i/, e.g., Old Rusian locative singular нозѣ of нога 'foot' and nominative plural пророци of пророкъ 'prophet'
    ii. Verbs: alternations before the ending /i/ in the imperative, e.g., Old Rusian imperative пьци of печи 'bake'
  e. Vowel fronting after soft consonants: development of different endings after soft consonants in the ŏ- and ā-declensions (section 11.9)

Notice that even if the second palatalization had important consequences for nouns in Old Rusian, the alternations in (25bi) have lost their importance in Modern Russian due to the loss of the vocative, while the alternations in (25d) have been wiped out by analogy. As a consequence, consonant alternations are not characteristic of nouns in Contemporary Standard Russian, but have been preserved in verbs.

11.11. For Further Reading

Most textbooks and historical grammars discuss the Pre-Slavic and Common Slavic consonant changes in some detail. Galinskaja (2009 and 2014) offers brief and reader-friendly overviews in Russian. In English, Townsend and Janda (1996) provide thorough discussions with comparisons to other Slavic languages. For more information, consult Shevelov 1964. In section 11.8, I mentioned that there are a number of different views on the relative chronology of the palatalizations. If you are interested in finding out more about this hotly debated topic in Slavic linguistics, the overview in Schenker 1995: 90ff. is a good place to start.

Chapter 12

Phonology: From Old Rusian to Modern Russian

Why does Modern Russian have mobile vowels, such as /o/ in сон 'dream', which disappear in inflected forms such as the genitive singular сна? Why can the letters к, г, х be followed by и, but not ы? Why is род 'family' pronounced with [t] at the end, when it is spelled with the letter д, and why is легко 'easy' spelled with the letter г? This chapter shows that this and many other problems you have struggled with in Modern Russian are the result of phonological changes in medieval times.

12.1. Overview: Phoneme Systems of Old Rusian and CSR

You have already seen the Old Rusian and Contemporary Standard Russian phoneme systems in sections 10.2 and 11.1. However, before we explore the sound changes from Old Rusian to Modern Russian it is helpful to take another look at these phoneme systems. From Tables 69–72 on pp. 245–46, you can see that the number of vowel phonemes goes down from 10 to 5, while the number of consonant phonemes displays the opposite tendency and rises from 24 to 33. The main task of this chapter is to explain the decrease in vowel phonemes and the increase in consonant phonemes. As a first step, consider the following lists of lost vowels and new consonants:

(1) Phoneme changes from Old Rusian to Contemporary Standard Russian:
  a. Lost vowels: /ě, ь, ъ, ä, y/
  b. New consonants:
   i. Soft labials: /p', b', f', v', m'/
   ii. Soft dentals: /t', d'/
   iii. Hard post-alveolar fricative: /š/
   iv. Labial fricative: /f/

With regard to vowels, you see that jat (/ě/) and the jers (/ь, ъ/) have disappeared. Of course, the letters ь and ъ are still used in Modern Russian, but these letters do not represent vowel sounds any more. In early Old Rusian, on the other hand, the jers were pronounced as vowels. The situation for /ä/ and /y/ is more complicated. Recall from section 10.7 that /ä/ is the Old Rusian vowel that developed from the Common Slavic front nasal vowel /ę/. Although, as pointed out in section 10.1, Contemporary Standard Russian has a fronted [ä] in words such as мять 'crumple', this sound is not an independent phoneme, but rather an allophone of /a/ that occurs between soft consonants. Similarly, Contemporary Standard Russian has the sound [y], but it can be analyzed as an allophone of the /i/ phoneme, since [y] and [i] are in complementary distribution. After hard consonants we have [y] (e.g., был 'he was'), while [i] is found after soft consonants (e.g., бил 'he hit'), as well as in the beginning of words (e.g., иск 'law suit').[1] Recall from section 10.1 that phonemes can be thought of as families of sounds in complementary distribution.

As shown in (1b), the increase in the number of consonants mostly has to do with soft and hard consonants. In the previous chapter, you learned that the palatalizations created soft consonants. Especially important was the *j*-palatalization, which affected a number of consonants, not just velars. Recall from section 11.6 that clusters of the sonorants /n, r, l/ + /j/ turned into soft /n', r', l'/. Clusters of the obstruents /k, t, g, d, z, x, s/ + /j/ became soft /č', ž', š'/. However, when the labials /p, b, v, m/ were followed by /j/, the result was a cluster consisting of labial + soft /l'/: /pl', bl', vl', ml'/. Therefore, *j*-palatalization did not create soft labials, and accordingly there were no such phonemes in early Old Rusian. There were no soft /t', d'/ either, because /tj/ and /dj/ became /č'/ and /ž'/, respectively. However, in Modern Russian the distinction between soft and hard phonemes has been extended to labials and to dental plosives. In this way, the difference between soft and hard consonants has become increasingly important in Russian phonology.

In (1biii) the hard /š/ is counted as a new phoneme. This is a simplification. It is more accurate to say that the old soft post-alveolar fricatives /š', ž'/ that Old Rusian inherited from Common Slavic became hard in medieval times, while a new, soft /š'/ developed. We can construct minimal pairs with the hard /š/ (written as ш) and the soft /š'/ (written as щ), e.g., /šok/, the nominative singu-

---

[1] Notice that according to the Leningrad (Petersburg) school of phonology, a tradition that goes back to the Polish linguist Jan Baudouin de Courtenay (1845–1929), who worked in St. Petersburg from 1900–18, /i/ and /y/ represent different phonemes. However, for the purposes of the present book I follow the Moscow school of phonology, which analyzes [i] and [y] as allophones of the same phoneme. For a recent overview of the "i-y problem" from a Leningrad/Petersburg perspective, the interested reader is referred to Popov 2004: 72–93.

lar of **шок** 'shock', and /š'ok/, the genitive plural of **щека** 'cheek'. The result is an increase in the number of consonant phonemes.

Finally, as shown in (1b), the emergence of /f/ (and its soft counterpart /f'/) has increased the number of consonant phonemes in Russian, so as to bring the total number up to 33. I hasten to add that different scholars have somewhat different analyses of Modern Russian phonology and assume different numbers of consonant phonemes. For instance, some scholars analyze soft /k', g', x'/ as phonemes, and some experts of Russian phonology assume an additional soft /ž'/ phoneme. On the other hand, some scholars argue that /š', ž'/ are not phonemes, but rather the phonetic realizations of sequences of two consonants. Since these questions do not affect the main point that the number of consonant phonemes has increased, a detailed discussion is beyond the scope of this book (but see discussion in Nesset 2008: 34–36 and references therein). For our purposes, the important question is how the number of consonant phonemes increased, while the number of vowel phonemes decreased. The clue to understanding this is to be found in the jers, to which we turn in the following section.

Table 69. Old Rusian vowel system

	Front		Non-front
	Unrounded		Rounded
High	i	y	u
High-Mid	ě		
Mid	e, ь		o, ъ
Low	ä	a	

Table 70. Contemporary Standard Russian vowel system

	Front	Non-front	
	Unrounded		Rounded
High	i		u
Mid	e		o
Low		a	

Table 71. Old Rusian consonant phoneme system

		labial	dental		post-alveolar	dorsal
			hard	soft	soft	
plosive	voiceless	p	t			k
plosive	voiced	b	d			g
affricate	voiceless			c′	č′	
fricative	voiceless		s	s′	š′	x
fricative	voiced		z	z′	ž′	
nasal	voiced	m	n	n′		
liquid	voiced		l, r	l′, r′		
glide	voiced	w				j

Table 72. Contemporary Standard Russian consonant phoneme system

		labial		dental		post-alveolar		dorsal
		hard	soft	hard	soft	hard	soft	
plosive	voiceless	p	p′	t	t′			k
plosive	voiced	b	b′	d	d′			g
affricate	voiceless			c			č′	
fricative	voiceless	f	f′	s	s′	š	š′	x
fricative	voiced	v	v′	z	z′	ž		
nasal	voiced	m	m′	n	n′			
liquid	voiced			l, r	l′, r′			
glide	voiced							j

12.2. The Fall and Vocalization of the Jers

12.2.1. Havlik's Law

The sound changes known as the fall and vocalization of the jers started in Late Common Slavic and have produced different results in different Slavic languages. It is believed that the changes started in the southeastern part of the Slavic territory and spread to East Slavic in the 11th century, or even as late as the 12th century (Isačenko 1970: 73–74). Since we are only interested in the consequences for Russian phonology, we will explore the fall and vocalization of the jers in the present chapter. Let us first consider the following examples:

(2) The fall and vocalization of jers—examples:
   a. дьнь → день 'day (nominative singular)'
   b. дьня → дня 'day (genitive singular)'
   c. сънъ → сон 'dream (nominative singular)'
   d. съна → сна 'dream (genitive singular)'

These examples show that the jers sometimes disappear. It is customary to refer to this as the "fall of the jers" (Russian: падение редуцированных). The positions where the jers fall are referred to as "weak positions." In other positions, which are called "strong," the jers undergo vocalization, i.e., they turn into other vowels. The questions we must ask are: which positions are strong and which are weak, and which vowels do jers turn into when they undergo vocalization?

We take the second question first, since it is simpler:

(3) The fall and vocalization of jers:
   a. /ь/ → /e/ in strong position
   b. /ъ/ → /o/ in strong position
   c. /ь, ъ/ → Ø ("zero") in weak position

As you can see from the examples in (2), the first jers in the nominative forms дьнь and сънъ undergo vocalization to /e/ and /o/. Since /ь, ъ/ go back to high vowels (/ĭ, ŭ/ in Proto-Slavic), while /e, o/ are mid vowels, the vocalization of the jers involves a lowering of the vowels from high to mid.

In order to identify weak and strong positions, a practical approach is to number the jers from right to left:

(4) Numbering the jers from right to left:
   a. дь²нь¹ → день
   b. дь¹ня → дня
   c. съ²нъ¹ → сон
   d. съ¹на → сна

As you can see, the jers that are assigned odd numbers fall, whereas jers with even numbers undergo vocalization. (If you are wondering why I say that the rightmost jer in дьнь falls even if it is still written in Modern Russian день, remember that the soft sign in this Modern Russian word is just an orthographic symbol indicating that the preceding consonant is soft. There is no vowel pronounced at the end of день, and therefore we say that the jer has fallen.)

Here are some examples with longer words:

(5) Numbering the jers from right to left:
    a. жь³нь²ць¹ → жнец 'reaper'
    b. отъ¹ходь¹нику → отходнику 'hermit' (dative sg)

The first example shows that the principle regarding even and odd numbers also holds for words with more than two jers. The second example is more complex, because отъходьнику also contains "normal" (non-jer) vowels. As you can see from the example, you have to restart the numbering from the "normal" vowels in order to arrive at the correct output. We are now in a position to state the following method for identifying weak and strong positions:

(6) How to identify strong and weak positions for jers:
    a. Number the jers from right to left.
    b. Restart the numbering from non-jer vowels.
    c. Jers with odd numbers are in weak position and fall.
    d. Jers with even numbers are in strong position and vocalize.

In Slavic linguistics, the sound law that describes the vocalization and fall of the jers is sometimes referred to as "Havlik's law" after the Czech linguist Antonín Havlík (1855–1925).

12.2.2. An Approach in Terms of Feet

Although the method in (6) is practical, it does not have much explanatory power. Clearly, speakers of Old Rusian did not decide the fate of the jers by counting them from right to left. In other words, (6) does not reflect what went on in the mental grammars of the speakers, and therefore does not offer a very insightful analysis of how and why this important language change took place. In order to make progress, the first observation we can make is that the vocalization and fall of the jers took place in a domain consisting of two syllables (cf. Bethin 1998: 95–107). For convenience, we may refer to these bisyllabic domains as "feet." What kinds of feet were acceptable in Old Rusian before the fall of the jers? There are four possible combinations of non-jer vowels (represented as V) and jers (represented as Ъ):

12.2.2. An Approach in Terms of Feet

(7) Old Rusian feet:
    a.   VЪ   (e.g., домъ 'house')
    b.   *ЪV   (not attested)
    c.   ЪЪ   (e.g., сънъ 'dream')
    d.   VV   (e.g., море 'sea')

The asterisk in (7b) indicates that ЪV was an illegitimate foot. In other words, a foot could not start with a jer unless both syllables in the foot were jers. Since ЪV was not a possible foot, words like дьня could not build a foot.

How were words divided into feet so as to avoid the illegitimate ЪV foot? Consider some longer words. Vowels that comprise a foot are included in parentheses:

(8) Feet in longer words:
    a. Ъ (Ъ Ъ)   b. (V Ъ)(V Ъ)(V V)   c. (Ъ Ъ) V
        | | | | | | | | | | | |
        жь³нь²ць¹   отъ¹ходь¹нику   съ²нь¹мы

In the two first examples, we can build feet from right to left. Since a foot consists of two syllables, the first vowel in жьньць in (8a) is not part of a foot. The remaining vowels in these words are part of a foot, and all the feet belong to the legitimate VЪ, ЪЪ, and VV types in (7). However, if we started building feet from right to left in сънъмы in (8c), we would construct a foot of the illegitimate ЪV type. In order to avoid this, we have to skip the syllable with the non-jer, and start building feet from the penultimate syllable. We can summarize the principles as follows:

(9) How to build feet in Old Rusian:
    a.   Build bisyllabic feet from right to left.
    b.   In order to avoid the illegitimate ЪV foot, skip a single non-jer.

With these principles in mind, we can state the rule for the fall and vocalization of the jers as follows:

(10) The fall and vocalization of the jers in terms of feet:
    a.   A jer undergoes vocalization if it is in the beginning of a foot.
    b.   All other jers fall.

12.2.3. Further Complications: Stress, Analogy, Tense Jers, and СЪRC Groups

If you find the analysis in terms of feet too technical, you may stick to the traditional formulation of Havlik's law in (6), which will enable you to predict which jers fall and which undergo vocalization. However, regardless of which approach you choose, you need to be aware of some complications. The first of them concerns the alleged effect of stress. It is sometimes stated in textbooks that a jer in a stressed syllable is always vocalized, regardless of other factors. According to Zaliznjak (1985: 169), this idea goes back to Šaxmatov. A frequently cited example is дъ́ску, the accusative singular of дъска́ 'board'. Since the jer in дъ́ску stands before a non-jer, it receives number 1, and we therefore predict that it will fall. However, Modern Russian has до́ску, where the jer has undergone vocalization. A possible solution of the problem would be to assume that the jer did not fall because it was stressed. However, Zaliznjak (1985: 168–72), who has analyzed a large body of examples, has demonstrated that the vast majority of jers in stressed syllables did indeed follow the normal rules (see also Isačenko 1970: 93). He therefore concludes that stress had no impact on the fall of the jers, and that apparent counterexamples either involve the avoidance of difficult consonant clusters, or are due to analogy. Дъ́ску belongs to the former type; the jer may have undergone vocalization in order to avoid the cluster /dsk/ in the beginning of a word.

In order to illustrate the effect of analogy on the fall of the jers, consider the Old Rusian noun шьвьць 'shoemaker'. As you would expect, this yields швец in Modern Russian, a somewhat archaic word for 'tailor'. For the genitive singular шьвьця, you would expect шевца in Modern Russian, but instead we get швеца. It stands to reason that this is the result of analogy, whereby the genitive has adopted the same stem as the nominative. As pointed out by Kiparsky (1963: 94–95), it is interesting to compare with Ukrainian, where the genitive has not undergone analogy. In other words, Ukrainian has швець in the nominative, but шевця in the genitive. In Polish, analogy has applied, but here the nominative has undergone change under the influence of the genitive so as to give *szewc* in the nominative and *szewca* in the genitive.

Another complication concerns so-called tense jers, i.e., jers before /j/. Of particular interest is the nominative singular masculine ending of adjectives. From -ъјь we expect -ой in Russian, since according to the rules for the vocalization and fall of the jers the last jer falls, while the second jer from the right vocalizes to /o/. In Contemporary Standard Russian, we have the ending -ой in stressed syllables: молодо́й 'young' and плохо́й 'bad'. However, how can we account for the ending -ый in unstressed syllables, as in бе́лый 'white'? The explanation is influence from Old Church Slavonic, where tense jers became /y/ and /i/. Accordingly, Old Church Slavonic has бѣлый, and this spelling of the adjectival ending was adopted in Russian. It is worth mentioning, though, that some speakers of the older generation pronounce this ending with an unstressed /o/ in Modern Russian, so for such speakers the influence from Old Church Slavonic has affected orthography, but not pronunciation (see section 6.3.2 for discussion).

A final complication concerns CЪRC groups, i.e., groups where a jer precedes a liquid. Recall from section 10.8.3 that in East Slavic the jer in such groups does not undergo metathesis or pleophony. However, with regard to the vocalization and fall of the jers, CЪRC groups are exceptional, since the jer in such groups consistently undergoes vocalization, regardless of the presence or absence of other jers in the word:

(11)   Vocalization of jers in CЪRC groups:
 a.   гърло → горло 'throat'
 b.   вълна → волна 'wave'

According to the general rules for the vocalization and fall of the jers, we would expect the jers in гърло and вълна to fall, but they nevertheless vocalize, because they are part of CЪRC groups.

Although /ь/ normally vocalizes to /e/ in CЪRC groups as elsewhere, /ъ/ becomes /o/ before /l/, as mentioned in section 10.8.3. By way of example, consider Modern Russian волк 'wolf', where /o/ goes back to /ъ/.

12.3. Some Consequences of the Fall of the Jers

The fall of the jers is traditionally considered a watershed event in the history of Russian, because a number of important changes are direct or indirect consequences of it. In the following, we will go through the most important consequences of the fall of the jers.

12.3.1. Mobile Vowels

A major problem when you learn Modern Russian is the existence of "mobile vowels" ("fleeting vowels", Russian: беглые гласные). Mobile vowels are vowels that occur in some of the inflected forms of a word, but are absent in other forms. By way of examples, consider the Modern Russian words день 'day' and сон 'dream', which lose the stem vowel in the inflected forms, as can be seen from the genitive singular forms дня and сна. From section 12.2.1 you understand that this is a direct consequence of the fall of the jers. In the nominative forms дьнь and сънъ, the jers in the stem were in strong position and underwent vocalization. In the genitive forms **дьня** and **съна**, on the other hand, the jers were in weak position and fell. The result was mobile vowels.

It is worth pointing out that we cannot always reconstruct jers on the basis of mobile vowels in Modern Russian. In some words, such as **лёд** 'ice' we have a mobile vowel today (cf. genitive **льда**). However, this appears to be due to analogy from words like **день** and **сон**. In Old Rusian the nominative singular was **ледъ** and the genitive singular **леду**, with no jer in the stem. Conversely, some words that had a jer in the stem have not developed a mobile vowel. A case in point is Modern Russian **сот** 'honeycomb' (genitive singular: **сота**), which goes back to Old Rusian **сътъ** (cf. Kiparsky 1963: 95–96).

12.3.2. Emergence of Closed Syllables

In chapter 10 you learned that Common Slavic is the period of open syllables. The fall of the jers represents the end of this period. Because jers in word-final position fell, the fall of the jers created numerous examples of closed syllables. Before the fall of the jers, **сънъ** 'dream' comprised two syllables: **съ–нъ**. Both syllables were open, since they had the structure CV. After the fall of the jers, on the other hand, the word had one syllable: **сон**. This syllable has the structure CVC, and since it ends in a consonant, it is a closed syllable.

12.3.3. Consonant Clusters: Assimilation and Dissimilation

As a consequence of the fall of the jers, consonant clusters emerged. Before the fall of the jers, **къде** 'where' consisted of two syllables, and /k/ and /d/ were separated by a vowel. After the fall of the jers, the two consonants ended up next to each other—they formed a consonant cluster. In consonant clusters, the first member frequently underwent change due to the influence of the second member. Two main types of processes are attested: assimilation, where the first member becomes more similar to the second member of the cluster, and dissimilation, where the first member becomes more different from the second member of the cluster.

Let us discuss assimilation first, since this is the most regular process. In clusters consisting of two obstruents, voicing assimilation took place:

(12) Voicing assimilation:
    a. Obstruent → voiceless / ___ voiceless obstruent
    b. Obstruent → voiced / ___ voiced obstruent

12.3.3. Consonant Clusters: Assimilation and Dissimilation

In other words, the first member adopts the same specification for voice as the second member of the cluster, so that both members are either voiceless or voiced. Recall that "obstruent" is a cover term for plosives, affricates, and fricatives. The effect of voicing assimilation can be seen from the examples in (13). In these and the following examples, the first arrow represents the fall of the jers, which created a consonant cluster. The second arrow represents the change in the consonant cluster, in this case assimilation. For convenience, the relevant segments are given in boldface:

(13) Voicing assimilation—examples:
   a. бъчела → бчела → пчела 'bee'
   b. къде → кде → где 'where'

As you can see, the voiced [b] in (13a) becomes voiceless before the voiceless [č'], while the voiceless [k] in (13b) becomes voiced before the voiced [d]. Voicing assimilation is not only a sound law that took place in medieval times, but has been preserved as an automatic pronunciation rule in Contemporary Standard Russian. Loanwords such as футбол 'football' illustrate this, insofar as the letter т is pronounced as [d] in front of [b].

There are also examples of softness/hardness assimilation, i.e., a process whereby the first member of a consonant cluster becomes soft before a soft consonant and hard before a hard consonant:

(14) Softness/hardness assimilation:
   a. Consonant → soft / ___ soft consonant
   b. Consonant → hard / ___ hard consonant

Here are a couple of examples:

(15) Softness/hardness assimilation—examples:
   a. [sьt'ixat'i] → [st'ixat'i] → [s't'ixat'i] 'calm down'
   b. [věr'ьno] → [věr'no] → [verno] 'true'

In (15a), the hard [s] undergoes softening to [s'] when it becomes adjacent to the soft [t']. In (15b), the soft [r'] becomes hard under the influence of the following hard [n]. It is worth pointing out that not all consonants were affected by the rule in (14a); soft [l'] has remained soft even when followed by a hard consonant. In words like польза 'use', for example, a soft [l'] is pronounced to this day, and the word is spelled with ь. (However, the jer is not pronounced as a vowel, of course; its function in Modern Russian **польза** is to indicate the softness of the preceding consonant.)

Dissimilation is less regular, but the following processes are attested:

(16) Dissimilation:
   a. Plosive → fricative / __ plosive
   b. Affricate → fricative / __ plosive

The following examples illustrate this:

(17) Dissimilation—examples:
   a. [l'ьgъko] → [l'egko] → [l'exko] 'easy'
   b. [č'ьto] → [č'to] → [što] 'what'

Notice that in these examples the dissimilation is not reflected in the orthography. *Легко* is still spelled with **г**, although it is pronounced with the fricative [x], and *что* is spelled with **ч**, although it is pronounced with the fricative [š]. In terms of pronunciation, however, in both examples the first member of the consonant cluster becomes more different from the second member.

12.3.4. Final Devoicing

From Modern Russian you know that words can end in vowels or consonants. While neuter nouns in the first declension (e.g., **лето** 'summer') and nouns in the second declension (e.g., **сестра** 'sister') end in a vowel, masculine nouns in the first declension (e.g., **род** 'family') and nouns in the third declension (e.g., **ночь** 'night') end in consonants. However, before the fall of the jers, all these words were pronounced with a vowel at the end, since at that time the final jers in **родъ** and **ночь** were still vowel sounds.

As a consequence of the fall of the jers, numerous words came to end in consonants, including voiced obstruents, such as [d] in **род**. However, these sounds underwent a process called "final devoicing", whereby obstruents become voiceless in word-final position. The # sign stands for a boundary between words, so "___ #": means "before a word boundary", i.e., at the end of the word.

(18) Final devoicing:
   Obstruent → voiceless / __ #

The development of Old Rusian **родъ** 'family' illustrates this:

(19) Final devoicing—example:

[rodъ] → [rod] → [rot] 'family'

In medieval texts we sometimes encounter words that are spelled with a voiceless obstruent instead of the corresponding voiced consonant. A case in point is the following example from the *Primary Chronicle*, where Jaroslav "the Wise" locks up his brother Sudislav in the **порубъ** 'dungeon' (where Sudislav had to spend the next twenty years of his life):

(20) a. В то же лѣто всади Ярославъ Судислава вь **порубь**, брата своего, Плесковѣ, оклеветань к нему. (PVL 1036 AD; 151,16)

b. В тот же год посадил Ярослав брата своего Судислава в темницу во Пскове — был тот оклеветан перед ним.

c. In the same year, Jaroslav put his brother Sudislav in the dungeon in Pskov, because someone had slandered him.

Compare the spellings of **порубъ** in two different sources of the *Primary Chronicle* (from Ostrowski 2003: 1198):

(21) a. *Laurentian Codex*: **порупъ** (PVL 1036 AD; 151,17)

b. *Hypatian Codex*: **порубь** (PVL 1036 AD; 151,17)

The fact that the scribe who wrote down the *Laurentian Chronicle* in 1377 used **п** instead of **б** suggests that in his speech this word was pronounced with a voiceless [p] at the end of the word. From this we can conclude, (a) that the fall of the jers had taken place so that the relevant consonant was in word-final position, and (b) that the rule of devoicing of obstruents was in place. This is an example of absolute chronology, insofar as we relate language change to a datable historical document, the *Laurentian Codex* from 1377 (cf. section 3.9 for discussion of absolute chronology). (The fact that the scribe who wrote down the *Hypatian Chronicle* about 50 years later, used **б** only tells us that he knew how to spell this word or at least managed to copy it correctly from the older source he was working with. But it is interesting to notice that this scribe uses **ь** instead of **ъ**. Since this was after the fall of the jers, it was probably easy to confuse the word-final jers that were no longer pronounced.)

12.3.5. Hard and Soft Consonants Word-Finally

In the beginning of this chapter, you saw that Modern Russian has more soft consonant phonemes than Old Rusian had before the fall of the jers. How did the development of these new phonemes depend on the fall of the jers? We need to take three steps into consideration:

(22) Three steps towards soft labials and plosives:
   a. *j*-palatalization
   b. Softening of semi-soft consonants ("смягчение полумягких")
   c. Fall of the jers

First, as mentioned in section 12.1, *j*-palatalization created soft phonemes from /n, r, l/ + /j/. In the prepositional phrase **къ нему** 'to him' we originally had a cluster of /nj/, which turned into /n'/, due to *j*-palatalization. In the aorist **принесе** 's/he brought', there was never a /j/, so here *j*-palatalization did not take place. It is customary to assume that the nasal consonant was "semi-soft" in words like **принесе**, since it was followed by a front vowel.

Subsequently, the semi-soft consonants became soft. This is referred to as **смягчение полумягких** in Russian. In the case of **принесе**, this process did not create any new phonemes, since /n'/ already existed.

However, for labials and plosives new phonemes emerged, but only after the fall of the jers. By way of an example, consider the word pair **кровъ** 'shelter' and **кръвь** 'blood', which Old Rusian inherited from Common Slavic (both words are attested in Old Church Slavonic). The first arrow represents the softening of the semi-soft consonants, and the second arrow stands for the fall and vocalization of the jers:

(23) a. [krovъ] → [krovъ] → [krov] 'shelter'
   b. [krъvь] → [krъv'ь] → [krov'] 'blood'

The result of the interaction of the softening of the semi-soft consonants and the fall and vocalization of the jers was to create minimal pairs. After the two processes had applied, there was only one difference between the two words in (23), namely the difference between a hard and a soft consonant at the end of the word. Since the final consonants distinguish between words with different meanings, the final consonants belong to different phonemes.

12.3.6. The Realization of /v, v'/ and the Emergence of /f, f'/

In (23) in the previous section I represented the labial consonant that ended up in word-final position as [v]. This is a simplification. As you may remember from section 11.1, in Proto-Slavic and Common Slavic we had [w]. While [v] is the symbol for a labio-dental fricative, i.e., a fricative where the air is released between the lower lip and the upper teeth, [w] represents a bilabial sonorant, where the airflow goes between the lower and upper lips. Although it is hard to pinpoint exactly when the bilabial sonorant [w] became the labio-dental fricative [v], there are good arguments for such a change in Old Rusian. Evidence comes from the use of the letter ф instead of the letter в. In the following example from Afanasij Nikitin's *Xoždenie za tri morja* (cf. section 2.3.5), the preposition в is spelled "ф":

(24) a. А жонки всѣ наги, толко на гузне фота, а иные **ф фотах**.

(Xoždenie)

b. И женщины все нагие, только фата на бедрах, а другие все **в фатах**.

c. The women are naked, too, save for a veil about their hips; others are all covered **by the veil**.

What does this spelling tell us about the pronunciation of [w] or [v]? It stands to reason that we find ф instead of в because the relevant consonant was pronounced as [f]. This pronunciation must be due to voicing assimilation, i.e., devoicing before a voiceless obstruent (see the rule in (12a) in section 12.3.3). Recall that this rule applies to obstruents, but not to sonorants. In other words, the sonorant [w] would not undergo assimilation, whereas the fricative [v] would. Since we have assimilation, we must conclude that we are dealing with a language with a labio-dental fricative, not a bilabial sonorant.

Spelling of ф instead of в is not found in the earliest Old Rusian sources (cf. Ivanov 1995: 72), so it is possible that the transition from [w] to [v] happened relatively late. It is worth mentioning that the transition did not take place in Ukrainian or Belarusian, nor did it happen in southwestern dialects of Russian.

When we classify the phoneme /v/ as a fricative in Contemporary Standard Russian, we are simplifying things somewhat. Like fricatives, /v/ is pronounced as voiceless [f] at the end of a word (e.g., **нов**—the short form of **новый** 'new') and before a voiceless obstruent (e.g., **входить** 'enter', where the prefix is pronounced as [f]). In other words, /v/ undergoes voicing assimilation and final devoicing like any other fricative. However, unlike fricatives (and other obstruents), /v/ does not trigger voicing assimilation. In Contemporary Standard Russian, both voiced and voiceless obstruents are possible before /v/, as illustrated by examples like **двоих** (the genitive of **двое** 'two', with voiced [d]) and **твоих** (the genitive plural of **твой** 'your', with voiceless [t]). The fact that /v/ does not trigger voicing assimilation in Contemporary Standard Russian sets it apart from (other) fricatives. In historical terms, we may say that /v/ in Contemporary Standard Russian has not changed completely from sonorant to fricative.

The transition from [w] to [v] paved the way for the emergence of the phonemes /f, f'/. As we have just seen, [f] was pronounced in the environments where /v/ underwent devoicing. Since the devoicing rule only introduces [f] at the end of the word and before voiceless obstruents, [f] would have remained an allophone of the /v/ phoneme if it had not been for loan words that included [f] in other positions. In the *Primary Chronicle* we find words such as **философъ** 'philosopher', as well as person names such as **Феодоръ** (from Greek Theodor) and **Фарлофъ** (from Old Norse Farulf) with [f] occurring in other positions. Since [f] occurred in a variety of positions, it was not in complementary distribution with [v], and we must conclude that we are dealing with two phonemes: /v/ and /f/. A similar argument can be constructed for the corresponding soft consonants, so we can assume the existence of the phonemes /v'/ and /f'/, too.

12.3.7. The Merger of /y/ and /i/

Common Slavic, Old Rusian, and Contemporary Standard Russian have the sounds [y] and [i], and the past-tense plural forms **были** 'were' and **били** 'hit' have been pronounced as they are today since Late Common Slavic. If, as pointed out by Galinskaja (2009: 122), we are interested in the history of the sounds themselves, there is not much to be said about [y] and [i]. Nevertheless, these sounds represent one of the most interesting consequences of the fall of the jers, since they demonstrate that two phonemes can become one even if the pronunciation of the relevant sounds themselves does not change.

In order to see this, it is helpful to consider three stages in the development of the words **конь** 'horse' and **конъ** 'game', where we are interested in the relationship between the nasal consonant and the following jer:

(25) a. Stage 1: [konь] vs. [konъ] (vowels distinguish between the words)
  b. Stage 2: [kon'ь] vs. [konъ] (both vowels and consonants are different)
  c. Stage 3: [kon'] vs. [kon] (consonants distinguish between the words)

12.3.7. The Merger of /y/ and /i/

In the first stage, before the softening of the semi-soft consonants (**смягчение полумягких**, see section 12.3.5), the only difference between the words was the front jer in **конь** and the non-front jer in **конъ**. In other words, we had a minimal pair where the final vowels distinguished between the two words. In Stage 2, after the softening of the semi-soft consonants, there are two differences between the words. At this stage, both the consonants (soft [n'] vs. hard [n]) and the following jers ([ь] vs. [ъ]) are different. In the third stage, after the fall of the jers, there is only one difference left. At this point only the nasal consonants distinguish between the two members of the minimal pair.

How did this affect the status of [i] and [y]? Consider the instrumental plural forms **кони** 'horses' and **коны** 'games'. After the softening of the semi-soft consonants, these words would be pronounced [kon'i] and [kony], respectively. There are two differences between the words, since both the nasal consonants and the final vowels are different. However, these two differences are not equally important. We know that /n/ and /n'/ are different phonemes, since in word final position they distinguish between words. Therefore, this difference is primary. We can predict the choice of [i] or [y] by a simple rule: "After soft consonant, use [i]; after hard consonant, use [y]." Since the choice between [i] and [y] is predictable from the preceding sounds, the two sounds are in complementary distribution. On this basis, we can conclude that they belong to the same phoneme, which it is customary to represent as /i/.

At this point, you may object: couldn't we assume that the difference between the vowels was primary, i.e., assume two vowel phonemes /i/ and /y/? Wouldn't it be possible to formulate a simple rule for the choice between soft and hard consonants, e.g., "use soft consonant before /i/ and hard consonant before /y/"? Unfortunately, this analysis would crash and burn, since it would not enable us to predict the choice between hard and soft consonant in word-final position. After the fall of the jers, there is no way to predict that there is soft [n'] at the end of **конь** 'horse', but hard [n] in **конъ** 'game'. In other words, we cannot predict the choice between soft and hard consonant from surrounding vowels, but we can predict the choice of vowel ([i] vs. [y]) from the preceding consonant. For this reason, we analyze [i] and [y] as allophones of the same phoneme /i/, while /n'/ and /n/ constitute different phonemes.

If you still aren't convinced, consider the following example concerning the prefixed verb **съискати** 'find'. After the jer fell in the prefix **съ-**, we get [s] followed by [i]. What happens next? The two analyses we have discussed above yield different predictions. If we treat soft and hard consonants as different phonemes, and predict [i] vs. [y] from the preceding consonant, we expect the hard [s] to force the [i] to become [y], since only [y] is found after hard consonants. This scenario is sketched in (26a). According to the alternative analysis, where we predict the softness of the consonant on the basis of the following vowel, we would expect [i] to force the preceding [s] to become soft, since only soft consonants are said to occur before [i]. This development is made explicit in (26b).

(26) Two scenarios for the development of **съискати** 'find':
    a. [sъiskati] → [siskat′i] → [syskat′i]
    b. [sъiskati] → [siskat′i] → [s′iskat′i]

From Contemporary Standard Russian you know that the verb in question is **сыскать**. Since the verb starts with a hard consonant followed by [y], we conclude that scenario (26a) is correct. The choice between [i] and [y] is predictable from the preceding consonant. We therefore analyze [i] and [y] as allophones of one phoneme, while hard and soft consonants represent different phonemes.

12.4. Dorsal Obstruents before /i/: [ky, gy, xy] → [k′i, g′i, x′i]

In this section, we consider a sound change that is related to the merger of /i/ and /y/, and concerns dorsal consonants. Recall that "dorsal" is an umbrella term for palatal [k′, g′, x′] and velar [k, g, x]. In Contemporary Standard Russian, there are words with the sound combinations [k′i, g′i, x′i], e.g., the plural forms **звуки** 'sounds', **круги** 'circles', and **орехи** 'nuts', but no words in [ky, gy, xy]. (Exceptions are foreign words, such as **Кыргызстан** 'Kyrgyzstan'.) In early Old Rusian, on the other hand, the sound combinations [k′i, g′i, x′i] did not exist, while [ky, gy, xy] were attested, inter alia in the accusative plural forms **звукы** 'sounds', **кругы** 'circles', and **орѣхы** 'nuts'. The difference between Contemporary Standard Russian and Old Rusian is summarized in Table 73. A simple generalization emerges from the table: Contemporary Standard Russian has [k′i, g′i, x′i] where Old Rusian had [ky, gy, xy]. In terms of natural classes this can be stated as follows: Contemporary Standard Russian has palatal obstruents + front [i] where Old Rusian had velar obstruents + non-front [y].

Table 73. Dorsal obstruents + [i] or [y] in Old Rusian and Contemporary Standard Russian

	[ky, gy, xy]	[k′i, g′i, x′i]
Old Rusian	звукы, кругы, орѣхы	—
Contemporary Standard Russian	—	звуки, круги, орехи

12.4. Dorsal Obstruents before /i/: [ky, gy, xy] → [k'i, g'i, x'i]

If you are wondering why early Old Rusian lacked the combinations [k'i, g'i, x'i], think about the first and second palatalizations. While the accusative plural forms were **звукы, кругы**, and **орѣхы**, the nominative plural had [i] in the ending. However, because of the palatalizations (in this case the second palatalization), the nominative plural forms were **звуци, крузи**, and **орѣси**. Other combinations of dorsal obstruents + front vowels had been removed by the first palatalization. For instance, **чистый** 'clean' started with [k] + front vowel in Proto-Slavic, but [k] turned into [č'] in Common Slavic, and Old Church Slavonic and Old Rusian had **чистъ** 'clean'.

We can assume that the following sound change took place in Old Rusian:

(27) From velar obstruent + non-front [y] to palatal obstruent + front [i]:
   a. [ky] → [k'i]
   b. [gy] → [g'i]
   c. [xy] → [x'i]

As you can see, both the consonant and the vowel undergo change. Was it the consonant or the vowel that triggered the change? Most likely, this is not the right question to ask. Rather, we seem to be dealing with a sound change that was motivated by the phonological system as a whole. The American linguist Jaye Padgett (2003) has worked out this analysis in detail. If we let P stand for any labial, T for any dental, and K for any dorsal consonant, we can describe the systems before and after the change as follows:

(28) Goodness of contrast and the change from [ky, gy, xy] → [k'i, g'i, x'i]:

Before			After		
P'i	Py	Pu	P'i	Py	Pu
T'i	Ty	Tu	T'i	Ty	Tu
	Ky	Ku	K'i		Ku

For labials and dentals, we have three-way contrasts:

(29) Three-way contrasts for labials and dentals:
   a. Labials: [b'i]—[by]—[bu] (**бити** 'hit', **быти** 'be', **буду** 'will be')
   b. Dentals: [t'i]—[ty]—[tu] (**ти** 'you [dative clitic]', **ты** 'you', **ту** 'that [acc sg feminine]')

For dorsal consonants, we have only two-way contrasts, since, as shown in (28) and Table 73, early Old Rusian lacked [k'i, g'i, x'i], while [ky, gy, xy] are not attested in Contemporary Standard Russian. The change from [ky, gy, xy] to [k'i, g'i, x'i] is motivated by a principle that Padgett (2003: 50) refers to as "goodness of contrast," whereby languages strive to make contrasts as easily perceptible as possible. Simply put, it is easier to hear the difference between K'i and Ku than between Ky and Ku, since K' and K are different and [i] is more different from [u] than [y] is. In order to make the contrast with Ku as easy to hear as possible Ky was replaced by K'i. The system after the change in Table 73 has improved the contrast for dorsals, and according to Padgett the change was triggered by the desire to make the contrasts as "good" (i.e., easily perceptible) as possible.

Why did fronting not take place with labials or dentals? It is generally agreed that this is motivated by the phonological system. As shown in (28), labials and dentals display three-way contrasts. If Py and Ty had turned into P'i and T'i, the P'i–Py and T'i–Ty contrasts would have been neutralized (lost). If we assume a principle of "neutralization avoidance," whereby languages strive to maintain phonological contrasts, we are in a position to explain why the changes from Py to P'i and Ty to T'i were blocked. Such changes would have undermined phonological contrasts.

Data from the northwestern dialects of Old Rusian provide additional evidence in favor of a "systemic approach" in terms of the "goodness of contrast" and "neutralization avoidance" principles. As you will learn in chapter 14, these dialects do not show traces of the second palatalization and preserved groups of the K'i type. A change from Ky to K'i in these dialects would therefore be at variance with the neutralization avoidance principle. As a consequence, we would expect the change from Ky to K'i to be inhibited in these dialects. This prediction is borne out by the facts; as pointed out by Galinskaja (2009: 128 and 2014: 125), the change from Ky to K'i occurs later in these dialects—presumably under the influence of the neighboring dialects where the change from Ky to K'i had already taken place.

12.5. Depalatalization of /š'/, /ž'/, and /c'/

As a result of the palatalizations discussed in chapter 11, Old Rusian inherited the following soft phonemes from Common Slavic: /š', ž', c', č'/. The first three of them became hard. We can refer to this process as "depalatalization":

(30) Depalatalization:
  a. Old Rusian /š'/ → Contemporary Standard Russian /š/
  b. Old Rusian /ž'/ → Contemporary Standard Russian /ž/
  c. Old Rusian /c'/ → Contemporary Standard Russian /c/

Depalatalization is an example of what we called an "unconditioned sound law" in section 3.5, since its application is not restricted to a certain phonological environment, but happens across the board. As a consequence of depalatalization, the first consonant in Modern Russian words like шить 'sew', жить 'live', and цена 'price' are hard. The fourth consonant in this group, /č'/, has remained soft in Contemporary Standard Russian, as shown by чистый 'pure', where the first consonant is soft.

The depalatalization of /š', ž', c'/ to /š, ž, c/ is evident from medieval texts where the relevant letters are sometimes followed by ы: шы, жы, and цы. Since only hard consonants occur before ы, such spellings indicate that the scribes pronounced шы, жы, and цы with hard consonants. As pointed out by Ivanov (1983: 235–36), шы and жы (e.g., жывите and Шышкина) are attested in sources from the late 14th century, while цы (e.g., концы) occurs in texts from the 16th century, so there is reason to believe that depalatalization took place earlier for /š', ž'/ than for /c'/. Notice that Contemporary Standard Russian orthography does not use ы after ш and ж (шить and жить), although the relevant consonants are pronounced as hard consonants. After ц, on the other hand, ы is possible in Contemporary Standard Russian orthography, as shown by words such as концы 'ends'.

12.6. Development of New Soft Post-Alveolar Fricatives

Old Rusian inherited the consonant clusters /š'č'/ and /ž'dž'/ from Common Slavic. The former had emerged in Common Slavic from /stj/ and /skj/, while the latter goes back to /zdj/ and /zgj/. These clusters underwent *j*-palatalization and then /s/ became assimilated to /š'/ and /z/ to /ž'/ under the influence of the following consonant. During the Old Rusian period, the clusters became simplified to [š'] and [ž']. The development can be summarized as follows:

(31) Development of new soft post-alveolar fricatives:
    a. [stj] and [skj] → [sč'] → [š'č'] → [š']
    b. [zdj] and [zgj] → [zdž'] → [ž'dž'] → [ž']

We find the resulting consonants in words such as щука 'pike' and дрожжи 'yeast'.

In the previous section you learned that /š', ž'/ underwent depalatalization. The development in (31) gave rise to a new soft /š'/ phoneme in Russian, and some scholars also assume a corresponding voiced soft /ž'/ phoneme. Yet other specialists of Russian phonology accept neither /š'/ nor /ž'/ as phonemes in Modern Russian, and instead analyze the relevant sounds as sequences of two phonemes that are pronounced as single fricatives (e.g., Halle 1959 and Isačenko 1969; for critical discussion, see Timberlake 2004: 65–67 and Nesset 2008: 36). There are two arguments for the sequence analysis. First, the relevant fricatives are about twice as long as other fricatives, which suggests that they represent sequences of two phonemes. Second, the relevant sounds often occur across a morphological boundary. In **считать** 'consider', which is pronounced as if it were spelled "**щитать**," it is clear that the fricative at the beginning of the word results from the merger of /s/ (the prefix **с-**) and the following /č'/ (cf. the related verb **читать** 'read').

12.7. Transition from /e/ to /o/: Relative Chronology

An important sound law in the Old Rusian period is the transition of /e/ to /o/. This sound law accounts for the pronunciation of [o] in Modern Russian words that are spelled with the letter **ё**, such as **нёс** 'he carried', **жёны** 'wives', **ёлка** 'fir tree', and **весёлый** 'cheerful'. We can write the sound law as follows:

(32) Transition from /e/ to /o/:

$$\overset{\acute{\sigma}}{\underset{|}{}}$$

/e/ → /o/ / ____ hard consonant

This formula captures two conditions that must be fulfilled for the rule to apply. First, the accented Greek sigma (ó) over the open place indicates that the transition takes place only if the relevant vowel is in a stressed syllable. (A sigma is often used in linguistics to represent the syllable.) Comparison of word pairs such as **нёс** 'he carried' vs. **несла́** 'she carried' and **жёны** 'wives' vs. **жена́** 'wife' shows that the /e/ to /o/ transition only took place in stressed syllables. Indeed, from Contemporary Standard Russian you know that the letter **ё** is only used in stressed syllables.

The second condition is that the transition from /e/ to /o/ only applies when followed by a hard consonant. Thus, in **ель** 'fir tree' and **весе́лье** 'merriment' the application of the rule is blocked, since the following consonant is soft, while in the related words **ёлка** and **весёлый** transition to /o/ takes place, because the vowel is followed by a hard consonant.[2]

---

[2] Notice that the sound law in (32) does not say anything about the consonant *preceding* the vowel that undergoes change. As you can see from the examples, the preceding consonant is always soft. However, it is not necessary to specify this in (32), since in Old Rusian /e/ did not occur after hard consonants.

Table 74 sums up the joint effect of stress and the following consonant. The transition to /o/ is attested in the plural form **сёла** 'villages', while /e/ is retained in the nominative and locative singular forms **село́** and **селе́**, as well as in the related adjective **се́льский**.

Table 74. The interaction of stress and a following hard consonant for the transition from /e/ to /o/

	Stressed vowel	Unstressed vowel
Before hard consonant	/o/: сёла	/e/: село́
Before soft consonant	/e/: се́льский	/e/: селе́

Table 74 does not say anything about vowels in word-final position. Since Modern Russian has words like **бельё** 'underwear', **копьё** 'spear', and **всё** 'all' with /o/ at the end of the word, it is tempting to assume that the transition from /e/ to /o/ took place in word-final position. However, all the relevant examples involve the neuter ending -o, and it is likely that /o/ in **бельё**, **копьё**, and **всё** is due to analogy from words where -o is preceded by hard consonants, such as **село** 'village', **окно** 'window', and **то** 'that'. An interesting example is the adverb **ещё** 'still'. Here /o/ at the end is not the neuter ending, so it is not likely that /o/ is due to analogy. However, since decisive examples are few and far between, we leave the question open as to whether word-final /o/ after soft consonants is the result of sound change or analogy.

The transition from /e/ to /o/ provides a good illustration of relative chronology (cf. section 3.9), since it allows us to establish the order in which a number of sound laws took place. Let us start with the fall and vocalization of the jers. From Common Slavic, Old Rusian inherited the word **пьсъ** 'dog', which corresponds to the Modern Russian word **пёс**. How can we explain the occurrence of /o/ in this word in Modern Russian? If we assume that **пьсъ** was first subjected to the fall and vocalization of the jers, which gave **пес**, and then underwent the transition of /e/ to /o/, we arrive at the correct form in Modern Russian, namely **пёс**. If we had ordered the transition from /e/ to /o/ before the fall of the jers, we would have ended up with **пес** pronounced with /e/ instead of /o/. In other words, **пёс** and similar words enable us to establish a relative chronology, whereby the fall and vocalization of the jers took place before the transition from /e/ to /o/.

In the next section, you will learn that /ě/ (jat) turned into /e/. Thus, Old Rusian words such as **дѣло** 'affair' and **бѣлый** 'white' which had jat, are now pronounced with /e/: **де́ло** and **бе́лый**. At this point, you may ask: why isn't there /o/ in these words? After all, the vowel is stressed and followed by a hard consonant, so the conditions for the transition to /o/ are fulfilled. Again, the key concept is relative chronology. If we assume that /ě/ became /e/ before the transition from /e/ to /o/, we would indeed get incorrect forms such as "де́ло" and "бе́лый." However, if we assume the opposite order, we predict the correct forms, де́ло and бе́лый. We are therefore forced to conclude that the transition from /e/ to /o/ took place before the change of /ě/ to /e/. At the time when the transition from /e/ to /o/ happened, words like дѣло and бѣлый still had /ě/ (not /e/), and therefore did not undergo the transition to /o/.

If you find the arguments about relative chronology hard to follow, take a look at Table 75, where the development from Old Rusian пьсъ 'dog', се́ла 'villages', and дѣло 'affair' is spelled out step by step. As an experiment, you may want to create a similar table, but change the order of the rules. The experiment will show you that you would get incorrect Modern Russian forms if you assume a different relative chronology.

Table 75. Relative chronology of fall/vocalization of the jers, the transition from /e/ to /o/ and the transition from /ě/ to /e/. The dash (—) is used when a rule does not change the relevant word.

Input	пьсъ	се́ла	дѣло
Fall/vocalization of jers	пес	—	—
/e/ → /o/	пёс	се́ла	—
/ě/ → /e/	—	—	де́ло
Output	пёс	се́ла	де́ло

We continue this *tour de force* of relative chronology with consideration of softness/hardness assimilation (see section 12.3.3). Modern Russian words such as мёртвый 'dead' and чёрный 'black' had a jer followed by soft /r'/ in early Old Rusian. Let us use the latter as an example. We can assume the following representation of the root: /č'ьr'n/. After the fall and vocalization of the jers, we get /č'er'n/. How can we explain that the modern word чёрный has /o/? The question is whether softness/hardness assimilation or the transition from /e/ to /o/ applied first. Recall from the discussion of softness/hardness assimilation in section 12.3.3 that a soft consonant became hard in front of a hard consonant. If we assume this process to transform /č'er'n/ into /č'ern/, which then undergoes the transition from /e/ to /o/, so that we get /č'orn/, we are in a position to predict the correct modern form. However, if we adopt the reverse order, we would get incorrect "черный" with /e/ instead of correct чёрный with /o/. In other words, softness/hardness assimilation before the transition from /e/ to /o/ is the correct relative chronology.

There is a snag, though. In words such as пе́рвый 'first' and верх 'upper part' we have /e/ even though the vowel is stressed and the following consonant is hard. Why don't Russians say "**пёрвый**" and "**вёрх**"? In Old Rusian, these words also contained a jer followed by a soft /r'/. If, as argued above, softness/hardness assimilation took place before the transition from /e/ to /o/, we would indeed predict the incorrect forms "**пёрвый**" and "**вёрх**." How can we explain /o/ in **мёртвый** and **чёрный**, but /e/ in **пёрвый** and **верх**? Take a look at the consonant after the vowel. Whereas in **мёртвый** and **чёрный** we have dental consonants (/t/ and /n/), **первый** has the labial /v/ and **верх** the velar /x/. If we assume that assimilation of soft /r'/ to hard /r/ took place earlier before dental consonants, we can establish a relative chronology that solves the problem. As shown in Table 76, we predict the correct forms if we order the transition from /e/ to /o/ after the hardening of soft /r'/ before dentals, but place it before the hardening of soft /r'/ elsewhere. (The softening of semi-soft consonants and the fall and vocalization of the jers are included in the table to provide a more complete picture.)

Table 76. Relative chronology of softness/hardness assimilation (hardening of /r'/) and the transition from /e/ to /o/. The dash (—) is used when a rule does not change the relevant word.

Input	/č'ьr'n/	/pьr'v/
Softening of semi-soft consonants	—	/p'ьr'v/
Fall/vocalization of the jers	/č'er'n/	/p'er'v/
/r'/ → /r/ / hard dental	/č'ern/	—
/e/ → /o/	/č'orn/	—
/r'/ → /r/ / hard consonant	—	/p'erv/
Output	/č'orn/	/p'erv/

If you are not convinced that the assimilation of /r'/ to /r/ before non-dental consonants was a very late sound change, travel to St. Petersburg and take a look at the Bronze Horseman, the monument on the Senate Square which figures prominently in Pushkin's poem *Mednyj Vsadnik*. You will find the following inscription: "**ПЕТРУ перьвому ЕКАТЕРИНА вторая лѣта 1782**." The soft sign in "**перьвому**" indicates that in the eighteenth century this word was still pronounced with soft /r'/.

As a final example of relative chronology, let us consider the depalatalization of soft /š', ž', c'/ to hard /š, ž, c/. As mentioned in section 12.4, it is customary to assume that depalatalization took place earlier for /š', ž'/ than for /c'/. The transition from /e/ to /o/ corroborates this assumption. Before /š, ž/, Modern Russian has /o/, as you can see from words such as **идёшь** 'you walk', несёшь 'you carry', and молодёжь 'youth'. Before /c/, on the other hand, we find /e/ in Modern Russian as is evident from words like отéц 'father', конéц 'end', and молодéц 'good boy'. We can explain this if we assume a relative chronology whereby depalatalization of /š', ž'/ takes place before the transition from /e/ to /o/, while depalatalization of /c'/ occurs after the transition from /e/ to /o/. This is shown in Table 77, which compares the development of the two related words молодёжь and молодéц.

Table 77. Relative chronology of depalatalization and the transition from /e/ to /o/. The dash (—) is used when a rule does not change the relevant word.

Input	/molodež'ь/	/molodьс'ь/
Softening of semi-soft consonants	/molod'ež'ь/	/molod'ьс'ь/
Fall/vocalization of the jers	/molod'ež'/	/molod'ec'/
/š', ž'/ → /š, ž/	/molod'ež/	—
/e/ → /o/	/molod'ož/	—
/c'/ → /c/	—	/molod'ec/
Output	/molod'ož/	/molod'ec/

Summarizing the discussion of relative chronology, we have established the following five stages of development:

(33) Relative chronology for transition from /e/ to /o/ and related changes:
   a. Softening of semi-soft consonants
   b. Fall and vocalization of the jers
   c. Assimilation of /r'/ to /r/ before hard dentals; depalatalization of /š', ž'/
   d. Transition from /e/ to /o/
   e. Transition from /ě/ to /e/; assimilation of /r'/ to /r/ before hard consonants; depalatalization of /c'/

Throughout the book you have seen examples that analogy and loanwords create (apparent) counterexamples to the sound laws. The transition from /e/ to /o/ illustrates this. For the effect of analogy, it is instructive to consider the present-tense forms of Modern Russian verbs like нести 'carry' given in Table 78. In the second person plural form несёте, /o/ occurs before the soft consonant /t'/, so here the conditions for the transition from /e/ to /o/ are not fulfilled. However, it stands to reason that /o/ in несёте is due to analogy from the other forms with /o/ in the ending. Recall from section 8.2 that in Old Rusian the first person plural had the ending /емъ/. Since /e/ was followed by hard /m/, the sound law for the transition from /e/ to /o/ applies here. In the second person singular, the ending was /eš'i/, which turned into /eš/ after the loss of the final vowel and the depalatalization of /š'/ to /š/. As shown in (33), depalatalization of /š'/ took place before the transition from /e/ to /o/. In other words, when the transition from /e/ to /o/ occurred, the second person singular ending contained a hard consonant, and accordingly the sound law for the transition from /e/ to /o/ could apply. The third person singular is somewhat more complicated. In Old Rusian, these forms ended in /et'/ with a soft /t'/. This /t'/ has become hard in northern and middle Russian dialects (which underlie the standard language), but have remained soft in southern dialects (see section 8.2 for discussion). The sound law for the transition of /e/ to /o/ can only have applied to dialects which had developed hard /t/. In southern dialects, we encounter forms such as **несéть** where /e/ has been preserved before the soft /t'/, as well as forms like **несёть** where /o/ is due to analogy from second person singular and first person plural.

Table 78. Present-tense forms of **нести** 'carry' in Contemporary Standard Russian

	Singular	Plural
1st person	несу́	несём
2nd person	несёшь	несёте
3rd person	несёт	несу́т

The effect of borrowing is evident in words that have stressed /e/ before a hard consonant, such as **цемéнт** 'cement', **памфлéт** 'pamphlet', and **берéт** 'beret'. The reason why the noun **берéт** 'beret' has /e/, while the verb form **берёт** 's/he takes' has /o/ is of course that the former is a relatively recent loanword, while the verb form is a Slavic word that has undergone the changes described above.

Sometimes we encounter word pairs like **нéбо** 'heaven, sky' and **нёбо** 'palate'. These words have the same root, and since the vowel is stressed and followed by a hard consonant, we would expect /o/. The reason why the word for 'heaven' has /e/ is that this religious term is borrowed from Church Slavic. The transition from /e/ to /o/ is an Old Rusian sound law, which did not affect Church Slavic.

12.8. The Fate of /ě/ (jat)

In the previous section, you saw that /ě/ (the vowel phoneme that corresponds to the letter ѣ 'jat') became /e/:

(34) Transition from /ě/ to /e/:

/ě/ → /e/

Examples illustrating this sound law include дѣло 'affair' and бѣлый 'white', which in Contemporary Standard Russian have /e/: де́ло and бе́лый. Notice that in both words /e/ is followed by a hard consonant. If you encounter a Modern Russian word with stressed /e/ before a hard consonant, it is likely that /e/ goes back to /ě/. The reason is that Old Rusian words that had /e/ in this position, underwent the transition from /e/ to /o/, as discussed in the previous section. But you cannot be sure; the word may be a loan word, as is the case for the Church Slavic loan не́бо, as well as for more obvious borrowings such as цеме́нт.

If a Modern Russian word has /e/ followed by a soft consonant, you cannot know whether this vowel goes back to /ě/, /e/, or /ь/. Thus, ве́тер 'wind' had jat (Old Rusian: вѣтръ), while вечер 'evening' did not (Old Rusian: вечеръ). In some cases, comparison with other words or forms of the same word is helpful. If, for instance, you wonder whether /e/ in the verb печь 'bake' goes back to jat in Old Rusian, you can look at the modern masculine singular past-tense form пёк. Since we have /o/ in this form where the vowel is stressed and followed by a hard consonant, the vowel cannot go back to jat in Old Rusian. In the Modern Russian verb петь 'sing', in contrast, we have /e/ in the masculine singular past-tense form пел, so here we can assume jat in Old Rusian.

Although the sound law in (34) is helpful when we compare Old Rusian and Contemporary Standard Russian, it is a simplification to say that /ě/ became /e/ in Russian. If we look at Russian dialects, the picture is more complicated — and more interesting:

(35) Development of Old Rusian /ě/ in dialects:
   a. /ě/ → /e/
   b. /ě/ → /i/
   c. /ě/ retained (but often pronounced as a diphthong [ie])

Dialects of type (a) include the central dialects that underlie Contemporary Standard Russian. Patterns (b) and (c) are attested in north Russian dialects.

In order to explain that /ě/ turned into /e/ or /i/ or was pronounced as [ie] it is customary to assume that the Old Rusian /ě/ was a high-mid vowel, i.e., that it was higher than /e/, but lower than /i/. It may have been pronounced as a diphthong already in Old Rusian, in which case we can sketch the following developments:

(36) Development of Old Rusian /ě/ in dialects:
　a. [ě] → [ie] → [e] (strengthening of the second part of the diphthong)
　b. [ě] → [ie] → [i] (strengthening of the first part of the diphthong)

The development in (36a) involved strengthening of the second part of the [ie] diphthong. The resulting sound [e] belongs to the /e/ phoneme, so /ě/ merged with /e/. In (36b), the first part of the diphthong was strengthened, and the result was [i], which belongs to the /i/ phoneme.

In (35), the change from /ě/ to /e/ is formulated as an unconditioned sound law, since its application is not restricted to certain phonological environments, but occurs in all positions in the word. However, in modern dialects [i] from Old Rusian [ě] is much more widespread before soft consonants than before hard consonants. Thus, in many dialects you may encounter [i] in the stressed syllable of ве́тер where the following consonant is soft, but [e] in the corresponding genitive form ве́тра where the vowel is followed by a hard consonant. In view of these facts, it is likely that the change from /ě/ to /e/ or /i/ started as a conditioned sound law that applied before soft consonants, and then spread to other environments.

12.9. Summary

In section 12.1, you learned that Contemporary Standard Russian has more consonant phonemes, but fewer vowel phonemes than Old Rusian. The consonant increase is mostly due to the expansion of soft consonant phonemes:

(37) Phoneme changes from Old Rusian to Contemporary Standard Russian:
　a. Lost vowels: /ě, ь, ъ, ä, y /
　b. New consonants:
　　i. Soft labials: /p', b', f', m', v'/
　　ii. Soft dentals: /t', d'/

(37) b. iii. Hard post-alveolar fricative: /š/
       iv. Labial fricative: /f/

The most important sound law in this chapter is Havlik's law for the vocalization and fall of the jers (section 12.2):

(38) Havlik's law for the vocalization and fall of the jers:
   a. Number the jers from right to left.
   b. Restart the numbering from non-jer vowels.
   c. Jers with odd numbers are in weak position and fall.
   d. Jers with even numbers are in strong position and vocalize.

The fall of the jers have a number of consequences for Russian phonology and grammar:

(39) Consequences of the fall of the jers:
   a. Mobile vowels (e.g., сон—сна, section 12.3.1).
   b. Closed syllables (e.g., CVC as in сон, section 12.3.2).
   c. Assimilation and dissimilation in consonant clusters (section 12.3.3):
      i. Voicing assimilation of obstruents (e.g., къде → где)
      ii. Softness/hardness assimilation of consonants (e.g., [sъt'ixat'i] → [s't'ixat'i])
      iii. Dissimilation of plosives and affricates (e.g., [č'ьto] → [što])
   d. Final devoicing of obstruents (e.g., [rodъ] → [rot] 'family', section 12.3.4)
   e. Minimal pairs with hard and soft consonants at the end of words (e.g., /krov/ 'shelter' vs. /krov'/ 'blood', section 12.3.5)
   f. Emergence of labial fricative phonemes (/v, v', f, f'/, section 12.3.6)
   g. Merger of /y/ and /i/ (section 12.3.7)

Sound laws that are less directly related to the fall of the jers include:

(40) Other important sound laws:
   a. [ky, gy, xy] → [k'i, g'i, x'i] (e.g., звукы → звуки, section 12.4)
   b. Depalatalization: /š', ž', c'/ → /š, ž, c/ (section 12.5)

(40) c. Development of new soft post-alveolar fricatives [š', ž'] (section 12.6)

d. Transition from /e/ to /o/ under stress and before hard consonant (e.g., нёс 'he carried', section 12.7)

e. Merger of /ě/ (jat) with /e/ (e.g., дѣло → дело, section 12.8)

Although this chapter emphasizes the importance of sound laws, we have seen numerous examples of the interaction of sound laws with analogy and borrowing. In sections 12.2.3 and 12.7, you saw that analogy has affected the fall and vocalization of the jers and the transition from /e/ to /o/. Illustrations of the role of loan words are found in section 12.7; Modern Russian has many loanwords with /e/ instead of /o/, e.g., Church Slavic loans such as небо 'heaven' and more recent borrowings such as цемент 'cement'. Section 12.7 furthermore demonstrated the importance of relative chronology in historical linguistics, since the transition from /e/ to /o/ enabled us to establish relative chronologies for a number of sound laws.

12.10. For Further Reading

A reader-friendly and up-to-date presentation of the phonological changes described in this chapter can be found in Galinskaja 2009 and 2014: 83–132. For the vocalization and fall of the jers, Kiparsky 1963 is a good source of information, with many illustrative examples (Kiparsky 1963 is in German; an English translation is available as Kiparsky 1979).

Chapter 13   Phonology: Stress and Vowel Reduction

Where do the complex stress patterns in Modern Russian come from? And why is **Москва** 'Moscow' pronounced with an unstressed [a] in the first syllable? In this chapter, you learn about the history of two related phenomena that cause problems for learners of Russian: stress patterns and vowel reduction in unstressed syllables.

13.1. Stress Patterns

13.1.1. Stress and Tone

When you listen to somebody speaking a language you do not know, you notice that some syllables stand out as more prominent than the rest. Different languages have different strategies for making syllables prominent. For our purposes, it is important to distinguish between two strategies: stress and tone.

Stress is used in Contemporary Standard Russian. In words like **сковорода́** 'frying pan', the final syllable is stressed. This means that it is louder and articulated with more respiratory force (more air from the lungs). Stressed vowels in Modern Russian are also longer than vowels in unstressed syllables.

Tone involves using differences in pitch (tone height). In Norwegian, for instance, the noun *vannet* 'the water' and the verb *vanne* 'to water' are pronounced the same, except that the first syllable has different tone contours. In Standard East Norwegian, the noun has a low tone on the first syllable, while the first syllable of the verb carries a falling contour from a high to a low tone (Kristoffersen 2000: 236–38).

Simply put, the history of Russian involves a transition from the tone-based system of Common Slavic to the stress-based system of Contemporary Standard Russian. In the modern Slavic languages, stress-based systems are dominant, but systems combining tone and stress have been preserved in Slovene and Bosnian, Croatian, and Serbian. The historical analysis of the tone- and stress-based systems of the Slavic languages has received considerable attention in Slavic linguistics. Important milestones in the field include the monograph *Slavonic Accentuation* (1957) by the Norwegian linguist Christian S. Stang, and works by the Moscow-based linguists Vladislav M. Illič-Svityč

(1963) and Vladimir A. Dybo (e.g., 1981). The exposition in the following subsections is mainly based on Andrej Zaliznjak's (1985) seminal monograph.

13.1.2. Contemporary Standard Russian Stress

The Modern Russian stress system has two properties that make it hard to acquire for foreigners:

(1) Modern Russian stress is

   a. lexical, i.e., unpredictable, and

   b. mobile, i.e., it shifts among the inflected forms of the same word.

Since Russian stress is lexical (unpredictable), you have to learn which syllable is stressed for each and every Russian word you acquire. The fact that **бáбушка** has stress on the first syllable (as opposed to what many foreigners believe) is just something you have to memorize when you learn this particular word. Mobile stress means that for many words the inflected forms have stress on different syllables. While **сковородá** 'frying pan' has stress on the ending in the nominative singular, stress shifts to the first syllable of the stem in the nominative plural: **скóвороды**.

Although Modern Russian stress is lexical and mobile, stress is not chaotic. We can distinguish between six main patterns, for which Zaliznjak (1977) uses the Latin letters a–f:[1]

(2) Main stress patterns in Contemporary Standard Russian:

   a. Immobile stress on the stem (e.g., **рак** 'crawfish')

   b. Immobile stress on the ending (e.g., **гриб** 'mushroom')

   c. Stem stress in the singular, stress on the ending in the plural (e.g., **мéсто** 'place')

   d. Stress on the ending in the singular, stem stress in the plural (e.g., **женá** 'wife')

---

[1] In addition, Zaliznjak (1977) considers some subpatterns (Russian: **второстепенные схемы ударения**). For instance, some of the nouns of pattern f belong to subpattern f' because they have stem stress in the accusative singular. Examples include **головá** 'head' (accusative singular: **гóлову**), **рукá** 'hand' (accusative singular: **рýку**), and **доскá** 'board' (accusative singular: **дóску**). Such subpatterns will not be discussed in this book.

(2) e. Stem stress except in the oblique cases in the plural (e.g., **гость** 'guest')

f. Stress on ending except in the nominative plural (e.g., **губа́** 'lip')

An example of each pattern is given in Table 79. Notice that we say that **гриб** has stress on the ending in the nominative singular, and that the stress is on the ending in the genitive plural form **мест**, even though strictly speaking these forms do not have an ending. Therefore, the stress is forced to fall on the stem. As you may have guessed, the historical explanation has to do with the fall of the jers. The relevant forms had the ending -ъ, but accent shifted to the preceding syllable and the jer disappeared. However, despite this, words such as **гриб** and **ме́сто** belong to stress patterns that assign stress to the ending in some or all forms of the paradigm as long as there is an ending that can carry stress. For this reason it is customary to say that **гриб** has stress on the ending throughout the paradigm, and that **ме́сто** has stress on the ending in all plural forms.

Table 79. Main stress patterns in Contemporary Standard Russian

		a	b	c	d	e	f
Sg	N	ра́к	гриб	ме́сто	жена́	го́сть	губа́
	A	ра́ка	гриб	ме́сто	жену́	го́стя	губу́
	G	ра́ка	гриба́	ме́ста	жены́	го́стя	губы́
	D	ра́ку	грибу́	ме́сту	жене́	го́стю	губе́
	I	ра́ком	грибо́м	ме́стом	жено́й	го́стем	губо́й
	L	ра́ке	грибе́	ме́сте	жене́	го́сте	губе́
Pl	N	ра́ки	грибы́	места́	жёны	го́сти	гу́бы
	A	ра́ков	грибы́	места́	жён	гостей́	гу́бы
	G	ра́ков	грибо́в	мест	жён	гостей́	губ
	D	ра́кам	гриба́м	места́м	жёнам	гостя́м	губа́м
	I	ра́ками	гриба́ми	места́ми	жёнами	гостя́ми	губа́ми
	L	ра́ках	гриба́х	места́х	жёнах	гостя́х	губа́х

We can divide the paradigms of Russian nouns into four parts ("subparadigms"): the nominative singular, the oblique cases singular, nominative plural, and the oblique cases plural. By "oblique cases," we mean the case forms that are different from the nominative. An important generalization is:

(3) Subparadigm uniformity:

Within a subparadigm, stress is uniform, i.e., falls on the same syllable in all forms of a subparadigm.

Figure 18 illustrates this. Each cell stands for a subparadigm. If a subparadigm has stem stress, the relevant cell is white, whereas subparadigms with stress on the ending have shaded cells.

Figure 18 shows that stress has a morphological function in Russian words with mobile stress (patterns c–f). In pattern c, stress is a plural marker; if you come across a form of **мéсто** with stress on the ending, you know that you are dealing with a plural form. Likewise, stress is a plural marker in pattern d. If you see a stem stressed form of **женá**, you know that it has to be a plural form. In pattern e, stress singles out the oblique cases in the plural, while stress is a marker of the nominative plural in pattern f. Since patterns c and d cover more words than pattern e, which in turn has more members than pattern f, we can state the following hierarchy, where "X > Y" means that "stress is more likely to mark X than Y":

(4) Hierarchy for stress as a morphological marker:

Plural > oblique cases plural > nominative plural

In other words, mobile stress is first and foremost a plural marker, but within the plural mobile stress can also single out the oblique cases or even the nominative.

Can we predict which morphological features stress marks in a given word with mobile stress? Not completely. However, as discussed at length in Nesset 1994, it turns out that whether the stem ends in a hard or soft consonant is relevant:

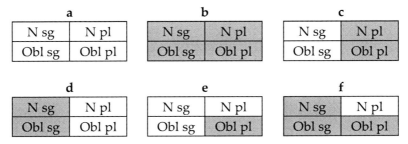

Figure 18. Main stress patterns in Contemporary Standard Russian (white cells: stem stress, shaded cells: stress on the ending)

(5) The hard/soft consonant stress rule:
   a. Hard = Plural: in nouns with a hard consonant in stem-final position, stress is a plural marker (patterns c and d, e.g., ме́сто 'place' and жена́ 'wife').
   b. Soft = Oblique cases plural: in nouns with a soft consonant in stem-final position, stress is a marker of oblique cases in the plural (e.g., гость 'guest' and кость 'bone').

This rule does not have anything to say about pattern f. While this class comprises a relatively small class of nouns that must be memorized, it is worth pointing out that they tend to be feminine or neuter nouns that denote body parts and/or have a velar consonant in stem-final position. Examples include губа́ 'lip', голова́ 'head', плечо́ 'shoulder', рука́ 'hand', and доска́ 'board'.

The patterns of mobile stress differ not only with regard to the morphological features they mark. Another difference is whether stress shifts from left to right or right to left. If we take the nominative singular as our starting point, we have rightward movement in patterns c (ме́сто – места́) and e (гость – гостей), but leftward movement in patterns d (жена́ – жёны) and f (губа́ – гу́бы). Whether the nominative singular form ends in a consonant or a vowel is relevant (as discussed in detail in Nesset 1994):

(6) The rightward/leftward stress shift rule:
   a. Consonant = rightward: in nouns where the nominative singular ends in a consonant, stress shifts to the right (patterns c and e, e.g., дом (pl: дома́) 'house' and гость 'guest').
   b. Vowel /a/ = leftward: in nouns where the nominative singular ends in the vowel /a/, stress shifts to the left (patterns d and f, e.g., жена́ 'wife' and губа́ 'lip').
   c. Vowel /o/ = rightward or leftward: in nouns where the nominative singular ends in the vowel /o/, stress shifts to the right (pattern c, e.g., ме́сто 'place') or to the left (pattern d, e.g., окно́ (pl: о́кна) 'window').

Rightward stress shift tends to go from the first syllable of the stem to the first syllable of the ending, as shown in examples such as го́род 'city' (nominative plural: города́, instrumental plural города́ми) and но́вость '(piece of) news' (genitive plural новосте́й, instrumental plural новостя́ми). Words with stress on the last syllable of the stem such as мото́р 'motor' and тетра́дь 'notebook' generally do not have mobile stress.

Leftward stress shift goes from the first syllable of the ending to either the first syllable of the stem (pattern f) or the final syllable of the stem (pattern d). The examples in Table 79 have monosyllabic stems, so we cannot tell the difference. However, longer words such as голова́ 'head' (pattern f, nominative plural: го́ловы) and величина́ 'size' (pattern d, nominative plural: величи́ны) show that stress lands on the first syllable of the stem in pattern f, but on the final syllable of the stem in pattern d.

You may have noticed that all the examples so far have been nouns. However, stress patterns are relevant for other parts of speech as well. Of particular interest are present-tense forms of verbs and short forms of adjectives. For verbs we can distinguish between patterns a, b, and c:

(7) Stress patterns in verbs (present-tense forms):
   a. Immobile stem stress, e.g., тра́тить 'spend' (тра́чу – тра́тит – тра́тят)
   b. Immobile stress on the ending, e.g., говори́ть 'speak' (говорю́ – говори́т – говоря́т)
   c. Mobile stress, e.g., купи́ть 'buy' (куплю́ – ку́пит – ку́пят)

The same three stress patterns are attested in short forms of adjectives:

(8) Stress patterns in adjectives (short forms):
   a. Immobile stem stress, e.g., интере́сный 'interesting' (интере́сен – интере́сна – интере́сно – интере́сны)
   b. Immobile stress on the ending, e.g., у́мный 'smart' (умён – умна́ – умно́ – умны́)
   c. Mobile stress, e.g., ве́рный 'faithful' (ве́рен – верна́ – ве́рно – ве́рны)

In pattern c, the variant with stress on the ending in the plural (верны́) is in the process of taking over for stem-stressed plural forms like ве́рны.

13.1.3. Common Slavic: Tone

Although Common Slavic distinguished between stressed and unstressed syllables, it was tone that played first violin, because three different tonal contours can be reliably reconstructed for stressed syllables in Common Slavic. Exactly how these contours were pronounced is not known, but for the purposes of this book we will assume the following, where H stands for a tone with high pitch, and L for a tone with low pitch (see Galinskaja 1997: 59 for discussion):

(9) Common Slavic tonal contours:
   a. Circumflex: HL (falling contour from H(igh) to L(ow))
   b. Acute: LHL (rising and falling contour from L(ow) to H(igh) to L(ow))
   c. Neoacute: LH (rising contour from L(ow) to H(igh))

In section 10.8.2, you learned that the tonal contours are important for the understanding of liquid diphthongs. If a word-initial liquid diphthong had the circumflex contour, the result in Russian was /lo/ as in **локотъ** 'elbow'. If, on the other hand, a word-initial liquid diphthong had the acute contour, Russian developed /la/ as in **лань** 'doe'.

13.1.4. Old Rusian: From Tone to Stress

The transformation of the Common Slavic tonal system to the Modern Russian stress-based system starts in early Old Rusian with the merger of the acute and the neoacute. On the assumption that the acute had an LHL contour, while an LH contour was characteristic of the neoacute, we can describe the merger of the acute and the neoacute as the loss of the final L in the acute:

(10) Merger of acute and neoacute:
   LHL → LH

The merger of the acute and the neoacute reduced the number of different patterns from three to two. In the course of time, the resulting two patterns were reinterpreted as stress patterns, known as "automatic" and "autonomous" stress:

(11) From tone to stress (first step):
   a. Circumflex tone → automatic stress (on the initial syllable)
   b. Acute/neoacute tone → autonomous stress (on any syllable)

It is important to notice that automatic and autonomous stress were different phonetically. In order to represent this difference it is customary to mark automatic stress as ¯ in front of the stressed syllable, while autonomous stress is marked with ˈ, which will be placed in front of the stressed vowel. The two patterns form minimal pairs. For instance, for the verb 'drink' language users could hear the difference between the participle ¯пити (with automatic stress) and the infinitive п'ити (with autonomous stress). Exactly what the difference was is uncertain, but it is likely that we are dealing with a combination of tone and stress. Jakobson (1963: 159–61; see also Zaliznjak 1985: 120) proposed that autonomous stress in fact was a combination of stress and a rising tone, while syllables with automatic stress were characterized in terms of stress only. To the extent that the early Old Rusian system combines stress and tone, the traditional term "autonomous stress" is somewhat misleading. However, for convenience we will continue using the traditional terms.

In order to see how this system works, let us first consider autonomous stress, which is lexical (i.e., unpredictable) in the same way as stress is in Modern Russian. Zaliznjak (1985) argues that each morpheme (roots and affixes) comes with its own stress properties. Simplifying somewhat, we can say that a morpheme either has stress on a certain syllable or is unstressed. It follows from this that the combination of a root + an ending can yield four different situations:

(12)   Assignment of stress in early Old Rusian:
   a.   Stressed root + stressed ending:
        дор'ог-'а → дор'ога 'road (nom sg)'
   b.   Stressed root + unstressed ending:
        дор'ог-у → дор'огу 'road (acc sg)'
   c.   Unstressed root + stressed ending:
        голов-'а → голов'а 'head (nom sg)'
   d.   Unstressed root + unstressed ending:
        голов-у → ¯голову 'head (acc sg)'

As you can see from (12), each word ends up with one and only one stressed syllable. If there are two syllables marked with ' as in (12a), the leftmost syllable wins out. If, on the other hand, there is no syllable with ' in the word (as in 12d), the word ends up with automatic stress on the initial syllable. We can formulate the following rule:

(13)   Basic stress rule in early East Slavic (simplified):
   a.   Autonomous stress: the leftmost syllable with ' receives stress.
   b.   Automatic stress: if there is no syllable with ', the word receives automatic stress on the initial syllable.

Words that receive autonomous stress are often referred to as "orthotonic words," while the inherently unstressed words that are assigned automatic stress are called "enclinomena."

While the rule in (13) illustrates the interaction between autonomous and automatic stress, it is simplistic in some respects (cf. Zaliznjak 1985: 123–24). Importantly, roots can attract autonomous stress in two different ways. In addition to "self-stressed" roots such as дор′ог, there are also what we may call "post-stressed" roots. While self-stressed roots attract autonomous stress to themselves, post-stressed roots direct autonomous stress to the following syllable, i.e., the first syllable of the ending. An example is жен of жена 'wife', which had the accusative singular form жен′у. Even if the ending -у is unstressed as shown in (12b and d), stress ends up on the ending, because жен is post-stressed, and thus directs stress to the following syllable.

An important property of Old Rusian stress is that it applies to the phonetic word as a whole. Recall from section 9.11 that a phonetic word can include a number of clitics, both proclitics that attach to the beginning of the word and enclitics that attach to the end of the word. In order to see that Old Rusian stress applies to the whole phonetic word, consider (a) enclinomena preceded by unstressed proclitics, and (b) enclinomena followed by a stressed enclitic:

(14) The phonetic word as the domain of Old Rusian stress:

    a. Unstressed proclitic + enclinomenon: ¯на слово 'on the word'

    b. Enclinomenon + stressed enclitic: продалъ с′я 'was sold'

As you can see from (14a), automatic stress falls on the proclitic, i.e., the first syllable of the phonetic word. We find reminiscences of this in Modern Russian expressions like зá городом 'out of town', where stress is on the preposition. In (14b), we see that autonomous stress can fall on an enclitic if it combines with an enclinomenon. Traces of this in Modern Russian include a few past-tense forms such as начался 'began' where stress falls on -ся.

In the beginning of this section, we saw that the merger of the acute and neoacute tonal patterns was the first step from a tonal to a stress-based system. The second step happened later in the Old Rusian period when the phonetic difference between autonomous and automatic stress was wiped out:

(15) From tone to stress (second step):

    Autonomous and automatic stress become phonetically indistinguishable.

If we adopt Jakobson's idea that autonomous stress involved a combination of stress and a rising tone, while syllables with automatic stress were characterized in terms of stress only, the sound law in (15) can be interpreted as the loss of the rising tone in autonomous stress. In any case, ever since the merger of autonomous and automatic stress, Russian has had a purely stress-based system. Since there is no longer a phonetic difference between autonomous and automatic stress, we can mark all stressed syllables with ´ from now on.

13.1.5. The Emergence of Modern Russian Stress Patterns: Analogy

The stress rules described in the previous subsection yielded a system of three so-called accentual paradigms, which it is customary to designate as a, b, and c. Accentual paradigm a consisted of words with self-stressed stems (autonomous stress on the stem), such as дорога 'way' in (12a, b). No matter what the stress properties of the ending were, such words received stress on the stem, since the leftmost stress mark always won out according to rule (13a). The Old Rusian accentual paradigm a is the ancestor of the Modern Russian stress pattern a (immobile stem stress).

Accentual paradigm b consisted of post-stressed stems such as жен in жена. This yielded stress on the ending, so this accentual paradigm is the ancestor of stress pattern b in Modern Russian (immobile stress on the ending). However, many post-stressed stems (including жен) developed stress on the final syllable of the stem in the plural. This became stress pattern d in Modern Russian. We return to this development below.

Accentual paradigm c consisted of unstressed stems that combined with stressed endings in some forms, and unstressed endings in other forms. As shown in (12c, d), such words will end up with stress on the ending in the forms with stressed endings, while automatic stress will be assigned to the word-initial syllable of the remaining forms. The result is mobile stress between the ending and the first syllable of the stem. This is characteristic of patterns c (гóрод – городá), e (нóвость – новостéй), and f (головá – гóловы) in Modern Russian.

How did the development from the three Old Rusian accentual paradigms to the six modern stress patterns take place? In one word, the answer is "analogy." As pointed out by Zaliznjak (1985: 371), two principles underlie the analogical changes:

(16) Principles governing analogical changes in stress patterns:
    a. Unification within the subparadigms: the forms of a subparadigm tended to develop stress on the same syllable.

(16) b. Polarization of singular vs. plural: the nominative singular and nominative plural tended to develop stress on different syllables.

Taken together, these two principles work toward a system of mobile stress where the singular and plural have stress on different syllables, i.e., where stress is a plural marker. This is indeed the hallmark of mobile stress in Contemporary Standard Russian, as you saw in section 13.1.2. A detailed discussion of all the individual analogical changes would take us too far afield, but an example from the ā-declension illustrates the mechanisms at work.

As shown by Zaliznjak (1985: 373), the development of stress pattern d in words such as **женá** 'wife' and **росá** 'dew' (nominative plural **жёны** and **рóсы** in Modern Russian) is the result of the convergence of Old Rusian accentual paradigms b and c. Paradigm c had different stress placement in the nominative singular and plural (**росá** – **рóсы**), and under the influence of this, words from paradigm b, such as **женá** developed stem stress in the nominative plural instead of the original **жены́**. In the singular, words like **росá** from paradigm c developed end stress in the accusative and dative (**росý** and **росé** instead of older **рóсу** and **рóсе**) under the influence of words from paradigm b, which had end stress (e.g., **женý** and **женé**). In the plural, the oblique cases in both paradigms originally had stress on the ending, but gradually developed stem stress under the influence of the nominative plural (e.g., dative plural **росáм** to **рóсам** and **женáм** to **жёнам**). We can summarize the analogical changes as follows:

(17) Analogical changes in **женá** (paradigm b) and **росá** (paradigm c):

a. Nominative plural: **жены́** → **жёны** under the influence of **рóсы**

b. Accusative singular: **рóсу** → **росý** under the influence of **женý**

c. Dative singular: **рóсе** → **росé** under the influence of **женé**

d. Oblique cases plural: e.g., **женáм** → **жёнам** and **росáм** → **рóсам** under the influence of nominative plural **жёны** and **рóсы**

As the result of all these changes the convergence of Old Rusian accentual paradigms b and c yielded the Modern Russian stress pattern d.

13.2. Vowel Reduction: The Emergence of Akan'e

One of the first things you learned about Russian pronunciation was that special rules apply to unstressed vowels. Simplifying somewhat, the unstressed vowel in **Москвá** is pronounced [a]. This phenomenon is called "vowel reduction" and is known as "**аканье**" in Russian. Vowel reduction patterns are different after soft consonants, but in the following we focus on the patterns after hard consonants, which suffice to illustrate the main historical processes at work.

Although for our purposes it is not necessary to go into detail, you should know that the vowel reduction pattern in Contemporary Standard Russian is merely the tip of the iceberg. Russian dialects display a plethora of patterns, which are both complex and interesting. By way of example, consider "dissimilative akan'e," which is attested in southwestern dialects of Russian. Table 80 compares dissimilative akan'e to the "strong akan'e" you are familiar with from Contemporary Standard Russian. Whereas under strong akan'e, the unstressed vowel is [a] in both the nominative form **Москва́** and the accusative form **Москву́**, dissimilative akan'e has different unstressed vowels in the two case forms. The rule is simple: unstressed [a] is pronounced before stressed high vowels (/i, u/), while unstressed [ъ] occurs before stressed low vowel (/a/). (For our purposes, it is not necessary to discuss what happens if the stressed syllable contains a mid vowel.) The symbol [ъ] represents a reduced e-like sound, which phoneticians call "schwa" and represent as [ə]. The symbol [ъ] is used here in order to emphasize that we are dealing with a vowel that is very similar to the Old Rusian phoneme /ъ/, which existed until the fall and vocalization of the jers.

Table 80. Strong vs. dissimilative akan'e

	Strong akan'e		Dissimilative akan'e	
Москва́	[a]:	[maskvá]	[ъ]:	[mъskvá]
Москву́	[a]:	[maskvú]	[a]:	[maskvú]

Today, various types of akan'e are attested in Belarusian and in southern and central dialects of Russian. Ukrainian and north Russian dialects do not have akan'e. In northern Russian, therefore, **Москва́** is pronounced [moskvá] with unstressed [o]. This is called "okan'e."

In texts from the end of the fourteenth century we can observe that the scribes sometimes mix up the letters **a** and **o**. For instance, Galinskaja (2009: 147 and 2014: 142) mentions the spelling **Маскву** for **Москву** in a document from 1389. Such incorrect spellings may be due to influence from the spoken language of the scribe, and therefore suggest that akan'e arose in the fourteenth century.

How did akan'e develop? This is a hotly debated question in Slavic linguistics, and a number of theories have been proposed. In the following, we consider a proposal advanced by the Russian linguist Sergej Knjazev (2000). Knjazev's point of departure is an idea formulated by the Norwegian linguist

13.2. Vowel Reduction: The Emergence of Akan'e

Olaf Broch (1916: 57–59): it is natural for long stressed vowels to be preceded by short unstressed vowels. Knjazev suggests that stressed vowels underwent lengthening in Old Rusian, whereas unstressed vowels became shorter. However, since high vowels (/i, u/) in general are shorter than non-high vowels (/e, o, a/), shortening only affected non-high vowels, which all became pronounced as [ъ] in unstressed syllables. The resulting system is a version of strong akan'e where **Москва́** and **Москву́** are pronounced with [ъ] in the first syllable. This system then developed into the strong akan'e we have in Contemporary Standard Russian, and the various types of dissimilative akan'e attested in dialects.

In order to understand the further development, you need to consider words with more than one unstressed vowel, such as **сковорода́** 'frying pan'. In Contemporary Standard Russian, the first two unstressed vowels are pronounced differently from the unstressed vowel immediately before the stressed syllable: [skъvъradá]. The unstressed vowel immediately before is somewhat longer than in the other unstressed syllables, and has [a] instead of [ъ] in Contemporary Standard Russian. Together with the stressed syllable, the immediately preceding unstressed syllable forms what we may call the "nucleus" of the phonetic word (Kodzasov 1999: 866). We can summarize the development so far as follows:

(18) Development of **сковорода́** 'frying pan':

[skovorodá]
↓   (lengthening of stressed vowels; a: = long vowel)
[skovorodá:]
↓   (shortening of unstressed [o] to [ъ])
[skъvъrъdá:]
↓   (emergence of nucleus; vowels in
[skъvъ(rъdá:)]   nucleus in parentheses)

As for the further development, Knjazev (2000: 88–89) suggests that the nucleus developed differently in the dialects with strong and dissimilative akan'e. The type of strong akan'e we have in Contemporary Standard Russian emphasizes the difference between unstressed vowels inside and outside the nucleus. Accordingly, unstressed [ъ] became lengthened and lowered to [a] inside the nucleus, while unstressed vowels outside the nucleus continued to be pronounced [ъ]. We can represent this as follows:

(19) Further development of **сковорода́** 'frying pan' – strong akan'e:

[skъvъ(rъdá:)]
↓   (lengthening of all unstressed vowels in
[skъvъ(radá:)]   nucleus: [ъ] → [a])

As you can see, the result is a system with different vowels inside and outside the nucleus.

Dialects that developed dissimilative akan'e, alternatively, focused on the relationship between the unstressed and stressed vowels inside the nucleus. The principle is simple: a short unstressed vowel precedes a long stressed vowel, and a long unstressed vowel precedes a short stressed vowel, so that the duration of all nuclei is the same. We may refer to this as the principle of isochrony ("equal length"), although Knjazev himself does not use this term. Recall that high vowels are generally shorter than low vowels. Accordingly, dialects with dissimilative akan'e have kept unstressed [ъ] before stressed low vowels like [á:]. Before a stressed high vowel like [ý], which is shorter than [á:], the unstressed vowel in the nucleus has undergone lengthening from [ъ] to [a] in order to satisfy the isochrony principle:

(20) Further development of **сковородá** 'frying pan' – dissimilative akan'e:

[skъvъ(rьdý)]
↓   (lengthening of unstressed vowel in
[skъvъ(radý)]   nucleus before [ý]: [ъ] → [a])

The result of (20) is the system of dissimilative akan'e with high unstressed vowels before stressed low vowels ([skъvъ(rьdá:)]), but low unstressed vowels before high stressed vowels [skъvъ(radý)]. In this way, the nucleus is either short + long or long + short.

We can summarize Knjazev's conception as follows:

(21) Development of akan'e according to Knjazev (2000):

  a. Lengthening of stressed vowels

  b. Shortening of non-high unstressed vowels to [ъ]

  c. Emergence of a "nucleus" consisting of the stressed syllable and the syllable preceding it

  d. In dialects with strong akan'e (as in Contemporary Standard Russian): lengthening of unstressed vowel inside nucleus to [a]

  e. In dialects with dissimilative akan'e (southwestern Russian): emergence of the principle of isochrony, whereby short (i.e., high) unstressed vowels precede long (i.e., low) stressed vowels and long (i.e., low) unstressed vowels precede short (i.e., high) stressed vowels within the nucleus

Whether Knjazev's theory will become generally accepted or the debate of akan'e will continue remains an open question.

13.3. Summary

In this chapter, you have learned about two related phenomena: stress patterns and vowel reduction in unstressed syllables. Here is the development of stress patterns in a nutshell:

(22) Development of stress patterns:
   a. Common Slavic: tone/stress → Modern Russian: stress (section 13.1.1)
   b. Common Slavic tones (13.1.3):
      i. Circumflex (probably a falling tone)
      ii. Acute (probably a rising and falling tone)
      iii. Neoacute (probably a rising tone)
   c. Important sound laws (13.1.4):
      i. Merger of the acute and neoacute
      ii. Reinterpretation of circumflex as "automatic" stress and the acute/neoacute as "autonomous" stress
      iii. Merger of automatic and autonomous stress
   d. Old Rusian accentual paradigms (13.1.5):
      Paradigm a: self-stressed stem (stem with autonomous stress)
      Paradigm b: post-stressed stem (autonomous stress directed to the syllable after the stem)
      Paradigm c: unstressed stem in combination with stressed and unstressed endings
   e. Development of six stress patterns in Modern Russian through analogy (13.1.5)

As for vowel reduction, you have learned that the type of akan'e we know from Contemporary Standard Russian is only one of many patterns attested in Russian dialects. We have seen that key concepts are "nucleus" and "isochrony," and that processes of shortening and lengthening have created different patterns in different dialects.

13.4. For Further Reading

If you want to learn more about stress patterns, Zaliznjak 1985 contains a wealth of information, both for Old Rusian and Modern Russian. A shorter presentation in German is Lehfeldt 2009. Most textbooks offer somewhat dated overviews of the history of vowel reduction, but Knjazev 2000 provides interesting perspectives.

Chapter 14   A Visit to Novgorod: The Language of the Birch Bark Letters

Today, Novgorod is a small provincial town in northwestern Russia.[1] However, in medieval times Novgord was a major city that served as a contact point between Rus' and Scandinavia, and later between Rus' and the Hanseatic League, the organization of German merchants that became an important trading partner for Rus'. From the perspective of Old Rusian language and literature, Novgorod is important because most of the birch bark letters have been found here. In section 2.3.7, you learned that these letters are a unique source of information about daily life in the Middle Ages. While birch bark letters can be fun to read, they display a number of dialect features that make them hard to penetrate. This chapter prepares you for the reading of birch bark letters by providing a survey of important dialect features. We explore orthography (section 14.1), phonology (sections 14.2–14.4), morphology (sections 14.5–14.6), and syntax (section 14.7). In section 14.8, we briefly discuss the role of the Old Novgorod dialect in the formation of the Russian language. This chapter is mainly based on Zaliznjak's monograph *Drevnenovgorodskij dialekt* (2004), which contains much more information than could be included in this short chapter.

14.1. Orthography: Бытовая система письма

When you read birch bark letters, the first obstacle you encounter is the orthography. Words are spelled in unexpected ways. In some cases, which we will discuss in the following sections, this is due to the phonological, morphological, and syntactic idiosyncrasies of the Old Novgorod dialect, i.e., the dialect spoken in medieval Novgorod. However, some of the unexpected spellings are simply due to a set of spelling conventions, which Zaliznjak (2004: 21) refers to as "**бытовая система письма**." According to this system, certain letters are used interchangeably (symbolized as ↔). Of particular importance is the distribution of letters for mid vowels:

---

[1] Don't confuse Novgorod in northwestern Russian with the much bigger city Nižnij Novgorod on the Volga. A third Novgorod is Novgorod-Seversk in present-day Ukraine, the hometown of the hero of *Slovo o polku Igoreve* (see section 2.3.3).

(1) **Бытовая система письма** – interchangeable vowel letters:
   a. ъ ↔ о (e.g., поклоно for поклонъ 'greeting')
   b. ь ↔ е ↔ ѣ (e.g., сьло for село 'village')
   c. ъ ↔ ь (in early birch bark letters, e.g., възьми for възьми/возьми 'take!')

From what you learned about the jers in section 12.2, you may not be surprised that the letters ъ and о are used interchangeably, and that the same holds for ь and е. After all, according to Havlik's law /ъ/ became /o/ and /ь/ became /e/ in strong position. However, as Zaliznjak (2004: 23–24) points out, it was not simply the case that the authors of birch bark letters wrote vowels as they pronounced them after the fall and vocalization of the jers. In the case of **поклоно** for **поклонъ** in (1a), for example, the final jer that is spelled as **о** is in weak position. In other words, according to Havlik's law, this jer falls. As such, if the person who wrote **поклоно** had just followed his or her pronunciation, s/he would have written **поклон**, with no vowel letter at the end of the word. In **сьло** for **село** in (1b), we are dealing with a word that never had an etymological jer, so this word was never pronounced with /ь/ — even before the fall of the jers. Again, if the writer was guided by his/her pronunciation, such examples are surprising. Zaliznjak (2004: 24) furthermore points out that the interchangeable use of ъ ↔ о and ь ↔ е is attested long after the fall and vocalization of the jers. He concludes that the use of letters reflects a set of purely orthographical conventions—hence the term "**бытовая система письма**."

The use of **е** and **ѣ** may not be surprising since in section 12.8 you learned that the two phonemes /e/ and /ě/ merged. However, for the same reasons as for the jers, we are presumably dealing with a purely orthographic convention.

The patterns in (1a–b) display a parallel development over time, as shown by Zaliznjak (2004: 25). While they are attested in the earliest birch bark letters from before 1100 AD, they are quite rare in the beginning, but show strong increase and peak between 1200 and 1300 AD, when about 9 out of 10 documents display the patterns in question. In the 14th century, the interchangable use of vowel letters decreases sharply.

The pattern in (1c), shows a very different development over time. This pattern, which is known as the "one-jer system" ("**одноеровое письмо**") is characteristic of the earliest birch bark letters, i.e., letters from the eleventh and the first part of the twelfth century. Interestingly, the one-jer system is not restricted to birch bark letters; the same system is attested in the *Novgorod Codex* (*Novgorodskij kodeks*) from between 1000 and 1025 AD.

The term "**бытовая система письма**" conveys three important properties of the spelling conventions. First, as suggested by the word **бытовой** 'domestic, everyday', these conventions are mainly found in writings pertaining to the domestic sphere and everyday life, as opposed to the **книжная система письма**, which was used in, e.g., religious texts. Second, the relevant conventions are systematic; the use of the **бытовая система письма** does not imply that the writer was uneducated, only that s/he followed a different and more flexible orthographic system than the norm in, e.g., religious texts. Third, the system is orthographic rather than phonetic, as suggested by the word **письмо** 'writing'.

14.2. Phonology: The Question of the Second and Third Palatalizations

An interesting question about the language of the birch bark letters concerns the second palatalization. Consider the following excerpt from birch bark letter no. 247, where a man is being accused of having caused damage to a house, although it turns out that the lock and the doors are "whole," i.e., undamaged:

(2) a. […] [п]о[клѣ](п)ает[ь] сего :м:ми рѣзанами а замъке **кѣле** а двьри **кѣлѣ** а господарь въ не тяжѣне дѣе
 (BBL 247; Zaliznjak 2004: 239–40)

 b. […] обвиняет этого [человека] в ущербе на 40 резан. А замок **цел** и двери **целы**, и хозяин по этому поводу иска не предъявляет.

 c. […] accuses this person of having caused 40 rezany [a monetary unit] worth of damage. But the lock is **whole** and the doors are **whole**, and the owner does not advance a claim regarding this case.

The crucial word here is 'whole', which in Modern Russian is **целый**. In section 11.7, you learned that the affricate at the beginning of this word is the result of the second palatalization. In Common Slavic, the diphthongs /āi/ and /ăi/ underwent monophthongization to /ě/, which then triggered the second palatalization, whereby /k, g, x/ turned into /c', z', s'/ before /ě/. As shown in Figure 19, the word for 'whole' had the root /kăil/ in Proto-Slavic, which turned into /kěl/ due to monophthongization, and then became /c'ěl/ after the second palatalization.

However, as shown in (2a), 'whole' is represented as **кѣле** and **кѣлѣ** in the birch bark letter from Novgorod. We will return to the endings -**е** and -**ѣ** in sections 14.5 and 14.6. Of particular interest here is the fact that the root has /k/ in front of /ě/. Going back to Figure 19, it seems that the Old Novgorod dialect stopped at the middle stage /kěl/, i.e., that the second palatalization never took

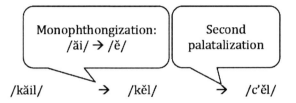

Figure 19. Development of целый 'whole'

place in the Old Novgorod dialect. This is indeed Zaliznjak's conclusion (Zaliznjak 2004: 45).

In section 3.10, you learned about the wave model of language change, which compares the spreading of a linguistic innovation to the waves in a pond when you throw a stone into it. Linguistic innovations start in central areas, and then gradually spread to the geographical periphery. This makes sense for the second palatalization and Novgorod. After all, Novgorod represented the northern periphery of the Slavic area, so it is not far-fetched to assume that the second palatalization never reached this peripheral area.

Another possibility is that it was the monophthongization of /āi/ and /ăi/ to /ĕ/ that reached Novgorod late. According to this scenario, which has been proposed by the Dutch linguist Willem Vermeer (2000: 18), words like 'whole' still had the shape /kăil/ at the time when the second and third palatalizations were active. Since there was no front vowel in /kăil/, it could not undergo palatalization. When later monophthongization took place and /kăil/ became /kĕl/, the second palatalization was no longer active, and /k/ therefore was not changed to /c'/. While this analysis is elegant, there is not much independent evidence in favor of it.

A different interpretation has been proposed by the Norwegian linguist Jan Ivar Bjørnflaten (1990), who suggests that the second palatalization did take place in the Old Novgorod dialect, but that its effect was subsequently cancelled out, possibly under the influence of surrounding Finno-Ugric languages, which lack affricates. However, as pointed out by Zaliznjak (2004: 43–44), this approach runs into problems with the relative chronology to other sound changes, and it has not been generally accepted.

In section 11.8, you learned that the third palatalization yielded the same results as the second palatalization: /k, g, x/ became /c', z', s'/. Given this similarity between the second and third palatalizations, it is reasonable to ask whether the third palatalization took place in Novgorod. The answer is not straightforward. With regard to /g/ the available data are limited and inconclusive. For /x/, it seems clear that the third palatalization did not take place, since the word corresponding to Modern Russian весь 'all' consistently shows /x/, and not /s'/. For instance, we find forms like **въхо** and **вьхемо** (Zaliznjak 2004: 46), which show no traces of the third palatalization.

However, for /k/ the effect of the third palatalization is evident from forms such as **отьць** 'father' (from Proto-Slavic /ătĭkăs/), where Proto-Slavic /k/ has turned into /c'/. The puzzling fact that we find evidence for the third palatalization for /k/ but not for /x/ is hard to explain. As Zaliznjak (2004: 47) laconically remarks, "это уже предмет гипотез" 'this is a topic for hypotheses'.

14.3. Phonology: Cokan'e

Here is a fragment from birch bark letter no. 550, which discusses taxation issues:

(3) a. [...] въдавоше собыславу **цетыри** гривне.
$$\text{(BBL 550; Zaliznjak 2004: 401–02)}$$
 b. [...] они отдали Сбыславу **четыре** гривны.
 c. [...] they gave Sbyslav **four** grivnas [a monetary unit].

As you can see from (3a), the word that corresponds to **четыре** 'four' is spelled with **ц** instead of **ч** in this birch bark letter. This reflects a phonological phenomenon called "cokan'e," whereby [c'] replaces [č']. We can write the following sound law:

(4) Cokan'e:
     /č'/ → /c/

Cokan'e is widespread in birch bark letters as shown by examples such as **пець** for **печь** 'bake' and **цисто** for **чисто** 'clean'. While other dialects of Old Rusian had two phonemes, /c'/ and /č'/, these two phonemes had merged in the Old Novgorod dialect, which had only one phoneme, namely /c'/. As shown by minimal pairs such as **цех** 'workshop' and **чех** 'Czech person', Contemporary Standard Russian has two phonemes, but cokan'e is attested in many contemporary dialects of Modern Russian, especially in the north.

14.4. Phonology: Secondary Pleophony in СъRC Groups

In section 12.2.3, it was shown that in so-called СъRC groups, i.e., groups where a jer precedes a liquid, the jer always vocalizes regardless of the presence or absence of other jers in the word. Thus **гърло** turns into **горло** 'throat' although the jer stands before a syllable with a non-jer vowel. According to

Havlik's law this jer should fall, but nevertheless vocalizes because it is part of a CЪRC group.

In the Old Novgorod dialect, CЪRC groups also show unexpected behavior, but not in the same way as other varieties of Old Rusian. For example, instead of **смьрди** 'peasant farmers' we find **смьрьди**, and instead of **дългъ** 'debt' we find **дълъгъ** (Zaliznjak 2004: 49). These forms are due to a sound law that is called "secondary pleophony":

(5) Secondary pleophony:
 CЪRC → CЪRЪC

The reason why this is called "secondary pleophony" is the similarity to the development we find in words such as **город** 'city', where a CORC group turns into COROC (see section 10.8.1). In both primary and secondary pleophony a liquid diphthong turns into a string of open syllables through the insertion of a vowel after the liquid, and in both cases the inserted vowel is the same as the vowel preceding the liquid. Although the dialects that underlie Contemporary Standard Russian never had secondary pleophony, a few words with secondary pleophony have been borrowed into the standard language from dialects. A case in point is **верёвка** 'rope', which go back to **вьрвька**.

14.5. Morphology: The Enigmatic e

In (2) in section 14.2, we discussed the example **замъке кѣле** 'the lock is whole', which has the unexpected /k/ before /ě/. However, this is not the only surprising fact about this example. The noun **замъке** is the subject, and **кѣле** is a predicative adjective agreeing with the noun. Since (as you saw in section 9.3) subjects and predicative adjectives were in the nominative case, **замъке** and **кѣле** must be nominative singular forms. But why do they both have the ending **-e**? Since the noun in question is a masculine noun and belongs to the ŏ-declension, we would instead expect the ending **-ъ**. Likewise, since short forms of masculine adjectives were inflected the same way as ŏ-declension nouns, we would expect the ending **-ъ** instead of **-e** in the adjective.

Although the ending **-e** occurs quite regularly in the nominative singular masculine ŏ-declension in birch bark letters, this ending is a bit of a mystery, since it lacks clear parallels in other dialects (or other Slavic languages for that matter). What makes the situation even more surprising is that there are no traces of the first palatalization before this **-e**. Recall from section 11.5 that the first palatalization turned /k, g, x/ into /č', ž', š'/ before front vowels (including /e/), so we would expect "**замъче**" instead of **замъке**. As opposed to the second palatalization, the first palatalization is widely attested in birch bark letters, so there is no doubt that the first palatalization took place in the Old Novgorod dialect. The only position where the first palatalization is consistently not attested, is before the nominative singular ending -e.

In short, the ending -e has two pecularities:

(6) The enigma of the ending -e:
 a. Not attested anywhere else in the Slavic world
 b. No traces of first palatalization in preceding consonant

Since -e appears not to trigger the first palatalization, it is tempting to suggest that we are not dealing with the phoneme /e/, but rather a mere orthographic variant of the ending -ъ found elsewhere in the Slavic world. However, Havlik's law provides strong evidence against this idea. Consider words with a jer in the last syllable of the stem, such as the masculine singular past-tense form of идти, which in early Old Rusian was шьлъ. In the standard language, this has turned into шёл. As predicted by Havlik's law (see section 12.2.1), the jer in the ending fell (it was number 1 from the end), while the jer in the root vocalized to /e/, which subsequently turned into /o/ (spelled as ё). If in the birch bark letters -e was an orthographic variant of -ъ, we would expect vocalization of the jer in the stem in forms with -e. If, alternatively, -e corresponded to a non-jer vowel in the Old Novgorod dialect, Havlik's law would lead us to expect a jer in the preceding syllable to fall. Recall from section 12.2.1 that jers fell before non-jer vowels. Thus, early Old Rusian шьла has turned into шла 'she came' in Contemporary Standard Russian. The evidence discussed by Zaliznjak (2004: 102) suggests that jers preceding -e fell in the Old Novgorod dialect. For instance, we find masculine singular forms such as пришле 'he came' with no jer in the root. Such forms strongly suggest that -e was not an orthographic version of a jer, but rather a full vowel pronounced by the speakers.

In order to explain the ending's inability to trigger the first palatalization, one might speculate that we are dealing with a different phoneme than /e/, perhaps a less fronted vowel that did not trigger palatalization. However, there is no independent evidence for this hypothesis. An alternative approach in terms of relative chronology would be to assume that the nominative singular ending -e came into being after the first palatalization had stopped being active. However, once again this hypothesis is not supported by independent evidence, and the ending -e remains shrouded in mystery.

14.6. Morphology: The Ubiquitous ě

Let us go back to birch bark letter no. 247 once more. As you remember from section 14.2, the phrase двьри кѣлѣ 'the doors are whole' is in the nominative. Since двьрь 'door' is a feminine noun, we would expect the nominative plural feminine ending -ы (from the ā-declension) on the adjective, but instead we have -ѣ. This is a general phenomenon in the ā-declension that involves the genitive, dative, and locative cases in the singular, as well as the nominative and accusative cases in the plural. Table 81 compares the Old Rusian endings given in section 4.2.3, with the endings you find in the Old Novgorod dialect. As you can see, the Old Novgorod dialect has generalized -ѣ to all these cases, after both hard and soft consonants.

Table 81. The ending -ѣ in the ā-declension—comparison between Old Rusian (left) and the Old Novgorod dialect (right)

	Old Rusian				Old Novgorod dialect			
	Hard		Soft		Hard		Soft	
Gen sg	-ы	(жены)	-ѣ	(землѣ)	-ѣ	(женѣ)	-ѣ	(землѣ)
Dat/Loc sg	-ѣ	(женѣ)	-и	(земли)	-ѣ	(женѣ)	-ѣ	(землѣ)
Nom/Acc pl	-ы	(жены)	-ѣ	(землѣ)	-ѣ	(женѣ)	-ѣ	(землѣ)

How can we explain this development? As you may have guessed already, the simple answer is: "analogy." Notice that in general in Old Rusian, -ѣ occurs both after hard and soft consonants; -ѣ is the "soft variant" of -ы, but at the same time -ѣ occurs after hard consonants in the dative and locative singular, where it corresponds to -и after soft consonants. The fact that -ѣ occurred in three out of six cells presumably motivated the analogy in the Old Novgorod dialect, whereby -ѣ was generalized to all six cells, as shown in the two rightmost columns in Table 81.

It is worth mentioning that the forms in Table 81 have undergone analogical change in Contemporary Standard Russian too. What happened is that the endings after hard consonants have replaced the endings after soft consonants, so that the same phoneme occurs after hard and soft consonants. In the genitive singular and the nominative and accusative plural, we have [y] in жены́/жёны and [i] in земли, but recall from section 12.1 that [y] and [i] are allophones of the same phoneme /i/ in Contemporary Standard Russian. In the dative and locative singular, we have /e/: жене́ and земле́.

While both the Old Novgorod dialect and Contemporary Standard Russian have undergone analogical change, the Old Novgorod dialect went further. In this dialect, the differences between the cases and between the hard and soft variants have disappeared. In Contemporary Standard Russian, the difference between the hard and soft variants have disappeared, but the cases have different endings.

14.7. Syntax: Clitics

Clitics are interesting in birch bark letters, because they offer particularly good examples of Wackernagel's Law, which is less consistently observed in other texts from Rus'. Recall from section 9.11 that according to Wackernagel's Law enclitics are incorporated in the first phonetic word in the clause. Birch bark letter no. 664 illustrates this. Here is the complete document with the relevant enclitics in boldface:

(7) a. От доброшькѣ къ прокъшѣ присъли **ми** гривьну а давыдъ **ти ми** не въдалъ велить възяти у вежьникъ.
(BBL 664; Zaliznjak 2004: 365–66)

   b. От Дорошки к Прокше. Пришли **мне** гривну: Давыд-**то** ведь **мне** не дал, велит взять у вежников.

   c. From Dobroška to Prokša. Send **me** a grivna [a monetary unit]: David didn't give it to **me**, but tells me to take it from the nomads.

As usual in birch bark letters, this letter first presents the sender and the addressee. After that, the first clause starts with the imperative присъли 'send!'. The enclitic ми 'to me' (the dative form of the personal pronoun) attaches to the first word in the clause as predicted by Wackernagel's Law. In the next clause, there are two enclitics attached to the first word: давыдъ ти ми. Here ти is a particle that emphasizes that the fact that David did not give Dobroška a grivna is important for the addressee (Zaliznjak 2008b: 32). The following enclitic, ми, is once again the dative form of the personal pronoun.

Notice that the clitics in давыдъ ти ми not only respect Wackernagel's Law, but also occur in the order predicted by the hierarchy in (46) in section 9.11. As you may remember, enclitics tend to occur in a particular order, and the hierarchy predicts that the particle ти (rank 4) occurs to the left of the clitic dative forms of personal pronouns (rank 6).

14.8. The Role of the Old Novgorod Dialect in the History of the Russian Language

Before leaving Novgorod, we must ask what role this dialect played in the formation of the Russian language. In section 1.8, you learned that Novgorod lost the battle of the political hegemony in northern Russia to Moscow, and it is therefore tempting to dismiss the Old Novgorod dialect as a regional phenomenon without important consequences for the history of the Russian language in general. However, there are indications that such an approach does not do justice to Novgorod.

Let us take the second palatalization as an example. Recall that this sound change turned /k/ into /c'/ before /ě/ and thus created Old Rusian dative/locative forms like **рѣцѣ** of **рѣка** 'river'. However, as mentioned in sections 3.6 and 4.2.1, Modern Russian has restored /k/ in the stem as is evident from modern dative/locative forms such as **реке**. This is traditionally considered an example of analogy, since the change back to /k/ made the dative/locative forms more similar to the remaining inflected forms which now all have /k/ in stem-final position.

Although the analysis in terms of analogy seems correct, it does not offer an answer to the question why the analogical change took place in Russian, but not in Belarusian and Ukrainian. In short, where did the impetus for the analogical change in Russian come from? A plausible answer is simply "from Novgorod." Recall from section 14.2 that the Old Novgorod dialect does not show traces of the second palatalization and accordingly had dative/locative forms like **рѣкѣ**. It is likely that this fact provided the motivation for the analogical change from **рѣцѣ** to **рѣкѣ** in Russian in general. Importantly, this Novgorod perspective explains why the analogy did not take place in Belarusian and Ukrainian. At the time when the three East Slavic languages were becoming separate languages, today's Belarus and Ukraine were part of the Grand Duchy of Lithuania, which made Belarusian and Ukrainian less susceptible to linguistic influence from Novgorod.

It is possible that the Old Novgorod dialect offers the key to explaining a number of features that separate Modern Russian from Belarusian and Ukrainian, and in a recent interview Andrej Zaliznjak laments the fact that the Novgorod perspective has not made its way into university courses on the history of the Russian language.[2] The present section is a first attempt to repair this weakness.

---

[2] The interview is available here: http://www.onlinetv.ru/video/1607/?playFrom=240.

14.9. Summary: The Language of the Birch Bark Letters

Reading birch bark letters is not easy, but with what you have learned in this chapter, you should be ready to start. Here are the essentials in summary:

(8) Important properties of birch bark letters and the Old Novgorod dialect:

　a. Orthography: the **бытовая система письма** used in birch bark letters displays a different distribution of letters representing mid vowels: ъ, ь, о, е, ѣ. (section 14.1)

　b. Phonology: there are no traces of the second palatalization, while the third palatalization is attested for /k/ → /c'/, but not for /x/ → /s'/. (section 14.2)

　c. Phonology: birch bark letters contain numerous examples of cokan'e, the merger of /č'/ and /c'/ to one phoneme. (section 14.3)

　d. Phonology: secondary pleophony (СЪRC → СЪRЪC) is well attested. (section 14.4)

　e. Morphology: in the ŏ-declension, the nominative singular had the ending -e. This ending did not trigger first palatalization of a preceding velar consonant. (section 14.5)

　f. Morphology: in the ā-declension, the ending -ѣ generalized in the genitive, dative, and locative cases in the singular, as well as the nominative and accusative cases in the plural, and is found after both hard and soft consonants. (section 14.6)

　g. Syntax: birch bark letters offer particularly good examples of Wackernagel's Law, which is less consistently observed in other texts. (section 14.7)

14.10. For Further Reading

If you want to know more about birch bark letters and the Old Novgorod dialect, Zaliznjak's monumental study *Drevnenovgorodskij dialekt* (2004) is an unsurpassable source of information, which includes a grammar, translations and analyses of individual letters, as well as several useful word lists and indices. You may also want to visit the webpage http://gramoty.ru/, which has pictures and translations of numerous letters from Novgorod and other cities. From this webpage you can also download a PDF version of Zaliznjak 2004.

Chapter 15   Epilogue: Reflections on a Triangle

Welcome to the other side! Thanks for travelling in time with me. Whether you read the whole book from beginning to end or just read selected chapters or sections, I hope you know more about the history of the Russian language than you did before you started reading. I will not review the contents of the book here, since each chapter contains a detailed summary. Instead, I offer some reflections on the three kinds of information you find in this book, and the relationship between them. Thinking about these issues will help you to go further in your study of the history of Russian—and historical linguistics in general.

The three kinds of information I have in mind are:

(1) Three components of the book:
     a. Facts about the history of the Russian language
     b. Historical background knowledge
     c. Tools from linguistic theory

The bulk of the book provides you with facts about the history of Russian from Proto-Slavic to Contemporary Standard Russian. You have learned about morphological developments in chapters 4–8, and then about syntax in chapter 9, and phonology in chapters 10–13. However, I have not just presented you with lists of hard facts, but also discussed various ways these facts can be interpreted. I hope you have learned that as we go back in time, hard facts become sparser, and the room for interpretation wider. Even when we have well-attested facts at hand, there is considerable room for interpretation, and in some cases there is no general consensus among the experts in the field. A case in point is the nominative singular ending **-e** in the Old Novgorod dialect discussed in section 14.5. Although this ending is well attested in birch bark letters, it is nevertheless shrouded in mystery. In order to interpret the facts about the history of Russian you need historical background knowledge (mentioned in (1b)) and tools from linguistic theory (mentioned in (1c)).

What exactly is the interplay of the three types of information in (1)? It is helpful to think of them as corners in a triangle, as shown in Figure 19. The left side of the triangle connects the facts about the history of Russian with historical background knowledge. Linguistic facts cannot be interpreted in a vacuum, and since language change takes place in time and space we need knowledge about the historical context in order to understand language change. Take loanwords, for example. In section 11.3, you learned that Germanic loanwords such as хлеб 'bread' can help us understand how Slavic developed a phoneme /x/. Is it reasonable to assume loanwords from Germanic for this period? In order to assess this hypothesis, you need to know about the whereabouts of Germanic and Slavic tribes in the relevant historical period. Summarizing, the crucial word here is "context." Without the historical context we cannot understand language change. That is why I included chapters 1 and 2 in the book.

However, knowledge of the historical context is not enough. We also need the tools of theoretical linguistics. Therefore I included chapter 3 in this book, which explains basic concepts such as "sound law" and "analogy." Without such theoretical concepts we would not know what to look for when we approach the facts. Theoretical concepts enable us to formulate precise hypotheses which we can confront with the data. For instance, we know from many languages that velar consonants often undergo palatalization before front vowels. With this in mind we can state a hypothetical sound law for Common Slavic and see to what extent this sound law accounts for the facts at hand. We will encounter apparent counterexamples for which we will have to devise other explanations (analogy? linguistic borrowing?), but if such explanations do not work, we will have to modify our sound law—or reject it altogether. In short, what linguistic theory has to offer are tools for hypothesis testing, as shown on the right side of the triangle in Figure 20.

What about the relationship between the two lower corners of the triangle? These two corners represent somewhat different approaches to scientific reasoning. As mentioned, historical background knowledge provides us with

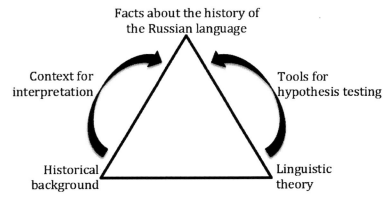

Figure 20. The three components of the book

context for interpretation. We ask: does our idea make sense given what we know about the historical context? This is what philosophers refer to as the "hermeneutic circle." You interpret a particular fact in the light of the whole context, and then go back to the context and ask to what extent your new understanding of the relevant fact changes the big picture, i.e., the context.

While the hermeneutic approach is characteristic of the arts (e.g., the study of literary texts), testing of hypotheses on the basis of concepts from linguistic theory brings us closer to experimental sciences, such as physics and chemistry. In the philosophy of science, the approach represented at the lower right corner of the triangle in Figure 19 is called the "hypothetico-deductive method." You devise a theory in terms of explicit hypotheses, and then test these hypotheses against data, whereafter you go back to your theory and modify or reject it.

After reading this book I hope you agree with me when I say that historical linguistics needs both hermeneutic-based interpretation and hypothesis testing in terms of the hypothetico-deductive method. Moreover, while the hermeneutic study of literary texts and the hypothetico-deductive testing of hypotheses about physical phenomena are very different enterprises, the two approaches converge in historical linguistics. While a student of literature is interested in texts, a physicist studies nature. Language is both a cultural phenomenon that manifests itself in texts, and a natural phenomenon that manifests itself in our brains. In order to understand language change we need to keep both aspects of languge in mind—and accordingly use a wide variety of methodologies. For this reason the bottom side of the triangle represents the methodological baseline of historical linguistics, which incorporates elements traditionally associated with both the arts and the hard sciences.

Emphasizing the importance of interpretation and hypothesis testing, I hope to have convinced you that historical linguistics is not just something you read about in books, but also something you do. Using the methods you have learned about in this book you can embark on your own research projects in historical linguistics. You do not necessarily need any groundbreaking new ideas from the start—a thorough application of well-known methods paired with a solid knowledge of the relevant facts in their historical context will take you far. A good example is Christian S. Stang's (1957) *Slavonic Accentuation*. Applying the traditional methods of historical linguistics to a large body of data, Stang arrived at conclusions that in the opinion of some scholars revolutionized the study of accentual systems in the Slavic languages. In this way, what Vermeer (1998: 250) refers to as Stang's "patently conservative approach" led to groundbreaking discoveries. Good luck with your research projects!

Appendix 1 — Morphological Tables

This appendix contains morphological tables from chapters 4–8 as a reference tool. If you need to identify a form in an Old Rusian text, it may be quicker and more efficient to look for it in this appendix than to locate the relevant paradigm in chapters 4–8.

A1.1. Nouns

A1.1.1. The ŏ-Declension (see section 4.2.1)

Sg	N	род-ъ	вълк-ъ	кон-ь	лѣт-о	мор-е
	A	род-ъ	вълк-ъ	кон-ь	лѣт-о	мор-е
	G	род-а	вълк-а	кон-я	лѣт-а	мор-я
	D	род-у	вълк-у	кон-ю	лѣт-у	мор-ю
	I	род-ъмь	вълк-ъмь	кон-ьмь	лѣт-ъмь	мор-ьмь
	L	род-ѣ	вълц-ѣ	кон-и	лѣт-ѣ	мор-и
	V	род-е	вълч-е	кон-ю	лѣт-о	мор-е
Du	NA	род-а	вълк-а	кон-я	лѣт-ѣ	мор-и
	GL	род-у	вълк-у	кон-ю	лѣт-у	мор-ю
	DI	род-ома	вълк-ома	кон-ема	лѣт-ома	мор-ема
Pl	N	род-и	вълц-и	кон-и	лѣт-а	мор-я
	A	род-ы	вълк-ы	кон-ѣ	лѣт-а	мор-я
	G	род-ъ	вълк-ъ	кон-ь	лѣт-ъ	мор-ь
	D	род-омъ	вълк-омъ	кон-емъ	лѣт-омъ	мор-емъ
	I	род-ы	вълк-ы	кон-и	лѣт-ы	мор-и
	L	род-ѣхъ	вълц-ѣхъ	кон-ихъ	лѣт-ѣхъ	мор-ихъ

A1.1.2. The *ŭ*-Declension (see section 4.2.2)

Sg	N	дом-ъ	врьх-ъ
	A	дом-ъ	врьх-ъ
	G	дом-у	врьх-у
	D	дом-ови	врьх-ови
	I	дом-ъмь	врьх-ъмь
	L	дом-у	врьх-у
	V	дом-у	врьх-у
Du	NA	дом-ы	врьх-ы
	GL	дом-ову	врьх-ову
	DI	дом-ъма	врьх-ъма
Pl	N	дом-ове	врьх-ове
	A	дом-ы	врьх-ы
	G	дом-овъ	врьх-овъ
	D	дом-ъмъ	врьх-ъмъ
	I	дом-ъми	врьх-ъми
	L	дом-ъхъ	врьх-ъхъ

A1.1.3. The ā-Declension (see section 4.2.3)

Sg	N	сестр-а	рук-а	вол-я	душ-а	дѣвиц-а
	A	сестр-у	рук-у	вол-ю	душ-ю	дѣвиц-ю
	G	сестр-ы	рук-ы	вол-ѣ	душ-ѣ	дѣвиц-ѣ
	D	сестр-ѣ	руц-ѣ	вол-и	душ-и	дѣвиц-и
	I	сестр-ою	рук-ою	вол-ею	душ-ею	дѣвиц-ею
	L	сестр-ѣ	руц-ѣ	вол-и	душ-и	дѣвиц-и
	V	сестр-о	рук-о	вол-е	душ-е	дѣвиц-е
Du	NA	сестр-ѣ	руц-ѣ	вол-и	душ-и	дѣвиц-и
	GL	сестр-у	рук-у	вол-ю	душ-у	дѣвиц-ю
	DI	сестр-ама	рук-ама	вол-яма	душ-ама	дѣвиц-ама
Pl	N	сестр-ы	рук-ы	вол-ѣ	душ-ѣ	дѣвиц-ѣ
	A	сестр-ы	рук-ы	вол-ѣ	душ-ѣ	дѣвиц-ѣ
	G	сестр-ъ	рук-ъ	вол-ь	душ-ь	дѣвиц-ь
	D	сестр-амъ	рук-амъ	вол-ямъ	душ-амъ	дѣвиц-амъ
	I	сестр-ами	рук-ами	вол-ями	душ-ами	дѣвиц-ами
	L	сестр-ахъ	рук-ахъ	вол-яхъ	душ-ахъ	дѣвиц-ахъ

A1.1.4. The ĭ-Declension (see section 4.2.4)

Sg	N	огн-ь	ноч-ь
	A	огн-ь	ноч-ь
	G	огн-и	ноч-и
	D	огн-и	ноч-и
	I	огн-ьмь	ноч-ию (-ью)
	L	огн-и	ноч-и
	V	огн-и	ноч-и
Du	NA	огн-и	ноч-и
	GL	огн-ию (-ью)	ноч-ию (-ью)
	DI	огн-ьма	ноч-ьма
Pl	N	огн-ие (-ье)	ноч-и
	A	огн-и	ноч-и
	G	огн-ии (-ьи)	ноч-ии (-ьи)
	D	огн-ьмъ	ноч-ьмъ
	I	огн-ьми	ноч-ьми
	L	огн-ьхъ	ноч-ьхъ

A1.1.5. The ū-Declension (see section 4.2.5)

Sg	N	букы	свекры
	A	букъв-ь	свекръв-ь
	G	букъв-е	свекръв-е
	D	букъв-и	свекръв-и
	I	букъв-ию (-ью)	свекръв-ию (-ью)
	L	букъв-е	свекръв-е
Du	NA	букъв-и	свекръв-и
	GL	букъв-у	свекръв-у (-ию)
	DI	букъв-ама	свекръв-ама
Pl	N	букъв-и	свекръв-и
	A	букъв-и	свекръв-и
	G	букъв-ъ	свекръв-ъ
	D	букъв-амъ	свекръв-амъ
	I	букъв-ами	свекръв-ами
	L	букъв-ахъ	свекръв-ахъ

A1.1.6. The C-Declension (see section 4.2.6)

		камы	сѣмя	дъчи	кол-о	осьля
Sg	N	камы	сѣмя	дъчи	кол-о	осьля
	A	камен-ь	сѣмя	дъчер-ь	кол-о	осьля
	G	камен-е	сѣмен-е	дъчер-е	колес-е	осьлят-е
	D	камен-и	сѣмен-и	дъчер-и	колес-и	осьлят-и
	I	камен-ьмь	сѣмен-ьмь	дъчер-ию	колес-ьмь	осьлят-ьмь
	L	камен-е	сѣмен-е	дъчер-е	колес-е	осьлят-е
Du	NA	камен-и	сѣмен-ѣ	дъчер-и	колес-ѣ	осьлят-ѣ
	GL	камен-у	сѣмен-у	дъчер-у (-ию)	колес-у	осьлят-у
	DI	камен-ьма	сѣмен-ьма	дъчер-ьма	колес-ьма	осьлят-ьма
Pl	N	камен-е	сѣмен-а	дъчер-и	колес-а	осьлят-а
	A	камен-и	сѣмен-а	дъчер-и	колес-а	осьлят-а
	G	камен-ъ	сѣмен-ъ	дъчер-ъ	колес-ъ	осьлят-ъ
	D	камен-ьмъ	сѣмен-ьмъ	дъчер-ьмъ	колес-ьмъ	осьлят-ьмъ
	I	камен-ьми	сѣмен-ы	дъчер-ьми	колес-ы	осьлят-ы
	L	камен-ьхъ	сѣмен-ьхъ	дъчер-ьхъ	колес-ьхъ	осьлят-ьхъ

A1.1.7. Overview of Old Rusian Declensions in Tabular Form (see section 4.2.7)

		ŏ-decl		ŭ-decl	ā-decl		ĭ-decl	ū-decl	C-decl
		Hard	Soft	Hard	Hard	Soft	Soft	Hard	Soft
Sg	N	-ъ/-о	-ь/-е	-ъ	-а	-я	-ь	-ы	-Ø
	A	-ъ/-о	-ь/-е	-ъ	-у	-ю	-ь	-ъ	-ь/-ъ/-Ø
	G	-а	-я	-у	-ы	-ѣ	-и	-е	-е
	D	-у	-ю	-ови	-ѣ	-и	-и	-и	-и
	I	-ьмь	-ьмь	-ьмь	-ою	-ею	-ьмь/-ию	-ию	-ьмь/-ию/-ьмь
	L	-ѣ	-и	-у	-ѣ	-и	-и	-е	-е
	V	-е/-о	-ю/-е	-у	-о	-е	-и		
Du	NA	-а/-ѣ	-я/-и	-ы	-ѣ	-и	-и	-и	-и/-и/-ѣ
	GL	-у	-ю	-ову	-у	-ю	-ию	-у	-у
	DI	-ома	-ема	-ьма	-ама	-яма	-ьма	-ама	-ьма
Pl	N	-и/-а	-и/-я	-ове	-ы	-ѣ	-ие/-и	-и	-е/-и/-а
	A	-ы/-а	-ѣ/-я	-ы	-ы	-ѣ	-и	-и	-и/-и/-а
	G	-ъ	-ь	-овъ	-ъ	-ь	-ии	-ъ	-ъ
	D	-омъ	-емъ	-ьмъ	-амъ	-ямъ	-ьмъ	-амъ	-ьмъ
	I	-ы	-и	-ьми	-ами	-ями	-ьми	-ами	-ьми/-ьми/-ы
	L	-ѣхъ	-ихъ	-ьхъ	-ахъ	-яхъ	-ьхъ	-ахъ	-ьхъ

A1.2. Pronouns

A1.2.1. Personal (1st and 2nd Persons) and Reflexive Pronouns (see section 5.1)

		1st person	2nd person	Reflexive
Sg	N	язъ, я	ты	—
	A	мене, мя	тебе, тя	себе, ся
	G	мене	тебе	себе
	D	мънѣ, ми	тобѣ, ти	собѣ, си
	I	мъною	тобою	собою
	L	мънѣ	тобѣ	собѣ
Du	N	вѣ	ва	—
	A	на	ва	—
	GL	наю	ваю	—
	DI	нама	вама	—
Pl	N	мы	вы	—
	A	насъ, ны	васъ, вы	—
	G	насъ	васъ	—
	D	намъ, ны	вамъ, вы	—
	I	нами	вами	—
	L	насъ	васъ	—

A1.2.2. Personal (3rd Person) and Relative Pronouns (see section 5.2)

		Masculine	Feminine	Neuter
Sg	N	и	я	е
	A	и	ю	е
	G	его	еѣ	его
	D	ему	еи	ему
	I	имь	ею	имь
	L	емь	еи	емь
Du	NA	я	и	и
	GL	ѣю	ѣю	ѣю
	DI	има	има	има
Pl	N	и	ѣ	я
	A	ѣ	ѣ	я
	G	ихъ	ихъ	ихъ
	D	имъ	имъ	имъ
	I	ими	ими	ими
	L	ихъ	ихъ	ихъ

A1.2.3. Demonstrative Pronouns (see section 5.3)

		Proximal			"Neutral" (?)			Distal		
		Masc	Fem	Neut	Masc	Fem	Neut	Masc	Fem	Neut
Sg	N	сь	си	се	тъ	та	то	онъ	она	оно
	A	сь	сю	се	тъ	ту	то	онъ	ону	оно
	G	сего	сеѣ	сего	того	тоѣ	того	оного	оноѣ	оного
	D	сему	сеи	сему	тому	тои	тому	оному	онои	оному
	I	симь	сею	симь	тѣмь	тою	тѣмь	онѣмь	оною	онѣмь
	L	семь	сеи	семь	томь	тои	томь	ономь	онои	ономь
Du	NA	сия	сии	сии	та	тѣ	тѣ	она	онѣ	онѣ
	GL	сею	сею	сею	тою	тою	тою	оною	оною	оною
	DI	сима	сима	сима	тѣма	тѣма	тѣма	онѣма	онѣма	онѣма
Pl	N	си	сиѣ	си	ти	ты	та	они	оны	она
	A	сиѣ	сиѣ	си	ты	ты	та	оны	оны	она
	G	сихъ	сихъ	сихъ	тѣхъ	тѣхъ	тѣхъ	онѣхъ	онѣхъ	онѣхъ
	D	симъ	симъ	симъ	тѣмъ	тѣмъ	тѣмъ	онѣмъ	онѣмъ	онѣмъ
	I	сими	сими	сими	тѣми	тѣми	тѣми	онѣми	онѣми	онѣми
	L	сихъ	сихъ	сихъ	тѣхъ	тѣхъ	тѣхъ	онѣхъ	онѣхъ	онѣхъ

A1.2.4. Possessive Pronouns (see section 5.4)

		Masc.	Fem.	Neuter	Masc.	Fem.	Neuter
Sg	N	мои	моя	мое	нашь	наша	наше
	A	мои	мою	мое	нашь	нашу	наше
	G	моего	моеѣ	моего	нашего	нашеѣ	нашего
	D	моему	моеи	моему	нашему	нашеи	нашему
	I	моимь	моею	моимь	нашимь	нашею	нашимь
	L	моемь	моеи	моемь	нашемь	нашеи	нашемь
Du	NA	моя	мои	мои	наша	наши	наши
	GL	моею	моею	моею	нашею	нашею	нашею
	DI	моима	моима	моима	нашима	нашима	нашима
Pl	N	мои	моѣ	моя	наши	нашѣ	наша
	A	моѣ	моѣ	моя	нашѣ	нашѣ	наша
	G	моихъ	моихъ	моихъ	нашихъ	нашихъ	нашихъ
	D	моимъ	моимъ	моимъ	нашимъ	нашимъ	нашимъ
	I	моими	моими	моими	нашими	нашими	нашими
	L	моихъ	моихъ	моихъ	нашихъ	нашихъ	нашихъ

A1.2.5. Вьсь 'all' (see section 5.5)

		Masculine	Feminine	Neuter
Sg	N	вьсь	вься	вьсе
	A	вьсь	вьсю	вьсе
	G	вьсего	вьсеѣ	вьсего
	D	вьсему	вьсеи	вьсему
	I	вьсѣмь	вьсею	вьсѣмь
	L	вьсемь	вьсеи	вьсемь
Pl	N	вьси	вьсѣ	вься
	A	вьсѣ	вьсѣ	вься
	G	вьсѣхъ	вьсѣхъ	вьсѣхъ
	D	вьсѣмъ	вьсѣмъ	вьсѣмъ
	I	вьсѣми	вьсѣми	вьсѣми
	L	вьсѣхъ	вьсѣхъ	вьсѣхъ

A1.2.6. Interrogative Pronouns: къто and чьто (see section 5.6)

		'who'	'what'
Sg	N	къто	чьто
	A	кого	чьто
	G	кого	чего
	D	кому	чему
	I	цѣмь	чимь
	L	комь	чемь

A1.3. Adjectives

A1.3.1. Short Forms of Adjectives (see section 6.2)

		Hard C in stem-final position			Soft C in stem-final position		
		Masc.	Fem.	Neuter	Masc.	Fem.	Neuter
Sg	N	добр-ъ	добр-а	добр-о	син-ь	син-я	син-е
	A	добр-ъ	добр-у	добр-о	син-ь	син-ю	син-е
	G	добр-а	добр-ы	добр-а	син-я	син-ѣ	син-я
	D	добр-у	добр-ѣ	добр-у	син-ю	син-и	син-ю
	I	добр-ъмь	добр-ою	добр-ъмь	син-ьмь	син-ею	син-ьмь
	L	добр-ѣ	добр-ѣ	добр-ѣ	син-и	син-и	син-и
Du	NA	добр-а	добр-ѣ	добр-ѣ	син-я	син-и	син-и
	GL	добр-у	добр-у	добр-у	син-ю	син-ю	син-ю
	DI	добр-ома	добр-ама	добр-ома	син-ема	син-яма	син-ема
Pl	N	добр-и	добр-ы	добр-а	син-и	син-ѣ	син-я
	A	добр-ы	добр-ы	добр-а	син-ѣ	син-ѣ	син-я
	G	добр-ъ	добр-ъ	добр-ъ	син-ь	син-ь	син-ь
	D	добр-омъ	добр-амъ	добр-омъ	син-емъ	син-ямъ	син-емъ
	I	добр-ы	добр-ами	добр-ы	син-и	син-ями	син-и
	L	добр-ѣхъ	добр-ахъ	добр-ѣхъ	син-ихъ	син-яхъ	син-ихъ

A1.3.2. Long Forms of Adjectives (see section 6.3)

		Hard C in stem-final position			Soft C in stem-final position		
		Masculine	Feminine	Neuter	Masculine	Feminine	Neuter
Sg	N	добр-ыи	добр-ая	добр-ое	син-ии	син-яя	син-ее
	A	добр-ыи	добр-ую	добр-ое	син-ии	син-юю	син-ее
	G	добр-ого	добр-ыѣ (-оѣ)	добр-ого	син-его	син-ѣѣ (-еѣ)	син-его
	D	добр-ому	добр-ои	добр-ому	син-ему	син-еи	син-ему
	I	добр-ымь	добр-ою	добр-ымь	син-имь	син-ею	син-имь
	L	добр-омь	добр-ои	добр-омь	син-емь	син-еи	син-емь
Du	NA	добр-ая	добр-ѣи	добр-ѣи	син-яя	син-ии	син-ии
	GL	добр-ую (-ою)	добр-ую (-ою)	добр-ую (-ою)	син-юю	син-юю	син-юю
	DI	добр-ыима	добр-ыима	добр-ыима	син-иима	син-иима	син-иима
Pl	N	добр-ии	добр-ыѣ	добр-ая	син-ии	син-ѣѣ	син-яя
	A	добр-ыѣ	добр-ыѣ	добр-ая	син-ѣѣ	син-ѣѣ	син-яя
	G	добр-ыихъ	добр-ыихъ	добр-ыихъ	син-иихъ	син-иихъ	син-иихъ
	D	добр-ыимъ	добр-ыимъ	добр-ыимъ	син-иимъ	син-иимъ	син-иимъ
	I	добр-ыими	добр-ыими	добр-ыими	син-иими	син-иими	син-иими
	L	добр-ыихъ	добр-ыихъ	добр-ыихъ	син-иихъ	син-иихъ	син-иихъ

A1.4. Numbers and Numerals

A1.4.1. The Number 1 (see section 7.2)

Одинъ was originally inflected in the same way as the demonstrative pronoun тъ, see sections 5.3 and A1.2.3.

A1.4.2. The Number 2 (see section 7.3)

		Masculine	Feminine	Neuter
Du	NA	дъва	дъвѣ	дъвѣ
	GL	дъвою	дъвою	дъвою
	DI	дъвѣма	дъвѣма	дъвѣма

A1.4.3. The Numbers 3 and 4 (see section 7.4)

		Masc.	Fem.	Neuter	Masc.	Fem.	Neuter
Pl	N	трье	три	три	четыре	четыри	четыри
	A	три	три	три	четыри	четыри	четыри
	G	трии	трии	трии	четыръ	четыръ	четыръ
	D	трьмъ	трьмъ	трьмъ	четырьмъ	четырьмъ	четырьмъ
	I	трьми	трьми	трьми	четырьми	четырьми	четырьми
	L	трьхъ	трьхъ	трьхъ	четырьхъ	четырьхъ	четырьхъ

A1.4.4. The Numbers 5 to 9 (see section 7.5)

Pl	N	пять	шесть	семь	осмь	девять
	A	пять	шесть	семь	осмь	девять
	G	пяти	шести	семи	осми	девяти
	D	пяти	шести	семи	осми	девяти
	I	пятию	шестию	семию	осмию	девятию
		(-ью)	(-ью)	(-ью)	(-ью)	(-ью)
	L	пяти	шести	семи	осми	девяти

A1.4.5. The Number 10 (see section 7.6)

	Singular	Dual	Plural
N	десять	десяти	десяте (-и)
A	десять	десяти	десяти
G	десяте (-и)	десяту	десятъ
D	десяти	десятьма	десятьмъ
I	десятью	десятьма	десятьми
L	десяте	десяту	десятьхъ

A1.5. Verbs

A1.5.1. The Present Tense: Thematic Verbs (classes I–IV, see section 8.2)

		I: нести	II: стати	III: знати	IV: хвалити
Sg	1	несу	стану	знаю	хвалю
	2	несеши	станеши	знаеши	хвалиши
	3	несеть	станеть	знаеть	хвалить
Du	1	несевѣ	станевѣ	знаевѣ	хваливѣ
	2	несета	станета	знаета	хвалита
	3	несета	станета	знаета	хвалита
Pl	1	несемъ	станемъ	знаемъ	хвалимъ
	2	несете	станете	знаете	хвалите
	3	несуть	стануть	знають	хвалять

A1.5.2. The Present Tense: Athematic Verbs (class V, see section 8.2)

		быти	дати	ѣсти	вѣдѣти	имѣти
Sg	1	есмь	дамь	ѣмь	вѣмь	имамь
	2	еси	даси	ѣси	вѣси	имаши
	3	есть	дасть	ѣсть	вѣсть	имать
Du	1	есвѣ	давѣ	ѣвѣ	вѣвѣ	имавѣ
	2	еста	даста	ѣста	вѣста	имата
	3	еста	даста	ѣста	вѣста	имата
Pl	1	есмъ	дамъ	ѣмъ	вѣмъ	имамъ
	2	есте	дасте	ѣсте	вѣсте	имате
	3	суть	дадять	ѣдять	вѣдять	имуть

A1.5.3. The Aorist (see section 8.3.1)

		I: нести	II: стати	III: знати	IV: хвалити	V: быти (Athematic)
Sg	1	несохъ	стахъ	знахъ	хвалихъ	быхъ
	2	несе	ста	зна	хвали	бы
	3	несе	ста	зна	хвали	бы
Du	1	несоховѣ	стаховѣ	знаховѣ	хвалиховѣ	быховѣ
	2	несоста	стаста	знаста	хвалиста	быста
	3	несоста	стаста	знаста	хвалиста	быста
Pl	1	несохомъ	стахомъ	знахомъ	хвалихомъ	быхомъ
	2	несосте	стасте	знасте	хвалисте	бысте
	3	несоша	сташа	знаша	хвалиша	быша

A1.5.4. The Imperfect (see section 8.3.2)

		знати	нести	хвалити	быти
Sg	1	знахъ	несяхъ	хваляхъ	бяхъ
	2	знаше	несяше	хваляше	бяше
	3	знаше(ть)	несяше(ть)	хваляше(ть)	бяше(ть)
Du	1	знаховѣ	несяховѣ	хваляховѣ	бяховѣ
	2	знаста	несяста	хваляста	бяста
	3	знаста	несяста	хваляста	бяста
Pl	1	знахомъ	несяхомъ	хваляхомъ	бяхомъ
	2	знасте	несясте	хвалясте	бясте
	3	знаху(ть)	несяху(ть)	хваляху(ть)	бяху(ть)

A1.5.5. The Imperative (see section 8.6)

		I: нести	II: стати	III: знати	IV: хвалити	V: дати	V: ѣсти
Sg	2–3	неси	стани	знаи	хвали	дажь	ѣжь
Du	1	несѣвѣ	станѣвѣ	знаивѣ	хваливѣ	дадивѣ	ѣдивѣ
	2	несѣта	станѣта	знаита	хвалита	дадита	ѣдита
Pl	1	несѣмъ	станѣмъ	знаимъ	хвалимъ	дадимъ	ѣдимъ
	2	несѣте	станѣте	знаите	хвалите	дадите	ѣдите

A1.5.6. Participles: Suffixes (see section 8.8.1)

	Participle suffix		Example (N sg feminine)
Present active	-ч		несучи, хвалячи
Past active	-въш	(after vowel)	знавъши
	-ъш	(after consonant)	несъши
Present passive	-м		несома, хвалима
Past passive	-т	(after rounded V or monosyllabic stem)	взята
	-н	(elsewhere)	несена
l-participle	-л		несла

A1.5.7. Participles: Agreement Endings (short forms in the nominative, see section 8.8.2)

		Masculine	Feminine	Neuter
Present active	sg.	неса (неся)	несучи	неса (неся)
	pl.	несуче	несучѣ	несуча
Past active	sg.	несъ	несъши	несъ
	pl.	несъше	несъшѣ	несъша
Present passive	sg.	несомъ	несома	несомо
	pl.	несоми	несомы	несома
Past passive	sg.	несенъ	несена	несено
	pl.	несени	несены	несена
l-participle	sg.	неслъ	несла	несло
	pl.	несли	неслы	несла

Appendix 2 Major Differences between Old Church Slavonic and Old Rusian

This appendix gives you a brief overview of the major differences between Old Church Slavonic and Old Rusian. This is obviously useful when you are working with Old Church Slavonic texts, but it also enables you to identify slavonicisms (Church Slavic elements) in Old Rusian and Modern Russian texts. For more information and examples, see Galinskaja 1997: 6–8.

A2.1. Morphology: Nouns, Pronouns, and Adjectives

Table 82. Differences between Old Church Slavonic and Old Rusian nouns, pronouns, and adjectives

	OCS	Old Rusian
G sg, ā-decl. (soft)	-ѧ (землѧ)	-ѣ (землѣ)
A pl, ŏ-decl. (soft)	-ѧ (конѧ)	-ѣ (конѣ)
I sg, ŏ-decl. (hard)	-омь (родомь)	-ъмь (родъмь)
I sg, ŏ-decl. (soft)	-емь (конемь)	-ьмь (коньмь)
D/L sg, personal pronoun:	тебѣ	тобѣ
D/L sg, reflexive pronoun:	себѣ	собѣ
G sg masc./neut., adjectives (long form)	-аѥго (добраѥго) -ааго (добрааго) -аго (добраго)	-ого (доброго)
D sg masc./neut., adjectives (long form)	-уѥму (добруѥму) -ууму (добрууму) -уму (добруму)	-ому (доброму)
L sg masc./neut., adjectives (long form)	-ѣѥмь (добрѣѥмь) -ѣѣмь (добрѣѣмь) -ѣмь (добрѣмь)	-омь (добромь)
G sg fem., adjectives (long form)	-ыѧ (добрыѧ)	-ыѣ, -оѣ (добрыѣ, доброѣ)

NB! The difference between -ѧ and -ѣ is also relevant for short forms of adjectives (which are inflected like nouns), as well as for demonstrative and possessive pronouns. For pronouns, Old Church Slavonic genitive singular forms include сеѧ, тоѧ, оноѧ, моеѧ, нашеѧ, and вьсеѧ, while the corresponding Old Rusian forms are сеѣ, тоѣ, оноѣ, моеѣ, нашеѣ, and вьсеѣ. The Old Church Slavonic accusative plural forms силѧ, молѧ, нашлѧ, and вьслѧ correspond to Old Rusian сиѣ, моѣ, нашѣ, and вьсѣ.

See sections 4.2 for more information about the declension of nouns, while sections 5.1–5.5 provide more details about pronouns. The long forms of adjectives are discussed in section 6.3.

A2.2. Morphology: Verbs

Table 83. Differences between Old Church Slavonic and Old Rusian verbs

	OCS	Old Rusian
3 sg present tense	-тъ (несетъ)	-ть (несеть)
3 pl present tense	-тъ (несѫтъ)	-ть (несуть)
Present active participle (N sg masc./neut.)	-ы (несы)	-а (неса)

See sections 8.2 and 8.8 for more information.

A2.3. Syntax: The Dative Absolute Construction

The dative absolute construction is an example of an Old Church Slavonic construction that is attested in Old Rusian texts that show some degree of Church Slavic influence. For examples, see section 9.9.

A2.4. Phonology: Liquid Diphthongs

Table 84. Liquid diphthongs in Old Church Slavonic and Old Rusian

Proto-Slavic	OCS	Old Rusian
CORC	CRAC (градъ, metathesis)	COROC (городъ, pleophony)
ORC, circumflex (falling tone)	RAC (работа, metathesis)	ROC (робота, metathesis)
CЪRC	CРЪC (врьхъ)	CЪRC (вьрхъ)

You can find more information about liquid diphthongs in section 10.8.

A2.5. Phonology: Prothetic Consonants in Word-Initial Position

Table 85. Prothetic consonants in Old Church Slavonic and Old Rusian

Proto-Slavic	OCS	Old Rusian
/ā/	/a/ (азъ)	/ja/ (язъ)
/eu/	/ju/ (юнъ)	/u/ (унъ)
/ĕ/	/je/ (ѥзеро)	/o/ (озеро)
/ē/	/ja/ (ѣхати)	/jě/ (ѣхати)

For more about prothetic consonants, see section 10.9.

A2.6. Phonology: *J*-Palatalization and Consonant Groups + Front Vowels

Table 86. *J*-palatalization in Old Church Slavonic and Old Rusian

Proto-Slavic	OCS	Old Rusian
/tj/	/š′t′/ (свѣшта)	/č′/ (свѣча)
/stj/	/š′t′/ (тьшта)	/š′č′/ (тьшча)
/skj/	/š′t′/ (пуштѫ)	/š′č′/ (пушчу)
/kt/ + front V	/š′t′/ (ношть)	/č′/ (ночь)
/gt/ + front V	/š′t′/ (мошти)	/č′/ (мочи)
/dj/	/ž′d′/ (межда)	/ž′/ (межа)
/zdj/	/ž′d′/ (ѣждѫ)	/ž′dž′/ (ѣзжу)
/zgj/	/ž′d′/ (дъждь)	/ž′dž′/ (дъждь)

NB! Although it is customary to assume that Proto-Slavic /zdj/ and /zgj/ were pronounced differently in Old Church Slavic and Old Rusian, the same letter combination жд were used in both languages, as illustrated by дъждь 'rain'. For more information about *j*-palatalization, see sections 11.6 and 12.6.

Appendix 3   Chronology of Major Sound Laws

In chapters 10–13, the sound laws were not described in strict chronological order, but this appendix will help you to establish the relative and absolute chronologies of the major changes. For Pre-Slavic and Common Slavic, the overviews in sections A3.1 and A3.2 are based on Shevelov 1964: 633–34. The chronologies for Old Rusian in section A3.3 are based on Kiparsky 1963: 153–54, as well as Gorškova and Xaburgaev 1981 and Ivanov 1983. You are advised to take the chronologies with more than a grain of salt, since data are often sparse and sometimes conflicting. Unsurprisingly, therefore, different handbooks provide different dates.

A3.1. The Pre-Slavic Period

Table 87. Chronology of Pre-Slavic sound laws

Sound law	Approximate chronology	Section
1. *Ruki* rule	By 6th–5th centuries BC	11.3
2. Satem assibilation	After *ruki* rule	11.2
3. *o/a* merger	6th–5th centuries BC	10.3

A3.2. The Common Slavic Period

Table 88. Chronology of Common Slavic sound laws

Sound law	Approximate chronology	Section
1. Loss of final consonants	1st–6th centuries AD	10.5
2. Emergence of prothetic consonants	1st–6th centuries AD	10.9
3. *j*-palatalization	5th–8th centuries AD	11.6
4. First palatalization of velars	5th–6th centuries AD	11.5
5. Monophthongization of oral diphthtongs	6th–7th centuries AD	10.6
6. Second palatalization of velars	6th–7th centuries AD	11.7

7.	Emergence of nasal vowels	7th century AD	10.7
8.	Third palatalization of velars	7th–mid 9th centuries AD	11.8
9.	Liquid diphthongs: ORC groups	8th–mid 9th centuries AD	10.8.2
10.	Liquid diphthongs: CORC groups	Mid 9th century AD	10.8.1

A3.3. The Old Rusian Period

Table 89. Chronology of Old Rusian sound laws

Sound law	Approximate chronology	Section
1. Softening of semi-soft consonants	11th century AD	12.3.5
2. Fall of weak jers	11th century AD	12.2
3. Vocalization of strong jers	11th–12th centuries AD	12.2
4. [ky, gy, xy] → [k'i, g'i, x'i]	13th century AD	12.4
5. Depalatalization of /š'/ and /ž'/	13th century AD	12.5
6. Transition from /e/ to /o/	13th–14th centuries AD	12.7
7. Transition from /ě/ to /e/	14th century AD	12.8
8. Emergence of akan'e	14th century AD	13.2
9. Depalatalization of /c'/	15th century AD	12.5

Appendix 4   Example of Text Analysis

This appendix provides some points for an analysis of a passage from the *Primary Chronicle*. The goal is not to offer an exhaustive analysis of the text, but rather give you an idea of how you can approach a medieval text. One thing you will notice when you start working with actual texts is that there is much more variation than you might expect from reading a book like the one you are holding in your hands. However, recall that, for example, the *Primary Chronicle* is the result of a long compilation process based on a multitude of sources, and that the text was then copied by different scribes at different places and times. Given this, abundant variation should not come as a surprise. Good luck with your own analyses!

A4.1. Text: Askold and Dir Attack Constantinople

В лѣто 6374. Иде Асколдъ и Диръ на Грѣкы, и приде въ 14 лѣто Михаила цесаря. Цесарю же отшедъшю на агаряны, и дошедшю ему Черное рѣкы, вѣсть епархъ посла ему, яко русь идеть на Цесарьград, и воротися цесарь. Си же внутрь Суда вшедъше, много убийство християномъ створиша, и въ двою сту кораблий Цесарьград оступиша. Цесарь же одва в городъ вниде, и с патриарьхом Фотиемъ къ сущий церкви святий Богородици Вълахерни всю нощь молитву створиша, такоже божественую ризу святыя Богородица с пѣснѣми изнесъше, в рѣку омочиша. Тишинѣ сущи и морю укротившюся, абье буря с вѣтром въста, и волнамъ великымъ въставшим засобь, и безъбожных руси корабля смяте, и къ берегу привѣрже, и изби я, яко малу ихъ от таковыя бѣды избыти и въсвояси възвратишася. (PVL 866 AD; 21,10)

A4.2. English Translation

In the year 6374 (866 AD) Askold and Dir went against the Greeks, arriving there during the fourteenth year of the reign of Emperor Michael. While the emperor was conducting a campaign against the Agarians and had reached the Black River, the eparch sent him word that the Rus' were approaching Constantinople, and the emperor turned back. Upon arriving inside the strait, the Rus' killed many Christians and attacked Constantinople in two hundred boats. The emperor just barely made it into the city and prayed all night with the Patriarch Photius at the Church of the Holy Virgin in Blachernae. They sang hymns and carried the sacred vestment of the Virgin to dip it in the sea. The weather was still, and the sea was calm, but a windstorm suddenly arose. Huge waves quickly scattered the boats of the godless Rus', and the storm threw them upon the shore and broke them up, so that few escaped such destruction to return to their home. (Adapted from Cross and Sherbowitz-Wetzor 1953: 60)

A4.3. Historical Context

This is the story about the first known Rus' attack on Constantinople, the capital of the Byzantine Empire. The attack is described in Byzantine sources, but it probably took place in 860 AD, not in 866 AD. The names *Askold* and *Dir* may correspond to Old Norse *Họskuldr* and *Dyri*, thus suggesting that the Rus' leaders were of Scandinavian origin—in accordance with the Normanist hypothesis discussed in section 1.6. However, Byzantine sources do not mention the names of the Rus' leaders.

A4.4. Morphology

The text contains a number of **nouns** from various declensions and in various cases. The following examples deserve mention:

(1) a. Accusative plural: на грѣк**ы**, на агарян**ы**; корабл**я**
     b. Instrumental sg: с патриарьх**ом** Фоти**емъ**, с вѣтр**ом**
     c. Genitive sg: Богородиц**а**

The examples in (1a) illustrate that Old Rusian had accusative plural forms in the ŏ-declension that were different from the nominative plural forms; the accusative plural had **-ы** (**грѣкы** and **агаряны**), while the nominative plural forms had **-и** (**грѣци, агаряни**). Notice that even if the nouns in the accusative denote animates, the accusative plural is different from the genitive plural (**грѣкъ** and **агарянъ**). In Contemporary Standard Russian, in contrast, the accusative plural has the same forms as the genitive for animate nouns.

The accusative plural form **корабля** is a Church Slavic form. As pointed out in A2.1, Old Church Slavonic had -ѩ (-я), whereas Old Rusian had -ѣ for nouns in the ŏ-declension (soft variety).

The instrumental singular endings with /o/ (hard variety) and /e/ (soft variety) in (1b) might arguably be due to Church Slavic influence (see A2.1), but a more likely explanation is that the jer in strong position has undergone vocalization. We will return to the jers in section A4.6 below.

While most nouns in the text about Askold and Dir are expected forms (either Old Rusian or Church Slavic), there are examples of unexpected forms, such as the genitive singular **Богородица** in (1c). From the context it is clear that we are dealing with a genitive singular form; this is a possessive construction (*the vestment of the virgin*), and the adjective **святыя** is clearly a Church Slavic genitive singular form. In the soft variety of the *ā*-declension, Old Rusian nouns have -ѣ while Church Slavic nouns have -ѧ (-я), so we would expect to find either of these endings on **Богородица**, but instead we have -**а**. A possible explanation is this. If we take the Church Slavic ending as our starting point, we expect **Богородицѧ** or **Богородиця**. However, since the *Hypatian Codex*, from which the example is taken, was written down as late as the 1420s, it is possible that the scribe pronounced a hard [c] rather than the original soft [c']. Accordingly, the scribe may have written **Богородица** instead of **Богородицѧ** or **Богородиця**, since the stem-final consonant was no longer soft. The result is a genitive singular ending that corresponds neither to the Church Slavic nor to the Old Rusian endings listed in A2.1. "Hybrid" endings of this type are quite common in Old Rusian texts.

Here is an interesting example with **numbers**:

(2) Locative dual: въ двою сту кораблий

The example contains the locative dual form **двою (дъвою) сту**, which is followed by the genitive plural noun **кораблий**.

As for **verbs**, we find one infinitive and one present-tense form, while the remaining forms are either aorists or active participles:

(3) a. Infinitive: **избыти**

   b. 3 sg present tense: **идеть**

   c. 3 sg aorist: **иде, приде, посла, воротися, вниде, въста, смяте, привърже**, and **изби**

   d. 3 pl aorist: **створиша, оступиша, омочиша**, and **възвратишася**

   e. Present active participle: **сущи**

   f. Past active participle: **отшедъшю, дошедъшю, вшедъше, изнесъше, укротившюся**, and **въставшим**

Notice that the 3 sg present tense ended in a soft /t'/ in Old Rusian, as shown in (3b). Old Church Slavonic had hard /t/ in this ending. In the 3 sg aorists, we have the expected /e/ at the end of verbs with consonant-final stems, such as **иде**. In **привѣрже** we have an alternation between /g/ and /ž'/ due to the first palatalization (see section 11.5).

A4.5. Syntax

A striking syntactic feature of the text is the frequent occurrence of the **dative absolute** construction:

(4) a. **Цесарю** же **отшедъшю** на агаряны
     b. **дошедшю** ему **Черное рѣкы**
     c. **Тишинѣ сущи**
     d. **морю укротившюся**
     e. **волнамъ великымъ въставшим** засобь

As pointed out in section 9.9, this Church Slavic construction consists of a participle in the dative and a logical subject in the same case. The logical subject can be a person as in (4a–b), but also inanimates are possible logical subjects, as demonstrated by (4c–e). The dative absolute resembles gerund constructions in Modern Russian, insofar as both constructions have a backgrounding effect. In the sentence that contains the constructions in (4a–b), for example, the foregrounded information is the fact that the eparch sent the emperor word about Askold and Dir's attack; the fact that the emperor was out of town represents background information conveyed by the dative absolute construction. As opposed to gerund constructions, the dative absolute does not normally have the same logical subject as the main clause. Again, the sentence with examples (4a–b) illustrates this, insofar as the eparch is the subject of the main clause, while the emperor is the logical subject of the dative absolute constructions. Stylistically, the dative absolute gives the text a bookish and learned flavor.

Another syntactic construction in the text that does not exist in Contemporary Standard Russian, is the use of **motion verbs with the prefix до- plus a noun phrase in the genitive**:

(5) дошедшю ему **Черное рѣкы**

In Contemporary Standard Russian, verbs like **дойти** take a prepositional phrase with **до** + genitive: **дойти до Черной реки** (see section 9.4).

As pointed out in section 9.11, in Old Rusian **enclitics** tended to occur in the so-called Wackernagel position at the end of the first phonetic word of a clause. The use of **же** in the text illustrates this:

(6) a. Цесарю **же** отшедъшю на агаряны

b. Си **же** внутрь Суда вшедъше

c. Цесарь **же** одва в городъ вниде

d. тако**же** божественую ризу святыя Богородица с пѣсньѣми изнесъше

In early Old Rusian, **ся** was an enclitic. However, in the present text **ся** appears immediately after the verb it modifies, rather than in the Wackernagel position:

(7) a. и вороти**ся** цесарь

b. морю укротившю**ся**

c. и въсвояси възвратиша**ся**

The text contains several interesting examples of **agreement** patterns. Since the subject of the first sentence is Askold and Dir, i.e., two persons, we would expect a verb in the dual or, maybe, plural. However, the verbs **иде** and **приде** are aorists in the 3rd person singular.

In section 9.10, it was pointed out that collectives may show either "formal agreement" in the singular or "semantic agreement in the plural." The text illustrates this; in (8a) **русь** agrees with the 3 sg present-tense verb form **идеть**, whereas in (8b) the agreement target is the plural adjective **безъбожных**:

(8) a. русь **идеть** на Цесарьград

b. и **безъбожных** руси корабля смяте

In Contemporary Standard Russian, **temporal adverbials** with the word for 'year' take the preposition **в** + locative case: **в этом году**. In Old Rusian, corresponding adverbials frequently occurred in the accusative, as illustrated by the following examples from the text, where **лѣто** 'year, summer' is in the accusative (see section 9.5 for discussion):

(9) a. В **лѣто** 6374

b. въ 14 **лѣто**

A4.6. Phonology

The text shows considerable variation with regard to the jers. Jers in weak position are sometimes preserved, sometimes omitted:

(10) a. въ 14 лѣто vs. в лѣто 6374

b. отшедъшю, вшедъше vs. дошедшю

c. Фотиемъ vs. патриарьхом

A likely explanation for this variation is the fact that the version of the text that has come down to us was copied long after the fall of the jers, and since the scribes did not pronounce the weak jers, they failed to include them consistently in their writing. Notice that in (10c), we would expect the front jer -ь in the instrumental sg ending. In Modern Russian, the nasal consonant in the ending has become hard, and this change seems to be in place in the text, where we find -ъ or no jer at the end of the relevant ending.

With regard to jers in strong position, examples from the text show that these have undergone vocalization:

(11) a. въ³шь²дъ¹ше → въшедъше

b. чьрное → черное

c. вълнамъ → волнамъ

In (11a), Havlik's law (section 12.2.1) predicts that jer number 2 undergoes vocalization to /e/, and the attested form in the text is in accordance with this. In (11b–c) we are dealing with СЪRС groups, where the jers always vocalize (see section 12.2.3). This prediction is borne out by the facts in (11b–c), where we find /e/ or /o/ instead of the jer.

In Contemporary Standard Russian, we find [i], not [y], after /k/. In (early) Old Rusian, alternatively, **/k/ was followed by [y]** (see section 12.4). The following examples from the text represent the situation before the change from [y] to [i]:

(12) a. Грѣкы

b. рѣкы

c. великымъ

As shown in section 10.8 on **liquid diphthongs**, characteristic of Old Church Slavonic and other South Slavic languages is metathesis, while Old Rusian has pleophony. In the text about Askold and Dir, we find pleophony forms such as **городъ** and **берегу**, but at the same time we find metathesis in the name **Цесарыград**:

(13) a. Pleophony: **городъ** and **берегу**

b. Metathesis: **Цесарьград**

Metathesis forms reveal Church Slavic influence.

In section 10.9 on **prothetic consonants** it was pointed out that Late Common Slavic (and Old Church Slavonic) have words in /je/, while the Old Rusian cognates have /o/. Examples include the word for 'one', which was /jedinъ/ in Old Church Slavonic, but /odinъ/ in Old Rusian. We find the same root in the adverb **едва** in Modern Russian—with the Church Slavic form with prothetic /j/. In the text about Askold and Dir, in contrast, we have the Old Rusian form **одва**. This form is also attested in Modern Russian dialects.

The root in the word for night had **/kt/ + a front vowel** in Proto-Slavic. In East Slavic, /kt/ became /č'/ as in **ночь**, while South Slavic developed /š't'/, often spelled as **щ** or **щ**: **нощь**. In the text about Askold and Dir, we find the South Slavic version—clearly a result of Church Slavic influence.

The Proto-Slavic consonant cluster /tj/ underwent *j*-palatalization, which gave /š't'/ in South Slavic, but /č'/ in East Slavic (Old Rusian), as pointed out in section 11.6. The present active participle **сущи** from the text about Askold and Dir is an example of a Church Slavic form.

A4.7. Sociolinguistics

The text about Askold and Dir illustrates the complex relationship between Church Slavic and East Slavic (Old Rusian) elements in texts from Kievan Rus'. In general, the text is heavily influenced by Church Slavic:

(14) Church Slavic elements:

a. Dative absolute construction: **Цесарю** же **отшедъшю** на агаряны

b. Metathesis: **Цесарьград**

c. /kt/ + front vowel → /š't'/: **нощь**

d. /tj/ → /š't'/: **сущи**

e. **-я (-ѧ)** for **-ѣ** in the accusative plural: **корабля**

At the same time, the text also contains some East Slavic elements:

(15) East Slavic (Old Rusian) elements:
   a. Pleophony: го́родъ and бере́гу
   b. Initial /o/ instead of /je/: одва
   c. 3 sg present tense in soft /t'/: идетъ

Even if there are arguments for assuming diglossia in Kievean Rus' (section 2.4), it is not the case that a given text contains either exclusively Church Slavic or exclusively East Slavic (Old Rusian) elements. Rather, quite often both types of elements are found in the same text—as shown in the text about Askold and Dir.

Bibliography

Printed Resources

Andersen, Henning. (1968) "IE *s after i, u, r, k in Baltic and Slavic." *Acta linguistica Hafniensia* 11: 171–90.
———. (1969) "Lenition in Slavic." *Language* 45(3): 553–74.
———. (1985) "Protoslavic and Common Slavic—Questions of periodization and terminology." *International journal of Slavic linguistics and poetics* 31–32: 67–82.
———. (1998) "Slavic." Anna Giacalone Ramat and Paolo Ramat, eds. *The Indo-European languages*. London: Routledge, 415–53.
———. (2006) "Grammation, regrammation, and degrammation: Tense loss in Russian." *Diachronica* 23(2): 231–58.
———. (2009) "On the origin of the Slavic aspects: Questions of chronology." Vit Bubenik, John Hewson, and Sarah Rose, eds. *Grammatical change in Indo-European languages*. Amsterdam: John Benjamins, 123–40.
———. (2012) "The new Russian vocative: Synchrony, diachrony, typology." *Scando-Slavica* 58(1): 122–67.
Anttila, Raimo. (1989) *Historical and comparative linguistics*. Amsterdam: John Benjamins.
Avanesov, Ruben I. (1984) *Russkoe literaturnoe proiznošenie*. Moscow: Prosveščenie.
Avvakum Petrovič. (1997) *Žitie protopopa Avvakuma im samim napisannoe i drugie ego sočinenija*. Moscow: ZAO "Svarog i K".
Baudouin de Courtenay, Jan. (1894) "Einiges über Palatalisierung (Palatalisation) und Entpalatalisierung (Dispalatalisation)." *Indogermanische Forschungen* 4: 45–47. (Relevant parts reprinted in Channon 1972.)
Bermel, Neil. (1997) *Context and the lexicon in the development of Russian aspect*. Berkeley: University of California Press.
Bethin, Christina Y. (1998) *Slavic prosody*. Cambridge: Cambridge University Press.
Bjørnflaten, Jan Ivar. (1990) "The birch bark letters redeemed." *Russian linguistics* 14(3): 315–38.

Borkovskij, Viktor I. (1978) *Istoričeskaja grammatika russkogo jazyka: Sintaksis. Prostoe predloženie*. Moscow: Nauka.
Borkovskij, Viktor I. and Petr S. Kuznecov. (1963) *Istoričeskaja grammatika russkogo jazyka*. Moscow: Izdatel'stvo Akademii Nauk SSSR.
Broch, Olaf. (1916) *Govory k" zapadu ot" Mosal'ska*. Petrograd: Imperatorskaja Akademija Nauk.
Bybee, Joan L. (2007) "Diachronic linguistics." Dirk Geeraerts and Hubert Cuyckens, eds. *The Oxford handbook of cognitive linguistics*. Oxford: Oxford University Press.
Bybee, Joan L., Revere Perkins, and William Pagliuca. (1994) *The evolution of grammar: Tense, aspect, and modality in the languages of the world*. Chicago: University of Chicago Press.
Børtnes, Jostein. (1988) *Visions of glory: Studies in early Russian hagiography*. Oslo: Solum Forlag A/S.
———. (1992) "The literature of old Russia 988–1730." Charles A. Moser, ed. *The Cambridge history of Russian literature*. Cambridge: Cambridge University Press, 1–44.
Campbell, Lyle. (1999) *Historical linguistics: An introduction*. Cambridge, MA: MIT Press.
Čekunova, Antonina E. (2010) *Russkoe kirilličeskoe pis'mo XI–XVIII vv.* Moscow: RGGU.
Channon, Robert. (1972) *On the place of the progressive palatalization of velars in the relative chronology of Slavic*. The Hague: Mouton.
Christensen, Svend Aage and Knud Rasmussen. (1986) *Rigets oprindelse: Politikens Ruslandshistorie indtil 1689*. Copenhagen: Politikens forlag.
Comrie, Bernard. (1976) *Aspect*. Cambridge: Cambridge University Press.
Corbett, Greville G. (1991) *Gender*. Cambridge: Cambridge University Press.
———. (2000) *Number*. Cambridge: Cambridge University Press.
Cross, Samuel H. and Olgerd P. Sherbowitz-Wetzor, trans. and eds. (1953) *The Russian Primary Chronicle: Laurentian text*. Cambridge, MA: The Mediaeval Academy of America.
Cruttenden, Alan. (2008) *Gimson's pronunciation of English*. 7th ed. London: Hodder Education.
Cubberley, Paul. (1993) "Alphabets and transliteration." Bernard Comrie and Greville Corbett, eds. *The Slavonic languages*. London: Routledge, 20–59.
Danièl', Mixail A. (2009) "'Novyj' russkij vokativ: Istorija formy usečennogo obraščenija skvoz' prizmu korpusa pis'mennyx tekstov." Ksenija L. Kiseleva, Vladimir A. Plungian, Ekaterina V. Rakhilina, and Sergej G. Tatevosov, eds. *Korpusnye issledovanija po russkoj grammatike*. Moscow: Probel-2000, 224–44.

Darden, Bill J. (1991/forthcoming) "Comments on Ivanov's *Istoričeskaja grammatika russkogo jazyka.*" *Studies in phonological theory and historical linguistics.* Bloomington, IN: Slavica.
Dickey, Stephen M. (2000) *Parameters of Slavic aspect.* Stanford, CA: Center for the Study of Language and Information.
———. (2008): "A prototype account of the development of delimitative *po* in Russian." Dagmar Divjak and Agata Kochanska, eds. *Cognitive paths into the Slavic domain.* Berlin: Mouton de Gruyter, 326–71.
Dostál, Antonín. (1954) *Studie o vidovém systému v staroslověnštině.* Prague: Státní pedagogické nakladatelství.
Dybo, Vladimir A. (1981) *Slavjanskaja akcentolgija.* Moscow: Nauka.
Eckhoff, Hanne M. (2011) *Old Russian possessive constructions: A construction grammar approach.* Berlin: De Gruyter Mouton
Eckhoff, Hanne M. and Laura A. Janda. (2014) "Grammatical profiles and aspect in Old Church Slavonic." *Transactions of the Philological Society* 112(2): 231–58.
Egeberg, Erik, trans. (2012) *Protopop Avvakums levned beskrevet av ham selv.* Oslo: Bokvennen.
Ferguson, Charles A. (1959) "Diglossia." *Word* 15: 325–40.
Flier, Michael S. (1984) "Sunday in medieval Russian culture: *Nedelja* versus *voskresenie.*" Henrik Birnbaum and Michael S. Flier, eds. *Medieval Russian culture.* Berkeley: University of California Press, 105–49.
———. (1985) "The non-Christian provenience of Slavic *nedělja.*" *International journal of Slavic linguistics and poetics* 31–32: 151–65.
Franklin, Simon. (2002) *Writing, society, and culture in early Rus, c. 950–1300.* Cambridge: Cambridge University Press.
Franks, Steven. (1995) *Parameters of Slavic morphosyntax.* New York: Oxford University Press.
Galinskaja, Elena A. (1997) *Istoričeskaja grammatika russkogo jazyka.* Moscow: Dialog–MGU.
———. (2009) *Istoričeskaja fonetika russkogo jazyka.* 2nd ed. Moscow: Izdatel'stvo moskovskogo universiteta.
———. (2014) *Istoričeskaja grammatika russkogo jazyka. Fonetika. Morfologija.* Moscow: URSS.
Gołąb, Zbigniew. (1973) "The initial *x-* in Common Slavic: A contribution to prehistorical Slavic-Iranian contacts." Ladislav Matejka, ed. *American contributions to the Seventh International Congress of Slavists.* Vol. 1. The Hague: Mouton, 129–56.
———. (1992) *The origins of the Slavs: A linguist's view.* Columbus, OH: Slavica.
Gorškova, Klavdija V. and Georgij A. Xaburgaev. (1981) *Istoričeskaja grammatika russkogo jazyka.* Moscow: Vysšaja škola.

Grannes, Alf. (1986) "Genitivus temporis in early 18th century Russian." *Russian linguistics* 10: 53–60.
Grekov, Boris D. (1949) *Kievskaja Rus'*. Moscow: Gosudarstvennoe učebno-pedagogičeskoe izdatel'stvo.
Halle, Morris. (1959) *The sound pattern of Russian*. The Hague: Mouton.
Harris, Alice C. and Lyle Campbell. (1995) *Historical syntax in cross-linguistic perspective*. Cambridge: Cambridge University Press.
Heyman, Neil M. (1993) *Russian history*. New York: McGraw-Hill.
Heine, Bernd, Ulrike Claudi, and Friederike Hünnemeyer. (1991) *Grammaticalization: A conceptual framework*. Chicago: University of Chicago Press.
Hock, Hans Henrich. (1991) *Principles of historical linguistics*. Berlin: Mouton de Gruyter.
Hockett, Charles F. (1958): *A course in modern linguistics*. New York: Macmillan.
Hopper, Paul J. (1991) "On some principles of grammaticization." Elizabeth C. Traugott and Bernd Heine, eds. *Approaches to grammaticalization*. Vol. 1. Amsterdam: John Benjamins.
Hopper, Paul J. and Elizabeth Closs Traugott. (2003) *Grammaticalization*. 2nd ed. Cambridge: Cambridge University Press.
Illič-Svityč, Vladislav M. (1963) *Imennaja akcentuacija v baltijskom i slavjanskom*. Moscow: Izdatel'stvo Akademii Nauk SSSR.
Isačenko, Alexander V. (1969) "The development of the clusters *sk', *zg', etc. in Russian." *Scando-Slavica* 15: 99–110.
———. (1970) "East Slavic morphophonemics and the treatment of the jers in Russian: A revision of Havlík's Law." *International journal of Slavic linguistics and poetics* 13: 73–124.
——— (Issatschenko). (1980) "Russian." Alexander M. Schenker and Edward Stankiewicz, eds. *The Slavic literary languages: Formation and development*. New Haven, CT: Yale Concilium on International and Area Studies, 119–42.
Istrin, Viktor A. (1988) *1100 let slavjanskoj azbuki*. Moscow: Nauka.
Ivanov, Valerij V. (1983) *Istoričeskaja grammatika russkogo jazyka*. Moscow: Prosveščenie.
———, ed. (1995) *Drevnerusskaja grammatika XXII–XXXIII vv*. Moscow: Nauka.
Jakobson, Roman O. (1936) "Beitrag zur allgemeinen Kasuslehre." *Travaux du Cercle linguistique de Prague* 6: 240–88.
———. (1963) "Opyt fonologičeskogo podxoda k istoričeskim voprosam slavjanskoj akcentologii." *American contributions to the Fifth International Congress of Slavists*. Vol. 2. The Hague: Mouton, 153–78.
Janda, Laura A. (1996) *Back from the brink*. Munich: Lincom Europa.

Jarceva, V. N., ed. (1997–2005) *Jazyki Rossijskoj Federacii i sosednix gosudarstv I–III*. Moscow: Nauka.
Kiparsky, Valentin. (1963) *Russische historische Grammatik*. Vol. 1: *Die Entwicklung des Lautsystems*. Heidelberg: Carl Winter Universitätsverlag.
———. (1967) *Russische historische Grammatik*. Vol. 2: *Die Entwicklung des Formensystems*. Heidelberg: Carl Winter Universitätsverlag.
———. (1979) *Russian historical grammar*. Ann Arbor, MI: Ardis.
Klenin, Emily. (1989) "On preposition repetition: A study in the history of syntactic government in Old Russian." *Russian linguistics* 13: 185–206.
Knjazev, Sergej V. (2000) "K voprosu o mexanizme vozniknovenija akan'ja v russkom jazyke." *Voprosy jazykoznanija* 1: 75–101.
Kodzasov, Sandro. (1999) "Russian." Harry van der Hulst, ed. *Word prosodic systems in the languages of Europe*. Berlin: Mouton de Gruyter.
Krasovitsky, Alexander, Matthew Baerman, Dunstan Brown, and Greville G. Corbett. (2011) "Changing semantic factors in case selection: Russian evidence from the last two centuries." *Morphology* 21: 573–92.
Kristoffersen, Gjert. (2000) *The phonology of Norwegian*. Oxford: Oxford University Press.
Krys'ko, Vadim B. (1994) *Razvitie oduševlennosti v istorii russkogo jazyka*. Moscow: Izdatel'stvo "Lyceum".
Larsen, Karin. (2005) *The evolution of the systems of long and short adjectives in Old Russian*. Munich: Verlag Otto Sagner.
Laver, John. (1994) *Principles of phonetics*. Cambridge: Cambridge University Press.
Lehfeldt, Werner. (2009) *Einführung in die morphologische Konzeption der slavischen Akzentologie*. 3rd ed. Munich: Verlag Otto Sagner.
Lunt, Horace G. (1981) *The progressive palatalization of Common Slavic*. Skopje: The Macedonian Academy of Sciences and Arts.
———. (1985) "On the progressive palatalization of Early Slavic: Synchrony versus history." *Studies in the linguistic sciences* 15(2): 149–69.
———. (2001) *Old Church Slavonic grammar*. 7th ed. Berlin: Mouton.
Martin, Janet. (2002) "From Kiev to Muscovy." Gregory L. Freeze, ed. *Russia – A history*. 2nd ed. Oxford: Oxford University Press.
———. (2007): *Medieval Russia 980–1584*. 2nd ed. Cambridge: Cambridge University Press.
Meillet, Antoine. (1897) *Recherches sur l'emploi du génitif-accusatif en vieux-slave*. Paris: É. Bouillon.
Mjakotin, Venedikt A. (2002) *Protopop Avvakum: Ego žizn' i dejatel'nost'*. Moscow: Zaxarov.
Mikhaylov, Nikita. (2012) *Tvoritel'nyj padež v russkom jazyke XVIII veka*. Uppsala: Uppsala University. [*Studia Slavica Upsaliensia*, 47.]

Müller, Ludolf. (1977) *Handbuch zur Nestorchronik*. Munich: W. Fink Verlag.
Nesset, Tore. (1994) *Russian Stress*. Oslo: Novus Press.
———. (1998a) *Russian conjugation revisited: A cognitive approach to aspects of Russian verb inflection*. Oslo: Novus Press.
———. (1998b) "Affiks eller klitikon?" *Norsk lingvistisk tidsskrift* 16: 185–206.
———. (2008) *Abstract phonology in a concrete model: Cognitive linguistics and the morphology-phonology interface*. Berlin: Mouton de Gruyter.
———. (2013) "The history of the Russian semelfactive: The development of a radial category." *Journal of Slavic linguistics* 21(1): 123–69.
Nuorluoto, Juhani. (2012) *De slaviska standardspråkens framväxt*. Uppsala: Uppsala Universitet.
Nørgård-Sørensen, Jens. (1997) "Tense, aspect, and verbal derivation in the language of the Novgorod birch bark letters." *Russian linguistics* 21(1): 1–21.
Obnorskij, Sergej P. (1947/1960) "Proisxoždenie russkogo literaturnogo jazyka starejšej pory." *Izbrannye trudy*. Moscow: Gosudarstvennoe učebno-pedagogičeskoe izdatel'stvo Ministerstva Prosveščenija RSFSR, 29–32.
Opeide, Gunnar. (2009) *Russisk historie fra Rjurik til Gorbatsjov: Fakta og resonnement*. Oslo: Solum.
Ostrowski, Donald, ed. (2003) *The Povĕst' vremennykh lĕt: An interlinear collation and paradosis*. 3 vols. Cambridge, MA: Harvard University Press.
Padgett, Jaye. (2003) "Contrast and post-velar fronting in Russian." *Natural language and linguistic theory* 21(1): 39–87.
Pavlova, Rumjana. (1977) *Prostranstvennye konstrukcii v drevnerusskom jazyke v sopostavlenii s drevnebolgarskim jazykom*. Sofia: Izdatel'stvo bolgarskoj akademii nauk.
Petruxin, Pavel V. and Dmitrij V. Sičinava. (2006) "'Russkij pljuskvamperfekt' v tipologičeskom perspektive." Aleksandr M. Moldovan, ed. *Verenica liter: K 60-letiju V. M. Živova*. Moscow: Jazyki slavjanskoj kul'tury, 193–214.
———. (2008) "Ešče raz o vostočnoslavjanskom sverxsložnom prošedšem, pljuskvamperfekte, i sovremennyx dialektnyx konstrukcijax." *Russkij jazyk v naučnom osveščenii* 15(1): 224–58.
Polnoe sobranie russkix letopisej. (1997) Vol. 1: Lavrent'evskaja letopis'. Moscow: Jazyki russkoj kul'tury.
Popov, Mixail B. (2004) *Problemy sinxroničeskoj i diaxroničeskoj fonologii russkogo jazyka*. St. Petersburg: St. Petersburg State University.
Press, Ian. (2007) *A history of the Russian language and its speakers*. Munich: Lincom Europa.
Saussure, Ferdinand de. (1916) *Cours de linguistique générale*. C. Bally and A. Sechehaye, eds. Lausanne: Payot.
Šapir, Maksim I. (1989) "Teorija 'cerkovnoslavjansko-russkoj diglossii' i ee storonniki." *Russian linguistics* 13: 271–309.

Šapir, Maksim I. (1997) "B. A. Uspenskij, Kratkij očerk istorii russkogo literaturnogo jazyka (XI–XIX vv.)." *Philologica* 4(8–10): 359–80.
Šaskol'skij, Igor' P. (1965) *Normanskaja teorija v sovremennoj buržuaznoj nauke*. Moscow: Nauka.
Šaskol'skij, Igor' P. (1967) "Vopros o proisxoždenii imeni *Rus'* v sovremennoj buržuaznoj nauke." O. L. Vajnštejn, ed. *Kritika novejšej buržuaznoj istoriografii*. Leningrad: Nauka.
Šaxmatov, Aleksej A. (1915) *Očerk" drevnějšago perioda istorii russkago jazyka*. Petrograd: Tipografija imperatorskoj akademii nauk.
Schenker, Alexander M. (1993) "Proto-Slavonic." Bernard Comrie and Greville G. Corbett, eds. *The Slavonic languages*. London: Routledge, 60–124.
———. (1995) *The dawn of Slavic: An introduction to Slavic philology*. New Haven, CT: Yale University Press.
Schmalstieg, William R. (1995) *An introduction to Old Russian*. Washington, DC: Institute for the Study of Man.
Ševeleva, Marija N. (2007) "'Russkij pljuskvamperfekt' v drevnerusskix pamjatnikax i sovremennyx govorax." *Russkij jazyk v naučnom osveščenii* 14(2): 214–52.
———. (2008) "Ešče raz ob istorii drevnerusskogo pljuskvamperfekta." *Russkij jazyk v naučnom osveščenii* 16(2): 217–45.
Shevelov, George Y. (1964) *A prehistory of Slavic: The historical phonology of Common Slavic*. Heidelberg: Carl Winter Universitätsverlag.
Sičinava, Dmitrij V. (2007) "Dva areala sverxsložnyx form v Evrazii: Slavjanskij pljuskvamperfekt meždu Zapadom i Vostokom." Vjačeslav V. Ivanov, ed. *Areal'noe i genetičeskoe v structure slavjanskix jazykov*. Moscow: "Probel".
———. (2013) *Tipologija pljuskvamperfekta: Slavjanskij pljuskvamperfekt*. Moscow: AST-PRESS.
Stang, Christian Schweigaard. (1957) *Slavonic accentuation*. Oslo: Aschehoug.
Stender-Petersen, Adolf. (1957) *Geschichte der Russischen Literatur: Erster Band*. Munich: C. H. Beck'sche Verlagsbuchhandlung.
Svane, Gunnar, trans. (1983) *Nestors krønike: Beretningen om de svundne år*. Højbjerg: Wormianum.
———. (1989) *Ældre kirkeslavisk litteratur*. Århus: Aarhus universitetsforlag.
Talev, Ilya. (1973) *Some problems of the second South Slavic influence in Russia*. Munich: Otto Sagner.
Timberlake, Alan. (2004) *A reference grammar of Russian*. Cambridge: Cambridge University Press.
Tixomirov, Mixail N. (1979) *Russkoe letopisanie*. Moscow: Nauka.
Toporov, Vladimir N. (1961) *Lokativ v slavjanskix jazykax*. Moscow: Izdatel'stvo akademii nauk SSSR.

Torke, Hans-Joachim. (2002) "From Muscovy towards St. Petersburg." Gregory L. Freeze, ed. *Russia: A history*. Oxford: Oxford University Press, 55–86.
Townsend, Charles E. and Laura A. Janda. (1996) *Common and comparative Slavic*. Columbus, OH: Slavica.
Trubetzkoy, Nikolay. (1922) "Essai sur la chronologie des certains faits phonétiques du slave commun." *Revue des études slaves* 2(3–4): 217–34.
Uspenskij, Boris A. (1994) *Kratkij očerk istorii russkogo literaturnogo jazyka (XI–XIX vv.)*. Moscow: Gnozis.
———. (2002) *Istorija russkogo literaturnogo jazyka (XI–XVII vv.)*. Moscow: Aspekt Press.
Vaillant, André. (1950) *Grammaire comparée des langues slaves*. Vol. 1. Lyon: IAC.
Vasmer, Max. (1964–1973) *Ètimologičeskij slovar' russkogo jazyka*. Moscow: Progress.
Vermeer, Willem. (1998) "Christian Stang's revolution in Slavic accentology." Jan Ivar Bjørnflaten, Geir Kjetsaa, and Terje Mathiassen, eds. *The Olaf Broch Symposium: A centenary of Slavic studies in Norway*. Oslo: The Norwegian Academy of Science and Letters, 240–54.
———. (2000) "On the status of the earliest Russian isogloss: Four untenable and three questionable reasons for separating the progressive and the second regressive palatalization of Common Slavic." *Russian linguistics* 24(1): 5–29.
Voyles, Joseph and Charles Barrack. (2009) *An introduction to Proto-Indo-European and the early Indo-European languages*. Bloomington, IN: Slavica.
Worth, Dean S. (1982) "Preposition repetition in Old Russian." *International journal of Slavic linguistics and poetics* 25–26: 495–507.
Xlevov, Aleksandr A. (1997) *Normanskaja problema v otečestvennoj istoričeskoj nauke*. St Petersburg: Izdatel'stvo S.-Peterburgskogo universiteta.
Zaliznjak, Andrej A. (1967) *Russkoe imennoe slovoizmenenie*. Moscow: Nauka.
———. (1977) *Grammatičeskij slovar' russkogo jazyka*. Moscow: Russkij jazyk.
———. (1985) *Ot praslavjanskoj akcentuacii k russkoj*. Moscow: Nauka.
———. (2004) *Drevnenovgorodskij dialect*. 2nd ed. Moscow: Jazyki slavjanskoj kul'tury.
———. (2008a) *"Slovo o polku Igoreve": Vzgljad lingvista*. 3rd ed. Moscow: Russian Academy of Sciences.
———. (2008b) *Drevnerusskie ènklitiki*. Moscow: Jazyki slavjanskix kul'tur.
Zarickij, Nikolaj S. (1961) *Formy i funkcii vozvratnyx glagolov*. Kiev: Izdatel'stvo kievskogo universiteta.
Zenkovsky, Serge A., ed. (1974) *Medieval Russia's epics, chronicles, and tales*. New York: Dutton & Co.
Živov, Viktor M. (1996) *Jazyk i kul'tura v Rossii XVIII veka*. Moscow: Jazyki russkoj kul'tury.

Electronic Resources

Biblioteka literatury drevnej Rusi (Institut russkoj literatury Rossijskoj Akademii Nauk): http://lib.pushkinskijdom.ru/Default.aspx?tabid=2070.
Drevnerusskie berestjanye gramoty: http://gramoty.ru/
Kievskaja letopis' (Institut russkogo jazyka Rossijskoj Akademii Nauk): http://www.lrc-lib.ru/rus_letopisi/Kiev/index.php
Kliment Std font, developed by Sebastian Kempgen: http://kodeks.uni-bamberg.de/aksl/Schrift/KlimentStd.htm
Povest' vremennyx let (Ostrowski's 2003 edition): http://pvl.obdurodon.org/pvl.html and http://hudce7.harvard.edu/~ostrowski/pvl/.
Russian National Corpus (historical subcorpus): www.ruscorpora.ru
Tromsø Old Russian and OCS Treebank (TOROT): http://nestor.uit.no/

Index of Names

Aleksej Mixajlovič 31, 57, 58, 60
Andersen, Henning 10, 12, 32, 65, 80, 94, 100, 150, 151, 153–54, 162, 216, 223–24, 230, 238
Anttila, Raimo 75
Attila the Hun 13
Avanesov, Ruben I. 119
Avvakum Petrovič 31, 32, 40–44, 60

Barrack, Charles 220, 222
Batu 23, 31, 47
Baudouin de Courtenay, Jan 238, 244
Bermel, Neil 153
Bethin, Christina Y. 248
Bjørnflaten, Jan Ivar 294
Boris and Gleb 42–43, 45
Boris Godunov 27
Borkovskij, Viktor I. 58, 88, 104, 105, 165, 167, 190, 193
Broch, Olaf 287
Bybee, Joan L. 69, 75
Børtnes, Jostein 42, 45, 46, 52, 60

Campbell, Lyle 75, 150
Čekunova, Antonina E. 39, 60
Channon, Robert 238
Chingiz Khan 23
Christensen, Svend Aage 22, 32
Claudi, Ulrike 75
Comrie, Bernard 149,
Constantine Porphyrogenitus 22
Corbett, Greville G. 97, 183
Cross, Samuel H. xxiv, 60, 332

Cruttenden, Alan 195
Cubberley, Paul 34, 35, 39, 60
Cyril (Constantine) 33–36, 59

Dan̄èl', Mixail A. 94, 100
Darden, Bill J. 100
Dickey, Stephen M. 154
Dmitrij, False (first) 27, 32
Dmitrij, False (second) 30, 32
Dostál, Antonín 153–54
Dybo, Vladimir A. 276

Eckhoff, Hanne M. 153–54, 178, 179, 193
Egeberg, Erik 60
Epiphanius "the Wise" 43

Ferguson, Charles A. 54–55, 56
Filofej 25
Flier, Michael S. 174
Franklin, Simon 60

Galinskaja, Elena A. 100, 210, 216, 242, 258, 262, 273, 281, 286, 325
Gołąb, Zbigniew 32, 222, 226
Gorškova, Klavdija V. 88, 100, 101, 111, 126, 134, 146, 162, 180, 329
Grannes, Alf 172
Grekov, Boris D. 20
Grigorij Camblak 58
Grimm, Jacob 66–67

Halle, Morris 264

Harald "Hardrada" 17
Harris, Alice C. 150
Havlík, Antonín 248
Heyman, Neil M. 32
Heine, Bernd 75
Hilarion 40–44
Hock, Hans Henrich 75
Hockett, Charles F. 96
Hopper, Paul J. 69, 75
Hünnemeyer, Friederike 75

Illič-Svityč, Vladislav M. 275
Isačenko (Issatschenko), Alexander V. 57, 60, 246, 250, 264
Istrin, Viktor A. 37
Ivan I "Moneybag" 24
Ivan III "the Great" 25, 26, 31, 48
Ivan IV "the Terrible" 16, 24, 26–27, 32, 47, 48, 49–51
Ivanov, Valerij V. 87, 88, 98, 100, 101, 105, 111, 120, 126, 134, 162, 193, 257, 263, 329

Jakobson, Roman O. 79, 282, 284
Janda, Laura A. 100, 153–54, 199, 216, 229, 230, 231, 237, 242
Jarceva, Viktorija N. 6
Jaroslav "the Wise" 17, 23, 24, 31, 48, 52, 255

Kempgen, Sebastian 36
Kiparsky, Valentin 111, 118, 122, 126, 131, 134, 182, 213, 250, 252, 273, 329
Kiprian 58
Klenin, Emily 175
Knjazev, Sergej V. 286–90
Kodzasov, Sandro 287
Krasovitsky, Alexander 165
Kristoffersen, Gjert 275
Krys'ko, Vadim B. 98, 100
Kurbskij, Andrej 49–51

Kuznecov, Petr S. 58, 88, 104, 105, 167, 190, 193

Larsen, Karin 126
Laver, John 198
Lehfeldt, Werner 290
Lunt, Horace G. 38, 39, 98, 141, 238

Martin, Janet 16, 17, 23, 24, 32
Meillet, Antoine 69, 98
Methodius 33–36
Mikhaylov, Nikita 170
Mjakotin, Venedikt A. 44
Müller, Ludolf xxiv

Nesset, Tore 70, 154, 187, 245, 264, 278, 279
Nestor 42–43, 45–46
Nikitin, Afanasij 48–49, 257
Nikon 30–31, 32, 57, 58, 60
Nil Sorskij 25
Nuorluoto, Juhani 60
Nørgård-Sørensen, Jens 153

Obnorskij, Sergej P. 54, 56
Opeide, Gunnar 32
Ostrowski, Donald xxiv, 21, 46, 166, 255

Padgett, Jaye 261–62
Pavlova, Rumjana 170
Pedersen, Holger 223
Peter I "the Great" 2, 5, 31, 32, 40
Petruxin, Pavel V. 149
Popov, Mixail B. 244
Press, Ian 60

Rask, Rasmus 67
Rasmussen, Knud 22, 32
Razin, Stepan (Stenka) 30, 32
Rjurik 16, 31

Romanov, Mixail 30, 31, 32

Saussure, Ferdinand de 61
Šapir, Maksim I. 54, 56
Šaskol'skij, Igor' P. 20
Šaxmatov, Aleksej A. 45–46, 54, 138, 250
Schenker, Alexander M. 11–13, 22, 32, 33, 35, 60, 122, 242
Schleicher, August 63
Schmalstieg, William R. 173, 193
Schuchardt, Hugo 72
Sergij Radonežskij 43
Ševeleva, Marija N. 149
Sherbowitz-Wetzor, Olgerd P. xxiv, 60, 332
Shevelov, George Y. 202, 205?, 209, 216, 226, 242, 329
Silvester 45
Sičinava, Dmitrij V. 149
Stang, Christian S. 275, 305
Stender-Petersen, Adolf 45
Svane, Gunnar 60
Svjatoslav 23, 31

Talev, Ilya 58
Taylor, Isaac 35
Timberlake, Alan 264
Tixomirov, Mixail N. 20
Toporov, Vladimir N. 170

Torke, Hans-Joachim 31
Townsend, Charles E. 100, 199, 216, 229–30, 231, 237, 242
Traugott, Elizabeth C. 75
Trubetzkoy, Nikolay 238

Uspenskij, Boris A. 54, 55–58, 60

Vaillant, André 238
Vasmer, Max 133
Vermeer, Willem 294, 305
Vladimir "the Holy" 16, 17, 31, 36, 40–41, 42–43, 52, 166
Vladimir Monomax 156
Voyles, Joseph 220, 222

Wackernagel, Jacob 184
Worth, Dean S. 175

Xaburgaev, Georgij A. 88, 100, 101, 111, 126, 134, 146, 162, 180, 329
Xlevov, Aleksandr A. 16, 32
Xmel'nic'kyj, Bohdan 30, 32, 58

Zaliznjak, Andrej A. 47, 51, 130, 175, 185, 186–87, 193, 250, 276, 282, 283, 284, 285, 290, 291–97, 299–301
Zarickij, Nikolaj S. 180
Zenkovsky, Serge A. xxiv, 60
Živov, Viktor M. 54, 56

Subject Index

ā-declension 80, 84–85, 88, 90, 91, 93, 95, 115, 125, 130, 133, 158, 165, 167 fn. 1, 177, 192, 225, 239, 240, 241, 285, 298, 301, 309, 312, 333
accentual paradigm 284–85, 289
accusative case 77, 78, 79, 80, 82–83, 89, 96–97, 102, 104, 105, 108, 114, 116, 119, 121–22, 129, 133, 164, 165, 168–70, 171–74, 176, 185, 187, 192, 202–03, 250, 260–61, 276 fn. 1, 283, 285, 286, 298, 301, 326, 332, 335, 337
actualization 70
acute 210, 281, 283, 289
adjective
    long form 103, 113–15, 116–123, 125–26, 130, 133, 158, 318, 325, 326
    short form 113–16, 118, 119, 121, 123, , 124, 125, 126, 133, 144, 158, 159, 257, 280, 296, 317, 323, 326
adverbial
    spatial 169–71, 192
    temporal 171–75, 192, 335
adverbial clause
    causal 185, 189–90
    conditional 190–91
    temporal 189, 192
adverbial participle, see gerund
agreement 96, 97, 127, 128, 129, 134, 157, 158–59, 160, 161, 163, 181–83, 192, 323, 335
akan'e 285–89, 330

Albanian 7, 10, 221
allophone 195, 196, 222, 224, 230, 244, 258, 259, 260, 298
alternation 68, 81–82, 84, 88, 108, 125, 135, 138–39, 142, 144, 155, 205, 206, 217, 222, 228, 232–33, 235, 241–42, 334
analogy 67–69, 70, 71, 74, 82, 84, 89, 105, 108, 111, 118, 120, 121, 122, 126, 138, 140, 143, 155–56, 161, 204, 214, 224–26, 242, 250, 252, 265, 268–69, 273, 284–85, 289, 298, 300, 304
Anatolian languages 7, 10, 221
animacy 77, 96–99, 100, 202
aorist 39, 140–43, 144, 146, 147–48, 149, 150, 152, 153, 156, 160, 161, 181, 183, 185, 224–25, 229, 241, 256, 321, 333, 335
Armenian 7, 10, 35, 221
aspect 140, 146, 148, 149, 152–54, 160
    imperfective, see imperfective aspect
    perfective, see perfective aspect
aspirated 217–18, 220, 221
assibilation 221–22, 240, 329
assimilation 116, 118, 126, 208, 211, 252–54, 257–58, 266–67, 268, 272
attributive 113–14, 115
Avars 13, 23, 31, 33

Baltic languages 7, 10, 12, 13–14, 65, 68, 72, 221

Belarusian 5, 6, 10, 59, 63, 64, 257, 286, 300
bilabial 212, 257
bilingualism 55–58, 60
birch bark letter 3, 51, 55, 59, 71, 175, 186, 236, 291–301, 303
borrowing 12, 67–69, 74, 125, 126, 214–15, 222, 226, 269, 270, 273, 304
Bosnian, Croatian, and Serbian (BCS) 5, 6, 34, 63, 64, 207–08, 210, 275
Breton 10
Bulgarian 5, 6, 10, 34, 57–58, 59, 60, 62, 63, 64
Byzantine Empire 16–17, 22–23, 25–26, 32, 33–34, 45, 52–53, 58, 332

C-declension 80, 88–90, 91, 92, 99, 132, 311, 312
case (grammatical category) 62, 68, 69, 77, 78–80, 81, 82, 88, 92–94, 96, 99, 101, 103, 105, 110, 113–14, 115, 116, 120, 122, 125, 128, 129–30, 133, 134, 163–70, 171–72, 175, 176, 177, 179–80, 186, 188, 202, 207, 214, 277–79, 285, 286, 296, 298–99, 301, 332, 334, 335
    accusative, see accusative case
    dative, see dative case,
    genitive, see genitive case
    instrumental, see instrumental case
    locative, see locative case
    nominative, see nominative case
    oblique, see oblique cases
    second genitive, see genitive, second
    second locative, see locative, second
category, inflectional 77–78, 81, 96, 127, 128, 129, 136, 145, 150
Celtic languages 7, 10, 221

centum languages 220–22
chronicle xxiv, 24, 31, 44–46, 55, 56, 59, 171, 175
    Hypatian Chronicle xxv, 45, 255
    Kiev Chronicle xxv
    Laurentian Chronicle 21, 22, 45, 255
    Novgorod Chronicle 131, 182
    Primary Chronicle (*Povest' vremennyx let*) xxiv, 16, 20, 21, 22, 31, 44–46, 54, 60, 146, 166, 255, 258, 331
chronology 329–30
    absolute 70–71, 74, 255
    relative 70–71, 74, 235–36, 238, 242, 264–69, 273, 294, 297
Church Slavic 36, 41, 43, 53–56, 57–58, 59, 60, 101, 102, 118, 119, 120, 122–23, 125, 126, 159–60, 175, 179, 180, 186, 209, 211, 215, 233–34, 269, 270, 273, 325, 326, 327, 332–33, 334, 337–38
circumflex 210, 281, 289, 326
clitic 102, 110, 163, 183–87, 189, 190, 192, 193, 204, 261, 283, 299, 334–35
closeness principle 83, 86, 92, 99, 100
codex
    Hypatian Codex 45, 255, 333
    Laurentian Codex 45, 255
    Law Codex 26, 30, 48
    Novgorod Codex 36, 40, 292
cognate 66, 73, 223, 337
cokan'e 295, 301
Common Slavic 10–11, 12, 13, 37, 61, 66, 68, 70, 77, 80, 82, 86, 90, 92, 94, 96, 97, 103, 109, 110, 113–15, 118, 127, 129, 134, 135–36, 137–39, 140–41, 143, 145, 153–54, 157, 161, 164, 177, 195–216, 217–42, 244, 246, 252, 256, 257, 258, 261, 262, 263, 265, 275, 280–81, 289, 293, 304, 329, 337

comparative degree 113, 123–25, 126, 158 fn. 3, 167 fn. 1
complementary distribution 55, 57, 59, 195–96, 230–31, 232, 244, 258, 259
complex sentence 163, 187–91, 192
conditioned sound law 66, 73, 271
conjunction 181, 185, 188, 189–91, 192
consonant
    loss of final 202–03, 215, 329
    prothetic 211–15, 327, 329, 337
consonant system 217–20, 240
converb, see gerund
CORC group 207–10, 211, 296, 326, 330
Cumans, see Polovtsians
Cyrillic alphabet xxiii, 34–39, 59, 60, 206
Czech 5, 6, 10, 63, 236
CъRC group 207, 211, 250–51, 295–96, 301, 326, 336

dative absolute construction 180–81, 186, 192, 326, 334, 337
dative case 22, 68–69, 71, 78, 79, 83, 84, 88, 102, 104, 105, 118, 119–22, 126, 130, 135, 164, 170, 176, 178–79, 180–81, 185, 186, 192, 204, 235, 261, 285, 298, 299, 300, 301, 326, 334, 337
declension 77–80, 81, 83, 84, 86, 87, 89–90, 92, 93, 99, 100, 101–02, 103, 106, 107, 108, 109, 110–11, 113, 115–22, 125–26, 129–33, 177, 202, 206, 225, 254, 326, 332
    declension, ā-, see ā-declension
    declension, C-, see C-declension
    declension, ĭ-, see ĭ-declension
    declension, ŏ-, see ŏ-declension
    declension, ŭ-, see ŭ-declension
    declension, ū-, see ū-declension
default 114, 125

demonstrative pronoun, see pronoun, demonstrative
dental 202, 217–19, 231, 243, 244, 246, 257, 261–62, 267–68, 271
depalatalization 228, 262–63, 267–69, 272, 330
devoicing 156, 254–55, 257–58, 272
deiotation, see j-palatalization
diachrony 61, 62, 72, 73
diglossia 54–58, 59, 60, 196, 338
diphthong 195, 216, 226, 230, 270, 271, 293
    liquid 207–12, 215, 234, 281, 296, 326–27, 330, 336
    nasal 137, 205–07, 211–12, 213, 215–16, 222, 224, 237
    oral 203–05, 215–16
diphthongization 230
dissimilation 252–54, 272
dorsal 218, 219, 220–221, 246, 260–62
Dregoviči 14, 15
Drevljane (Derevljane) 14, 15, 45
dual 81, 92–94, 99, 100, 101, 103, 109, 116, 119, 129–30, 132–33, 134, 136, 137, 154–55, 182, 224, 320, 333, 335

East Slavic languages 3, 5, 6, 10, 13, 34, 36, 53, 101, 118, 153, 186, 207–11, 213 fn. 3, 214, 231, 232, 233–34, 246, 251, 282, 300, 337–38
enclitic 184–87, 204, 283, 299, 334–35
ending 1, 39, 64, 68, 69, 77–84, 86–91, 94–97, 100, 104, 105, 108, 110, 115, 116, 118, 119–24, 125, 126, 130, 134, 135, 136–44, 155, 157–59, 161, 167 fn. 1, 183, 202–04, 224–25, 229, 231, 235, 239–40, 241, 250–51, 261, 265, 269, 276–80, 282–85, 289, 293, 296–99, 301, 303, 323, 332–33, 336

family tree model 63–65, 72, 73

feature, inflectional 77–78
Finno-Ugric language family 7, 13, 294
foot 248–49, 250
frequency principle 93, 99, 100
fricative 37, 105, 120, 201, 217–24, 229–30, 233, 234, 240, 243, 244, 246, 253, 254, 257–58, 263–64, 272–73
future tense 69–70, 150–52, 153, 160, 161, 162

gender (grammatical category) 77, 78, 86, 88, 91, 96–98, 99, 103–04, 109, 115–16, 127–29, 130, 135, 145, 150, 158, 177, 203
genetically related languages 61–62, 63, 65–66, 72, 73
genitive case 1, 78–79, 82–84, 87, 88, 90, 92, 94–95, 96–97, 102, 105, 107, 108, 109, 118, 119–24, 126, 127–28, 130–31, 132–33, 134, 164, 166, 168, 171, 172, 174, 176, 177–79, 192, 195, 202, 214, 243, 245, 247, 250, 251–52, 258, 271, 277, 279, 298, 301, 326, 332–33, 334
genitive, second 78–79, 84, 90, 94, 99
Germanic languages 7, 10, 12, 62, 66, 68, 209, 221, 226, 237, 304
gerund 157, 159–60, 181, 334
Glagolitic alphabet 34–36, 59, 60, 206
glide 217–20, 246
Gothic 226
grammaticalization 69–70, 71, 74, 75, 102, 110, 151, 161, 187
Greek 7, 10, 34–35, 37, 39, 52–53, 59, 65, 199, 221, 223, 227, 258, 264
Grimm's law 66–67
Gutturalwechsel 222

hagiography 42, 52, 59
haplology 116, 118, 120, 121–23, 126

Havlik's law 246–48, 250, 272, 292, 296, 297, 336
hermeneutic circle 305
Hindi 10
historical dialectology 62–63, 73
Hittite 7, 10
Huns 13, 23, 31
hypothetico-deductive method 305

$\check{\imath}$-declension 80, 86–87, 88–89, 90, 91, 92, 93, 131, 225, 310, 312
imitatio Christi 43, 44, 45
imperative 154–56, 160, 161, 204, 235, 241, 299, 322
imperfect 140, 142–44, 145–46, 148–49, 150–51, 152, 153, 156, 160, 161, 322
imperfective aspect 70, 140, 146, 147, 148, 149, 150–51, 153–54, 159, 160, 161, 180
Indo-European language family 5, 7, 10, 12, 65, 198, 220, 221, 223
Indo-Iranian languages 7, 10, 12, 68, 221, 226
infinitive 70, 135–36, 140–43, 150–51, 160, 161, 165–66, 192, 205, 207, 231, 234, 282, 333
inflection 68–69, 77–78, 80, 81–82, 84, 87, 88, 90, 91, 96, 116, 121, 123–24, 127–29, 131, 137, 145, 229
instrumental case 78, 79, 83, 86, 88, 95, 104, 108, 115, 121–22, 130, 166–70, 172–73, 176, 179, 192, 259, 279, 332, 336
interrogative pronoun, see pronoun, interrogative
Irish 10
isochrony 288, 289
isogloss 71–72, 74

j-palatalization 139, 144, 177, 204, 231–34, 239, 241, 244, 256, 263, 327, 329, 337
jotation, see *j*-palatalization
jers 37, 82, 104, 118, 119, 135, 156, 198, 207, 211, 244, 245, 246–56, 258–59, 265–68, 272–73, 277, 286, 292, 295–96, 297, 330, 333, 335–36

Kashubian 5, 6, 63, 206
Khazars 19, 23, 31, 34
Kiev 11, 15, 16–17, 18, 23–24, 26, 28, 30, 31, 41, 42, 45, 170
Kriviči 14, 15, 21 fn. 4

labial 217, 218, 219, 232, 243, 244, 246, 256–57, 261–62, 267, 271–72
labialized 217, 218, 220, 221
Latvian 7, 10
Law of Open Syllables 200–03, 205, 206–07, 212, 213, 214, 215, 226, 230
Law of Syllabic Synharmony 226–28, 230, 232, 234, 238–39, 240
lax vowels 198, 200
lenition 229, 234
liquid consonant 207–09, 210, 211, 218, 219, 246, 251, 295, 296
liquid diphthong, see diphthong, liquid
Lithuanian 7, 10, 223
locative case 68–69, 71, 78, 79, 82–83, 84, 87, 88–89, 94, 102, 105, 119–21, 122, 127, 128, 130, 132, 165, 168–69, 170, 171–72, 173, 174, 176, 188, 192, 225, 235, 241, 265, 298, 300, 301, 333, 335
locative, second 79, 84, 90, 94, 99

Macedonian 5, 6, 34, 59, 63, 64
metathesis 207–10, 211, 215, 251, 326, 336–37

Middle Russian 10, 11, 150, 151, 161
minimal pair 195–96, 244, 256, 259, 272, 282, 295
mobile vowel 243, 251–52, 272
Modern Russian, see Contemporary Standard Russian
Mongols 17, 23–26, 27, 31–32, 47, 48, 49
monophthong 204
monophthongization 137, 203–05, 209, 215, 222, 234–36, 293–94, 329
Moravian mission 33–36, 59, 60
morphology 68, 69, 74, 77–162, 195, 228, 235, 241, 291, 296–99, 301, 325–26, 332–34
Moscow 11, 14, 17, 19, 23–27, 28, 30–32, 43, 47, 57, 58, 177, 244 fn. 1, 300
Muscovy 24–27, 28–29, 33–60

N-stem 88–89
nasal consonant 202, 205–07, 216, 217–19, 237, 246, 256, 258–59, 336
nasal diphthong, see diphthong, nasal
nasal vowel 37–38, 205–07, 213, 222, 224, 236–37, 244, 330
natural class 196, 217, 223, 260
neoacute 281, 283, 289
nominative case 1, 22, 77, 78, 79, 80, 81, 82–83, 84, 86, 87, 88, 89, 94, 95, 96, 97, 100, 101, 103–04, 105, 108, 109–10, 111, 113–15, 116, 119, 121–22, 124–25, 126, 128, 129–30, 132–33, 134, 144, 145, 156, 157, 158–59, 163, 165, 166–67, 183, 192, 195, 202–03, 204, 206, 214, 235, 239, 241, 244, 247, 250, 251–52, 261, 265, 276–80, 285–86, 296–97, 298, 301, 303, 323, 332

Novgorod 3, 14 fn. 2, 15, 16, 17, 18, 21, 24–25, 27, 28, 31, 32, 46, 51, 71, 236, 291–301
Novgorod Codex, see codex, *Novgorod*
Novgorod-Seversk 18, 46, 291 fn. 1
Novgorod Chronicle, see chronicle, *Novgorod*
nucleus 287–88, 289
number (grammatical category) 77, 80, 81, 92–94, 96, 99, 104, 109, 129, 136, 145, 177
numeral 1, 127–34, 174, 182–83, 319–20

ŏ-declension 80, 81–83, 84, 86, 89, 90, 91, 92, 93, 95, 100, 105, 115, 121, 125, 130, 133, 155, 158, 177, 203, 204, 225, 228, 235, 239–40, 241, 296, 301, 307, 312, 332
o/a merger 198–200, 203, 215, 329
object 80, 104, 164–66, 167, 168, 192
object clause 188
oblique cases 101, 103, 105, 110, 113–15, 116, 122, 128, 130, 133, 134, 207, 277–79, 285
Old Believers 31, 43, 58
Old Church Slavonic (OCS) 3, 33–37, 59, 60, 102, 118, 120, 137, 141 fn. 1, 153–54, 158, 199, 206, 208, 210, 214 fn. 3, 233–34, 250–51, 256, 261, 325–27, 332, 333, 336–37
Old Novgorod dialect 3, 71, 236, 291, 293–94, 295–98, 300, 301 (291–301??), 303
Old Rusian (definition) 10, 11
Opričnina 27, 32
ORC group 207, 210–11, 326, 330
Ostrogoths 13
Ostromir Gospel 36, 40, 41

palatal 217, 218, 220, 221–22, 229, 260–61
palatalization
  first 82, 109, 139, 142, 228–31, 234, 235–36, 238, 239, 241, 261, 296–97, 301, 329, 334
  j-, see j-palatalization
  progressive 228, 237, 238
  regressive 228, 237, 238
  second 68, 82, 108, 155, 234–36, 237, 238, 239, 241, 242, 261, 262, 293–95, 296, 300, 301, 329
  third 236–38, 239, 241, 293–95, 301, 330
palatalized xxiii, 208, 217–18, 224
paradigm
  accentual 284–85, 289
  inflectional 77–78, 121
participle 70, 124 fn. 1, 150, 156–60, 161, 167 fn. 1, 179, 180–81, 186, 233, 282, 322–23, 326, 333, 334, 337
  l-participle 144–45, 149–50, 152, 156, 157, 158, 159, 160, 161, 322–23
passive construction 179–80, 187, 192
past tense 64, 70, 135, 140–50, 152–53, 156, 157, 160, 258, 270, 283, 297
paucal 130 fn. 1
Pechenegs 23, 147
Pedersen's rule (ruki rule) 223
perfect 140, 144–45, 146, 148, 149, 150, 152, 153, 156, 157, 160, 161
perfective aspect 140, 146, 148, 149, 153–54, 159, 160, 181
periphrastic 144, 149, 150, 151–52, 153, 161, 162
Persian (Farsi) 10
personal pronoun, see pronoun, personal
phoneme 37, 95, 195–96, 198–200, 203, 217, 218, 219, 220, 221, 222, 223–24,

230–31, 232, 239, 240, 243–46, 256–60, 262, 263–64, 270, 271, 272, 286, 292, 295, 297, 298, 301, 304
phonology 120, 126, 195–290, 291, 293–96, 301, 303, 326–27, 335–37
pleophony 207–10, 211, 215, 251, 326, 336–37, 338
   secondary 295–96, 301
pletenie sloves 43
plosive ("stop") 201, 217, 218, 219, 220–24, 229–30, 240, 244, 246, 253–54, 256, 272
pluperfect 140, 144, 145–46, 149, 150, 152, 153, 156, 157, 160, 161
Polabian 5, 6, 63
Polish 5, 6, 63, 125, 206, 207–09, 210, 250
polysemy 191, 192
Poljane 14, 15
Polovtsians (Cumans) 23, 46, 149
possessive construction 175–79, 192, 193, 333
possessive pronoun, see pronoun, possessive
post-alveolar 217–18, 219, 243, 244, 246, 263–64, 272–73
Pre-Slavic 10, 11, 63, 195, 198, 217, 220–26, 240, 241, 242, 329
predicative 113–15, 123, 125, 166–69, 192, 296
preposition 37, 79, 82, 101, 104, 132, 154, 165, 168–72, 175–76, 179, 184, 187, 188, 233, 256, 257, 283, 334, 335
present tense 135, 136–40, 143, 144, 148, 149, 152–53, 155, 156, 157, 160, 161, 183, 205, 229, 231, 232–33, 241, 268, 269, 280, 320–21, 326, 333, 335, 338
primordial home of the Slavs 11–13, 32, 68
proclitic 184, 283

pro-drop 163–64, 192
progressive palatalization, see palatalization, progressive
prominent (in prosody) 275
pronoun
   demonstrative 101, 103, 105–07, 109, 110, 114, 116, 120, 129, 131, 138, 172, 174, 315, 319, 326
   interrogative 101, 104, 108–09, 317
   personal 101–05, 107, 109–10, 163, 164, 183, 299, 313–14, 325
   possessive 101, 107–08, 109, 110, 183, 316, 326
   reflexive 101–02, 110, 313, 325
   relative 103–05, 188, 314
prothetic consonant 211–14, 215, 327, 329, 337
Proto-Indo-European 7, 62–63, 66, 73, 133, 196–200, 203, 205, 207, 215–16, 217–18, 220, 222–25, 240
Proto-Slavic 5, 10, 61–63, 66–67, 123–24, 135, 137, 139, 142, 177, 196–99, 202–08, 212–13, 217, 219–20, 223, 228, 230–33, 235–37, 239–40, 247, 257, 261, 293, 295, 303, 326–27, 337

quantity, loss of vowel 198–200

R-stem 88, 89, 92, 132
Radimiči 14, 15
reanalysis 70, 74, 150, 157, 160, 161
Re-Bulgarization 57, 60
reconstruction (linguistic) 65–67
redaction 45–46
   Laurentian Redaction 21–22
reflexive pronoun, see pronoun, reflexive
regressive palatalization, see palatalization, regressive
relative clause 104, 188, 190

relative pronoun, see pronoun, relative
"rich get richer, poor get poorer" principle 84, 86, 92, 99, 100
Romance languages 7, 10, 62, 68, 221
ruki rule 142, 223–26, 229, 240, 241, 329
Rus' 10, 13, 14–25, 31, 32, 33, 36, 40–43, 45–48, 52–56, 58, 60, 62, 141 fn. 1, 175, 186, 209, 291, 299, 331–32, 337–38
Russkaja Pravda 48, 54, 56, 150–51
Rusyn 5, 6, 63

S-stem 88–89
Sarmatians 12–13, 226
satem assibilation 221–22, 240, 329
satem languages 220–22
Scythians 12–13, 226
Severjane 14, 15
sibilant 221
Slavic languages 5–10, 12, 13, 34, 37 fn. 3, 53, 61, 63–64, 100, 154, 198, 206, 207, 208, 210, 211, 212, 214, 216, 221, 231, 233, 236, 242, 246, 275, 296, 300, 305, 336
Slovak 5, 6, 63, 64
Slovene (East Slavic tribe) 14, 15, 21 fn. 4
Slovene (Slovenian) 5, 6, 14 fn. 2, 34, 63, 64, 275
Slovincian 5, 6, 63
Slovo o polku Igoreve (*Lay of Igor's Campaign, Igor Tale*) 46–47, 291 fn. 1
Slovo o zakone i blagodati 41
softening of semi-soft consonants 256, 259, 267, 268, 330
sonority 201–02, 204–08, 212, 215, 230
sonority hierarchy 201
Sorbian, Lower 5, 6, 63
Sorbian, Upper 5, 6, 63

sound correspondence 65–67, 73
sound law 65–71, 73, 82, 108–09, 119, 123–25, 137–39, 155–56, 161, 195, 200, 202, 204, 206, 214, 215, 220, 221, 223–25, 228, 234, 241, 248, 253, 263, 264–65, 268–73, 284, 289, 295–96, 304, 329–30
South Slavic 5–6, 14 fn. 2, 53, 63–64, 101, 119, 179, 186, 208, 210, 233, 336, 337
South Slavic influence
  first 57, 60
  second 57, 58, 60
  third 57, 58, 60
standard language 33, 52–58, 59, 60, 62–63, 73, 138, 296, 297
stem 1, 39, 68–69, 77, 78, 81, 82, 83, 84, 88, 89, 95, 115–17, 123, 124–25, 130 fn. 1, 133, 135–36, 138–44, 146, 155, 157–58, 161, 177, 186, 217, 224, 229, 231, 235, 239, 250, 251–52, 276–77, 278–80, 284–85, 289, 297, 300, 317, 318, 322, 333–34
stress 1, 3, 70, 102, 119, 130 fn. 1, 135, 183–84, 213 fn. 3, 214, 250–51, 264–65, 266, 269–70, 271, 273, 275–90
  automatic 281–84, 289
  autonomous 281–84, 289
subgender 96–99, 202
subject 22, 80, 96, 114, 145, 163–64, 167, 180–83, 186, 192, 296, 334–35
subjunctive 135, 156, 157, 160, 161, 184, 185
superlative degree 113, 123–25, 231
supine 135–36, 160, 161, 166, 192
suppletion 103, 110
syllable 104, 121, 195, 200–08, 211–15, 226–28, 230, 237, 239, 240, 248–50, 252, 264, 271, 275–89, 295, 297
  closed 202, 252, 272

open 195, 200–02, 206–08, 212, 215, 226, 252, 296
synchrony 61, 72
synharmony 226–28
synonymy 191, 192
syntax 113, 163–193, 195, 291, 299, 301, 303, 326, 334–35

T-stem 88–89, 92
tense 62, 149, 152–53, 160
    tense, past see past tense
    tense, present see present tense
tense jers 250–51
tense vowels 198
theme vowel 136, 138, 161
Third Rome 25–26, 32, 58
Tocharian 7, 10, 221
tone 210, 275, 280–84, 289, 326
TORT group, see CORC group
typologically related languages 61–62, 73
TЪRT group, see CЪRC group

ŭ-declension 80, 83–84, 85, 90, 91, 92, 93, 94, 99, 100, 170, 178, 202–03, 225, 308, 312
ū-declension 80, 87–88, 90, 91, 92, 93, 99, 310, 312
Ukrainian 5, 6, 10, 59, 64, 151, 211, 250, 257, 286, 300
unconditioned sound law 66, 73, 263, 271
Urdu 10

Varangians (varjagi) 16, 20, 21

velar 81, 82, 83, 124, 138, 142, 155, 217–18, 220, 222, 228–29, 231, 234–38, 241, 244, 260–61, 267, 279, 301, 304, 329–30
verb
    athematic 136, 139–40, 141, 142, 155, 321
    thematic 136–41, 320
Vjatiči 14, 15
Vladimir (city) 17, 19, 23, 24
vocative 79–82, 94–95, 99, 100, 186–87, 229, 241–42
voiced consonant 217–19, 222, 246, 252–53, 254–55, 258, 263
voiceless consonant 217–19, 222, 246, 252–53, 254–55, 257–58
vowel reduction 275, 285–89, 290
vowel system 196–98, 206, 245

Wackernagel position 185–86, 189, 192, 334–35
Wackernagel's law 184–85, 187, 299, 301
wave model 71–72, 74, 294
Welsh 10
West Slavic 5, 6, 13, 34, 53, 63, 207–10, 236

Xoždenie za tri morja 48–49, 257

yers, see jers
yodization, see *j*-palatalization

Zadonščina 46–47
žitie 42–44